Archival Narratives for Canada

Archival Narratives for Canada
RE-TELLING STORIES IN A CHANGING LANDSCAPE

edited by
Kathleen Garay and Christl Verduyn

Fernwood Publishing • Halifax and Winnipeg

Copyright © 2011 Kathleen Garay and Christl Verduyn

All rights reserved. No part of this book may be reproduced or transmitted in any form by any means without permission in writing from the publisher, except by a reviewer, who may quote brief passages in a review.

Editing and design: Brenda Conroy
Cover design: John van der Woude
Printed and bound in Canada by Hignell Book Printing

Published in Canada by Fernwood Publishing
32 Oceanvista Lane
Black Point, Nova Scotia, B0J 1B0
and 748 Broadway Avenue, Winnipeg, Manitoba, R3G 0X3
www.fernwoodpublishing.ca

Fernwood Publishing Company Limited gratefully acknowledges the financial support of the Government of Canada through the Canada Book Fund, the Canada Council for the Arts, the Nova Scotia Department of Tourism and Culture, the Manitoba Department of Culture, Heritage and Tourism under the Manitoba Publishers Marketing Assistance Program and the Province of Manitoba, through the Book Publishing Tax Credit, for our publishing program.

Library and Archives Canada Cataloguing in Publication

 Archival narratives for Canada : re-telling stories in a changing landscape / [edited by] Kathleen Garay, Christl Verduyn.

Includes bibliographical references.
ISBN 978-1-55266-455-1 (bound).--ISBN 978-1-55266-446-9 (pbk.)

1. Archives--Canada. 2. Canada--History--Archival resources.
3. Canada--Archival resources. I. Garay, Kathleen E., 1945- II. Verduyn, Christl, 1953-

CD3621.A725 2011   020'.971   C2011-902778-X

Contents

Introduction
Kathleen Garay and Christl Verduyn 7

Section I Overview — Mapping the Archival Landscape 19

Preface: Archives and the Canadian Narrative
Doug Rimmer 21

Stories, Buildings and Maps: A Canadian Archive
Noah Richler 25

Section II Archives and Narratives for Canada — International, National and Regional 39

Archives as Narrative: The Politics of Ethnographic Archiving at the National Museum
Andrew Nurse 41

Our Records, Ourselves: Documenting Archives and Archivists
Kristan Cook and Heather Dean 56

Les enjeux historiographiques de l'usage des archives littéraires
Manon Brunet 74

Les archives sonores dans les provinces de l'Atlantique un patrimoine en perdition?
Ronald Labelle 87

Money Is Time: Case Studies in Small Canadian Regional Archives
Grant Hurley 98

Section III Re-Producing, Re-Presenting the Archival Narrative — Mapping the Virtual World   115

Marshland Memories: Constructing Narrative in an Online Archival Exhibition
Robert Summerby-Murray 117

Connected Constructions, Constructing Connections: Materiality of Archival Records as Historical Evidence
Ala Rekrut 135

Physicality as Apotheosis: The Changing Roles of Atoms and Bits in the Digital Age
Melissa McCarthy..158

A New Build: Digital Tools for Archives, Commons, and Collaboration
Dean Irvine and Meagan Timney 173

Respect des fonds and the Digital Page
Emily Ballantyne and Zailig Pollock 184

Section IV Case Studies in Archives and the Canadian Narrative   203

Titling *He Drown She in the Sea:* The Archive as Paratext
Jocelyn Hallman 205

The Letters of Frances Stewart: Two Centuries of Layered Representation
Jodi Aoki 222

From Bath to Birchbark: The Peregrinations of a Marriage Poem
Gwendolyn Davies and Carole Gerson...238

Unearthing an Erased Poet: Gathering up The Fragments of James McCarroll
Michael Peterman..253

The Many Deaths of Tom Thomson
Gregory Klages 274

Contributors 299

Introduction

Kathleen Garay and Christl Verduyn

Canadian archival repositories are memory institutions whose function is to ensure the acquisition, preservation and dissemination of the many narratives that constitute Canada. These institutions have been shaped by the country's past and defined by its present and are centrally engaged in forming its future. While these repositories, and the archives which they house, are the professional domain of archivists and scholars, their holdings are also usually made available to the interested public, either for consultation in traditional reading rooms or virtually, via the Internet. The collection we present here is the outcome of a series of conversations about archives in Canada, which began at McMaster University in 2005.[1] The first gathering in what was to become the biennial Archives in Canada Conference Series focused on literary archives. The discussion continued in 2007 at Library and Archives Canada (LAC) in Ottawa, this time with a focus on Canada's radical archives.[2] And the final conference was held in 2009 at Mount Allison University.

Our first objective in establishing the Archives in Canada Conference Series was to bring together archivists, scholars and the wider community to exchange ideas and to engage in discussions about our shared passion for archives. The goal of the series, echoed in this collection, was to provide a forum for all users of archives to reflect on their practice, be it traditional or grounded in new media, and to share their ideas. It was at our last gathering, organized around the theme of archives and the Canadian narrative, that earlier versions of many of these essays were first presented. Also identified for discussion and designated as subthemes at the 2009 conference, and hence represented here, were the importance of regional archives and, inevitably, the role of new digital initiatives in framing narratives of and for Canada.

This collection reflects our engagement with the theme of narrative. Its contributions reveal scholars, archivists and all those concerned with Canada and its meanings seeking out its defining stories. While we make no claim that those stories are to be found only in written sources — indeed, we readily acknowledge that Canada's narratives may be found in its oral tradition and even in the land itself — our primary focus is on the narratives to be found in archival collections, be they national, provincial or local. The ways in which those narratives are shaped, in both traditional and non-traditional forms, are the shared concern of the scholars and archivists whose essays appear here.

On a conceptual level, the archive may be considered as a cultural technology in the Foucauldian sense, an example of the contingent arrangements of ideals, artefacts and practices that order forms of knowledge and seek to guide practices of learning.[3] While the telling of Canada's stories is a long established and traditional activity, it is a pursuit that also demonstrates dramatic change, as techniques and technology transform familiar rituals. The time-honoured archival monologue, in which the lone voice of archival authority speaks, has become a dialogue, including its users, and, as the arc of conversation widens, it has even become a multilogue. The expanding narrative accentuates the need to chart the unfamiliar territory. This collection offers an assortment of maps for a changing landscape.

Our contributors, more fully identified in their biographies, bring a variety of perspectives to this conversation about archives. They include professional archivists at all stages of their career and young researchers alongside some of Canada's most distinguished writers and scholars. They represent archival institutions and universities from across Canada, and their essays draw upon archival resources both national, from institutions coast to coast, and international.

Section I — Overview — Mapping the Archival Landscape

In his preface, Doug Rimmer, representing Library and Archives Canada, discusses new patterns of knowledge creation and sharing as he foregrounds the country's most powerful memory institution's role in supporting "the process of formation, dissolution, change and challenge in our Canadian narratives." LAC's mandate, Rimmer observes, "rests on a narrative conception of Canadian society — not a static, fixed narrative but one composing many strands and shifting over time." Referencing the concept of conversation theory, Rimmer's opening words situate Canada's national archives firmly within an approach facilitating "knowledge-creating conversations."

Appropriately for our opening essay, Noah Richler, one of Canada's most thoughtful authors and essayists, in "Stories, Buildings, and Maps: A Canadian Archive," takes a wide and inclusive view of archives, suggesting that the landscape itself is an archival text from which Canadian narratives are constructed and that in Canada "we feel history through what is inferred." Because, he suggests, so much of Canada's history is not written, we behave as "archaeologists of the present day," divining our past from the landscape. Convinced by Robert Bringhurst's assertion that "stories are the first maps" and that "the text is already here" in the form of "the clouds, the mountains, the rivers and the lakes," Richler invites us to honour our own songlines and enjoins us to seek out our archives, not just in books and papers and photographs but also in the land.[4]

Section II — Archives and Narratives for Canada — International, National and Regional

In our second section we shift focus to approach the archival narrative in ways that are at once more traditional, in that they deal with the more conventional archival resources of artefacts and paper, but that are also less normative, in their emphasis on archival meta-narratives — that is, narratives of the archival stories themselves rather than of the evidential stories contained in them. In their different ways, these contributions present the relationship between archives and prevailing narratives of power, past, present and future, demonstrating that archives are shaped by prevailing political and social narratives and exposing any remnant of the myth of archival neutrality.

In his historical examination of the archiving practices of Canada's National Museum, Andrew Nurse looks to recent reconceptualizations of archives, which no longer see them as neutral or apolitical repositories but rather as institutions that "embed specific narratives of understanding, conceptions of knowledge, and definitions of what constitutes evidence, while literally calling this 'evidence' into being" (Cook and Schwartz 2002). In "Archives as Narrative: The Politics of Ethnographic Archiving at the National Museum," responding to calls from archival theorists for an approach that looks at archives as a subject of study, as opposed to a site where other subjects are investigated, Nurse attempts to show, not only how the National Museum embodied the prevailing social and power relations of the time in which it was established, but how it also functioned as an agency of culture transformation and even culture creation.

Further pursuing the approach that sees significant value in the study of archives themselves, and in particular the significance of the archivist's role in shaping evidence, "Our Records, Ourselves: Documenting Archives and Archivists," by Kristan Cook and Heather Dean, examines contemporary rather than historical practices. Their concern is with institutional documentation in archives. With one of the authors based at a Canadian government institution — the Provincial Archives of Alberta — and the other at a private U.S. university — the Beinecke Rare Book and Manuscript Library at Yale University — they are well placed to compare the different legislative environments and administrative practices that give rise to the varying content of administrative files. Yet, despite the significant international differences between these administrative environments and the consequent variation evident in the documentation preserved in their internal files, the authors make the same proposal for both institutions. Indeed, it is a proposal that they apply to archives in general: that archivists provide researchers with a "complete narrative" of a donation. In keeping with current attitudes promoting accessibility and transparency beyond the world or archives, Cook and Dean suggest that the information contained in these files be made available to interested researchers. As working archivists, however, the authors recognize that such openness cannot be achieved without resolving potential obstacles, and they examine the potential legal, ethical and administrative barriers to implementing such a proposal.

Manon Brunet writes from the perspective of a researcher in yet another provincial archives. Her essay, "Les enjeux historiographiques de l'usage des archives littéraires,"[5] considers how literary historians in Quebec today are turning to archives to augment their work and to make their research more amenable to literary theory and criticism. Brunet reports that when she began conducting archival research on Quebec literature, she encountered few other scholars paying attention to the importance of archives. Like a lonely *coureur des bois*, she met mainly genealogists and a few historians. She is glad to observe that this situation has now changed, and she predicts that researchers' use of archives will continue to increase as access becomes easier via the Internet. Increased scholarly attention, Brunet suggests, will significantly assist in the ongoing work of redefining Quebec literary history.

While Cook and Dean, in comparing practices at the archives of the Province of Alberta with those at an American institution, and Brunet, in examining archives in Quebec, shift our investigations from the national archival focus of Rimmer and Nurse, Ronald Labelle's essay moves our focus still deeper into the area of regional archives, one of the two subthemes at our Mount Allison conference. Labelle's essay, "Les archives sonores dans les provinces de l'Atlantique: un patrimoine en perdition?" is an example of a less well known regional archive, located away from the centre of Canada's archival world in Ottawa (LAC). Labelle reminds us that Canada is one of the world's most decentralized nations and that we should therefore expect small regional archives to contain many of its significant stories. He estimates there is a total of some 20,000 hours of sound material contained in archives in the Atlantic Provinces, much of it residing in very small institutions such as la Société historique du Madawaska and the New Brunswick Woodsmen's Museum. While recognizing the importance of recent joint efforts between universities and community groups, Labelle makes a plea for the further development of the necessary skills to preserve this valuable material and for greater coordination of preservation and dissemination efforts at a national level.

Grant Hurley also is concerned with regional archives and the rich stories waiting there to be explored. In "Money Is Time: Case Studies in Small

Canadian Regional Archives," his focus is on the Charlotte County Archives in St. Andrew's, New Brunswick (where, as will be seen below, contributors Gwen Davies and Carole Gerson also found stories of considerable interest) and the archives of Mount Allison University. Reminding us that archives are spaces that hold an enormous amount of power over "memory and identity," Hurley argues for the vital importance of small regional archives in preserving narratives that contrast sharply with those emerging from the national, centralized collective memory. And yet, despite their significance, the two examples that he explores in some depth indicate that "while small regional archives are integral to maintaining the histories of Canada," they are, nonetheless, "under constant threat." Hurley offers some specific recommendations for strengthening small archives in the face of such dangers.

Section III Re-Producing, Re-Presenting the Archival Narrative — Mapping the Virtual World

The issue of narrative is a central theme in Martin Hand's study, *Making Digital Cultures: Access, Interactivity and Authenticity*. He argues that "dominant tropes do not simply live in the academy: they 'script' digitization in particular ways, and operate as rhetorical vehicles for institutional actors seeking to embrace and implement digitization for locally specific ends" (2008: 6). The "scripting" of digitization is the concern of all of the essays in this segment of our collection, most explicitly in the first contribution, "Marshland Memories: Constructing Narrative in an Online Archival Exhibition," by Robert Summerby-Murray. Grounding his observations in a digitization project developed using those same Mount Allison University archives used by Grant Hurley as a small archives case study in the previous section of this collection, Summerby-Murray points out that while the "construction of narrative… in the archival record has been keenly debated in the theoretical literature over the past decades," there are "relatively few examples of researchers applying these theoretical positions to a set of archival resources." Like Noah Richler, Summerby-Murray's thematic concern in his digital archive project is the physical landscape. As he makes clear, telling the stories of the Tantramar marshlands in a way that faithfully represents the archival "reality" was an elusive goal, one which led the project team to question the very nature of archival truth and to appreciate more fully the ways in which the cherished archival tenets of organization, order and accountability present only a flawed and partial meta-narrative, whether in conventional or online archival representation.

Discussion of aspects of archival "reality" continues in Ala Rekrut's essay "Connected Constructions, Constructing Connections: Materiality of Archival Records as Historical Evidence." She suggests that recent shifts, especially in the field of history, to more theoretical and interdisciplinary approaches to analyzing sources appear to have distanced historians from records as physical phenomena. Positing that the "materiality of records is anchored in the social circumstances surrounding their physical creation" and is therefore a significant part of the reconstructive and interpretive process, Rekrut develops a tight focus on the physical aspects of two versions of a Hudson's Bay Company journal from the Moose Fort trade post, compiled between 1789 and 1791. Her finely detailed analysis of the differences in physical composition between the two artefacts is a classic example of the value of evidence provided by material analysis. As researchers increasingly use archival materials only through their digitized surrogates, we need to be cautioned by Rekrut's observation that "those who have access only to an image of a record have access to significantly less materially manifested evidence than those who can use the original records."

Rekrut's celebration of materiality and her cautionary words about the loss of evidentiary value in any form of archival reproduction find echoes in "Physicality as Apotheosis: The Changing Roles of Atoms and Bits in the Digital Age," by Melissa McCarthy. Attempting to steer a course between the practical and the philosophical and to integrate analysis of both the material and the digital in the construction of an online exhibit, McCarthy dismisses poorly planned exhibits of randomly chosen images, mounted without consideration or context, and instead suggests that any online project first define "its goal, its intended audience and, vitally, its maintenance plan." Her discussion then shifts to the question of the material versus the virtual, the real versus the fake and, following the work of Walter Benjamin, "the ways in which, in creating virtual exhibits, we are allowing many more people to see our holdings than would otherwise be the case, but at the same time, we are harming the authenticity and authority of the objects we are reproducing." Addressing the tensions between the real and the virtual, as well as the lack of consensus among archivists concerning the value of virtual exhibits, McCarthy suggests that a "properly designed exhibit with sufficient description and meta-data to clarify each item's informational content can offer enough information to most researchers, but some researchers may need to examine the physical object to gain, for instance, clues as to its method of production." Her essay also considers the varying approaches to exhibit site design implicit in Web 1.0 and 2.0 developments and, in conclusion, offers hope and even some encouragement for archives, however small, that are considering construction of virtual exhibits.

The question of constructing a virtual presence for archives is also the theme of Dean Irvine and Meagan Timney's essay "A New Build: Digital Tools for Archives, Commons and Collaboration." As architects of the Editing Modernism in Canada project (EMiC), they have been concerned

with the creation of a digital media commons and, in particular, with the development of collaborative editing tools to facilitate their own project and other such virtual initiatives. While McCarthy's essay explores some of the preliminary conceptual and practical issues to be considered in establishing an online presence for archives, Irvine and Timney's contribution, based on an already well developed project involving a number of partner institutions, considers issues arising at a considerably more advanced stage. There is also a significant conceptual shift from discussion of how best (if at all) to present online versions of archival collections, to the concept of the digital commons, a project collectively produced by and distributed among those who contribute their labour to the project. Irvine and Timney's comprehensive discussion of currently available and developing digital tools, together with examples of Canadian projects making use of them, provides a valuable "real time" snapshot of the most advanced technological approaches to shaping new archival narratives of Canada.

Completing the section on mapping archives in the virtual world, Emily Ballantyne and Zalig Pollock's essay, "*Respect des fonds* and the Digital Page," provides an inside look into their work as editors of a sophisticated digital project focused on the work of a single Canadian poet and writer, P.K. Page. Central to their discussion is an aspect of digitization present in the highly varied approaches of Summerby-Murray, Rekrut, McCarthy and even, although more tangentially, Irvine and Timney, namely the question of context. How does a virtual rendering of an archival fonds, either in whole or in part, convey the content and ordering of the archival original? And is it important that it do so?[6] The authors, carefully distinguishing the concept of fonds from that of the collection, the product of clearly defined activities from the artificial construct," align digital archives with the artificial collection and call them "in effect, anti-archives." However, they also make clear that the basic archival tenet of the fonds, with its accompanying respect for provenance and original order, has itself been the subject of interrogation in these uncertain postmodern times and, from this perspective, the fonds is as much a "conceptual principle" as a "physical entity" (Cook 1992: 33). Citing Lyotard's definition of postmodernism as "incredulity towards metanarratives," the authors follow Cook in arguing that archival principles such as *respect des fonds*, are "historically contingent, not universal or absolute. The record is now perceived as… reflecting the narrative intentions of its author and the receptivity of its contemporary audience as much as its actual informational content" (2001: 27).

Ballantyne and Pollock pursue the idea of the author's "narrative intentions" into their virtual presentation of the collected works of P.K. Page. Echoing Richler's earlier discussion of the relationship of maps to archives and the relationship of both to the land, they acknowledge that "If it is true that the map is not the territory, it is equally true that the database is not the archive." They describe their project as a "kind of archaeological investigation" at the heart of which "will be a database whose data will be largely (though not exclusively) drawn from the Page fonds." The authors reflect upon the subjectivity inherent in the organization of a database, an element they observe to parallel that inherent in archival organization and description, and they accept the responsibility to make this subjectivity clear to users of the digital *Collected Works*: "Inevitably the editors' choice of texts to include will reflect their sense of what is artistically and biographically significant, and their focus on genesis and social context will highlight certain aspects of the texts at the expense of others. In any case, the narrativized organizations embedded in the Digital Page will be very different indeed from Page's own self-narrative embedded in her fonds." This conclusion aligns closely with Martin Hand's prediction that since "technologies are inseparable from institutional and organizational cultures then we would expect digitization to bring alternative cultural conventions and practices into being" (2008: 6). The final part of Ballantyne and Pollock's essay provides a case study example of the digital transcription of one of Page's poems, supplying both the "genetic" text as well as an example of the editor's adherence to the central doctrine of *respect des fonds*.

Section IV — Case Studies in Archives and the Canadian Narrative

Ballantyne and Pollock's paper, which closes the previous section, provides a classic example of the conversations to which Doug Rimmer's preface referred — scholars and archivists sharing their expertise in the pursuit of new ways of presenting and exploring archives. These fruitful discussions are further demonstrated and developed in this final section where we more fully explore the case study approach. As our first essayist observes: "The literary archive is a space of transaction. In this space, the producers, arrangers, describers and interpreters of texts exchange ideas about words and collaborate in the production of literary meaning." Authors in this section send what are essentially reports from the field, or, more accurately, reports from the archives, about the process and progress of their research.

Jocelyn Hallman's essay, "Titling *He Drown She in the Sea*: The Archive as Paratext," once again invokes consideration of power and control — by archivists and scholars — counterpoised in relation to authorial intent, as she considers the archival context of Shani Mootoo's work. Once again the vocabulary of mapping recurs, in this case in relation to the physical placement of Mootoo's fonds. "Does it matter," Hallman asks, "that Mootoo's fonds were placed at a Vancouver institution, in a Canadian collection, rather than in a Trinidadian or diasporic context; does this alter or insert the archive into the dialogue about an author and her 'place' according to literary discourse?" Citing the works of both archivists and literary theorists, Hallman's analysis focuses on Mootoo's search for a title for her novel and what the archival traces of this search reveal about the novel itself. Using Gérard Genette's "peritext + epitext = paratext" equation as her starting point, Hallman makes clear that "reading the archive as epitext reveals a more fraught relationship between peritext and epitext than this equation suggests," and in tracing, through the archival evidence, the search for the novel's title, she argues that "we do not see a simple equation of peritext + epitext = paratext; instead, the epitext shapes our reading of the peritext, altering its role in interpretation." Further, Hallman argues that the case of Mootoo's search for a title can be seen as an example of a particularly Canadian search for identity — the archive considered as epitext "alters our understanding of the novel's peritexts but also our understanding of Mootoo's role in the Canadian literary canon. The discourses that locate her as an Indian, Trinidadian, Caribbean or diasporic writer are disrupted by the archival process as much as are our readings of her work."

In "The Letters of Frances Stewart; Two Centuries of Layered Representation," Jodi Aoki returns us to consideration of the concept of authenticity and the difficulties of searching for the "original" authorial voice and reminds us that these are not concerns arising only out of relatively recent attempts at digital representation of archival material. As her meticulous research reveals, the letters of early Canadian settler Frances Stewart, housed in the archives at Trent University, have been copied, edited and altered over the two hundred years since they were written, perhaps most extensively by Stewart's daughter, Ellen. Aoki observes that "Ellen unobtrusively weaves her own commentary in and out of the principal text, sometimes without distinguishing punctuation, an effect that contributes to the re-description of her mother's life." In her contextualization of these repeated editorial interventions, Aoki draws on the work of both archival and historical/literary theorists, once again providing an example of the fruitful results of such cross-disciplinary conversations. Her essay also emphasizes the continuing importance of materiality in archival research. Some contemporary scholars, primarily concerned with the interpretation of the new digital universe, question the role of the more traditional skills: in considering the archival object Martin Hand asks "what is it which remains resilient? Is it the materiality, the texture of the thing? Is it the congealed form of knowledge encased within it? Is it the form of representation presented through it? Or, is it the skill and competence required in putting it to use?" In cases such as the Frances Stewart letters considered here we should be forced to respond that it is the combined resilience of both interpretive skill and the evidence provided by materiality that is essential to the search for understanding.

Materiality is also a significant component of Gwen Davies and Carole

Gerson's essay "From Bath to Birchbark: The Peregrinations of a Marriage Poem." While they describe their quest for the origins and authorship of an eighteenth-century marriage poem as taking them "from graveyards to Google," Davies and Gerson vividly recall an archival encounter, "admiring the binding, feeling the texture of the paper, and appreciating the typesetting." The authors trace the poem, which they had first discovered written on birchbark in St. John, New Brunswick, in 1786, and considered as an authentic early Canadian "original," back to a first publication in England in the *Bath Journal* of May 25, 1752. As they recount, their research, starting with the "original" discovered in the Mowat Papers in the Charlotte County Archives in St. Andrews, New Brunswick (the same small archives that provides Grant Hurley with one of his case study justifications for the importance of small local collections), included all types of media, from birchbark through rare book repositories, old newspapers and journals to sophisticated electronic databases. And yet, as they carefully acknowledge, their breakthrough in the search for the poem's origin was finally made through personal contact with another distinguished researcher. The most stereotypically scholarly and traditional as well as the most up-to-date electronic archival sleuthing methods were both upstaged by an invaluable personal connection. The authors' comprehensive research, tracing the many iterations of their poem from New Brunswick through Pennsylvania, Scotland, London, New York, Quebec and finally to Bath, also gives this local Canadian discovery an international context and reveals how unexpectedly porous were the boundaries of the Atlantic world in the eighteenth century.

Porous boundaries, somewhat less extensive although no less engaging, are a significant element in Michael Peterman's archival quest. In his essay, "Unearthing an Erased Poet: Gathering Up the Fragments of James McCarroll," Peterman shares the fruits of his research into the life and work of a transplanted Irishman who, after arriving in North America in 1831, first made his primary living, not by his pen, but as a Customs Officer in Peterborough, Toronto and elsewhere in Canada West, before leaving to spend the last twenty-five years of his life in the United States, first in Buffalo and then in New York City. Peterman's search for traces of this erased writer, musician and poet has all of the elements of detective fiction as he describes the pursuit of this "pre-Confederation Humpty Dumpty" from a well-established creative and artistic career in Toronto to his almost total disappearance from the Canadian cultural scene after 1864. The struggle to eke out a living, following the loss of his customs position, resulted in his move to the United States in 1866. Subsequently, partly as a result of this relocation and suspicions of his Fenian sympathies, McCarroll was "dropped from the record of cultural achievement by the country in which he had done his best literary work."

Peterman's ongoing work of reconstruction has encountered more than the usual share of archival roadblocks: the lack of any surviving family papers and the disappearance of many of the journals, magazines and newspapers to which McCarroll contributed. Without the powerful searching capacity of the Internet and the careful work of archivists in digitizing their "plain vanilla" finding aids, tracing McCarroll's contributions in obscure and long defunct publications and identifying McCarroll letters in other collections would have been an all but impossible task.

Geoffrey Klages has also had cause to turn to obscure local newspapers as well as many other unpublished archival resources in his efforts to solve a much more famous Canadian conundrum — the mysterious death of the celebrated painter Tom Thomson. Klages's efforts, however, have not been prompted by any lack of evidence or cultural erasure — quite the contrary. In his essay, "The Many Deaths of Tom Thomson," Klages attempts to uncover the truth about one of Canada's most enduring and well known mysteries — the circumstances surrounding the death of the artist Tom Thomson at Canoe Lake in the summer of 1917. This researcher's efforts have been hampered rather than assisted by all of the attention accorded the event. Klages's examination surveys the "myth-making" and "rescripting" that has taken place in what has been almost a century since Thomson's death. However, as his careful and comprehensive research into the "original" evidence reveals, returning to the authenticity of archival sources and government records does not always reveal a single, uncomplicated truth: the "primary" accounts of contemporaries close to Thomson, of those close to the scene of the tragedy, and even of professionals such as the park ranger and the examining coroner, are sometimes unclear and contradictory. Nonetheless, Klages's forensic archival sleuthing does provide, for the first time in almost a century, some degree of certainty surrounding this event. As the author observes: "The primary documents available from the time of Tom Thomson's death, particularly those in publicly accessible archival collections, many of which have been available for over sixty years, are integral to an accurate understanding of how this leading figure of Canadian art died." The link between archives and the formation of an accurate Canadian narrative could not be more clearly established than in the case of this mythic mystery.

These case studies of archival quests conclude our collection. In surveying aspects of the archival landscape in Canada we have been able to map but a small portion of its extensive terrain. Although the Archives in Canada Conference Series has concluded, the conversations to which it gave rise continue. These conversations continue through the essays presented here and, more widely, through the ongoing work of archivists and scholars in acquiring, arranging, describing and distributing, in both traditional and new digital forms, the primary materials that make possible the accurate and insightful construction and dissemination of narratives for Canada.

Notes

1. Selected papers from this conference were published as a special issue of the *Journal of Canadian Studies* (40, 2, 2006).
2. Selected papers from this conference were published in two journals, *Topia* (20, Fall, 2008) and *Archivaria* (67, 2009).
3. See Martin Hand, *Making Digital Cultures: Access, Interactivity and Authenticity* (Aldershot, U.K.: Ashgate, 2008, 8). He observes that "the library, financial services, and the archive can all be considered cultural technologies in the Foucauldian sense."
4. The idea of the Archive of Place, "the ways in which people interpret material traces to reconstruct past events, the conditions under which such interpretation takes place and the role this interpretation plays in historical consciousness and social memory" is thoughtfully explored by William J. Turkel in *The Archive of Place: Unearthing the Pasts of the Chilcotin Plateau* (Vancouver: UBC Press, 2007, xix).
5. We are delighted to represent the work of Francophone scholars and archivists by including two French language essays in this collection. In order to integrate these essays into a volume that is presented primarily in English, we present them with the English-language system of punctuation, citation and reference listing. We have, however, maintained French accents on place names where applicable.
6. Compare the view of Daniel J. Caron, Librarian and Archivist of Canada, "the value, utility, and mediation of information resources transcend the status, medium or mode of their creation. In the digital age, communication is primarily all about the production and consumption of the information resource and not about the nature or status of the information resource container (*Memory Institutions in the 21st Century: The Need for Convergence and Collaboration*, Address to Archives Society of Alberta, May 2010 <http://www.collectionscanada.gc.ca/lac/012007-1000.007-e.html>.

Section I

Overview — Mapping the Archival Landscape

Preface: Archives and the Canadian Narrative

Doug Rimmer

The Archives in Canada Conference Series was formed after the first conference, "Turning the Knobs on Writers' Closets," was held at McMaster University in May 2005. Former Librarian and Archivist of Canada, Ian Wilson, gave a plenary address, following which he pledged the support of LAC for a continued series. I was very pleased to speak briefly at the second conference in the series, "Taking a Stand: Activism in Canadian Archives," held at LAC's main building in Ottawa in June 2007, and I am even more pleased to have had the opportunity to make a substantive contribution to the third conference, Archives and the Canadian Narrative, at Mount Allison University, June 2009. The following remarks are based on the plenary address I gave at that meeting.

One of the true strengths of this conference series is its multidisciplinary focus. The series welcomes archivists, librarians, literary and historical scholars, and the practitioners who create archives. This reflects a larger pattern that is taking shape at LAC and in many other memory institutions — a new pattern of sharing and knowledge creation, driven more by conversations between those interested in a given topic and less by issues arising from access to specific items in our collection. We are continuing to understand and work within this shift, and it makes participating in this conference series very important to us.

The 2009 conference invited participants to reflect on the role archives have in the telling of Canadian stories and the creation of narratives about Canada. The concept of narrative, in its postmodern sense, implies that we tell a story but at the same time we understand that, by choosing the direction of that story, we must necessarily leave out details and omit individuals because our scope or focus has not allowed them in. A postmodern concept of narrative does not let recorded history or a canon rest as a final form. These narratives are always in a process of formation, dissolution, change and challenge from other viewpoints or interests.

By way of example, John Ralston Saul, in his latest book, *A Fair Country: Telling Truths about Canada* (2008), challenges what he sees as the prevailing narrative about Canada: "We are not a civilization of British or French or European inspiration. We never have been…. To accept and even believe such fundamental misrepresentations of Canada and Canadians is to sever our mythologies from our reality" (xi). In the next breath, asserting the importance of narrative, Ralston Saul writes:

> We are a people of Aboriginal inspiration organized around a concept of peace, fairness and good government…. If we can embrace a language that expresses that story, we will feel a great release. We will discover a remarkable power to act and to do so in such a way that we will feel we are true to ourselves. (xii)

To underline the importance of narrative, Ralston Saul cites two Canadian novelists, Guy Vanderhaeghe: "The narrative is how you think of things," and Thomas King: "The truth about stories is that that's all we are" (21). Narratives, or "mythologies" to use Ralston Saul's term, are important because they shape how we understand, think and act. And they do so regardless of whether they are real or true.

What better subject for a conference, then, than the telling of Canadian stories — how, why and by what means — including the use of archives and other memory resources in the search for verisimilitude. LAC, as part of our national and regional archival and library communities, can harness the power of the digital era to support that effort.

It can support the process of formation, dissolution, change and challenge in our Canadian narratives and stories with a richer body of content that is better contextualized than before, easier to access and to link together — either to reinforce or to contest the strands of narratives. Today LAC is working, on our own and in partnership with others, to enable discovery of, and access to, a more diverse and comprehensive range of material.

In many ways, LAC's mandate to acquire cultural, social and historical material in order to document Canadian society rests on a narrative conception of Canadian society — not a static, fixed narrative but one composing many strands and shifting over time. Our task is to constantly revisit our collections' directions to better understand the complexities of what needs to be documented. That self-questioning needs to recognize what narrative elements we have missed in the past, Aboriginal and multicultural records, for example. Our task is to engage others as well, such as those present at this conference, in the work of questioning, so that we are better able to see what we have not yet seen and so that we better understand how our fonds and our collections fit with the broader national collection that is the composite of all the material held by all of our memory institutions.

There is, it could be argued, a narrative about the Canadian narrative, which is that, as Canadians we seek to be inclusive, to be open to new stands and to address our mistakes. The very way we choose to understand our narrative is part of the story of who we believe ourselves to be. LAC's winter 2009 exhibition on Inuit residential schools demonstrates this point. All memory institutions are engaged in the effort to allow the Canadian narrative to be as rich, complex and evolving as it needs to be. LAC actively supports that effort. Returning to the idea that "knowledge is created through conversation" and to the implications of this statement for libraries and archives, the 2007 *Information Research* article, "Participatory Networks: The Library as Conversation" neatly summarizes my starting point:

> Knowledge is created through conversation. People converse, organizations converse, states converse, societies converse. Different communities have different standards for conversations, from the scientific community's rigorous formalisms to the sometimes impenetrable dialect of teens.
>
> Conversations can take place between friends and colleagues in the "here and now." However, they can also take place over centuries, with the participants changing but the theme remaining the same.
>
> "Conversation Theory" is a means of explaining cognition and how people learn. Put simply: people learn through conversation where conversation is defined as an act of communication and agreement between a set of agents who can be individuals, organizations, societies, or even different aspects of oneself....
>
> The lasting results of these conversations are the books, videos, and artefacts that document, expand, or result from conversations.
>
> Institutions such as libraries and archives have been the places that facilitate conversations, though often implicitly. Facilitation not only enriches conversations with diverse and deep information, it also serves as a memory keeper, documenting agreements and outcomes to facilitate future conversations.
>
> If theory states that conversation creates knowledge, memory institutions have added a corollary: the best knowledge comes from an "optimal information environment," one in which the most diverse and complete information is available to the conversant(s), which lead to principles such as intellectual freedom and unfettered access.[1]

This extract supports my view that one of the fundamental shifts that LAC and other libraries/archives/museums must make is to increasingly become facilitators of "conversations" in which we may or may not be an active participant, as opposed to current conversations which are either bilateral between LAC and individual clients or where LAC is seen merely as a source of resources, hardly conversations at all.

Understanding that "knowledge-creating conversations" must involve an internal-to-the-individual component as each participant arrives at his or her own point of "knowing" something new, these "conversations" can take place solely within an individual, supported and triggered by information from our collection, or they may be highly participatory conversations involving many, many people using our collection and the information within it as a point of departure or reference.

The continuing evolution of the Internet provides a powerful set of tools for making these conversations and our role in generating or supporting them more explicit, shifting them from bilateral exchanges to a broader dialogue. We recognize that LAC is but one of many memory institutions working to determine how best to use these tools to accomplish our shared objectives. We aim to learn from the work of our other national and regional partners in the creation of narratives and counter narratives for Canada and to share our own successes with the broader community. Conferences such as this are an important conversational occasion for sharing our ideas and initiatives.

Narratives and conversation — the stories we tell and the ways in which we learn — these concepts were at the heart of our 2009 discussions and will provide a sturdy frame for the papers which follow in this collection.

Note

1. R. David Lankes, Joanne Silverstein, Scott Nicholson and Todd Marshall <http://informationr.net/ir/12-4/colis/colis05.html>.

Stories, Buildings and Maps
A Canadian Archive

Noah Richler

The Digby Neck is a spit of land that extends out from the ridge of the North Mountain, at the back of Nova Scotia's fertile Annapolis Valley, a wharf of the natural world that gradually sinks over the course of forty kilometres into the frigid waters of the Bay of Fundy. The region is a historic part of Canada. In the dictionary sense of the term, it is one of the country's earliest historic sites, insofar as stories of Samuel de Champlain and the Mi'kmaq chief Membertou, and their meeting in nearby Annapolis-Port Royal, are remembered in the written diaries that provide us with some idea of the hardships that Champlain and his not-immediately-cheery bunch endured a bit more than four hundred years ago. But of course history reaches back much further than writing — unless we take a broader view of what constitutes a script.

The replica of the French *habitation* that now stands at Port Royal is a National Historic Site, and a very beautiful one — especially in winter, when the truth of living in this country is so much more in evidence. It came into being mostly because of the passions of an American summer visitor, Harriet Taber Richardson. This is ironic for a couple of reasons, not the least of which is that the original buildings were sacked by marauding settlers from Virginia, then one of the Thirteen Colonies, now the United States of America — first a pillaging and then the restoration of a settlement that stood at a natural crossroads of land and sea.

The Annapolis Valley and, further to the south, the Digby Neck, as well as what is now called the French Shore, on the Acadian (east) side of St. Mary's Bay, are at the heart of a part of the country that saw a remarkable confluence of Canada's founding nations — Mi'kmaq, Acadians, English, French and then African-American United Empire Loyalists all arrived in the region before today's constant waves of new Canadian immigrants seeking the fortune of a second chance.

Often, driving from Halifax to Digby through the Annapolis Valley — Ernest Buckler country — I am reminded of the Mississippi, not because of any civil rights injustices, though Canada had these too, but because of the layered, occupied and even haunted feeling of the place. The valley, like the Mississippi, is a flood plain where the soil is rich with sediments and memories of the absent. The silt that accounts for the valley's incredible fertility acts as a quiet metaphor for the peoples who also passed over and left their faint traces. Great tides washed over the valley's flood plain, salt water that was finally kept at bay — the language serves us well, here — by the system of dikes that the Acadians called *aboiteaux*. The tides deposited layers upon layers of fecund soil — just as the sum of the various peoples who made up Canada laid their own strata, rich with memory and possibility, and continue to do so.

In Nova Scotia — in so much of Canada — we feel history through what is inferred. It is a ghostly feeling, certainly, though not one that is spooky so much as mysterious and compelling. This sense that any of us has today of arriving at the back of a train of families who will never be known by name, and whose actions are so often rendered generic when they are remembered at all, is at the very essence of being Canadian. Not only Newfoundland's Beothuk, and all evidence of them, have disappeared from our landscape. We ask, "Who was Membertou? Who was Shawnadithit? Who were the Acadians and the French and the English and the Scottish and the Irish, and then the Poles and the Ukrainians, and all the other anonymous peoples who built this place?"

Along the Digby Neck, the foundations of pioneers' houses that might have provided scant clues are rubble beneath the undergrowth of once-cultivated fields, hard-won from the rocky promontory and now returned in a messy state back to nature. Larry, a lobster fisher friend of mine, knows where some of them are and takes me on walks occasionally to find them. The weathered stones — at least the ones that have not been taken to serve a similar purpose again — lie in roughly oblong formation, and trees slightly younger than the surrounding ones sprout from soil that was once the floor of a house. Of the shack that the hermit George inhabited on the sandy shore, he who was said to put a hex on passing ships for the salvage that would then wash up on the beach, there is only a photograph and stories that grow more vague with each passing day. The man who remembers George, who can identify the face in the photograph, will be dead soon and more history will be lost.

Along the neck, even recent history is falling down. It is shocking, to me, how many of the beautiful wooden barns, untended, have fallen down in just the few years that I have been living in the region. One long barn, by Lake Midway, was built over a running stream. Two more, along Highway 217, at the head of St. Mary's Bay and below Seawall, are just piles of useless lumber now, with the carcasses of motor cars as their rejoinders.

More fall down and no one seems to care.

Out in the water — at Seawall, on the St. Mary's Bay side, and further down the neck at Sandy Cove, on the Bay of Fundy side — are occasional herring weirs. These are beguiling arrangements of high timbers, two bound spruce trunks high, that have nets strung between them and are planted into the sea bed in a bass clef–like formation. The herring that swim into them at high tide are trapped when the waters recede. They are beautiful to behold, these weirs, though fewer and fewer of them operate because of the seiner boats that come in and, having located the schools of fish with sonar and GPS, suck them out unceremoniously and in ruthless, unthinking quantity. In winter, treacherous weather makes the weirs impossible to manage, and in recent summers those along the Digby Neck have yielded no herring at all. The fishers blame the weather, the tides, the warm air and the seals — anything but themselves, though that is another story. The point is that there has been less work for local fishermen (though the son of a fisher will most likely want to travel to the city now — and can) and less herring to draw the bigger catch in.

The weirs, too, will fall down soon.

These buildings, these constructions — the barns, the weirs — are a part of Canada's historical archive. They are a script upon the land. We all know what a barn is, and when we see one we know what kind of activity is undertaken there. If we are on the prairie, we see not just barns but settlers' homes tilting away from the wind and then collapsing, and in their sparsity we understand not just the vicariousness of weather and the ephemeral grip of peoples on an unyielding land but also the devastating change that occurred in the way that labour and settlements were organized when mechanized farming replaced smaller homesteads. When we do this, we are entering into a conversation with the land, just as we do when we look out over the Bay of Fundy and see that herring weir for the first time and ask what it is and who put it there. We try to imagine what purpose it served, the sort of work that was done there and what it says of the munificence beneath the surface of the water.

In Canada, we divine our past and read the landscape more often than we know. We behave as archaeologists of the present day. We have to do so because so much of our history and so many of our documents are not written — and so we prick up our ears and listen for stories, and read the trails and monuments and buildings that are our mute writing upon the land, instead. It is a conversation beyond words that we are having, for not just First Nations or Inuit read the land this way. An adage of what some have come to call psycho-geography, an idea that at its simplest recognizes the interaction of topography and human sentiment, is that a place without stories is merely a landscape. As Ted Chamberlin argued in *If This Is Your*

Land, Then Where Are Your Stories? and John Ralston Saul did later in *A Fair Country*: *Telling Truths about Canada*, merely by virtue of living here, of having entered into the stories of this place, we are becoming aboriginal in our world view and in the way we interpret the land if we are not actually native already. Each of us erects our own *inuksuit*. Consider, for instance — sadly an all too easy example — those places along the highway where a cross and flowers mark the spot of an accident. The cross remembers a death, but it also presents a story. It tells you that the turn is dangerous and to watch out and to slow right down. This is not at all different from the way we assume that a ranch hand on the prairie reads the information of a coulee and what it says about water in a parched place, or the way that an Inuk reads an *iqalurait*, the snow cut by the prevailing wind into low, tongue-shaped drifts pointing northwest. The land and all the things upon it are a library and an archive waiting to be read.

In Canada, in our psyche as much as in our literature, we are fascinated by maps because we understand them as stories.

Think of those early sixteenth- and seventeenth-century maps of Canada — of how so much in them was invented, maps filled with the monsters and natives and great big seas that were fruits of the imagination of cartographers often working back in France or England from explorers' and missionaries' notes. Think of how these maps were gradually displaced by more scientific ones such as James Cook charted. And think of how even our supposedly objective maps are disputed now — how the Gail-Peters protection challenged conventional maps that usually had England or the United States at their centre.

Stories work this way too. We invent a place with stories or by drawing a picture of a rock or a herd of animals as the first cave painters did, or of a house and a tree as a child does, and then we mark our place in the world by adding ourselves as hunters in the field or as a little girl in a dress in the garden of the house beneath a bright sun. Over time, we chart the territory completely — or so we think, before someone else disputes the picture we have presented of a place with a competing story. In this way we invent, map and then argue a place, and we describe a city like Montreal or Vancouver or New York as "storied" because so many have laid claim to it and given it life, and then others have revised its life with competing stories of their own. In this constantly evolving, amoebic set of stories is the essence of a place, a story that will not be settled until the place is dead, finished — just a landscape again. Even then, a single story is unlikely.

This cultural argument is the lively present end of history, and it is one of the great excitements of living in Canada, perhaps as a result of our having so little official history — no single, definitive map — that so many kinds of stories vie for attention. Spoken ones, written ones, silent ones. We are, here, still finding our way through — still learning the place, still learning the trails.

Robert Bringhurst, the British Columbian classicist, poet, scholar of typography and translator of the Haida canon, helped make this clear to me one day, when I found myself following him on a trail through woods that he knew better than I. We were on the east side of Quadra Island, in B.C., not far from Heriot Bay.

Bringhurst is one of the country's literary treasures, a brilliant linguist whose passions are ignited with temper. He is an artist to the point of eclectic near-absurdity. He has written a play that uses English, Ancient Greek and Cree simultaneously. I cannot imagine this ever being a Broadway hit, but still I pay attention to everything Bringhurst writes. His interest in typography is fascinating, given his obsession — what he has elsewhere called "pure wonder" (1986: 17) — with stories that are not written. In his poem "Hóng Zìchéng," Bringhurst writes:

> So you can read
> a book full of words.
> Can you read one without words?
> You can bring music
> out of that lute after tuning
> the strings. Can you play one without strings?

Bringhurst's great endeavour, the one for which he stands to be remembered, is *A Story as Sharp as a Knife*, his verse translation of a substantial portion of the extant canon of the Haida, the northwest coastal First Nation. After his trilogy was published, Bringhurst was excoriated by angry Haida. The rallying call was that Bringhurst, a white man, had stolen Native stories, even if what he had really done was breathe new life into the work of Ghandl, Skaay and several other Haida myth-tellers whose work had been transcribed by the ethnologist John Reed Swanton in 1900–1. (Archivists take note — and feel vindicated if ever you feel that your vocational duty prompts you to transgress: because Swanton was not allowed to listen to the women, only the male Haida storytellers' work has survived. We are at a loss.)

Bringhurst's Haida opus enraged both Aboriginals and academics defending their territory against trespass, but Bringhurst was undeterred. His trilogy thrust forgotten Haida masters into a previously segregated canon of European greats. He compared the Haida storytellers whose work he had resuscitated with Aristotle, Tolstoy and Flaubert. With bold authority, Bringhurst wrote, "In my attempts to set the best Haida poets in a global context, I have found Bach and Titian and Velásquez more immediately helpful than Racine" (Richler 2006: 50).

Bringhurst rehabilitated old furrows that the Haida oral stories had travelled before the Europeans criss-crossed the continent and controlled it with stories of their own. His translations animated the forest with spirits and stories that had been largely forgotten and, spoken by a minority of Haida and otherwise withering in the dusty files of various library archives, had only the possibility of a diminishing circulation. His translations gave Haida poets identity and proved that Haida oral poetry was not some loose, folksy set of stories passed on by anyone in the community, but a rigorous canon of brilliantly honed poems of frequently considerable length performed by a small number of highly skilled orators. This did not mean that Bringhurst believed that this small number of Haida storytellers invented the stories they told. He believed, as I do, that stories exist outside of us and that those who write or speak them, Haida or not, are shamans of a kind in the service of stories who articulate them as a means of a society finding its way.

Maps, I suggested to Bringhurst, were the first stories.

"No," said Bringhurst. "Stories are the first maps" (Richler 2006: 50).[1]

"If we stop telling stories," he continued, "the forest will shrivel up and die. We won't find our way, not only because we don't have the maps that stories are for us, but because without the wisdom of these stories there won't be a world for us to live in any more…. In myth-telling culture, the material embodiment of the stories is the landscape — the forest, the oceans; it's the clouds, the mountains, the rivers and the lakes. They're the script, the literature of reality, so that learning to write is not on the agenda. Learning *to read* is the important thing. *The text is already here*. When we pass through the forest and make up stories about it, we're deciphering the stories that are already in it. Articulating those stories is as much a part of the process of living as deer passing through here and munching leaves" (Richler 2006: 51, 53).

In Canada, we have a problem — or at least we have two competing tendencies that the work of archivists is helping to resolve.

On the one hand, our dearth of a formal history leaves us with an overwhelming curiosity about who we are and how we arrived here. On the other, we have a tendency to disregard the evidence of history and even to act against it as it can seem an abnegation of our present of that second chance so many people came to Canada to find. I do not believe those who accuse Canadians of being ignorant of their history and use this charge to howl down our general intelligence. There is a certain indifference to our formal history in Canada, as it was mostly written elsewhere by people and institutions that were our colonial masters. Canada was, and is still, a nation of peoples who have fled governments or hard times and come here for a fresh start, snubbing the powers that be — what I have described in my own work as the "distant authority," the power that started with the Hudson's Bay Company, governed from faraway London, and then became Ottawa, though some would say Washington, and that in all its permutations seemed to have so little to do with Canadians' work as pioneers and the day-to-day struggles of the work they did. The Hudson's Bay Company, then Ottawa, was certainly not telling the story of that work — not in their annals, anyway. This is the reason, I believe, that novelists and local historians have come to have such importance and high standing in Canada, why writers such as David Adams Richards, Fred Stenson, Guy Vanderhaeghe, Alice Munro, Bernice Morgan and Alistair MacLeod have the place that they do. There is no history that sings how the loggers of New Brunswick worked the woods in the days before gasoline changed the industry; there are no writers who put the people of New Brunswick and the stories they tell onto the page and into the imagination, so fully formed and unforgettable, as David Adams Richards does, or as a host of other writers do for other vital parts of Canada's present — and history — elsewhere.

Time and again, in Canada, we prove ourselves a nation in which the heroics that matter are those of ordinary people — whether in the woods around us, in the waters off Nova Scotia or in the trenches of Vimy and now Afghanistan. When the novel that is to be written comes out of Fort McMurray, out of Alberta's tar sands, the chances are that it will not, as was Upton Sinclair's *Oil!* — the book that inspired the Paul Thomas Anderson movie *There Will Be Blood* — be a story about an oil magnate taming the frontier, but about a Newfoundland worker enduring it. And we will want to know that story because, as with so much of the Canadian narrative, it will be a story about a fascinating "ordinary" life. The evidence for it will be slight — that is the nature of our country — and no one else will be telling it.

So, as a fundamental aspect of our culture, we have a tremendous interest in the sum of extraordinary ordinary stories that make up the quilt of our identity, each of these lives a stitch in its fabric, a stitch in time. It is an interest that has — since the 1960s especially (a decade that was as important to Canadian life and unity as the year 1917) — reached further back and outwards to include in its embrace our Aboriginal history. Our Aboriginal history, because, as I have already suggested, merely by being here we are all, whatever our origins, affected by it. In no small part because of our dearth of a formal written history, in the absence of a mythology or a *magna carta* that proves our provenance from way back, we want our own stories to be grafted on to the bark of the aboriginal tree. This is why Joseph Boyden's first novel, *Three Day Road*, was such a terrific and deserving success. It took one of Canada's founding creation myths — the story of Canadians' participation in the First World War — and put Cree right into the middle of it. In the trenches at Vimy in 1917, we are told, is where Canadians of all kinds first met each other and, in the crucible of battle, bonded. It is the moment, historians insist, when the character of the nation was forged. Until Boyden's

Three Day Road was published in 2005, however, there were no Aboriginals in this story. Of course the stories of Aboriginal soldiers that inspired Boyden — one was a relative — were true, and yet these stories were not an active part of Canadians' collective memory. But now, after Boyden's novel and its brilliant intertwining of Canadian with Cree myths and histories, it is impossible to exclude them.

Our resistance to a formal history has its sociological roots in a resentment of governments and overly powerful institutions — typically, in Canada, the company in a town where other employment is extremely hard to come by — even as Canadians know that they depend upon these imbalanced relationships. Canadians have a fascination with stories of arrival, the archives of which are likely to be sitting in boxes in the attic, but outside of this very intimate relationship to history we have little compunction in wasting the evidence of a less personal past that appears to be a shackle on that opportunity of a fresh start. We regularly contribute to a wasting of the evidence. Often, the challenge is to even recognize what is historic in the new land before we raze that which we have built and start again. Those stones along the Digby Neck are taken from the foundations of old houses to use in new ones, and community memory mostly dies with their displacement. It was ever this way, from ancient empires forward, where the building blocks of houses are precious and practically are used again. But I see the same thing happening all around me, in Toronto, where the site of Upper Canada's first parliament sits, perhaps aptly for a city where business reigns paramount, beneath a Porsche vendor's lot. Regent Park, the city's first social housing project, is being demolished to make way for new houses, towers and community space. I am probably one of the few who are of two minds about this: I see the demolition of more history and housing that might have been refurbished and kept standing and contributed to the panoply of the city. The mostly three-storey buildings stand deliberately in green spaces. The idea, nearly sixty years ago, had been to find a way to put the poor of the city in what we would, today, call a "green" environment; but certain mistakes of urban engineering were made, and Regent Park became a ghetto and a den of crime and, pointed as we ever are towards a new world, what is being levelled now is a piece of urban history — and our embarrassment.

This levelling of our history and how it makes detectives out of historians and archivists can be seen all over the place. The Nova Scotian writer Leo McKay Jr.'s novel *Twenty-Six* remembers the twenty-six miners buried, near Stellarton, after the shafts of an improperly run coal mine collapsed in the Westray mining disaster of May 1992. For a while, the closed mine stood as its own inadvertent memorial, but more embarrassment, this time of the political kind, meant that the surface buildings were demolished and now McKay Jr.'s novel stands in their place as memorial and testament. Lisa

Moore's *February* is another example of this kind. A fine and beautifully written novel, it has at its core the terrible loss, to Newfoundland, of the Ocean Ranger in February 1982, all eighty-four members of the ocean oil rig's crew lost in a disaster that might have been prevented had the men on board been trained at all in what to do in the face of such a storm. The resentment of authority is expressed in what I have described *This Is My Country, What's Yours?* as our "myths of disappointment," the idea that we are let down by the authority that should properly be our steward (Richler 2006: 269). The ill feeling is profound.

A lot of the time the problem of scant evidence is more routine and even comic. In Newfoundland, I visited the mining town of Buchans with another wonderful writer from that province, Michael Crummey. Buchans was where Michael had grown up, a busy mining town then that (a common Canadian story) was closed and packed up after the resource — in this case, iron ore — was depleted and the town's *raison d'être* undone. The town's pointlessness was familiar to me, and would be to anyone who has travelled through the depopulated hamlets of the Atlantic provinces, northern Ontario, the Prairies, B.C. or the North — places where the few who remain stay behind to fish or hunt or hang onto memories and the impossible hope of the town's revival. The town business closes, and we move on — today, from Nova Scotia, Newfoundland and New Brunswick to Fort McMurray and the oil sands of Alberta, and perhaps thirty years hence, from Athabasca to some new Canadian Nirvana.

We do not linger much, in Canada; it is not our way. Elsewhere in Newfoundland, the writer Michael Winter told me of standing where a mining town had been, and all that was left of it was a hundred yards of tarmac on miles of what was otherwise a rural dirt road. It was the only piece of the town that had not been ripped up and moved. Drive at a normal speed and you perhaps notice a sudden smooth moment in the car's passage over what had been, before and after, dusty gravel, unknowingly passing over a place that had been life for hundreds in a split second.

The Saskatchewan writer Guy Vanderhaeghe is another novelist who has used the art of the novel (in this case, *The Englishman's Boy*) to explore and bring into the forefront of our collective consciousness key moments of our history, such as the Cypress Hills Massacre of June 1873, in which twenty-three Nakota were slaughtered by marauding American and Canadian wolf hunters and whiskey traders — leading to the establishment of Fort Walsh and, eventually, of "peace, order and good government" there. Vanderhaeghe, tellingly, in the epigraph to *The Last Crossing*, dedicated the novel to "all those local historians who keep the particulars of our past alive."

"I started school in a place called Mercoal, Alberta," the Cape Breton novelist Alistair MacLeod once told me in a conversation that he and I and

David Adams Richards and Guy Vanderhaeghe were having about the importance of work to the history of Canada — how it has shaped the very way we have settled the country, but is also the sort of history that is forgotten or left to archivists and novelists to remember after such towns are closed up.

"Mercoal was one of those typical company towns," Macleod said. "We lived in company houses that were built on skids, and when the price of coal dropped, the town went away. I remember, a number of years ago, driving from Banff to where Mercoal was, and there was absolutely nothing there. I drove into this little clearing and I said to my children, 'This is where I started school.' And they all laughed. They thought, 'Here is Dad being funny.' They were thinking, 'Well, where's the school?' and a woman came out of one of these hunting lodges and said, 'What are you looking for?' and I said, 'Well, I am looking for the school,' and she said, because she had gone to school there too, 'Go over there on your hands and knees and if you crawl around in the grass you will find the foundation of the school'" (Richler 2006: 230).

"My father was from Nova Scotia," said Macleod, remembering Cape Breton. "We had come from a place that was very rooted, but here was this very different kind of place. There are people who cannot find where they were born, because it was a Company Town that just vanished" (230).

In South Asian novels, a typical setting is of the busy street; in the spirit of the *Mahabharata*, the great book of India, on the busy street is where all things happen all the time. In the Middle East, the block of apartments does the job — an appropriate setting in stories by Arabs and Jews of tenants who cannot choose their neighbours but must find a way to live with them. In Canada, our fundamental literary metaphor is of the house. In stories emanating the length and breadth of the country — from Ami McKay's *Birth House* to the stories of Carol Shields or the ominous apartment blocks and hotels to be found in the work of the Vancouver writers Annabel Lyon and Timothy Taylor — the house rules.

In Vancouver, I drove with the novelist Michael Turner along the Kingsway, a busy road that was initially created as a route of emergency for English troops towards the sea. He narrated the Kingsway — he had written a book of poems by that name — as others would have done a mountain trail. He was one of Robert Bringhurst's deer munching his way through the forest.

"I like to think that I'm in a dialogue with the space around me," said Turner. "For me, the city is a novel — but one with many authors. It's an anthology. Some people get more pages than others, but everybody's contributing. The idea of my collection *Kingsway* was that reading is like driving, and writing is like thinking. I feel like I'm reading a book right now" (Richler 2006: 162).

I have an idea about what to do about the book of Canada as it is laid out on the land, a fantasy that comes out of my love of the country and its novels, and the experiences I have had of relearning the place after having been away from it so long. It comes from my work in radio, too, a medium that, at its best, is all about a love of story and ordinary lives made great — the sorts of stories that you are collecting in the archive, whether as photographs or letters or bits of recorded testimony, or the ones that inspire many Canadian novelists to write their versions of who we are. This fantasy of mine is derived from travels and conversations in places where the history that is being preserved is entirely oral — such as Igloolik, in Nunavut, where the work that John MacDonald and Leah Otak and a small group of Inuit has done under the aegis of the Igloolik Oral History Project, or IOHP, preserving local memory for the rest of us. Bruce Chatwin, the English romantic writer and traveller who died in 1989, once hypothesized that story was invented by humans staying up at night around a jungle fire to keep the dreaded tiger at bay. Chatwin was the author of *The Songlines*, a meld of fiction and travelogue that can probably be described as revolutionary for the way that it honoured how oral stories and their mnemonics written upon the land "sing" a place into existence. In Nunavut, I learned the validity and the importance of both these ideas — not just to Aboriginal Canada but also to the country in its present incarnation. In Nunavut, the tiger is the cold in the dark months of winter, called *siqinnaarut*, the time of year Iglulingmiut — the Inuit of Igloolik — waited for the sun to rise up above the horizon after its long absence and staved off hardships when the hunting was likely not so good and supplies were running out, with amusements, games and stories.

Another age.

Now snowmobiles take Inuit to where the caribou are and make winter camps less necessary, and the elders from whom the young would have learned their history and practical knowledge are either dying or being moved into retirement homes — inadvertently, away from the community. The stories are less necessary, as the Iglulingmiut are able — and need — to travel farther and farther to find the caribou, who are learning to travel in a wide arc around the humans' fixed settlements. The hunters return by evening to insulated homes, as they should, where the creation myths and cautionary tales that once kept order in the community have been subverted by the new technology. No need to visit when you can use the telephone. No need to weave into the knit of a story the things to be remembered — the valley where a catch is effortlessly made, a couple of tricks to snare your intended prey. New technology means your message and your bearings can be conveyed immediately.

"All the hunters take these [GPS] radios with them when they go hunting," said Louis Tapardjuk, one of IOHP's founders. "So everybody is constantly informed as to what's happening and there's no good stories coming back from the land anymore." He sighed. "Memory is so different now" (Richler 2006: 87).

The work that the IOHP is doing, collecting stories and knowledge and lore, is all about memory, and it is being replicated all over the country by Canadians looking in their own backyards and finding the treasure trove of living history there. Across Canada and not just the North, many concerned Canadians — as Archives Canada recognizes on its own website — are recording the memories of elders and doing what they can "to keep the particulars of our past alive."

Imagine, then, if a deliberate and concerted effort were made between three parties — the CBC, government and storytellers — to honour our own song lines and to solidify the effort that such groups are making in order to map the country through stories wholeheartedly. It would be a national mission that had, as its purpose, the charting of the territory in all languages and forms. Call this accumulative project the Canadian Canon, one that recorded the names (they say so much), the paintings, songs, stories, films, remembrances and imaginings of all kinds that make up the trails and the library of our country. Imagine that these were posted to an interactive website and digitally stored. Our project would function both as an archive of collective memory and as the museum of our aspirations. Tap on Beechey Island, Dorset, Carcross or Ross River, and we would be able to see, or listen to, the well of our affection and anxieties — and, ultimately, bask in the light of our relationship of belonging.

And do not make the canon merely retrospective. Let Canadians add to it — and artists reside in it. Fund, every year, a new singing of the country: a musician, a writer and a painter, each an artist resident with a *carte blanche* (a fitting colour) to travel, learn, add to the canon and sing his or her part of Canada anew.

But there is another element that is needed to make this work, a bigger idea about song and trails and the script of the country that we are learning, day by day, to read. It is the germ of a commons policy, really, the kind that Britain and New Zealand already have but that we do not, with the result that the fundamental character of our country is being altered as we speak.

In Quebec, where I grew up, a credit in French — French 432 — is a necessary requirement to graduate from high school. What if we were to do the same, today, with Aboriginal studies — so that a course in Cree or some aspect of probably local First Nations culture was a mandatory requirement to graduate? Education is a provincial and not a federal matter, and in some parts of the country local initiatives along these lines have been taken. But what if we used the clout of law to meld our country this way — to have all three of our founding nations meet and thrive and remember and debate?

What if, alongside this measure of inclusion, this way of meeting and sharing the cultural territory, another step was taken to further the learning of Canada and the library that is the land's text? What if, instead of royalties from gas pipelines and the like, our First Nations fought for their traditional right of passage — of being able to freely travel the country and its parks and coastlines and rivers in a national and binding commons policy of trails and reserves? Not just books and papers and photographs but these trails and all we have built upon them are our archive, and having them accessible to all lays the way for Canadians to be able to learn their country properly.

Canadians, I believe, would back such a measure, and if we did, then we would be far less likely to let those weirs, barns and buildings — those pieces of the Canadian script — all fall down. From the Digby Neck to Sackville — from Regent Park to the Arctic and the West Coast — we would be able to read from the library of the land… and remember it.

Notes

1. Bringhurst's comments here are reproduced from taped conversations, circa 2004, and also documented in my book, *This Is My Country, What's Yours?* (2006).

References

Anderson, Paul Thomas (Dir.). 2007. *There Will Be Blood*. Ghoulardi.
Boyden, Joseph. 2005. *Three Day Road*. Toronto: Penguin.
Bringhurst, Robert. 1999. *A Story as Sharp as a Knife: The Classical Haida Mythtellers and Their World*. Vancouver: Douglas and McIntyre.
_____. 1986. *Pieces of Map, Pieces of Music*. Toronto: McClelland and Stewart.
Chamberlin, J. Edward. 2003. *If This Is Your Land, Where Are Your Stories?* Toronto: Knopf.
Chatwin, Bruce. 1986. *The Songlines*. London: Franklin.
McKay, Ami. 2006. *The Birth House*. Toronto: Random House.
McKay, Leo, Jr. 2003. *Twenty-Six*. Toronto: McClelland and Stewart.
Moore, Lisa. 2009. *February*. Toronto: House of Anansi.
Richler, Noah. 2006. *This Is My Country, What's Yours? A Literary Atlas of Canada*. Toronto: McClelland and Stewart.
Saul, John Ralston. 2008. *A Fair Country: Telling Truths About Canada*. Toronto: Viking.
Sinclair, Upton. 2007. *Oil!* New York: Penguin.
Vanderhaeghe, Guy. 1996. *The Englishman's Boy*. Toronto: McClelland and Stewart.
_____. 2001. *The Last Crossing*. Toronto: McClelland and Stewart.

Section II

Archives and Narratives for Canada — International, National and Regional

Archives as Narrative
The Politics of Ethnographic Archiving at the National Museum

Andrew Nurse

In her study "Colonial Archives and the Arts of Governance," Ann Stoler (2002) argues that archives need to be reconceptualized as key elements of state power that are better considered "intricate technologies of rule" than as simply repositories. Stoler's work is part of a wider reconsideration of archives that looks to explore both their history and function from alternative perspectives. As Terry Cook and Joan Schwartz note, archives can no longer be considered simply as repositories that preserve the past in a neutral — or apolitical — manner. Instead, they embed specific narratives of understanding, conceptions of knowledge and definitions of what constitutes evidence, while literally calling this "evidence" into being (Cook and Schwartz 2002). In Stoler's view, archives are tied to imperialist technologies of power serving, at once, to encapsulate the dynamics of cultural, political and economic inequality and as sites through which the biopolitics of colonized subject positions are, in fact, created. Both Stoler and Cook and Schwartz call for a new approach to archival practice, whether oriented to historiography or to the present, which looks at the archives as a subject of study as opposed to a site where other subjects are investigated.

In this essay, my aim is to work within the investigative space created by Stoler, Cook and Schwartz, and others, but to move their analytic focus in a different direction. Archives, as Cook and Schwartz explain, can be — and have been — conceptualized in a variety of ways, from repositories to technologies of power to sites of performance related to the enactment of historiographic principles. I treat archives as the institutional mechanism that serves to organize a series of cultural practices. My goal is to link these cultural practices to wider dynamics of cultural history in order to show how archives are tied to and contribute to broader processes of cultural change. This analysis focuses on the practices of state cultural archiving in Canada; more specifically, it looks to explore the effects of professionalized cultural collecting and archiving on First Peoples cultures. I seek to make the general conclusions drawn by critical archival theory more specific, in that my aim is not simply to show that the archives encapsulated social and power relations. I also aim to show how the archiving practices of the National Museum worked in culture at a specific time.

This discussion focuses on the emergence of professional cultural archiving in Canada in the first half of the twentieth century. It begins by sketching out the rise of professional ethnographic archiving by looking at the creation of the Anthropology Division of the Geological Survey of Canada (GSC), the primary institution responsible for ethnographic collection and preservation in the National Museum. Next, it examines the way the Museum's archiving practices affected First Nations cultures. I argue that the cultural effects of archiving were both varied and significant. Finally, this essay concludes by looking at the relations between collectors and First Peoples in order to demonstrate the conditions under which cultural archives were fashioned. My goal is to show that cultural archives were themselves a product of unequal power relations between First Peoples and white Canadians.

From the time they arrived in what became Canada, European explorers, traders, missionaries and state officials collected Native cultures (Dickason 1984). Their rationale for collecting varied and included both a scientific and philosophical impetus as well as more pragmatic considerations. The scope of Native cultural elements collected by Europeans was similarly broad, ranging from languages to information on economic practices, to conceptions of authority or proper gender relations (Colpitts 2002; Dickason 1984; Jaenen 1974; Phillips 1998). Over time, increased European settlement and the concomitant marginalization of Native peoples in eastern Canada changed the scope, rationale, and intensity of collecting. By the last quarter of the nineteenth century, anthropologists from a range of countries came to regard Canada as a central site for ethnographic collecting (Cole 1995; McGee 1897). Their rationale was multifold: the degree to which Aboriginal peoples in western and northern Canada remained separated from European settlement supposedly increased the "authenticity" of their cultures — that is, they were supposedly less "corrupted" by outside influences, hence their cultural practices and traditions were deemed to be more genuine — and the specific character of Canadian Aboriginal peoples supposedly bore directly on contested issues in anthropological theory relating to cultural development (MacCurdy 1909; Sapir 1911). These two rationales combined into a third: the supposed imminent demise of traditional Aboriginal cultures in Canada. While not all collectors shared this view, most tended to believe that the collapse of traditional culture was only a matter of time. Aboriginal cultures, in brief, were viewed as incompatible with modernity and, in this regard, fated to disappear (GSC 1909: 9). One turn-of-the-century report on Aboriginal culture in Canada noted "the exceptional circumstances surrounding the Indians of British Columbia; the fact that it is becoming more and more difficult each year to obtain reliable accounts of these people; the rapid disappearance of old customs, dress, and modes of living... have seemed sufficient reasons for devoting to their study a much larger share of [research] resources... than might otherwise appear justifiable" (Anon. 1899: 211). Beginning in the last two decades of the nineteenth century, British and American anthropologists and institutions began to collect Native cultures extensively in Canada. By the first decade of the twentieth century, international and domestic scholars were urging the Canadian government to take more direct action to preserve — that is, to collect and store or archive — what they viewed as endangered Aboriginal cultures.[1]

Within Canada, cultural collecting remained idiosyncratic until the beginning of the second decade of the twentieth century. Cultural collecting was carried out by a variety of local, provincial and federal institutions as well as by interested individuals working largely in the private sector (Anon. 1899; Ganong et al. 1903; Wintemberg 1907). On an individual level, collecting more resembled the older "cabinet of curiosities" than the modern archive or museum (Young 2000), but at least some collectors took their work seriously, compiling information on different religious beliefs or other cultural traditions and histories (e.g., Hale 1889; 1890). Federal involvement in culture collecting was organized through the GSC and linked more directly to the broader rubric of natural history than to the new and evolving discipline of anthropology.[2] GSC culture collecting remained piecemeal and limited to the interests of scientists who worked primarily in other fields. In addition, little provision was made for the storage or display of material collected (GSC 1909).

Under international and domestic pressure, the federal state initiated a series of reforms designed to organize, systematize and modernize cultural collecting in Canada in the first decade of the twentieth century. As part of a broader reorganization of government science, then GSC director, R.W. Brock, established the Survey's Anthropology Division in 1910 (Zaslow 1975). His aim was to mobilize the latest developments in anthropology in support of a broader and more intensive archiving, research and publication program. From its creation until after World War II, the Anthropology Division — and, then, after a reorganization of state scientific bureaucracy, the National Museum — remained the pre-eminent anthropological research institution in Canada. Its permanent staff, publication series, connections to the state and financial resources combined to allow it to supplant private, local and provincial cultural archives and museums.

A key Divisional goal was to shift processes of cultural collecting from amateur and localized initiatives to a professional and scientific basis (Barbeau 1913). Its research staff included some of the best-known figures in North American anthropology in the first half of the twentieth century. Edward

Sapir, a student of Franz Boas, served as its first director. He was replaced by Diamond Jenness, who had originally worked with the Canadian Arctic Expedition, in 1925, when he returned to the United States to take up a university appointment. Other staff members included, at various times, Marius Barbeau, Harlan Smith, Frank Speck and A.A. Goldenweiser. The specific nature of staff training and interests varied, but professional certification and standing were important to all members. Sapir held a doctorate from Columbia and became one of the leading figures in the history of linguistics. Smith was an archaeologist who had worked extensively with Boas, while Speck, like Sapir, had advanced training under Boas in the United States. Barbeau's credentials were lower but included education under R.R. Marett at Oxford and Marcel Mauss at the Sorbonne. Like Barbeau, Jenness trained at Oxford before spending a number of years doing fieldwork in the Canadian arctic.[3]

What all these figures shared was a commitment to a reorganized practice of cultural collection. The Division was housed in and responsible for the ethnographic collections of the National Museum. Their primary task, as Brock had earlier indicated, was both to reorganize existing collections and to extend the scope of the ethnographic archives. In Sapir's view, this included systematizing current collections as well as an active fieldwork program designed to extend the Museum's collection to include those peoples not currently (or under) represented (Sapir 1911). Barbeau seconded this view and opined that very little good cultural collecting had, in fact, actually been done before the Division was established. It was vital, Barbeau noted in one essay on this subject, to preserve the cultures of what he viewed as moribund First Peoples for posterity (Barbeau 1913).

It would be difficult to catalogue the broad range of materials collected by the Anthropology Division. They included oral traditions, songs, legends, recipes, family genealogies, histories, cultural practices relating to education and totemism, and religious views and languages. By himself, Barbeau, as just one example, amassed an archive that still constitutes a core element of a new revamped Museum of Civilization research collection. Material objects were also important, and staff collected clothing, religious masks, toys, weapons, tools and furniture as well as black slate carvings from the Northwest Coast and totem poles. Divisional staff collected materials from across Canada. Jenness worked in the Arctic, among the Ojibwa of Ontario and in British Columbia. Barbeau spend several field seasons over the course of the interwar period among the Tsimshian and Gitsan peoples in northern B.C. and also worked among the Huron at Lorette in Quebec and Anderdon, Ontario. Other staff worked in the Maritimes, Quebec, Labrador and western Canada, among the Mi'kmaq, Six Nations, Innu, Salish and Assiniboine. To further extend the Division's work, it employed assistants to collect material to send to Ottawa, the best known of whom is likely William Beynon. He collected Aboriginal legends and information on the potlatch among the Tsimshian speaking peoples of the Pacific Northwest. In Ontario, Sapir employed local amateur enthusiasts, whose work he closely supervised, to assess and purchase Six Nations material culture for the Museum. Finally, Divisional staff also assessed donations and larger amateur collections, some of which were bought and transferred to the Museum if they were seen to be of value.

The diverse activities and extensive work of the Divisional staff never completely effaced older, localized and more individualized approaches to cultural collecting. In important ways, in fact, the professional anthropologists who staffed the Division relied on popular support for their work in the face of what they viewed as the periodic indifference of civil servants and GSC staff working in the "harder" sciences (Nurse 2007). Nevertheless, the development of the Anthropology Division and the work of its staff brought with it clear changes in the history of cultural archiving. Most significantly, it changed the way in which archives functioned in Canadian culture in marked ways. A series of observations are important in this regard.

First, the creation of the Anthropology Division established a new system of authority in Canadian culture, defining who could legitimately collect culture and speak about those collections. All Division anthropologists shared a commitment to anthropology as a "modern" social science that needed to be differentiated from previous ethnographic practices. Culture collecting, in other words, was the work of professionals and this commitment carried with it a new system of authority supported by the state that recognized the voice of the professional as the legitimate spokesperson for culture. For early twentieth-century Canadian anthropologists, it was necessary to establish the authority of their voices on two different levels. On the first level, professional anthropologists needed to establish their voices against the previous grid of significance that did not differentiate easily between cultural and other forms of archiving. Through the support of the state, which provided the resources needed to collect and maintain archives, government anthropologists were able to dramatically broaden the work of collecting, centralize it and publish results (Cole 1973). In addition, carefully developed and maintained international connections tied Canadian anthropologists to a wider international scholarly community in the United States, Britain and France. In effect, the evolution of the Anthropology Division served to displace other local, private and institutionalized collectors, museums and archives as the central authority in such matters for Canada (Smith and Thériault 2008). Divisional staff spoke with the authority of a key Canadian cultural institution supporting their words and actions.

On a second and more problematic level, this new system of authority upholding the voices and activities of professional culture collectors also needed to be maintained against the voices of the very Aboriginal peoples from whom anthropologists collected materials. Canadian anthropologists were, in fact, remarkably distrustful of Aboriginal informants. All Canadian anthropologists shared this view, but Barbeau, perhaps, put it most bluntly in a 1917 paper read before the Royal Society of Canada. "The ethnologist," he said, "is a fool who so far deceives himself as to believe that his field notes and specimens gathered in the raw from half-breeds or the decrepit survivors of a past age, still represents the unadulterated knowledge of the prehistoric races of America" (Barbeau 1927: 52–53). Sapir intoned the same message to an amateur researcher whose work he was directing for the National Museum: "even the older Indians are not quite clear… as to what is merely comparatively old and what is thoroughly aboriginal."[4] Owing to this confusion, the determination of authenticity was made by the anthropologist. References to "half-breeds," "decrepit survivors" and "confused Indians" rhetorically served to reinforce the authority of anthologists over the very people they were studying and whose culture came to constitute the cornerstone of the Museum archives.

The high water mark of this cultural practice came with the implementation of Canadian antiquities legislation written by Jenness in the latter half of the 1920s and applied to Canada's northern territories (Richling 1995). In effect, this legislation legalized the authority of the Division over the collection of material culture in the Canadian Arctic, requiring the approval of the Division head — in this case Jenness himself — before collecting could take place. This would permit, Jenness told one correspondent, control over the collection process, ensuring that it was done by accredited scholars and that accredited scholars would have continued access to collected material by ensuring it was maintained in an approved repository or museum. It was a shame, Jenness felt, that federalism prevented the extension of this type of legislation to the provinces and he urged anthropologists working in Ontario to pressure their provincial government to enact similar laws.[5] In some ways, this legislation seems self-evident. Contemporary Canadians treat it as common sense that the state should guard the patrimony of the nation. On the other hand, its implications need to be more fully considered. The effect of Jenness's legislation was to place northern material culture — primarily but not exclusively Inuit — under the legal control of the professional anthropologists working in a state institution. The effect disempowered the Inuit to use or dispose of their cultural heritage as they saw fit at the same time that it augmented the power and authority of the state over not only collection and archiving processes but Aboriginal archaeological and material culture itself. Moreover, the key interested parties were assumed to be scholars, whose access to material was assured through this process, and not the Inuit or other First Peoples. In other instances, Barbeau made similar recommendations (Barbeau 1919) while other anthropologists and civil servants were involved in securing control over totem poles in British Columbia (Darling and Cole 1980).

Second, as a cultural practice, the development of the Anthropology Division de-historicized and created specific conceptions of what constituted Aboriginal cultures. Within the Museum a series of different strategies served to affect this end. Culture group displays, for example, were used to present to the public specific images of what constituted traditional Aboriginal cultures. In terms of collecting, the weeding out of the "authentic" from the supposedly confused perceptions of Aboriginal peoples served the same end. In part, these distinctions showed up in the publications as the result of collecting, which were written up and edited to eliminate culture traits deemed not to be authentic (Barbeau 1915). In another instance, the reorganization of existing cultures was built into the collection process as Division staff focused their attention on specific culture traits while ignoring or discarding others. Barbeau confronted precisely this issue during fieldwork he conducted in 1911 and 1912 at the Lorette Huron reserve near Quebec City. In the course of his research, Barbeau found the reserve residents friendly and supportive of his work but, he complained to Sapir, they insisted on donating things to the Anthropology Division for inclusion in its collection that, in his view, were clearly not authentic. His solution was to accept material so as not to offend informants, but not include it in the Museum's collections.[6] During the period of his fieldwork among the Bella Bella fifteen years later, T.F. McIlwraith encountered the same situation. In the course of two field seasons living in an Aboriginal community, McIlwraith remarked in his correspondence on the range of modern cultural practices used by Aboriginal people, including but not limited to musical instruments (Barker and Cole 2003: 106, 134).

Third, archival practices worked in culture through a process of relocation. Relocation is an inherent element of archiving: material is moved from one location to another for storage, preservation or research purposes. In the case of the National Museum's cultural archives, the relocation of material had other effects: it served to alter the meaning of the collected materials. For example, within communities, a legend cycle, a traditional song, a geneaology or a material object had a specific meaning. This meaning varied from community to community and depended on the specific object. The purpose of oral traditions, for example, could be historiographic, the delineation of a genealogy could define family or clan rights, and masks or other traditions and songs could have religious purposes. The point is that the collected materials had meanings within communities and those meanings were part of living cultures. In the archives these meanings were effaced. Storage, maintenance and display redefined songs, family histories, recipes and material objects, among other things, as artifacts, maintained in an archives precisely to ensure their disconnection from historical change in the communities from which they came. Anthropological skepticism about the future of First Peoples and the supposedly already corrupted nature of their cultures and traditions, meant, in the view of Divisional staff, that Aboriginal communities could no longer guarantee their own cultural integrity and continuity. Relocation, in this sense, was designed to preserve the past but what it actually did was to make cultures into artifacts. In the museum or archives, the song, black slate carving, tool or legend was transformed, by virtue of its new location, into an artifact, to be understood and appreciated on that ground. In this process, relocation transforms materials from part of a living culture into a sign of that culture's demise. In the archives or museum, cultural objects are signifiers of history, of culture that has been lost, as opposed to elements of vibrant cultural practices. The relocation of cultures to archives and museums made cultural objects into part of a supposedly vanishing history, the authenticity of which no longer existed (Frank 2000).

Fourth, relocation established new systems of authority over culture in another way. The voice of the anthropologist, as already noted, is one part of the evolving system of cultural authority in modern Canada in which archival practices were embedded. Another important element of the changing dynamics of Canadian culture to which archival practices contributed related to the use of culture and the legal authority to determine how different aspects of Aboriginal cultures functioned in Canada. In their communities, First Peoples maintained different systems of control over culture. Not all elements of Aboriginal cultures were public goods. Certain songs, for example, were, in effect, the property of specific individuals or clans. Symbols could be passed down (in effect, willed) to others. The reciting of oral traditions could be a specialized office, as in the keeper of the wampum. This is not to suggest some pan-Aboriginal practice of cultural control but rather to indicate that these practices existed for different communities and nations. The process of archiving embedded cultures in different systems of control. Once archived, the institution and its staff, as well as the Canadian legal system, exercised control over access and use. In the case of the National Museum, the strong emphasis on publication added a further complication: copyright. Copyright functioned as a legalized system of control in which the force of the state could be mobilized to ensure that unauthorized use — that is use without the authority of the copyright holder — was prohibited.

The close connection between the National Museum and its personnel and Canadian culture industries in the first half of the twentieth century illustrated how this process could be tied to other cultural dynamics. During this period, the National Museum lent materials — songs, clothing and other objects — to professional performers for both artistic and tourist promotion purposes. In these instances, the performer did not gain a permanent right to perform forever a traditional song. National Museum approval tended to be on a one-time-use basis. The point, however, is not the frequency but the process: the performer did not have to seek permission from Aboriginal individuals, clans, families or nations to use and perform traditional music collected by anthropologists. Instead, this permission was accorded by the Museum. In effect, the Museum established itself as an intermediary between First Peoples and professional vocalists, but an intermediary that did not act on instruction from First Peoples or even with consideration of their cultural practices and preferences in mind.

Closely connected to this process, cultural archiving in Canada facilitated another practice: commoditization. In loaning materials for tourist promotion, the Museum transferred culture from its traditional community setting and embedded it in consumer culture. The most significant example of this process was the close support provided by the National Museum for the Canadian Folk-Song and Handicraft Festival run by the Canadian Pacific Railroad at the Chateau Frontenac in Quebec City in the late 1920s. The Festival was the brainchild of CPR Chief Publicity Agent John Murray Gibbon and National Museum anthropologist Marius Barbeau. Gibbon was originally looking for some sort of event he could use to attract media attention to the re-opening of a wing of the Chateau that had been damaged by fire. The event could also serve as a lure to attract a foreign travelling public to the CPR resort. In addition, he was himself enthusiastic about folk music and decided to hire the French-Canadian soprano Juliette Gaulthier to sing at the opening and at an event in New York designed to promote the Chateau among potential American tourists. Barbeau augmented Gaulthier's repertoire with selections from his fieldwork that included both traditional Euro-Canadian and Aboriginal music. In addition, he arranged the loan of traditional clothing for Gauthier to add effect to her performances. Gibbon continued this model in other cities across Canada, dramatically expanding and commercializing it over the next two years (Henderson 2005; Slominska 2008). In other instances, National Museum staff worked with the CPR, the CNR and the Department of Indian Affairs in British Columbia to relocate and display totems poles in northern B.C. to provide a scenic vista for vacationers travelling to that region (Darling and Cole 1980). And archaeologist Harlan Smith published and spoke frequently to various clubs and services groups about their possible use of Aboriginal culture in industrial and consumer good design (Smith 1923). In all of these instances, Aboriginal cultures took on new traits as older traits were effaced. Moreover, the effect of this process was to place Aboriginal culture in the service of white Canadian businesses and to contribute to their profits. Native peoples were never consulted about Gauthier's use of their songs, nor does Smith seem to have considered it necessary to secure the permission of First Peoples before recommending Aboriginal motifs to designers. In the case of totem pole relocation, First Peoples were viewed more as a problem to manage than as active contributors or participants to the process. In these diverse ways, First Peoples cultures were connected more directly to the matrix of consumerism.

These changes highlight the place of cultural collecting and the National Museum in the changing cultural dynamics of Canada in the first half of the twentieth century. The National Museum served, in these processes, not a single function but instead worked in a number of different ways. It institutionally organized a series of practices that carried with them significant effects for First Peoples cultures. In different ways, the practices connected to the National Museum's cultural collecting redefined systems of authority over culture (who had the right to speak for and about First Peoples cultures), established legal control over at least some aspects of northern Aboriginal material culture and heritage, transformed living cultures into signs of their own demise and facilitated the connection between Aboriginal cultures in the legal matrix of copyright and consumer culture. In all of this, but perhaps most evidently in the work of Smith, Jenness and Barbeau, Aboriginal cultures were treated as a scarce resource, an element of public heritage and as the fading shards of vanishing cultures, fated to disappear before the political, economic, social and cultural practices of modernity. In constructing Aboriginal cultures as a national resource, anthropologists repositioned cultures in yet other ways that superseded and legitimized other practices. In effect, the colonial state appropriated First Peoples cultures and claimed the right to redirect them as it saw fit.

In recent work, questions have been raised about the degree to which appropriation can be considered a legitimate description of the way in which the state and white Canadian artists and companies made use of Aboriginal cultures. Robert Fulford, for example, has argued that artists traditionally draw inspiration from a broad range of cultures and that Canadian artists who made use of Aboriginal motifs were doing nothing unethical (Fulford 1996; see also Cole 2000).

Be this argument as it may, the issues with regard to the cultural practices facilitated by the archive need to be considered in a different light. The issue, in this sense, might not be the legitimacy of artistic inspiration but the world view that needs to be in place to claim control over other people's culture. What is more, I contend that the interaction between First Peoples and the National Museum cannot be considered either a simple case of inspiration or a form of cultural exchange. Instead, it needs to be seen as a manifestation of unequal power relations and collecting processes that were, from their beginning, disturbing in their implications.

Staff at the National Museum paid informants and assistants for information, a practice that was both well-established and, it seems, considered a fair way of compensating informants for their time as the information they provided was recorded, transcribed and archived. Likewise, collectors paid First Peoples for material objects and likely felt that this exchange established a contractual basis for the archiving of culture. In many instances, First Peoples willingly contributed materials to the Museum's collection: in some instances taking the initiative by contacting Museum staff or offering items for sale (Phillips 1998: 58–59). In other instances collecting practices were also organized through a different set of imperatives.

As Barbeau's concerns about supposedly non-authentic Huron culture and Sapir's injunction to distrust Aboriginal informants make clear, Canadian anthropologists were not always honest with their informants. In these instances, professional collectors accepted material with the intention of neither displaying it nor making it part of a supposedly authentic culture collection. In such cases, the information and materials taken from informants and archived involved an editing process about which informants were unaware, with material put to different uses than informants assumed. In other instances, the collection process involved other practices that Canadians today would find problematic. Barbeau, for example, one time secretly observed and photographed Aboriginal rituals to which he was denied access (Kemp 1948) and on another occasion he had potential informants meet him at an out-of-the-way location so he could obtain information that would have been otherwise denied him by community norms.[7] Nor were anthropologists above manipulation, using their research budgets to coerce types of behaviour from assistants by withholding funds or refusing to renew contracts for a period of time in order to provide an object lesson in what they viewed as appropriate work habits (Nowry 1995: 213). Another way in which money was used to purchase cultural materials was to take advantage of bad economic times to secure aspects of material culture at lower prices than their owners had originally stated (Cole 1985: 268). In this case, pressing material needs convinced Aboriginal people to part with goods out of necessity. And, finally, as Tina Loo's work on potlatch prosecutions notes, cultural goods impounded in RCMP raids on potlatches made their way to the National Museum and other repositories after having been confiscated as part of criminal prosecutions (Loo 1992).

What this demonstrates is that the process of cultural collecting through which materials were archived involved a variety of different processes. These included practices that collectors at the time knew to be ethically problematic because they hid them from their informants or otherwise worked surreptitiously. In addition, and from a more historical perspective, the archiving processes were clearly facilitated by the marginalized condition of First Peoples and the coercive authority of the Canadian state. The idea that

First Peoples were fast disappearing appeared to legitimize these processes. Because Canadian culture collectors believed they were "working against time," they made use of practices that, in other circumstances, they might have avoided. In this sense, the supposed imminent collapse of authentic Aboriginal cultures legitimized the extreme measures taken to build the Museum's cultural archives.

In his work on cultural exchange and fieldwork in anthropology, Paul Rabinow argued that some degree of symbolic violence — some degree of implicit or explicit coercion — is inherent in the ethnographic research process (Rabinow 1977). Current work in archival theory suggests a very similar conclusion. As Ann Stoler argues, archives are an institutional element of imperialist technologies of power. The argument that I have set out here does not replicate this conclusion but instead, I believe, adds to a critical scholarship interrogating the way in which archives operated in culture. Archives are best seen as institutional mechanisms that served — by virtue of their very institutionalization — as the means through which a series of different cultural practices were organized. These practices affected Canadian Aboriginal cultures in diverse ways. Their effect, in other words, was not singular. As archivists grapple with the legacy of their institutional past and consider new approaches to archival practice, the historical dynamics that brought archives as institutions to this point in history need to be borne in mind. Current efforts to repatriate cultural materials — including bodies — are one indication of the shifting parameters of archival and museological practice, changes essential to building a new relationship with First Peoples (Clifford 1988). A clear recognition of the diverse cultural affects of archives is another such necessary element. In this regard, our goal is not to condemn the past or pass simple moral judgment on it. The work of professional cultural collectors, the fashioning of archives and the development of modern disciplinary-based and authoritative museums are linked to wider processes of cultural change In this change, the archive is central. It is part of the narrative of First Peoples cultures and the interaction between Canada and First Peoples. As has been shown here, in the process of accumulating cultures, archiving practices transformed the very cultures they sought to preserve.

Notes

1. My discussion of the origins of the National Museum draws on primary material I have discussed in Nurse 2007.
2. On the established scientific paradigms displaced by the rise of modern disciplines, see Sheets-Pyenson 1988; Waiser 1989; Zaslow 1975.
3. Biographical information on figures mentioned as well as information on Anthropology Division personnel is drawn from Darnell 1990; Hancock 2006; Jenness and Jenness 2008; Nowry 1995.

4. Edward Sapir to F.W. Waugh, 3 October 1911, Edward Sapir Fonds, Canadian Museum of Civilization, box 430, file 62.
5. Diamond Jenness to T.F. McIlwraith, 26 May 1939, Thomas McIlwraith Papers, University of Toronto Archives, box 79, file 2.
6. Marius Barbeau to Edward Sapir, 16 May 1911, Sapir Fonds, box 425, file 19.
7. Marius Barbeau to Edward Sapir, 7 September 1924, Sapir Fonds, box 425, file 24.

References

Anon. 1899. "Anthropology at the British Association Dover Meeting: September 13th and 20th, 1899." *Journal of the Anthropological Institute of Great Britain and Ireland* 29: 198–223.

Barbeau, C. M. [Marius]. 1913. "Indian Tribes of Canada." *Man* 13: 122–27.

_____. 1915. "Wyandotte Tales, Including Foreign Elements." *Journal of American Folk-Lore* 28, 57: 83–95.

_____. 1919. "The Indian Reserve at Lorette (Quebec): A Report Concerning Its Proposed Disestablishment." Marius Barbeau Fonds, Canadian Museum of Civilization, box 91, file 3.

_____. 1927. "The Native Races of Canada." *Transactions of the Royal Society of Canada* 3rd Ser., 21, Sec. II: 41–53.

Barker, John, and Douglas Cole (eds.). 2003. *At Home with the Bella Coola: T.F. McIlwraith's Field Letters, 1922–4*. Vancouver: University of British Columbia Press.

Clifford, James. 1988. *The Predicament of Culture: Twentieth-Century Ethnography, Literature, and Art*. Cambridge, MA: Harvard University Press.

Cole, Douglas. 1973. "The Origins of Canadian Anthropology, 1850–1910" *Journal of Canadian Studies* 8,1: 33–45.

_____. 1985. *Captured Heritage: The Scramble for Northwest Coast Artifacts*. Vancouver: University of British Columbia Press.

_____. 1995. *Captured Heritage: The Scramble for Northwest Coast Artifacts*. Vancouver: University of British Columbia Press.

_____. 2000. "The Invented Indian/The Imagined Emily." *BC Studies* 125/6 (Summer): 147–62.

Colpitts, George. 2002. "'Animated Like Us by Commercial Interests': Commercial Ethnography and Fur Trade Descriptions in New France, 1660–1760." *Canadian Historical Review* 85, 3 (September): 305–37.

Cook, Terry, and Joan M. Schwartz. 2002. "Archives, Records, and Power: From (Postmodern) Theory to (Archival Performance." *Archival Science* 2: 1–19.

Darling, David, and Douglas Cole. 1980. "Totem Pole Restoration on the Skeena, 1925–1930: An Early Exercise in Heritage Conservation." *BC Studies* 47: 29–48.

Darnell, R. 1990. *Edward Sapir: Linguist, Anthropologist, and Humanist*. Berkeley and Los Angeles: University of California Press.

Dickason, Olive P. 1984. *The Myth of the Savage and the Beginnings of French Colonialism in the Americas*. Edmonton: University of Alberta Press: 261–91.

Frank, Gloria Jean. 2000. "'That's My Dinner on Display': A First Nations Reflection

on Museum Culture." *BC Studies* 125/6 (Spring/Summer): 163–79.
Fulford, Robert. 1996. "The Trouble With Emily." In Donald Avery and Roger Halls (eds.), *Coming of Age: Readings in Canadian History Since World War II*. Toronto: Harcourt Brace: 24–31.
Ganong, W.F. et al. 1903. "Algonkian Words in American English." *Journal of American Folklore* 16, 61 (Apr.-Jun.): 128–29.
GSC (Geological Survey of Canada). 1906. *Summary Report of the Geological Survey of Canada for the Calendar Year 1906*. Ottawa: S.E. Dawson.
——. 1909. *Summary Report of the Geological Survey Branch of the Department of Mines for the Calendar year 1908*. Ottawa: C.H. Parmalee.
Hale, Horatio. 1889. "Huron Folk-Lore: The Story of Tijaiha, the Sorcerer." *Journal of American Folk-Lore* 2, 7: 249–54.
——. 1890. "Huron Folk-Lore. Cosmogonic Myths. The Good and Evil Minds." *Journal of American Folk-Lore* 3, 10: 177–83.
Hancock, Robert L.A. 2006. "Diamond Jenness's Arctic Ethnography and the Potential for a Canadian Anthropology." In R. Darnell and F.W. Gleach (eds.), *Histories of Anthropology Annual* 2: 155–211.
Henderson, Stuart. 2005. "'While There Is Still Time...': J. Murray Gibbon and the Spectacle of Difference in Three CPR Folk Festivals, 1928–1931." *Journal of Canadian Studies* 39, 1 (Winter): 139–74.
Jaenen, Cornelius J. 1974. "Amerindian Views of French Culture in the Seventeenth Century." *Canadian Historical Review* 55, 3: 261–291.
Jenness, Diamond, and Stewart E. Jenness. 2008. *Through the Darkening Spectacles: Memoires of Diamond Jenness*. Mercury Series History Paper 55. Gatineau: Canadian Museum of Civilization.
Kemp, Hugh. 1948. "Top Man in Totem Poles." *Macleans* (1 May), 66–71.
Loo, Tina. 1992. "Dan Cranmer's Potlatch: Law as Coercion, Symbol, and Rhetoric in British Columbia, 1884–1951." *Canadian Historical Review* 73, 2: 125–65.
MacCurdy, George Grant. 1909. "Anthropology at the Winnipeg Meeting of the British Association." *American Anthropologist* 11, 3: 456–77.
McGee, W.J. 1897. "Anthropology at Detroit and Toronto." *American Anthropologist* 10, 10: 317–45.
Nowry, Laurence. 1995. *Marius Barbeau: Man of Man*. Toronto: NC Press.
Nurse, Andrew. 2007. "Making Anthropology: Reconsidering the Politics of Disciplinary Autonomy in Anthropology's Museum Age, 1910–1949." *Scientia Canadensis* 30, 2: 37–53.
Phillips, Ruth B. 1998. *Trading Identities: The Souvenir in Native North American Art from the Northeast 1700–1900*. Montreal and Kingston: McGill-Queen's University Press.
Rabinow, Paul. 1977. *Reflections on Fieldwork in Morocco*. Berkeley: University of California Press.
Richling, Barnett. 1995. "Politics, Bureaucracy, and Arctic Archaeology in Canada, 1910–39." *Arctic* 42, 2 (June): 109–17.
Sapir, E. 1911. "An Anthropological Survey of Canada." *Science* NS 34, 884: 189–93.
Sheets-Pyenson, Susan. 1988. *Cathedrals of Science: The Development of Colonial Natural History Museums During the Late Nineteenth Century*. Kingston: McGill-Queen's

University Press.

Slominska, Anita Marie. 2008. "Interpreting Success and Failure: The Eclectic Careers of Eva and Juliette Gauthier." Ph.D. thesis, McGill University.

Smith, Derek G., and Benoît Thériault. 2008. "The French Connection: Marius Barbeau, the *Année Sociologique*, and the Société des Américanistes, 1911–30." In Lynda Jessup et al. (eds.), *Around and About Barbeau: Modelling Twentieth Century Culture*. Mercury Series Cultural Studies Paper 83. Gatineau: Canadian Museum of Civilization, 65–78.

Smith, Harlan I. 1923. *An Album of Prehistoric Art*. National Museum Bulletin 37. Ottawa: National Museum of Canada.

Stoler, Ann Laura. 2002. "Colonial Archives and the Arts of Governance." *Archival Science* 2: 87–109.

Waiser, W.A. 1989. *The Field Naturalist: John Macoun, the Geological Survey, and Natural Science*. Toronto: University of Toronto Press.

Wintemberg, W.J. 1907. "Alsatian Witch Stories." *Journal of American Folklore* 20, 78 (Jul.–Sep.): 213–15.

Young, Brian. 2000. *The Making and Unmaking of a University Museum: The McCord, 1921–1996*. Montreal: McGill-Queen's University Press.

Zaslow, Morris. 1975. *Reading the Rocks: The Story of the Geological Survey of Canada, 1842–1972*. Toronto: Macmillan.

Our Records, Ourselves
Documenting Archives and Archivists

Kristan Cook and Heather Dean

Contemporary writing in archival literature posits that archivists serve as authors and editors actively shaping archives rather than as objective conduits of the historical record.[1] This essay builds upon this argument through an examination of the institutional documentation that archivists and archives produce and argues that this kind of documentation, revealing the roles that archivists play, could affect how users of archives perceive and interpret archival materials, and also represents an important narrative about the records, a narrative that is not readily available to archival users.

The first section of this essay introduces current theories regarding methods to increase transparency and accountability in archives. These theories focus on illuminating archivists' work in order to demonstrate the importance of providing users with a more complete understanding of the context of the records. In the second section, by comparing the types of documentation produced in archivists' working files at a Canadian government archives, the Provincial Archives of Alberta (PAA), and at an American private academic archival institution, the Beinecke Rare Book and Manuscript Library at Yale University, this essay identifies the value of institutional documentation and the benefits of providing this kind of information to researchers. The final section of this essay discusses the challenges of making institutional documentation available to researchers, arguing that while opening our institutional documentation could better reveal the roles that archivists play by making openly available the formerly "private" narrative of their activities, undoubtedly, this proposal presents a myriad of challenges to both public and private archives. Ultimately, archivists will have to chart new courses to sail through the legal, ethical and administrative barriers to making such information available to researchers.

The archivist's quest for transparency and accountability is the foundation of sound archival practice. As professionals, archivists must ensure that they document their decisions, not simply to remain accountable to the users that they serve, but also to ensure that future archivists who will care for the records will be able to understand why and how decisions have been made. To achieve greater accountability and transparency, archivists have increasingly begun to acknowledge their role in actively shaping archives and have sought to find new methods or suggest changes to archival practices.[2] Some of the changes archivists have promoted include adding more contextual information to existing documentation, such as descriptions found in finding aids and catalogue records. For example, Michelle Light and Tom Hyry propose the addition of "colophons" to finding aids, defined as a "statement regarding the creation of a work written or printed after the main text has concluded to be implemented in archives as a note about the collection not only about the finding aid itself" (Hyry and Light 2002: 223). Others have lobbied for the creation of additional kinds of institutional documentation. For example, Terry Cook has suggested that archivists should be formally documented and linked to their work "with a curriculum vitae placed in accessible files, complemented by autobiographical details of the values that they used in appraisal and that they reflected in description" (2001: 34).

Archivists have also begun to employ technology as a tool, not only to facilitate greater transparency and accountability, but also to foster a more collaborative relationship between users and archives. The increasingly participatory nature of the current Web 2.0 environment provides opportunities for archivists to supply insight into their practices, to engage with researchers as collaborators and to use technologies to "transcend the archival limits imposed by current description practices" (MacNeil 2005: 274). In a Web 2.0 world, traditional archival description can become a more dynamic tool, showing the continued documentation that archivists create regarding an acquisition, as well as how archival material has been acquired, appraised, arranged and described. This kind of documentation may also illuminate if and what kind of conservation treatment it has received, if and why some of the material was de-accessioned, where the material has been exhibited and what changes might have been made to its physical order or to an archival description.

These kinds of technologies not only create opportunities for archivists to share information about how archives are created and managed, but they also facilitate a dynamic conversation between archivists and users. Archivists now engage in an array of emergent technologies, such as blogs,[3] microblogs (Twitter), video sharing (YouTube) and image sharing (Flickr). The Beinecke Library, for example, has a number of blogs covering various topics from new acquisitions to exhibits and announcements of recently processed collections. The Beinecke Library has also created podcasts highlighting particular collections, established a photostream on Flickr displaying select digital images from collections and uses Twitter to promote collections and events at the Library.[4] Some institutions using blogs include the Harold Pinter Archive blog <http://britishlibrary.typepad.co.uk/pinter_archive_blog/> at the British National Archives and the Processing the Chew Family Papers blog <http://chewpapers.blogspot.com/> at the Historical Society of Pennsylvania. The Massachusetts Historical Society is using Twitter to share John Quincy Adams' nineteenth-century line-a-day diary <http://twitter.com/JQAdams_MHS>. The Library of Congress <http://www.youtube.com/LibraryOfCongress> and the National Library of Scotland <http://www.youtube.com/user/NLofScotland> are examples of cultural institutions with channels on YouTube. A number of institutions are also sharing their photograph archives through Flickr. The Library of Congress established "The Commons" on Flickr, in collaboration with a number of institutions, including the National Library of New Zealand, the New York Public Library and the Smithsonian Institution, in order to show "hidden treasures in the world's public photography archives" <http://www.flickr.com/commons>. The use of these kinds of technologies simultaneously allows archivists to share information about their work and creates a location for users to interact with each other, as well as with archivists.

Technology can also enable users to add their interpretations and research to documentation about an acquisition, including theories about the acquisition and links to other related records. One example of this kind of work is the Polar Bear Expedition Digital Collections Project at the Bentley Historical Library, University of Michigan (Yakel, Reynolds and Shaw: 2007), which employs the inclusion of user-generated "annotations" to finding aids, a practice first conceived by Light and Hyry. Light and Hyry argue that annotations, created by both archivists and users, could enhance an understanding of the context of the records by linking the records to related items, collections and pieces of scholarship, and drawing attention to other "individuals, families, and organizations that are relevant to an understanding of the records" (Hyry and Light 2002: 228).

While many of the current trends in archives, as noted above, focus on employing technology and creating additional documentation to offer users a privileged view of archival work, one of the greatest as yet untapped sources of information for users can be found within archivists' working files. To demonstrate the value of narratives that are found in the internal documentation of archivists' files, the following section discusses two institutions: the Provincial Archives of Alberta and the Beinecke Rare Book and Manuscript Library. Analysis of these two institutions offers a comparison of archival practices at Canadian and American institutions and public and private institutions. An examination of the differences and similarities between the type of information contained in archivists' internal files helps to illuminate the richness of these narratives. To limit the scope of this analysis, examples found in the following sections only refer to information generated as a result of working with private records at both institutions.

Depending on its collecting policy and legislative mandate, an archival institution may acquire public and/or private records. Public records are "documents created or received by public authorities in the course of carrying out their public functions" whereas private records are "archives of non-governmental provenance."[5] Archival institutions — as repositories of records — may be public or private. That is, a public archives is an entity of a government body (at the federal, provincial or municipal level) that serves as the official repository of that body's public records. Many public institutions also collect private records. Private archival institutions, on the other hand, are unaffiliated with the government and acquire records from the private sector rather than from the government.

As a branch of the Government of Alberta with the mission "to preserve the collective memory of Alberta, and to contribute to the protection of Albertans' rights and the sense of the Alberta identity," the Provincial Archives of Alberta acquires records from both private and government sources.[6] Records schedules, created by ministries of the Government of Alberta, dictate the disposition of records of the twenty-five ministries of the Government of Alberta such as transfer to the PAA for permanent retention, transfer to inactive storage, transfer to another Ministry, alienation (transferring the custody and control of the records to an entity outside of the Government of Alberta) or destruction. Private records held at the PAA, on the other hand, are acquired from individuals, associations, boards, organizations, corporations and unions. Local public bodies are also included under the umbrella of "private records." Local public bodies refer to educational bodies (school boards), health care bodies (health regions) and local government bodies (municipalities).[7]

The Beinecke Rare Book and Manuscript Library, unlike the PAA, is a private library located on the campus of Yale University, a private post-secondary institution. As such, the Beinecke Library is neither authorized nor mandated to acquire government records. Instead, the Beinecke Library is Yale University's principal repository for literary papers, early manuscripts and rare books in the fields of literature, theology, history and the natural sciences. In addition to its general collection of rare books and manuscripts, the Library also maintains the Yale Collection of American Literature, the Yale Collection of German Literature, the Yale Collection of Western Americana and the James Marshall and Marie-Louise Osborn Collection, which consists of English literary and historical manuscripts from the Anglo-Saxon period to the twentieth century. All of the Beinecke Library's collections derive from private rather than government provenance.

In the course of acquiring, processing, preserving and making records accessible, archives create documentation about records, donors and creators. This kind of work is normally captured in correspondence, institutional forms, contracts, reports and research notes and is collected in various files, such as processing files and curator's files. Many of the archivist's records are also captured in accession files, perhaps the most potentially valuable file to users and the file to which we direct this discussion. The accession file documents activities associated with "the initial steps of processing by establishing rudimentary physical and intellectual control over the materials by entering brief information about those materials in a register, database, or other log of the repository's holdings."[8] The file may also contain information about provenance and custodial history as well as details about how a repository acquired and manages a fonds. These types of records would help users gain an understanding of the context of the records, or in other words, how the records were created, used, stored and received while in the custody of their creators and custodians.

Correspondence in accession files includes communication with donors and, in the Beinecke Library's case, book and manuscript dealers, which provides background about how the institution obtained particular records. The accession file may also contain internal correspondence regarding initial evaluations of the records' intellectual and cultural value and whether or not the institution should acquire the material. At the PAA, accession files rarely contain information relating to the purchase of archival records; the PAA acquires most of its records via donation from private donors and from the transfer of government records.

Accession files also contain information regarding donor agreements and negotiations. At the Beinecke Library, purchases and donations are captured in the "Gift/Deposit Authorization and Processing Form" while at the PAA, the "Certificate of Gift" encapsulates negotiation between the donor and the archives. While both institutions sign contracts with their donors, the Beinecke Library does not routinely obtain copyright for its collections; rather, the Library obtains physical but not intellectual custody of materials. The Beinecke Library does own copyright for some of its collections, but this is not the norm.[9] Since the majority of the Beinecke Library's fonds derive from writers and other artists, it is important for the Library to ensure that authors and their designated literary executors retain the financial benefits and artistic rights pertaining to their creative work. At the PAA, on the other hand, when donors sign a "Certificate of Gift," they transfer copyright and ownership of the records from the donor to the PAA. If the material pertains to an artistic endeavour such as a film, which still brings in revenue for the donor, donors to the PAA, like some of those who donate to the Beinecke Library, will sometimes negotiate the date of copyright release.

Accession files at the PAA also contain archivists' appraisal reports. Archivists at the PAA are responsible for the appraisal of Government of Alberta records' schedules as well as for conducting appraisals of potential acquisitions from private donors. In Canada, private donors are eligible to apply for a federal government tax credit, whereas in the U.S. there is no such incentive provided to donors. Once or twice a year, the National Archival Appraisal Board (NAAB) visits the PAA and provides a monetary appraisal of private acquisitions. Records documenting this process are also added to the accession file. Since no comparable program is in place in the U.S., archivists at the Beinecke Library do not systematically appraise fonds, and consequently, this type of documentation is not present in the accession files unless it is supplied by a third-party appraiser.

Accession files may also contain further information about records such as preliminary lists and other contextual material, which the donor, dealer or other third party provides to the institution during negotiations. The Beinecke Library often obtains this kind of material from donors and book dealers, and it may include appraisals providing varying degrees of information about the intellectual and monetary value of a fonds as well as preliminary lists of the fonds' contents. Donors or dealers may also provide newspaper clippings, copies of articles from books or periodicals, obituaries and correspondence.

Records related to the "arrangement, description, and housing of archival materials for storage and use by patrons" or processing of acquisitions also comprise a large amount of institutional documentation in archives.[10] Archivists generate additional material, such as research notes, during the course of gathering information about the donor, creator and contents of the acquisition. Archivists' research notes may range from basic historical or biographical information relating to the records to more extensive investigations into the people, places and organizations represented in the records. At the PAA, archivists include records regarding processing, such as decisions relating to arrangement and description, to the accession file. While the Beinecke Library creates similar documentation, it distinguishes between accession and processing files and houses this information in separate locations; material pertaining to acquisition is placed in the accession file whereas material regarding arrangement, description and preservation is put into the processing file.

The complexity of the records' provenance also affects the amount of information recorded in institutional files. Sometimes, the complete provenance of records is unknown. It may take consultations with donors and creators or biographical research to discover the full narrative of the records. These consultations and research document the story of the records, including determining who received the records, where they have been stored, who used them and why the records were created.

Institutional procedures and the development of professional archival practices also influence the information created and retained about records. Accession files often contain varying degrees of information about a fonds and its creator/donor; information is frequently much more limited in the case of those files created before the days of standardized institutional forms and during a time when acquisitions were often not processed until decades after they had arrived at the archives.

Overall, an institution's documentation, and in particular the accession file, traces provenance[11] and custodial history[12] as well as decisions about how an acquisition is managed, including appraisal, processing and preservation. This documentation constitutes a narrative that can help users research and interpret archives and could also affect a researcher's understanding of the people and places documented therein.

In some instances, viewing institutional documentation can help a user gather a more balanced portrait of the individuals chronicled in the records. Most donors are aware when they donate material to an archives that the material they choose to donate presents a certain view of themselves. They have selected the material that documents their best thoughts, awards and achievements. As we might expect, it is rarer for donors to provide records that reflect the less successful or admirable aspects of their lives. Accession files, however, are a potentially excellent resource to find out the "behind the scenes" story of a donor's life.

Sometimes institutional documentation helps to provide a more nuanced and complex family portrait. As previously noted, accession files from private donors often contain correspondence from family members to the archives. This correspondence, while perhaps intended by the donors to provide more insight into the records, can sometimes reveal more about the personality of the donors. Suppose, for example, that a file documenting the acquisition of a family fonds contains not only family correspondence but also copies of transcripts of a court case to settle the disposition of the family's records.[13] In this story, a brother donates his family's records after his father bequeaths the records to him; a sister complains to the archives and to the courts that the father did not have the right to donate *her* records; the sister then declares her brother crazy and incompetent; a brother similarly declares his sister crazy and incompetent; the brother dies; and another brother enters the fray. Undoubtedly, access to this institutional documentation would enable users to better understand the family's story and would help place the fonds within a broader context. Researchers may, in fact, want to know whether family members intended their individual records to be included in the family fonds and made publicly accessible. In addition, this rather negative characterization of a seemingly cohesive family may also be of significance to researchers.

An accession file can also reveal information regarding the provenance of an acquisition. For example, an accession file for a collection of material relating to the Klondike at the Beinecke Library illuminates why the donors collected the material and why they donated their collection to an American institution. The accession file reveals that the donors collected material relating to early commerce in Canada and early Canadian settlements due to a family connection to this period of Canadian history. A personal connection — this time to Yale University — motivated the donors to present their collection to the Beinecke Library rather than another institution.

Just as the stories that document the acquisition of records provide valuable contextual information to users, institutional records can also demonstrate to users how or why archivists have created and arranged collections or why archivists describe some acquisitions in little detail and some in great depth. No doubt, to some users, arrangement and description decisions appear arbitrary and inconsistent. However, access to institutional documentation could avoid misconceptions about the inconsistency of the arrangement and description of a fonds and a collection.

Though most users may not be familiar with the differences between a "fonds" and a "collection," the distinction between the two influences the way that an archivist arranges and describes material, as well as how a researcher interprets the material. A fonds constitutes the "entire body of records of an organization, family, or individual that have been created and accumulated as the result of an organic process reflecting the functions of the creator."[14] In a fonds, an "archival bond" intellectually fuses records together through a web of interrelations that "links each record, incrementally, to the previous and subsequent ones and to all those which participate in the same activity" (InterPARES 2002: 5). A collection, on the other hand, consists of "materials assembled by a person, organization, or repository from a variety of sources."[15] When archivists arrange and describe a fonds, they are attempting to document the relationship between the activities of the creator and records those activities generated. However, when archivists arrange and describe a collection they try to reflect the artificial connection between the records designed by creators and/or custodians, or they may try to unify disparate pieces of material into a grouping of records of similar subject matter or form. While researchers do not need to know textbook definitions of archival terms, access to institutional documentation would enable researchers to understand arrangement and description decisions and to more appropriately decipher the meanings imbedded in a fonds' arrangement.

Institutional documentation can also reveal how archivists construct finding aids. While standards for finding aids and institutional practices vary somewhat from institution to institution, most finding aids provide similar types of information to users. This information describes how the archives acquired the records, who created the records, who donated the records, which activities the creator undertook to create the records, what type of conservation treatment the material has received, and the form of the records. When archivists create finding aids, they attempt to provide an impartial narrative of the story of the records. However, despite the best efforts of archivists to present an unbiased picture of the records, archivists often make decisions that affect a researcher's perspective on the records, decisions that may or may not be described in finding aids.

Some of the decisions that are not documented in a finding aid relate to the processing of archival material. Processing an archival acquisition involves collaboration between various professionals throughout the institution who help determine and perform activities related to physically storing, caring for, and treating archival material. However, not all finding aids identify by whom and how archival acquisitions have been processed. Institutional documentation, on the other hand, discloses the collaborative nature of processing archival material as well as the decisions made by archivists and their colleagues.

Without access to institutional documentation, users fail to see the relationship between the processing of an acquisition and what they read in a finding aid. For example, larger archival institutions assign the intellectual and the physical and/or administrative work to different individuals. One employee might appraise and make decisions regarding arrangement and description, while another may take over the practical concerns of physically re-foldering and storing the records. During these transactions, if an employee fails to communicate pertinent information regarding the physical arrangement of the records, this omission might result in an alteration of the physical arrangement that destroys the order of the records. If the archivist neglects to tell a colleague responsible for physically processing the seemingly "disorganized" files not to "sort" the files during the re-housing or re-foldering process, the colleague could make a change to the physical arrangement that erases the way the creator/custodian used or stored the records. Thus, if the user read only the finding aid, they might assume that the creator lived an orderly life instead of, perhaps, the wild and scattered life that the physical order revealed. Most archivists, out of a desire to preserve their professional reputation, would be unlikely to reveal the story of this kind of miscommunication in their archival descriptions.

Whether archivists will admit it or not, finding aids are a public tool that reflects how the archivists have done their job. Archivists with a strong sense of self preservation might search for a way to explain "mistakes" without implicating themselves. As Wendy M. Duff and Verne Harris note:

> Each archivist must decide what information about which records to highlight; what transitory data to capture and make visible. When describing records archivists will remember certain aspects and hide or forget others." (2002: 275)

While archivists do their best to create unprejudiced and unbiased finding aids, inevitably, archivists omit information in finding aids that users might find beneficial to their work.

As suggested previously in this discussion, internal documentation provides invaluable evidence about the story of the records to users, from their creation, custody, use, acquisition, appraisal and preservation, to their arrangement and description. However, despite the obvious value of institutional documentation to users, archivists cannot and should not open their files to public scrutiny and study without the consideration of several factors. In determining what and when institutional documentation can be made accessible, archivists must first carefully consider the constellation of legislation, professional ethics and institutional policies regarding recordkeeping.

Balancing access with privacy is one of archivists' most important roles in both Canada and the United States and in public and private institutions. Both fonds and institutional documentation are subject to access and privacy legislation. However, public and private institutions are subject to different legislation. For example, while the Beinecke Library is subject to some federal privacy laws, much of American legislation regarding access and privacy pertains to government institutions and records. The Beinecke Library, as a private institution, is not required to comply with many federal and state laws, such as the *Privacy Act* and the *Freedom of Information Act* (FOIA), which are applicable to government records. These laws are only pertinent in rare cases where Yale University operates as a government entity, such as the Yale University Police Department.[16]

Many of the federal laws that are pertinent to private institutions concern particular types of records; for example, health records are subject to the *Health Insurance Portability and Accountability Act* (HIPAA) and educational records are subject to the *Family Educational Rights and Privacy Act* (FERPA). While the Beinecke Library does not create health or educational records it does acquire collections containing such material. In these cases the Beinecke Library adheres to HIPAA and FERPA and restricts access to health and student records as legally required. For example, the William Carlos Williams Papers (YCAL MSS 116) contain material relating to his work both as a poet and as a doctor. Documents pertaining to Williams' career as a poet are open and accessible to researchers whereas those relating to his work as a doctor, namely medical records, are restricted in accordance with HIPAA. Since the Beinecke Library does not create student or health records, HIPAA and FERPA do not apply to the Library's institutional documentation.

The Beinecke Library is accountable to the internal policies and procedures of Yale University. The president and the Yale Corporation comprise the university's governing body and are vested with overall supervision of the affairs of the university. Day-to-day administration falls to seven offices — including the secretary, the general counsel and the vice-president for finance and business operations, all of whom in some aspect or another are responsible for developing policies and procedures regarding university records. In reality, several departments and offices across the university administer guidelines and policies regarding recordkeeping, all of whom, in turn, rely on the University Archives to manage university records.

The Yale Corporation outlines general policies regarding university records in its "Miscellaneous Regulations."[17] Written in consultation with University Archives, these policies determine, at a high level, which records to retain and destroy and outline access procedures. Most records created and maintained within university units and offices are open after a thirty-five-year period. Exceptions include, for example, records relating to donors, which are closed permanently (although the secretary can review requests for access to donor records on a case-by-case basis). If interpreted narrowly this exception applies to all of the Beinecke Library's dealings with its donors — whether the donation of financial gifts or records. In addition to these policies, the Beinecke Library maintains a number of internal policies regarding access. For example, the Library deems records pertaining to the financial value of its collections as confidential. Ultimately, the default restriction on institutional records is thirty-five years unless the "Miscellaneous Regulations" denote an exemption; this exemption often applies to information routinely found in accession files.

Two laws govern access and privacy in the Province of Alberta: the *Freedom of Information and Protection of Privacy Act* (FOIP) and the Personal Information Protection Act (PIPA). FOIP governs public bodies such as any department or branch of Government of Alberta, agencies, boards, commissions, Executive Council, Legislative Assembly Office, Office of Auditor General, Ombudsman, Chief Electoral Office, Ethics Commissioner and the Information and Privacy Commissioner (FOIP, s. 1 (p)). PIPA governs "organizations" or more specifically corporations, unincorporated associations, trade unions (as defined in the *Labour Relations Code*), a partnership (as defined in the *Partnership Act*) and an individual acting in a commercial capacity, but does not include "an individual acting in a personal or domestic capacity" (PIPA, s. 1 (j)).

In terms of how these two laws affect privacy and access at the PAA, as a branch of the Government of Alberta, the PAA is subject to FOIP but not to PIPA. Essentially this means that all the records that the PAA creates in conjunction with acquiring, accessioning, processing and preserving records (all those records that can be found in the accession file) are subject to FOIP as well as all of the records it receives from those bodies subject to FOIP. Accordingly, the PAA is not legally obligated to protect the privacy rights of individuals featured in records from bodies not subject to FOIP, nor is it under any legal obligation to protect the privacy of "an individual acting in a personal or domestic capacity."[18]

To access records subject to FOIP, including accession files, users can wait the seventy-five-year restriction period or they may make a formal FOIP request. However, section 43 includes a special provision for archives to disclose information in acquisitions if the information has been in existence for over twenty-five years, if the records do not contain personal information that would cause harm or is deemed an unreasonable invasion of privacy according to section 17 or section 42, or if the records are over seventy-five years old (FOIP, s. 43(1) a). The PAA can also disclose information in a record that does not contain personal information if the information in the record has been in existence for twenty-five years and if the disclosure of the information would not cause harm to third-party business interests according to section 16, if the release of the information would not cause harm to law enforcement according to section 20 and if the information is not subject to any type of legal privilege under section 27 (FOIP, s. 43(1) b).

However, despite the array of privacy and access laws in both countries, archivists are often confronted with situations when they must determine access conditions. When access and privacy legislation presents holes and gaps, archivists must instead reflect on their ethical rather than legislative responsibilities. For instance, in both institutions, while records from private individuals and organizations are not subject to FOIP or FOIA, these donors may request that some of the records remain closed for a pre-determined amount of time. In other instances, donors, particularly the aged or those acting on behalf of someone else, may not know the contents of their donation. In these situations, archivists must rely on their own sense of personal ethics to help determine access conditions.

Professional codes of ethics also assist archivists in making access and privacy decisions. Codes of ethics of the Association of Canadian Archivists (*Code of Ethics*) and the Society of American Archivists (*Code of Ethics for Archivists*) require archivists to conduct their affairs with professional judgment regarding privacy and confidentiality. According to the Association of Canadian Archivists "archivists [must] make every attempt possible to respect the privacy of the individuals who created or are the subject of records, especially those who had no voice in the disposition of the records."[19] Similarly, the Society of American Archivists states: "archivists protect the privacy rights of donors and individuals or groups who are the subject of records."[20] It is clear that although, ethically, archivists must respect the privacy rights of those represented in records as well as donors and users of archives, neither professional organization provides detailed guidance on how archivists should safeguard the privacy of donors, creators and third parties, leaving archivists to depend on their own judgment and interpretation of their profession's code of ethics.

Effective communication with creators and donors constitutes an important element in the fulfilment of archivists' legal obligations. Archivists must be vigilant during donor interviews to ensure that donors understand the full implications of transferring their records to an archival institution and what it means to contribute to the institution's archival record — a record that, if requested under access and privacy legislation, could also become accessible to the public. Archivists must negotiate access in cases where donors feel that both the records and the institutional documentation surrounding the records' transfer to an archival institution are sensitive.

In order to appropriately create, retain and make accessible institutional documentation, for the sake of institutional memory and accountability and to ensure the preservation of the story of the records, archives must competently manage their own records. In most cases this requires implementing and sustaining a records management program. A good records management program includes policies and regulations that dictate the types of decisions that institutional documentation should capture and manage. If archives consistently apply these kinds of policies, when users view institutional documentation, they can trust that they are viewing an accurate reflection of how an archives operates.

Unfortunately, fully operational records management programs do not exist in all archival institutions. Even where institutional policies on records management exist, many archival institutions do not have the resources to employ staff dedicated to implementing them. However, institutions such as the Beinecke Library have identified records management as a priority and are in a transition toward managing records more effectively.

The Yale University Archives serves as the official repository for all university records — including those of the Beinecke Library. The University Archives currently does not employ a records manager, and the department, while providing advice on such matters, is not mandated to perform records management services. However, the University Archives does facilitate the Records Services Program, which is Yale's first university-wide records management initiative. The program provides support to carry out appraisal, selection and preservation of the institutional records of Yale University and its affiliated agencies. The University Archives is currently revising the collection development policy for the various libraries and archives on campus. The existing records schedule for libraries and archives, while no longer active, provides insight into the activities and records the university deems of enduring value — many of which provide contextual information about the library's holdings.[21] While the Beinecke Library has not utilized the Records Services Program, the library has identified records management as a priority and aims to implement a more formalized records management program in the near future.

Two pieces of legislation direct records management within the Government of Alberta. *The Government Organization Act* stipulates that the Government of Alberta is subject to records management policies relating to the creation, handling, control, organization, retention, maintenance, security, preservation and disposition of records (s. 14 (2)). The *Act*'s subordinate legislation, the Records Management Regulation, indicates who will be responsible and how records management policies will be implemented in the Government of Alberta. The regulation states that a committee of representatives of the records management community, known as the Alberta Records Management Committee, is responsible for approving the retention and disposition of schedules created by ministries of the Government of Alberta (s. 6). Ministries create schedules for their records, and, subject to various approvals, the schedules are enacted and their disposition managed. Departments are expected to comply with these pieces of legislation and to employ enough resources to meet the requirements of the legislation.

As previously discussed, the documentation archivists create about records varies greatly, ranging from very little information to rich resources providing invaluable insights concerning the records' provenance, custodial history, acquisition, appraisal, processing and preservation. Ideally, legislation or internal policies should allow archivists to make this kind of internal documentation routinely available. This documentation, if made available to researchers, could affect their perception of archivists as well as the organizations and individuals featured in the records.

While archival tools for the public, such as finding aids, provide archivists with an opportunity to describe provenance, custodial history and decisions regarding appraisal and processing, finding aids often fail to provide the kind of detail found in institutional documentation. While archival descriptive standards could be amended to require archivists to include more information about the ways in which archives manage records, ultimate transparency and accountability can only come through opening our own archives — our internal documentation — to researchers.

In some cases, viewing internal documentation is not vital for users. For some researchers, the finding aid may be a good enough substitute for linking and describing what has happened to the records before they arrived at the archives. Other researchers, however, may have questions regarding the records that are not answered in the finding aid. In such cases, researchers may benefit from viewing institutional information. It is archivists' obligation to at least provide researchers with the choice to consult such information.

From the widespread acceptance and use of technology in archives, it is clear that archivists are seeking innovative ways to encourage the discoverability of their holdings, to provide insight into the ways in which archival institutions acquire, arrange and describe their holdings and to foster more proactive and participatory outreach. Employing technology to increase transparency demonstrates the profession's ability to think innovatively and to adapt to a rapidly changing environment with creativity and thoughtfulness.

However, the use of technology and enhancing finding aids does not remove the archivists' imprint from the context of the record; archivists continue to mediate and shape information about their work and records. Online descriptions and Web 2.0 technologies are limited in their ability to provide the same kind of information regarding the context in which archives are acquired and managed as is found in institutional documentation. Most archivists simply do not have the capability to impartially document their own processes in finding aids and other tools. Institutional documentation, on the other hand, provides a more accurate and less self-conscious snapshot of archivists' roles in creating and managing archives.

Rather than launching costly projects to enhance descriptive information and engage in new technologies, even though these kinds of projects have much value to users, a more cost-effective and routine means of recording archivists' functions could be achieved through maintaining and making institutional documentation accessible. Considerable potential exists to provide patrons with insight into archivists' decisions and practices if we utilize the documentation already created as part of the day-to-day administration of archives.

However, while this documentation already exists — to varying degrees — the realities of making institutional records accessible to patrons, as we have demonstrated in this discussion, is not always straightforward, given the juridical, ethical and institutional context of an archivists' working environment. If institutional documentation about archives is valuable for interpreting archives, archivists will need to grapple with the number of legalities and ethics inherent in making such material routinely available to researchers. Archivists will need to communicate and negotiate effectively with creators and donors in order to ensure the donors understand the implications of donating to an archives. Institutions must also rely on effective records management of their own records in order to guarantee that the complete narrative of the records is retained and is made available appropriately and equitably.

Notes

1. For example, a succinct discussion of the postmodern perspective in archival theory can be found in Terry Cook 2001 and 1997.
2. Articles exploring these themes include Duff and Harris 2002, Kaplan 2002, and Yakel 2003.
3. A more comprehensive list of various Web 2.0 technologies archives have embraced can be found on the "Archives 2.0" <wiki (http://archives2point0.

wetpaint.com/>.
4. To view the Beinecke Library's blogs and podcasts visit <http://www.library.yale.edu/beinecke/brblevents/blogspodcasts.html>. To see the Beinecke Library's photostream on Flickr visit <http://www.flickr.com/photos/beinecke_library/>. To follow the Beinecke Library's tweets see <http://twitter.com/BeineckeLibrary>.
5. School of Library, Archival and Information Studies, University of British Columbia, "Select List of Archival Terminology," <http://www.slais.ubc.ca/RESOURCES/students/Archival_Terminology.pdf>.
6. Provincial Archives of Alberta, "Homepage," <http://culture.alberta.ca/archives/>.
7. Government of Alberta, *Freedom of Information and Protection of Privacy Act* (FOIP), s. 1 (j). <http://foip.alberta.ca/legislation/act/section1.cfm>.
8. Society of American Archivists, *Glossary of Archival and Records Terminology* <http://www.archivists.org/glossary/index.asp>.
9. For example, the Beinecke Library owns the copyright to the Alfred Stieglitz\Georgia O'Keefe Archive and the Eugene O'Neill Papers. For a comprehensive list see <http://www.library.yale.edu/beinecke/brblresearch/copyright_list.html>.
10. Society of American Archivists, *Glossary of Archival and Records Terminology*, <http://www.archivists.org/glossary/index.asp>.
11. "Provenance is a fundamental principle of archives, referring to the individual, family or organization that created or received the items in a collection. The principle of provenance or the *respect des fonds* dictates that records of different origins (provenance) be kept separate to preserve their context." Society of American Archivists, *Glossary of Archival and Records Terminology* <http://www.archivists.org/glossary/index.asp>.
12. "The Custodial history gives information about the chain of agencies, officers, or persons, if different from the creator(s), that have exercised custody or control over the records at all stages in their existence." Canadian Council on Archives, *Rules for Archival Description* (Ottawa: Bureau of Canadian Archivists, 2008), <http://www.cdncouncilarchives.ca/RAD/RAD_Chapter01_July2008.pdf>.
13. In accordance with privacy and access legislation, these examples have been anonymized.
14. Society of American Archivists, *Glossary of Archival and Records Terminology*, <http://www.archivists.org/glossary/index.asp>.
15. Ibid.
16. In fact, the Freedom of Information Commission of Connecticut voted unanimously on February 13, 2008, that the Yale University Police Department is accountable to the same rules as public police departments including FOIA (FIC 2007-370). Freedom of Information Commission of Connecticut <http://www.state.ct.us/foi/2008FD/20080213/FIC2007-370.htm>.
17. Yale Corporation, "Miscellaneous Regulations" <http://www.yale.edu/about/corporation/regulations.html>.
18. Despite the absence of legislation, the PAA endeavours to use consistent privacy practices.
19. Association of Canadian Archivists, "Code of Ethics" <http://archivists.ca/

about/ethics.aspx>.
20. Society of American Archivists, "Code of Ethics for Archivists" <http://www.archivists.org/governance/handbook/app_ethics.asp>.
21. See "Records Schedules," Manuscripts and Archives, Yale University <http://www.library.yale.edu/mssa/ua_sched_libraries.html>.

References

Association of Canadian Archivists. *Code of Ethics.* <http://archivists.ca/about/ethics.aspx> (accessed on January 10, 2010).

Canadian Council on Archives. *Rules for Archival Description.* Ottawa: Bureau of Canadian Archivists, 2008. <http://www.cdncouncilarchives.ca/RAD/RAD_Chapter01_July2008.pdf> (accessed on January 5, 2010).

Cook, Terry. 2001. "Fashionable Nonsense or Professional Rebirth: Postmodernism and the Practice of Archives." *Archivaria* 51 (Spring): 14–35.

_____. 1997. "What is Past is Prologue: A History of Archival Ideas Since 1998 and the Future Paradigm Shift," *Archivaria* 43 (Spring): 17–63.

Duff, Wendy, and Verne Harris. 2002. "Stories and Names: Archival Description as Narrating Records and Constructing Meanings." *Archival Science* 2.3-4 (September): 263–85.

Freedom of Information Commission of Connecticut. Docket FIC 2007-370. <http://www.state.ct.us/foi/2008FD/20080213/FIC2007-370.htm> (accessed on January 21, 2010).

Government of Alberta. *Freedom of Information and Protection of Privacy Act.* <http://foip.alberta.ca/legislation/act/section43.cfm> (accessed on January 10, 2010).

_____. *Government Organization Act.* <http://www.qp.alberta.ca/574.cfm?page=g10.cfm&leg_type=Acts&isbncln=9780779736188> (accessed on January 27, 2010).

_____. *Records Management Regulation.* <http://www.qp.alberta.ca/574.cfm?page=2001_224.cfm&leg_type=Regs&isbncln=9780779735600> (accessed on January 10, 2010).

_____. *Personal Information Protection Act.* <http://pipa.alberta.ca/index.cfm?page=legislation/act/index.html> (accessed on January 10, 2010).

Hyry, Tom, and Michelle Light. 2002. "Colophons and Annotations: New Directions for the Finding Aid." *American Archivist* 65.2 (Fall/Winter): 216–30.

InterPARES (International Research on Permanent Authentic Records in Electronic Systems). 2002. *The Interpares Glossary: A Controlled Vocabulary of Terms Used in the Interpares Project.* Vancouver: University of British Columbia. <http://www.interpares.org/documents/Interpares%20Glossary%202002-1.pdf> (accessed on January 27, 2010).

Kaplan, Elisabeth. 2002. "'Many Paths to Partial Truths': Archives, Anthropology, and the Power of Representation." *Archival Science* 2: 209–20.

MacNeil, Heather. 2005. "Picking Our Text: Archival Description, Authenticity, and the Archivist as Editor." *American Archivist* 68.2 (Fall/Winter): 264–78.

Provincial Archives of Alberta. "Homepage." <http://culture.alberta.ca/archives/> (accessed on January 15, 2010).

School of Library, Archival, and Information Studies. University of British Columbia. "Select List of Archival Terminology." <http://www.slais.ubc.ca/

RESOURCES/students/Archival_Terminology.pdf> (accessed on January 10, 2010).
Society of American Archivists. *Code of Ethics for Archivists*. <http://www.archivists.org/governance/handbook/app_ethics.asp> (accessed on January 10, 2010).
_____. *Glossary of Archival and Records Terminology*. <http://www.archivists.org/glossary/index.asp> (accessed on January 27, 2010).
Yakel, Elizabeth. 2003. "Archival Representation," *Archival Science* 3: 1–25.
Yakel, Elizabeth, Polly Reynolds and Seth Shaw. 2007. "Creating the Next Generation of Archival Finding Aids." *D-Lib Magazine* 13.5/6 <http://www.dlib.org/dlib/may07/yakel/05yakel.html> (accessed on August 2, 2010).
Yale Corporation. 2006. "Miscellaneous Regulations." September. <http://www.yale.edu/about/corporation/regulations.html> (accessed on January 10, 2010).

Les enjeux historiographiques de l'usage des archives littéraires

Manon Brunet

> "Ah! fiez-vous à l'expérience
> d'un vieux coureur des bois à qui
> la solitude et le désert ont appris
> une science qui ne se trouve pas dans les livres."
> —Henri-Raymond Casgrain, *La Jongleuse*

Au-delà de ce que la lecture de milliers d'archives épistolaires m'a permis d'apprendre empiriquement sur des hommes, des femmes, des événements et des oeuvres entre 1850 et 1900, de ce qu'elle m'a amenée à connaître de leur vision de la littérature et du monde, et de ce qu'elle m'a conduite à développer comme théorie des réseaux littéraires, il me reste le souci de comprendre comment l'histoire littéraire québécoise d'aujourd'hui utilise les archives pour se mettre à jour et se rendre utile à la théorie et à la critique littéraires. Voilà le but des réflexions qui suivent sur l'état présent de l'historiographie littéraire québécoise, basées sur mon parcours dans les archives à des fins de recherche qui ne sont pas seulement historiques.

Un parcours dans les archives

Quand, il y a 30 ans, j'ai commencé, jeune étudiante au doctorat dans la vingtaine, à explorer par curiosité, ensuite par grand intérêt, les fonds d'archives dans les institutions religieuses, comme le Séminaire de Québec et le Séminaire de Nicolet, dans des dépôts gouvernementaux, comme les Archives nationales du Québec ou les Archives publiques du Canada alors ainsi nommées ainsi que chez d'anciens artisans du livre au Québec, comme la Librairie Beauchemin, la papetière de Jean-Baptiste Rolland, me rendant même là où des familles descendantes d'écrivains québécois du 19e siècle m'ouvraient leurs archives et leurs mémoires, dans toutes les régions du Québec, de l'Outaouais jusqu'au Bas-Saint-Laurent, je ne pensais pas que cela me mènerait au bout du monde, au bout de bien des mondes. Comment imaginer qu'un chercheur qui paraît isolé, quand il se retrouve si souvent trop seul dans ces archives à mille lieux de toutes terres, apparemment scientifiquement habitées, peut, en parcourant des feuillets jaunis, des lettres en liasses à la tonne, aux mille et une calligraphies, conservées n'importe comment, n'importe où, dans n'importe quel état, en France, en Allemagne, en Irlande, en Louisiane, partout au Canada, jusque dans les archives du Vatican, peut donc trouver un sens, une unité à tous ces fragments d'histoire mal fagotée?

Nous y allions avec nos propres moyens, nos propres intuitions de recherche. Nous fabriquions nos propres outils de recherche, car peu d'inventaires existaient et, bien sûr, aucun moteur de recherche du genre PISTARD. L'ordinateur n'existait même pas. La numérisation non plus, il va sans dire. Tout se lisait et se faisait à la main ou presque, à cause de contraintes matérielles, techniques ou… politiques. L'accès aux archives était toujours compliqué et nous ne réussissions qu'au prix de toutes sortes de patiences et de précautions diplomatiques développées au contact d'archivistes de diverses trempes et de divers tempéraments. Nous suivions des pistes que nous n'étions que quelques-uns alors à ouvrir, à découvrir et à en imaginer tout le potentiel historiographique. Qu'est-ce qui nous motivait tant, malgré tous ces obstacles?

Dans les années 1980, je rencontrais rarement des chercheurs dans les archives, sauf des généalogistes et quelques historiens. Des littéraires, jamais, sauf dans les pays étrangers. Cela m'interrogeait: pourquoi là et pas chez nous? pourquoi s'intéressent-ils à l'histoire de leur littérature et, nous, pas à la nôtre? pourquoi les autres ont-ils une tradition en histoire littéraire et pas nous? À l'heure encore du structuralisme, l'ère de la théorie littéraire battait son plein dans nos universités québécoises et, par conséquent, l'histoire littéraire était un discours laissé pour compte par rapport à la sémiologie, à la poétique, à la narratologie, enfin par rapport à toute approche de la littérature qui privilégiait le Texte, appelé alors l'"interne" de la littérature en opposition à l'"externe," l'Histoire. Derrida, Barthes, Kristeva et les Formalistes russes étaient plus populaires que Lanson ou que ceux qui cherchaient à renouveler la "méthode" de celui-ci.

C'est pour trouver des réponses théoriques, méthodologiques et épistémologiques à toutes ces questions que j'ai persisté à travailler dans et avec les archives et, plus particulièrement, avec les correspondances des écrivains québécois de la deuxième moitié du 19e siècle, période qui correspond au processus d'institutionnalisation de la littérature québécoise. Voilà le sens profond de mes démarches qui m'ont guidée dans les archives. Je suis encore à la recherche d'une unité épistémologique au sein de ma discipline, parfois trop, parfois pas assez humaine. J'ai l'impression que les historiens sont parvenus plus que nous à cette unité, avec l'École des Annales et les nouvelles tendances. Il leur semble plus aisé de conjuguer le sujet avec l'objet de leurs recherches. L'usage courant qu'ils font des archives les aiderait-il à créer ces liens tout naturellement? Car, à fréquenter les archives, on découvre vite que le privé et le public sont enchevêtrés, qu'ils sont des vases communicants et que l'on ne peut parler d'"interne" ou d'"externe" d'un individu, d'une société, d'un fait sans manquer à la relativité générale et restreinte qui est la marque de tous les phénomènes historiques.

Dans les études littéraires, en revanche, l'objet a trop tendance à se confondre avec le sujet recherché et le sujet-chercheur. Comment parler de la littérature sans trop en faire? Comment être une science sans en avoir trop l'air? C'est pourquoi nous avons tendance à passer d'un extrême à l'autre dans nos approches scientifiques: nous hésitons entre des théories très restrictives, mais plus fiables et des interprétations trop personnelles, mais plus justes. Ceci est peut-être encore plus vrai dans le cas québécois qui peine à développer, malgré la très haute compétence de nos chercheurs, des modèles théoriques qui seraient adoptés par l'institution littéraire scientifique internationale. Un véritable mythe de Sisyphe! Les Européens se méfient injustement de nos modèles inspirés de notre corpus national archivistique. Nous en venons presque alors à nous méfier de nous-mêmes, à agir avec des prudences extrêmes dans nos analyses et interprétations de nos corpus et des leurs, tant nous désirons paraître plus rigoureux que l'institution qui nous boude.

Aurions-nous démissionné de notre capacité à voir autrement notre histoire littéraire? Par exemple, malgré les multiples recherches menées par plusieurs équipes depuis la Révolution tranquille, nos histoires littéraires ajusteraient difficilement leur discours. Nous commençons à peine, par exemple, à voir le 19e siècle comme une période ouverte sur le monde et à la modernité :

> Loin de l'Europe et isolés en Amérique, les écrivains canadiens-français du 19e siècle se heurtent à des contradictions[…].
> Les idées débattues sont largement nourries de celles qui circulent aux États-Unis et en Europe où plusieurs écrivains séjournent. […] De sorte qu'il faut décidément nuancer l'image de repli que conserve le siècle. (Biron, Dumont, Nardout-Lafarge 2007: 59)

Or, les archives apportent beaucoup d'éclairages circonstanciés qui rendent caduques des interprétations faites à la surface de ce qui est trop empiriquement visible, mais limité. La censure, par exemple, a joué un rôle important au Québec. Mais les archives révèlent jusqu'au 20e siècle des écritures et des pratiques aussi très libres. Par exemple, au 19e siècle, l'abbé Henri-Raymond Casgrain fréquentait chaque hiver passé à Paris des salons dreyfusards et féministes et il ne couchait pas toujours chez des religieux…; l'univers religieux lui semblait trop restrictif. Son réseau de 850 correspondants s'étendait sur les cinq continents et les allégeances littéraires, religieuses et politiques étaient très diversifiées (Brunet 2002). Grâce à l'abbé, la première romancière québécoise, Laure Conan, a pu être publiée et être payée pour son travail (Brunet 1997), ce qui étonna des écrivains pourtant aussi libéraux que Louis Fréchette. La correspondance publiée de Laure Conan en témoigne (Conan 2002). Un autre exemple d'ouverture sur la modernité, du 20ᵉ siècle cette fois: le *Journal* (Ringuet 1998) et *Le carnet du cynique* (Ringuet 1998) de Ringuet révèlent dix ans avant la parution du très conservateur roman de la terre de ce dernier, *Trente arpents* (Ringuet 1938), un intellectuel gaillard, très ouvert aux courants modernes, et aux idées anticléricales très libérales. Qui oserait dire, même aujourd'hui, ceci:

> Mettez en contact un Canadien français et un étranger. Infailliblement au bout de quelques instants on parlera Canada. C'est-à-dire que l'étranger, après avoir avoué son ignorance, au grand reproche de son interlocuteur, l'écoutera parler.[…] Et nous, que trouvons-nous à dire du Gabon? (Ringuet 1998: 77)

Les documents sont là, en grand nombre, les analyses existent de réseaux intellectuels actifs et ouverts à la différence, des archives ont été publiées ces dernières années, d'autres attendent encore de servir sur des milliers de mètres linéaires de tablettes et la relève est là. Les différents savoirs dans les études littéraires gagneraient donc à créer davantage de ponts entre elles: le savoir théorique, le savoir critique et le savoir historique. Un plus grand et meilleur usage de la richesse archivistique du Québec pourrait y contribuer, comme cela fut le cas ici pour l'histoire et pour l'histoire littéraire en France. Là, une tradition en histoire littéraire s'est poursuivie et renouvelée, au-delà du structuralisme et même grâce à lui dans sa tangente sociologique. Barthes n'a-t-il pas lui-même défendu l'importance d'une "histoire de l'*idée* de littérature" (Barthes 1981: 265)? De même en Allemagne, autour des théoriciens de l'esthétique de la réception de l'École de Jauss (Jauss 1978), à la fois herméneutes et historiens de la littérature: un souci historiographique sous-tend les débats théoriques.

Un parcours de l'historiographie littéraire québécoise

Au début des années 1970, les instruments de recherche en histoire littéraire du Québec étaient fort limités. En réalité, nous n'avions comme guide que l'*Histoire de la littérature française du Québec* de Pierre De Grandpré, parue en quatre tomes entre 1967 et 1969 (De Grandpré 1967–69). Cette histoire classique ne faisait pas l'usage d'archives et mettait l'accent sur les hommes et les œuvres. C'est à Laurent Mailhot que l'on doit d'avoir lancé le signal en 1974 de la nécessité d'une réécriture de l'histoire littéraire du Québec avec son fameux *Que sais-je?* sur *La littérature québécoise* (Mailhot 1974). L'historien engagé n'hésite alors pas à dire, pour montrer tout le travail encore à faire, que: "Nous avons à la fois moins et plus qu'une littérature. Un iceberg dont les documents immergés communiquent en profondeur. Un héritage sous bénéfice d'inventaire" (Mailhot 1974: 6). À la fin de cette décennie politisée, nous disposions de deux ouvrages de référence qui s'avérèrent d'une importance capitale dans le développement de la nouvelle histoire littéraire du Québec. Ils sont d'ailleurs désormais accessibles directement sur le web, dans leur version numérisée grâce à BAnQ. Un premier, paru en 1976, le *Dictionnaire pratique des auteurs québécois* (Hamel et al. 1976) (l'ancêtre du DALFAN, *Dictionnaire des auteurs de langue française de l'Amérique du Nord*, Hamel et al. 1989) dont les auteurs des universités de Montréal et d'Ottawa, Réginald Hamel, John Hare et Paul Wyczynski, avaient une expérience archivistique. L'autre ouvrage, réalisé sous l'initiative de Maurice Lemire à l'Université Laval, est le premier tome, publié en 1978, de l'incontournable série du *Dictionnaire des œuvres littéraires du Québec* (Lemire 1978). Ces ouvrages ne fournissent pas de pistes archivistiques, mais ils procèdent d'un dépouillement de très nombreuses sources primaires, comme les journaux, ce qui a rendu de grands services aux chercheurs. Ils ont constitué le corpus national commun de référence. Le *DOLQ* a aussi ouvert la porte à la recherche en grande équipe en histoire littéraire au Québec, comme le démontrent aussi les cinq tomes parus depuis 1991 de *La vie littéraire au Québec* (Lemire and Saint-Jacques 1991–2005), qui en sont le prolongement analytique.

Au moment donc où je débutais mes recherches archivistiques, je disposais de ces deux guides historiques dont la parution témoignait, malgré le fort courant structuraliste, d'une volonté de réintégrer l'histoire littéraire dans le champ scientifique littéraire. Ce qui contribua le plus à cette actualisation fut concurremment le développement des études sociologiques en littérature et, en particulier, celui de la perspective institutionnelle. L'histoire littéraire du Québec s'est ainsi renouvelée en même temps que la sociologie de l'institution littéraire s'est développée et a provoqué une réflexion en historiographie littéraire. Qu'on se rappelle, dans les années 1980, les nombreux colloques et publications sur le sujet. Au Québec, par exemple, Clément Moisan de l'Université Laval se pose la question en 1987, *Qu'est-ce que l'histoire littéraire?* (Moisan 1987), dans un ouvrage édité aux Presses universitaires de France. Un collectif en 1989 rassemblait les réflexions de chercheurs, auxquelles j'ai participé, sur *L'histoire littéraire: théories, méthodes, pratiques* (Moisan 1989). En Europe, ce retour à l'histoire littéraire se faisait également, avec des représentants en sociologie de la littérature comme le Belge Jacques Dubois, auteur de *L'institution de la littérature: introduction à une sociologie* (Dubois 1978) ou les Français Alain Viala, *Naissance de l'écrivain: sociologie de la littérature à l'âge classique* (Viala 1985) et Antoine Compagnon, *La Troisième République des Lettres: de Flaubert à*

Proust (Compagnon 1983). L'histoire littéraire des 18ᵉ et 19ᵉ siècles français se renouvelait; tous étant à la recherche du moment-clé de la constitution de l'institution littéraire, indépendante des institutions politiques et religieuses. Nos études critiques au Québec ont suivi cette pente sociohistorique; l'impact majeur qu'eut l'ouvrage de Lucie Robert, *L'institution du littéraire au Québec* (Robert 1989) est révélateur.

Cependant, cette réorientation sociologique de l'histoire littéraire se faisait en Europe en prenant en considération l'importance des archives littéraires: correspondance d'Alfred de Vigny (Vigny 1989) ou de Zola (1978, 1986, 1987 and 2003), carnets de notes de Flaubert (Flaubert 1977, 1987, 1988, 1993, 1995, 1999, 2001 and 2008), manuscrits bigarrés de Francis Ponge (Ponge 1984 and 2005), les éditions et rééditions d'archives, de même que des analyses critiques se multiplièrent très rapidement en France à partir des années 1980. L'ITEM (Institut des textes et manuscrits modernes, CNRS), sous la direction de Michel Contat (Contat 1991) et de Louis Hay (Hay 1989 and 1990), propulsa la nouvelle génétique textuelle. Or, cette préoccupation pour les archives fut plus tardive dans le milieu québécois. L'équipe du GRÉLQ (Groupe de recherche sur l'édition littéraire au Québec), créée par Jacques Michon et Richard Giguère en 1982, fut une pionnière avec sa préoccupation pour les archives éditoriales du 20ᵉ siècle. Les deux volumes parus depuis 1999 de l'*Histoire de l'édition littéraire au Québec* (Michon 1999) qui doit en totaliser trois, sont les synthèses des nombreux travaux réalisés par cette équipe dynamique. Les éditions critiques ouvrirent aussi le chemin, comme celles de la collection de la "Bibliothèque du Nouveau-Monde" des Presses de l'Université de Montréal lancée en 1986 par Roméo Arbour, Jean-Louis Major et Laurent Mailhot. Mais il fallut attendre les années 1990 pour observer la création de groupes de recherche reliés directement à la mise en valeur d'archives personnelles d'écrivains, comme l'entreprise d'édition de la riche correspondance de Louis Fréchette par Jacques Blais (Blais et al. 1992) qui est sur le point de voir le jour, et comme le Projet Casgrain que j'ai créé en 1989 avec comme but de faire connaître la correspondance des 5 000 lettres du réseau casgrainien (Brunet 1993, 1995 and 1999). Les travaux "archéologiques" de l'ALAQ (Archéologie du littéraire au Québec), menés patiemment par Bernard Andrès (Andrès 2001, 2003, 2005 and 2007) et son équipe depuis 1990 dans les mémoires et la correspondance de Pierre de Sales Laterrière notamment, et d'autres d'entre 1759 et 1839, ont permis de revisiter significativement les débuts de la littérature québécoise. À l'heure actuelle, l'ARCHÈ, Centre québécois de recherche sur l'archive littéraire, sous la direction de Jacinthe Martel à l'UQAM, est très actif. Il a notamment produit en 2005 un bien utile *Répertoire des archives littéraires et des manuscrits d'écrivains* (Martel 2005 and 2008) lequel est venu compléter les bibliographies de Yvan Lamonde sur la littérature personnelle (Lamonde 1983 and 2000). Il faut reconnaître que les contributions majeures de ce dernier à l'histoire culturelle, qui reposent sur de la documentation archivistique de première importance, comme la correspondance de Louis-Antoine Dessaulles (Lamonde 1978, 1991 and 1994) ou les archives Papineau (Lamonde 1998), ou encore à l'histoire du livre qui ont conduit au collectif de l'*Histoire du livre et de l'imprimé au Canada* (Fleming and Lamonde 2004–2007), sont toutes des modèles à suivre.

Or, étant donné que, depuis 1991, l'histoire littéraire du Québec vit une phase de réécriture, comme en témoignent les cinq tomes déjà parus de *La vie littéraire au Québec* (Lemire and Saint-Jacques 1991–2005) sous la direction de Maurice Lemire et de Denis Saint-Jacques, *La littérature québécoise depuis ses origines* (Mailhot 1997) de Laurent Mailhot chez Typo, et la toute récente *Histoire de la littérature québécoise* (Biron et al. 2007) de Michel Biron, François Dumont et d'Élisabeth Nardout-Lafarge, la question qui se pose à la lumière des recherches actuelles menées sur le terrain en histoire littéraire est celle-ci: comment intégrer à notre historiographie littéraire nos connaissances acquises grâce à la fréquentation des archives? La question mérite d'être posée, car bien que d'une utilité tout à fait incontestable, force est d'admettre que nos récentes histoires littéraires font peu ou pas référence au patrimoine archivistique, même celui qui est connu, si l'on se réfère à leurs analyses et bibliographies. Il appert alors que non seulement nous avons de la difficulté à nous intéresser aux archives québécoises plus que des chercheurs de littératures étrangères, mais que la réflexion sur nos archives littéraires et leur usage analytique semble demeurer à l'écart par rapport à nos autres pratiques savantes littéraires au Québec — ce qui produit un effet de décalage dans l'historiographie. Pourquoi? Cela pouvait s'expliquer il y a 30 ou même 20 ans, mais plus difficilement à l'heure actuelle où les sources primaires et secondaires archivistiques sont là. Nous n'aurons pas le temps d'approfondir la question sur le plan socio-épistémologique. Néanmoins, une partie de la réponse se trouve sûrement du côté de notre manque de formation archivistique et, par ricochet, de celle de nos étudiants. On ne travaille pas dans les archives comme dans une bibliothèque ou sur internet.

J'ai eu l'occasion de former plusieurs générations d'étudiants aux archives, mais cela demande du temps et du flair car les documents ne sont jamais aussi précisément localisés et décrits que pour des livres; il faut une capacité de lire des écritures manuscrites parfois à la limite d'hiéroglyphes et une capacité de faire des liens entre des informations très éparses. Enfin, en somme, cela demande une sensibilité à ce qui ne ressemble à rien du tout fait, bien imprimé, lisible et compréhensible. Le caractère fragmentaire, décousu et toujours inachevé des archives, leur éloignement, en rebute plus d'un et cela est compréhensible. Et, pour couronner le tout, on dirait qu'un document en appelle toujours un autre, existant peut-être, ailleurs sûrement et, plus souvent qu'autrement, perdu à jamais. Souvent, un vrai labyrinthe; parfois, de vrais culs-de-sac. Néanmoins, la cause profonde de notre indifférence vis-à-vis de nos archives me semble plus profonde, car nos histoires littéraires pourraient au moins puiser davantage dans les travaux publiés de ceux qui aiment ce travail ingrat. Les archivistes qui nous voient travailler en auraient sûrement long à dire... Quel est notre rapport au patrimoine? Par quoi est-il conditionné, à l'heure actuelle? Préférerait-on oublier plutôt que de se souvenir? Croirait-on encore que nous avons si peu de littérature et d'histoire véritables avant la Révolution tranquille? Cet article ne peut répondre à lui seul à toutes ces questions de fond. Néanmoins, il vise à suggérer un questionnement qui s'impose à la lecture de l'historiographie littéraire québécoise qui connaît, comme on l'a vu, un regain d'activité.

Pour terminer, nous aimerions suggérer quelques pistes d'usage d'archives en fonction des buts visés par l'histoire littéraire contemporaine, en insistant, cette fois, sur l'apport nécessaire des milieux archivistiques. Car, l'autre raison pour laquelle les historiens de la littérature délaissent trop souvent les archives est la difficulté d'accès à ces matériaux.

Dans *Qu'est-ce que l'histoire littéraire?*, Clément Moisan posait clairement la question corollaire: "Pourquoi écrit-on l'histoire littéraire?" Les réponses apportées en 1987 demeurent les mêmes, soit: "I. Pour construire l'histoire (littéraire); II. Pour ordonner les faits littéraires; III. Pour interpréter (valoriser) l'histoire (littéraire)" (Moisan 1987: 98). Ce qui change à l'heure actuelle, du numérique notamment, c'est la façon d'atteindre ces objectifs propres à l'histoire littéraire.

La numérisation des archives privées, de fonds d'auteurs, aiderait beaucoup à l'histoire littéraire, que cette dernière se fasse dans une perspective sociologique ou plus critique. La construction, l'ordonnance et l'interprétation des phénomènes littéraires dépendent autant des matériaux disponibles que des choix épistémologiques. Sur le web, le *Réseau de diffusion des archives du Québec (RDAQ)* (Réseau des archives du Québec 2009) ainsi que PISTARD (Programme informatisé servant au traitement des archives et à la recherche documentaire) de BAnQ (Bibliothèque et Archives nationales du Québec 2009), de même que le moteur de recherche d'archives de Bibliothèque et Archives Canada (BAC) et celui du Réseau canadien d'information archivistique (Bibliothèque et Archives Canada 2009), pour ne nommer que ceux-là, sont certes des interrogateurs nationaux et collectifs très utiles pour localiser des fonds d'archives. Toutefois, l'accès à distance aux documents archivistiques eux-mêmes nécessite leur numérisation et, donc, la conception de sites de consultation d'archives en direct.

Pour les livres et les journaux, de tels accès à leurs supports numérisés existent et se multiplient sur les sites des bibliothèques nationales ou spécialisées, ou même dans des bases de données comme *Notre mémoire en ligne*

(Canadiana.org 2009), bibliothèque numérique qui, depuis 1997, a diffusé près de 3 millions de pages du patrimoine imprimé du Canada. Des bibliothèques prêteuses de partout au Canada enrichissent cette base dont le corpus original est tiré de la collection de microfiches de l'Institut canadien de micro-reproductions historiques qui existait depuis 1978. La numérisation des ces imprimés anciens a beaucoup stimulé les recherches historiques récentes chez les universitaires et, auprès du grand public, elle a ouvert des portes à des trésors largement méconnus.

Pour les archives, des bases de données de ces envergures sont encore à développer. Jusqu'à maintenant, ce sont les documents visuels (photos) ou audio-visuels (musique, films, reportages, séries télévisées) qui ont été les plus ciblés par les programmes de numérisation. Les archives écrites, comme les fonds d'auteurs, contenant les manuscrits des œuvres, les notes, les journaux de voyage ou la correspondance des écrivains, qui sont d'une grande richesse pour l'histoire littéraire, devraient être davantage mis en valeur que seulement lors d'expositions trop rares. Cela encouragerait les chercheurs à découvrir de nouveaux textes, des auteurs mal connus, des réseaux intellectuels beaucoup plus dynamiques qu'on ne l'aurait cru, des processus d'écriture qui ont échappé à l'interprétation juste des œuvres, des influences littéraires difficilement repérables autrement, des conditions éditoriales spécifiques, bref, la lecture de ces riches archives nous conduirait à améliorer, voire à corriger dans certains cas, notre vision de l'écrivain, de la littérature et du monde dont ils ont fait partie et qu'ils ont créée.

En fonction de ces besoins immenses, le fait, par exemple, que le Programme de numérisation de la communauté archivistique (PNCA) subventionné par le ministère du Patrimoine canadien n'existe plus depuis 2011, est plus que décevant: il marque un recul certain par rapport aux autres pays qui, même en période de récession économique, poursuivent leur support de la culture.

Les conditions de conception et de réalisation de l'histoire littéraire ont changé depuis la Révolution tranquille. L'homme, la femme et l'œuvre ne sont plus singuliers. La société non plus. Les débats foisonnent sur toutes sortes de tribunes, de forums réels ou virtuels. Ils sont observables en fonction des conditions de production, de diffusion et de réception propres à la vie littéraire. Les textes et les auteurs valorisés ont des factures et des visages différents. L'histoire littéraire a évolué au rythme de la réflexion en littérature, mais aussi à celui de la littérature elle-même, de ses formes, de ses questionnements, de ses supports. Qui, du temps de l'*Histoire de la littérature française du Québec* (De Grandpré 1967–69) en 1967, aurait cru exactement trente ans plus tard, que les littératures médiatiques (radio, télévision, cinéma, revues), le fantastique, la science-fiction et la bande dessinée, la chanson et l'édition en chiffres et en lettres, composeraient l'essentiel de l'imposant *Panorama de la littérature québécoise contemporaine* (Hamel 1997) de 822 pages réalisé sous la direction de Réginald Hamel?

Les instruments de recherche ont, eux aussi, changé de nature, de fonction. Les catalogues de bibliothèques et les dictionnaires biographiques sont maintenant accessibles par internet. Nous les utilisons autant pour l'enseignement supporté par les nouvelles technologies que pour la recherche, et ils servent autant aux particuliers qu'aux universitaires. La numérisation démocratise encore plus le savoir. Plusieurs œuvres des écrivains sont numérisées, surtout celles des plus anciens. Tous peuvent lire aujourd'hui sur le site de BAnQ dans leur édition originale, *La légende d'un peuple* (Fréchette 1887) de Louis Fréchette, *Angéline de Montbrun* (Conan 1884) de la première romancière québécoise Laure Conan, ou les *Légendes canadiennes* (Casgrain 1861) de Henri-Raymond Casgrain. Mais à quand la numérisation des archives de ces écrivains importants? L'utilité en est aussi cruciale pour celles d'écrivains du 20e siècle. La numérisation faciliterait grandement le travail critique, qu'il soit d'édition ou d'analyse, théorique ou historique. Ainsi, parce que nous n'avons encore que très peu d'accès aisé aux archives manuscrites, des chercheurs passent des années dans des fonds d'archives et des décennies à les éditer pour les besoins collectifs. Peut-on alors vraiment reprocher à l'histoire littéraire actuelle de ne pas en faire assez de cas?

Sur le plan épistémologique, certes, l'histoire littéraire doit poursuivre sa réflexion sur ce qu'elle est, sur ce qu'elle cherche à connaître comparativement aux autres savoirs des études littéraires ou historiques, sur le public qu'elle vise. Inévitablement, cette réflexion multidimensionnelle et interdisciplinaire profitera de l'état des usages de nos archives, en aval comme en amont. D'une part, les conservateurs et diffuseurs d'archives doivent prendre les moyens pour rendre le patrimoine manuscrit plus accessible. D'autre part, les historiens de la littérature, écrivant une histoire, patrimoniale malgré eux et leur désir d'autonomisation vis-à-vis des institutions politiques, doivent se faire plus entendre à des tables de concertation ou à des rencontres sur les archives publiques. Le but commun est de dévoiler le plein potentiel historique et littéraire des archives manuscrites, ces écrits-ratures qui n'attendent qu'une présence, qu'un énigmatique flâneur. Car, comme le disait Félix Leclerc, dans son *Calepin d'un flâneur*: "Rature et lit font bien littérature" (Leclerc 1988: 146).

References

Andrès, Bernard. 2001. *Écrire le Québec, de la contrainte à la contrariété: essai sur la constitution des Lettres*. Montréal: Éditions XYZ.

_____. 2003. *Les Mémoires de Pierre de Sales Laterrière,* suivi de *Correspondances*. Montréal: Triptyque.

_____. 2005. "Pour une juste mémoire de l'archive canadienne du 18e siècle." *Tangence* 78 (Été): 9-19.

_____. 2007. *La Conquête des lettres au Québec, 1759-99: anthologie*. Québec: Presses de l'Université Laval.
Barthes, Roland. 1981. "Littérature et signification (1963)." *Essais critiques*. Paris: Seuil.
Bibliothèque et Archives nationales du Québec (BAnQ). 2009. "PISTARD (Programme informatisé servant au traitement des archives et à la recherche documentaire)." Available at <http://pistard.banq.qc.ca> (accessed on March 13, 2009).
Biron, Michel and François Dumont and Élisabeth Nardout-Lafarge. 2007. *Histoire de la littérature québécoise*. Montréal: Boréal.
Blais, Jacques and Hélène Marcotte and Roger Saumur. 1992. *Louis Fréchette épistolier*. Québec: Nuit Blanche.
Brunet, Manon. 1997. "Henri-Raymond Casgrain et la paternité d'une littérature nationale." *Voix et Images* 65 (Hiver): 205–24.
_____. 1999. *Érudition et passion dans les écritures intimes*. Québec: Nota bene.
_____. 2002. "Prolégomènes à une méthodologie d'analyse des réseaux littéraires: le cas de la correspondance de Henri-Raymond Casgrain." *Voix et Images* 80 (Hiver): 216–37.
Brunet, Manon et al. 1995. *Henri-Raymond Casgrain épistolier: réseau et littérature au 19e siècle*. Québec: Nuit Blanche.
Brunet, Manon, and Serge Gagnon (ed.). 1993. *Discours et pratiques de l'intime*. Québec: Institut québécois de recherche sur la culture.
Canadiana.org. 2009. "Notre mémoire en ligne." Available at <http://www.canadiana.org/nml.php> (accessed on March 13, 2009).
Casgrain, Henri-Raymond. 1861. "*Légendes canadiennes*. Québec: J.-T. Brousseau." Available at <http://collections.banq.qc.ca/bitstream/52327/2022426/1/174730.pdf> (accessed on March 13, 2009).
_____. 1912. *La Jongleuse* (1861). Montréal: Beauchemin.
Compagnon, Antoine. 1983. *La Troisième République des Lettres: de Flaubert à Proust*. Paris: Seuil.
Conan, Laure. 1884. "*Angéline de Montbrun*. Québec: Léger Brousseau." Available at <http://bibnum2.banq.qc.ca/bna/numtexte/17239.pdf> (accessed on March 13, 2009).
_____. 2002. *J'ai tant de sujets de désespoir: correspondance, 1878–1924*. Jean-Noël Dion (ed.). Montréal: Varia.
Contat, Michel. 1991. *L'auteur et le manuscrit*. Paris: Presses universitaires de France.
De Grandpré, Pierre (ed.). 1967–69. *Histoire de la littérature française du Québec*. Montréal: Beauchemin. 4 vol.
Dubois, Jacques. 1978. *L'institution de la littérature: introduction à une sociologie*. Bruxelles: Labor.
Flaubert, Gustave. 1977. *Plans, notes et scénarios d'Un cœur simple*. François Fleury (ed.). Rouen: Éditions Lecerf.
_____. 1987. *Cahier intime de jeunesse: souvenirs, notes et pensées intimes*. J.-P. Germain (ed.). Paris: Nizet.
_____. 1988. *Carnets de travail*. Pierre-Marc de Biasi (ed.). Paris: Balland.
_____. 1993. *Correspondance: Gustave Flaubert – Guy de Maupassant*. Yvan Leclerc (ed.). Paris: Flammarion.
_____. 1995. *Carnet de voyage à Carthage*. Claire-Marie Delavoye (ed.). Rouen: Publications de l'Université de Rouen.

_____. 1999. *Plans et scénarios de Madame Bovary*. Yvan Leclerc (ed.). Paris and Cadeilhan: CNRS and Zulma.

_____. 2001. *Correspondance*. Giovanni Bonaccorso (ed.). Saint-Genouph: Librairie Nizet, 2 vol.

_____. 2008. *Lettres à sa maîtresse*. Sylvain Kerandoux (ed.). Rennes: Part Commune. 3 vol.

Fleming, Patricia Lockhart, and Yvan Lamonde (ed.). 2004–07. *Histoire du livre et de l'imprimé au Canada*. Montréal: Presses de l'Université de Montréal. 3 vol.

Fréchette, Louis. 1887. *La légende d'un peuple*. Paris: La Librairie illustrée. Available at <http://collections.banq.qc.ca/bitstream/52327/2022064/1/93301.pdf > (accessed on March 13, 2009).

Hamel, Réginald (ed.). 1997. *Panorama de la littérature québécoise contemporaine*. Montréal: Guérin.

Hamel, Réginald, and John Hare and Paul Wyczynski. 1976. *Dictionnaire pratique des auteurs québécois*. Montréal: Fides.

_____. 1989. *Dictionnaire des auteurs de langue française de l'Amérique du Nord* (DALFAN). Montréal: Fides.

Hay, Louis. 1989. *De la lettre au livre: sémiotique des manuscrits littéraires*. Paris: Éditions du CNRS.

_____. 1989. *La naissance du texte*. Paris: José Corti.

_____. 1990. *Carnets d'écrivains, 1: Hugo, Flaubert, Proust, Valéry, Gide, du Bouchet, Pérec*. Paris: Éditions du CNRS.

Jauss, Hans Robert. 1978. *Pour une esthétique de la réception*. Paris: Gallimard.

Lamonde, Yvan. 1983. *Je me souviens: la littérature personnelle au Québec, 1860–1980*. Québec: Institut québécois de recherche sur la culture.

_____. 1994. *Louis-Antoine Dessaulles, 1818–95: un seigneur libéral et anticlérical*. Montréal: Fides.

_____. 1994. *Louis-Antoine Dessaulles: Écrits*. Montréal: Presses de l'Université de Montréal: Bibliothèque du Nouveau-Monde.

_____. 1998. *Louis-Joseph Papineau, un demi-siècle de combats: interventions publiques*. Montréal: Fides.

Lamonde, Yvan, and Éliane Gubin (ed.). 1991. *Un Canadien français en Belgique au 19e siècle: correspondance d'exil de L.-A. Dessaulles, 1985–1878*. Bruxelles: Palais des Académies.

Lamonde, Yvan, and Sylvain Simard (ed.). 1978. *Inventaire chronologique et analytique d'une correspondance de Louis-Antoine Dessaulles, 1817 [i.e. 1818]–95*. Québec: Ministère des affaires culturelles, Archives nationales.

Lamonde, Yvan, and Marie-Pier Turcot. 2000. *La littérature personnelle au Québec, 1980-2000*. Montréal: Bibliothèque nationale du Québec.

Leclerc, Félix. 1988. *Le calepin d'un flâneur* (1961). Montréal: BQ.

Lemire, Maurice (ed.). 1978. *Dictionnaire des œuvres littéraires du Québec: des origines à 1900* (DOLQ). Montréal: Fides.

Lemire, Maurice, and Denis Saint-Jacques (ed.). 1991–2005. *La vie littéraire au Québec*. Québec: Presses de l'Université Laval. 5 vol.

Mailhot, Laurent. 1974. *La littérature québécoise*. Paris: Presses universitaires de France.

_____. 1997. *La littérature québécoise depuis ses origines*. Montréal: Typo.

Martel, Jacinthe (ed.). 2005. *Répertoire des archives littéraires et des manuscrits d'écrivains*.

Québec: Nota bene.
_____. 2008. "Les archives du vent." *Tangence* 87 (Été): 89.
_____. 2008. *Archives littéraires et manuscrits d'écrivain: politiques et usages du patrimoine.* Québec: Nota bene.
Michon, Jacques (ed.). 1999. *Histoire de l'édition littéraire au Québec au 20ᵉ siècle.* Montréal: Fides. 2 vol.
Moisan, Clément. 1987. *Qu'est-ce que l'histoire littéraire?* Paris: Presses universitaires de France.
_____. 1989. *L'histoire littéraire: théories, méthodes, pratiques.* Québec: Presses de l'Université Laval.
Ponge, Francis. 1984. *Pratiques d'écriture ou l'inachèvement perpétuel.* Paris: Hermann.
_____. 2005. *Pages d'atelier, 1917–82.* Bernard Beugnot (ed.). Paris: Gallimard.
Réseau des archives du Québec (RDAQ). 2009. Available at <http://www.rdaq.qc.ca> (accessed on March 13, 2009).
Ringuet [pseud. de Philippe Panneton]. 1938. *Trente arpents.* Paris: Flammarion.
_____. 1998. *Carnet du cynique.* Francis Parmentier and Jean Panneton (ed.). Montréal: Guérin.
_____. 1998. *Journal.* Francis Parmentier and Jean Panneton (ed.). Montréal: Guérin.
Robert, Lucie. 1989. *L'institution du littéraire au Québec.* Québec: Presses de l'Université Laval.
Viala, Alain. 1985. *Naissance de l'écrivain: sociologie de la littérature à l'âge classique.* Paris: Éditions de Minuit.
Vigny, Alfred de. 1989. *Correspondance.* Madeleine Ambrière (ed.). Paris: Presses universitaires de France. 4 vol.
Zola, Émile. 1978. *Correspondance.* B.H. Bakker and Colette Becker (ed.). Montréal and Paris: Presses de l'Université de Montréal and Éditions du CNRS. 10 vol.
_____. 1986. *La fabrique de* Germinal*: dossier préparatoire de l'œuvre.* Colette Becker (ed.). Paris: SEDES.
_____. 1987. *Carnets d'enquête: une ethnographie inédite de la France.* Henri Mitterand (ed.). Paris: Plon.
_____. 2003. *Les manuscrits et les dessins de Zola.* Olivier Lumbroso and Henri Mitterand (ed.). Paris: Textuel. 3 vol.

Les archives sonores dans les provinces de l'Atlantique
un patrimoine en perdition?

Ronald Labelle

L'expression "archives sonores," telle que je l'emploie, désigne en général les collections archivistiques composées d'enregistrements sonores, quel que soit leur support de conservation. Ces collections constituent un véritable patrimoine culturel au Canada, puisqu'on y trouve les témoignages de milliers de gens qui racontent leurs souvenirs et leurs expériences rattachés à notre passé collectif.

J'ai commencé mon investigation sur l'état des archives sonores dans les provinces de l'Atlantique avec un esprit plutôt pessimiste. Je m'attendais à découvrir qu'au plus 10% des collections sonores conservées par divers établissements avaient été soumises à un processus de numérisation visant leur préservation à long terme. J'ai découvert, à ma grande surprise, qu'un travail extraordinaire avait été accompli au cours des quatre ou cinq dernières années. À la fin de 2009, j'estimais qu'environ un tiers des archives sonores avaient été reproduites en format numérique. Si j'avais à décrire l'état des archives sonores dans l'est du Canada, je ne dirais donc pas qu'elles sont en perdition, mais je constate quand même qu'elles se trouvent dans une situation chaotique.

Il ne faut pas se surprendre de l'état chaotique des archives au Canada: notre pays est l'un des plus décentralisés au monde. Les Archives nationales du Canada ont comme unique mandat de conserver la documentation jugée d'importance nationale. Lors d'un stage de formation en archivistique offert à Ottawa en 1991, j'ai questionné les représentants des Archives nationales afin d'apprendre au juste ce que voulait dire "d'importance nationale" et j'ai appris que ce concept se limitait à tout ce qui touchait de près ou de loin au gouvernement fédéral. Les centres d'archives régionaux qui documentent la vie des Canadiens à travers le pays doivent donc se débrouiller seuls pour trouver les moyens de conserver leurs précieuses collections.

Il faut dire qu'au Québec, la situation est peut-être meilleure, car cette province s'est dotée de ses propres institutions culturelles dites "nationales." Le Québec est aujourd'hui divisé en 17 régions administratives et on y trouve un réseau d'archives financé par l'état. Dans les Maritimes et à Terre-Neuve-et-Labrador, il existe bien sûr des chapitres provinciaux du Conseil canadien des archives (CCA) et chaque institution membre peut participer aux programmes de subventions du CCA, mais les modestes sommes disponibles sont loin de leur permettre de réaliser des travaux d'une grande complexité, telle la numérisation des fonds sonores.

Survol des archives dans l'Atlantique

Afin de tracer un portrait de l'état des archives sonores dans les provinces de l'Atlantique, j'ai pris comme point de départ le *Guide des fonds d'histoire orale au Canada*, publié par la Société canadienne d'histoire orale en 1993 et maintenant disponible en ligne. Ce guide décrit 1 816 fonds d'archives sonores détenus par 354 institutions canadiennes. Quarante-six dépôts d'archives situés dans les quatre provinces de l'Atlantique y sont représentés. En 1993, on n'avait pas encore commencé à numériser les documents sonores et les 1 816 fonds et collections avaient donc tous comme supports des bandes magnétiques ou des cassettes sonores.

Mon but était de savoir en quel état se trouvent aujourd'hui les collections sonores constituées avant le début de l'ère numérique. J'ai concentré mon étude sur les collections représentant au moins une dizaine d'heures d'enregistrements sonores. J'ai fini par examiner 30 dépôts d'archives, dont deux à l'Île-du-Prince-Édouard, 11 au Nouveau-Brunswick, 14 en Nouvelle-Écosse et trois à Terre-Neuve-et-Labrador:

Île-du-Prince-Édouard
    Musée acadien et Centre de recherches acadiennes de l'Î-P.-É.
    University of Prince Edward Island, Robertson Library

Nouveau-Brunswick
    Archives provinciales du N.-B. / N.B. Provincial Archives
    Conseil de conservation du N.-B. / Conservation Council of N.B.
    Grand Manan Museum and Archives
    Mount Allison University Library, Mount Allison Archives
    Musée historique du Madawaska
    New Brunswick Woodsmen's Museum
    Saint John Jewish Historical Museum
    Société historique du Madawaska
    Société historique Nicolas-Denys
    Université de Moncton, Centre d'études acadiennes Anselme-Chiasson

University of New Brunswick Library, Archives and Special Collections

Nouvelle-Écosse
    Alexander Graham Bell National Historic Site
    Canadian Parks Service, Historical Research
    Cape Breton University, Beaton Institute for Cape Breton Studies
    Cape Sable Historical Society
    Cumberland County Museum
    Fisheries Museum of the Atlantic
    Maritime Museum of the Atlantic
    Nova Scotia Archives and Records Management
    Nova Scotia Museum of Industry
    Nova Scotia Museum Library
    St. Francis Xavier University Library
    Shambhala Archives
    Thomas Raddall Research Centre
    Université Sainte-Anne, Centre acadien

Terre-Neuve-et-Labrador
    College of the North Atlantic, Learning Resource Centre
    Memorial University, Folklore and Language Archive
    "Them Days" Labrador Archive

Il y a au Canada peu de dépôts d'archives dont la fonction principale est la conservation des collections sonores. En dehors des institutions fédérales comme la Division des archives visuelles et sonores des Archives nationales du Canada, le Musée canadien des civilisations et la Société Radio-Canada, il n'existe que les quelques archives de folklore, comme celles de l'Université Laval, qui pourraient être considérées comme étant avant tout des dépôts d'archives sonores. Ailleurs, les collections sonores se trouvent dispersées dans une multitude de bibliothèques, de centres d'archives provinciaux ou régionaux, de musées et de locaux de sociétés historiques. Il en est de même dans les provinces de l'Atlantique. Si l'on consulte la liste des trente dépôts d'archives qui ont fait partie de la présente étude, on se rend compte qu'à part le Memorial University Folklore and Language Archive, aucune institution n'a comme principale fonction la conservation des archives sonores.

    En gros, j'estime qu'il existe près de 20 000 heures d'enregistrements sonores dans l'ensemble des dépôts d'archives des provinces de l'Atlantique. Bien que 90% des enregistrements se trouvent soit dans les archives provinciales ou dans les universités de la région, il ne faut pas sous-estimer l'importance des collections dispersées dans les musées régionaux ou les locaux de sociétés d'histoire régionale. Les collections d'entrevues qu'on y trouve reflètent les travaux de chercheurs qui jettent un regard intime sur leur propre communauté. C'est un héritage culturel à la fois précieux et unique.

Afin d'avoir une idée juste de l'état des archives sonores dans la région de l'Atlantique, plutôt que de faire circuler un formulaire à remplir par les responsables des dépôts, j'ai choisi de les contacter par téléphone et de discuter avec eux de leurs succès, échecs et défis.[1] L'expérience a été très révélatrice. J'ai constaté que les archivistes sentaient souvent le besoin de parler de leurs problèmes. Nos conversations leur ont fourni l'opportunité de se confier à une oreille sympathique. Ils avaient investi beaucoup d'efforts dans la conservation de leurs collections et s'inquiétaient justement de leur avenir.

Les archives universitaires

C'est en milieu universitaire que l'on peut constater les meilleures réussites en termes de conservation d'archives sonores. Trois institutions mènent aujourd'hui des projets d'excellence dans ce domaine. À l'Université St. Francis Xavier à Antigonish, un projet bilingue intitulé *Gael Stream / Sruth nan Gaidheal* vise à développer des ressources numériques centrées sur la culture écossaise en Nouvelle-Écosse. La collection la plus importante, soit les 375 heures de folklore gaélique enregistrées par John Shaw entre 1977 et 1982, a déjà été numérisée et saisie dans une banque de données prête à mettre en ligne sur le site internet du projet. Les travaux entrepris à St. Francis Xavier impliquent un partenariat entre le Celtic Studies Department et la bibliothèque universitaire. De plus, des partenaires communautaires comme le Iona Highland Village aident à financer le projet, bien que Bibliothèque et Archives Canada soit le principal bailleur de fonds.

Au Cape Breton University, le centre d'archives situé au Beaton Institute for Cape Breton Studies possède 4 000 bandes sonores dans ses collections. D'importants projets de numérisation y ont été réalisés, dont le *Ethnic Resources Inventory*. Tout comme à St. Francis Xavier, le Beaton Institute entretient des liens avec des organismes communautaires qui aident à fixer ses priorités. De plus, l'expertise technique disponible au laboratoire sonore du Centre for Cape Breton Studies assure que les travaux de numérisation soient menés de façon professionnelle. On entrevoit qu'à l'avenir certaines collections pourront être mises en ligne grâce à un partenariat avec le *Digital Archives Initiative* de Memorial University à Terre-Neuve.

Enfin, le Centre d'études acadiennes Anselme-Chiasson de l'Université de Moncton (CEAAC) possède aussi plus de 4 000 bandes sonores dans ses archives et encore là un projet global de numérisation est en cours. Depuis deux ans, l'équipe du CEAAC a réussi à numériser la moitié de ses collections dans le cadre du projet *Collections acadiennes en ligne*. Des milliers de fiches analytiques ont aussi été saisies dans la banque de données où l'on pourra éventuellement trouver à la fois des enregistrements sonores et les données textuelles qui y correspondent. Il m'arrive déjà de faire usage de cette nouvelle ressource: lorsque je veux présenter en salle de classe un enregistrement sonore numérisé, j'en fais la demande à l'archiviste qui me transmet par courriel une copie en format compressé MP3. Je suis donc en mesure d'apprécier les aspects pratiques de ce nouveau service.

Les trois grands projets décrits ici sont en voie de réalisation grâce à la présence dans les universités d'une infrastructure comprenant un personnel qualifié, de l'équipement spécialisé et de l'expertise permettant d'organiser les travaux et de trouver le financement nécessaire. Mais il ne faut pas croire que tous les dépôts d'archives sonores déposées dans des universités sont en si bon état. À Terre-Neuve, le Memorial University Folklore and Language Archive (MUNFLA) contient plusieurs milliers d'heures d'enregistrements sonores. Jusqu'à date, très peu ont été numérisées, le travail étant accompli dans le cadre de projets ponctuels au département de folklore de l'université. Les archives ne possèdent ni les moyens financiers, ni l'expertise et l'équipement technique nécessaires à l'accomplissement d'un projet de numérisation soutenu, ce qui surprend, étant donné l'existence du *Digital Archives Initiative* qui est rattaché à la bibliothèque universitaire. Un autre exemple à mentionner est celui du Centre acadien de l'Université Sainte-Anne en Nouvelle-Écosse, où l'on a reproduit sur disque compact numérique la collection complète de plus de 1 000 bandes et cassettes sonores portant sur le folklore acadien, mais là aussi, la qualité technique du travail accompli est inégale.

Lorsqu'on entreprend un projet de numérisation sans s'assurer de suivre les normes techniques les plus élevées, on peut perdre une partie de la qualité sonore des enregistrements originaux. Si à l'avenir ces documents se détériorent ou sont élagués, on aura perdu à jamais l'opportunité de les préserver correctement. Certaines bandes sonores se trouvent déjà dans un état avancé de détérioration physique et doivent être restaurés avant d'être reproduites. C'est le cas de centaines de bandes magnétiques touchées par le "sticky shed syndrome," un problème de détérioration qui est particulièrement fréquent dans le cas de bandes sonores datant des années 1980, à cause de défauts techniques associés aux bandes sonores fabriquées à cette époque. Un traitement de restauration temporaire n'est pas nécessairement coûteux ni compliqué, mais il exige que l'on soit bien informé à propos des mesures à prendre pour résoudre le problème.

Avant de considérer les archives situées en dehors des universités, je mentionnerais que certaines bibliothèques universitaires conservent des enregistrements sonores originaux sans trop savoir quoi en faire et qu'il leur arrive même d'en perdre la trace. Il suffit de mentionner une entrée dans le *Guide des fonds d'histoire orale* intitulée "Micmac-Maliseet Resource Collection" déposée à l'Université du Nouveau-Brunswick à Fredericton. Lorsque j'ai tenté de retracer les 20 heures d'enregistrements faisant partie du fonds, j'ai appris qu'en 1998, cette collection avait été transférée par le département d'éducation à la bibliothèque universitaire. Les bibliothécaires ont toutefois cherché en vain les enregistrements. Personne n'en connaissait l'existence et les entrevues sont donc maintenant impossibles à repérer.

La gestion des archives sonores au Nouveau-Brunswick et en Nouvelle-Écosse

Étant donné que l'on trouve partout au Canada des archives provinciales ayant comme mandat de coordonner les activités des conseils provinciaux des archives, on s'attendrait à y trouver des normes et des procédures communes, contrairement à la situation qui prévaut dans les universités. Mais là encore, une grande divergence existe d'un endroit à l'autre. Il suffit de consulter les sites internet des conseils provinciaux des archives dans les quatre provinces de l'Atlantique pour constater qu'il n'existe en apparence aucune concertation entre les quatre bureaux provinciaux. Chaque conseil coordonne les activités de ses membres et gère le budget qui lui est transmis par le Conseil canadien des archives, mais il n'existe pas de projet commun dans le domaine de la conservation des collections.

La gestion des archives sonores n'a jamais été une priorité pour les archives provinciales, mais deux dépôts provinciaux préservent quand même des collections importantes. En Nouvelle-Écosse, deux fonds sonores de grande importance sont conservés au Nova Scotia Archives and Records Management (NSARM), soit ceux de la folkloriste Helen Creighton et de l'éditeur du *Cape Breton's Magazine*, Ronald Caplan. Dans le cas d'Helen Creighton, les archives ont entrepris un travail exhaustif d'indexation du fonds au moment de leur dépôt et un certain nombre d'enregistrements ont ensuite été numérisés, mais le travail est loin d'être complet. Le fonds du *Cape Breton's Magazine* est en voie d'être numérisé grâce au dépositaire lui-même qui obtient les subventions nécessaires à travers le programme Jeunesse Canada au Travail de Patrimoine canadien. Une des priorités du NSARM est présentement la numérisation de leurs fonds vidéo. Les archivistes consultés m'ont appris que leurs usagers cherchent plus souvent des images que des enregistrements sonores. C'est pour répondre à cette demande que les projets de numérisation mettent présentement l'accent sur tout ce qui est visuel.

NSARM joue un rôle passif dans l'acquisition et le traitement des archives sonores. Au Nouveau-Brunswick, il en est tout autrement. Là, les archives provinciales cherchent activement à acquérir des enregistrements sonores et le personnel s'intéresse de près aux techniques de conservation spécifiques au son. Le principal fonds sonore déposé aux Archives provinciales du Nouveau-Brunswick est celui des chansons folkloriques de la Miramichi, dont les premiers enregistrements remontent aux années 1940. Mais le volet le plus important du travail accompli par les archives est le service de numérisation offert aux institutions membres du Conseil provincial des archives.

Depuis quatre ans, on invite les centres d'archives régionaux à planifier la numérisation de leurs collections sonores dans le cadre de leur demande de subvention provinciale annuelle. Les Archives provinciales utilisent ensuite leur financement provenant du Conseil canadien des archives pour effectuer le travail. Une copie numérisée selon de très hauts standards techniques (48 bit, 96Mhz) est ensuite conservée sur disque dur à Fredericton et les institutions membres en reçoivent une copie compressée qu'elles peuvent reproduire au besoin. Bien sûr, les bandes originales leur sont aussi retournées.

En 2009, par exemple, chaque institution membre qui en faisait la demande pouvait faire numériser environ 20 heures d'enregistrements sonores. Ce n'est pas énorme, mais cela signifie qu'une petite société historique possédant, par exemple, une quarantaine de vieilles cassettes sonores qui risquent de se détériorer, peut sans difficulté les faire transférer sur un nouveau médium dans l'espace de deux ans. Des centres que nous avons contactés comme le Saint John Jewish Museum et le Grand Manan Museum and Archives se réjouissent de ce service qui apporte une solution idéale à un de leurs problèmes.

Les besoins en termes de conservation sont très variés et cela, même dans les petites institutions. On a choisi à plusieurs endroits de concentrer ses efforts sur la numérisation des documents manuscrits ou photographiques, pour remettre à plus tard le transfert des bandes sonores. C'est le cas, par exemple, à la Société historique du Madawaska et au New Brunswick Woodsmen's Museum. Les responsables de ce dernier musée sont frustrés de voir languir leurs précieuses collections sonores dans des armoires, mais ils sont aux prises avec les nombreux problèmes encourus dans la conservation de vieux édifices, d'artéfacts et de documents de toutes sortes. Ils sont loin de posséder les ressources nécessaires à l'accomplissement de leur mandat.

Alors qu'au Nouveau-Brunswick, il existe au moins un service public permettant d'envisager la numérisation des bandes sonores, cela n'est pas le cas dans les autres provinces de l'Atlantique. Les responsables des centres d'archives régionaux en Nouvelle-Écosse tiennent tous le même discours: ils regrettent de ne pouvoir rien faire pour assurer la conservation de leurs collections sur cassettes audio. Que l'on s'adresse au Cape Sable Historical Association, au Cumberland County Museum d'Amherst ou au Thomas Raddall Research Centre de Liverpool, c'est partout la même histoire. Des bénévoles apportent bien sûr leur support aux organisations concernées, mais ceux-ci ne peuvent pas tout faire, faute d'équipement et d'expertise technique. Les personnes contactées lors de mon sondage regrettent ne pas pouvoir mettre en valeur leurs collections sonores et déplorent le fait qu'aucune solution au problème ne semble être envisageable prochainement.

Même les institutions qui sont financées directement par la province de la Nouvelle-Écosse n'arrivent pas à traiter leurs collections sonores en vue d'une préservation à long terme. Au Nova Scotia Museum d'Halifax, on cite des réductions de budget comme étant le problème principal. Alors qu'il y existait pendant les années 1980 un poste de bibliothécaire à plein temps et deux postes d'adjoints, une seule bibliothécaire y est maintenant affectée à deux jours par semaine. Au Fisheries Museum of the Atlantic de Lunenburg, la plupart des enregistrements sonores ont été transcrits, mais rien n'est préservé sous forme numérique, ce que déplore le conservateur, car les entrevues représentent de beaux exemples de l'ancien dialecte anglais du comté de Lunenburg, un patrimoine oral qui est aujourd'hui en voie de disparition. Enfin, certaines institutions ont réussi au moins à produire des copies de leurs cassettes sonores sur disques compacts. C'est le cas, notamment, du Nova Scotia Museum of Industry à Stellarton.

Les archives à l'Île-du-Prince-Édouard et à Terre-Neuve-et-Labrador

La situation est semblable dans les deux autres provinces de la région. Le Musée et centre d'archives acadien de l'Île-du-Prince-Édouard possède 280 entrevues orales sur cassettes audio surtout, mais aucune n'a été numérisée à date. Comme c'est le cas dans plusieurs centres régionaux, la numérisation des collections de photos monopolise présentement les maigres ressources disponibles. Dans cette province, comme partout ailleurs sauf au Nouveau-Brunswick, aucun programme de financement ne vise spécifiquement la conservation sonore. Quelques centaines de cassettes et rubans sonores se trouvent aux archives provinciales à Charlottetown, ainsi qu'au Robertson Library de la University of Prince Edward Island. Le Robertson Library espère pouvoir procéder bientôt à la numérisation de ses collections sonores grâce au *Inukshuk Wireless Learning Plan*, une initiative de Bell Wireless et de Rogers Communications.

À Terre-Neuve-et-Labrador, le campus du College of the North Atlantic situé à Stephenville possède 350 cassettes audio traitant principalement du folklore de la côte ouest de la province. Dû à un manque de personnel et de ressources, la collection ne fait objet d'aucun traitement de conservation et l'on prévoit que cet état de stagnation va se poursuivre dans l'avenir immédiat. Enfin au Labrador, les archives de la revue *Them Days* contiennent maintenant environ 800 entrevues sur cassettes audio enregistrées depuis les années 1960, dont la moitié a été transcrite. De plus, quelques dizaines d'entrevues récentes ont été réalisées en format numérique. C'est un des très rares cas d'un organisme qui continue à générer de nouveaux fonds sonores. Un projet de numérisation de photographies était en cours pendant l'été 2009 grâce au programme de projets communautaires Katimavik, mais aucun plan à long terme n'existe en ce qui a trait à la conservation des documents sonores. La détérioration éventuelle de ces enregistrements serait une grande perte pour la culture des habitants du Labrador.

Avant de conclure le survol, il faut mentionner qu'il existe dans la région de l'Atlantique un centre d'archives entièrement financé par des fonds privés et qui possède des archives sonores organisées selon les plus hauts standards techniques. Il s'agit du Shambhala Archives d'Halifax, où sont conservés des milliers d'enregistrements sonores de chefs spirituels bouddhistes. Les rubans magnétiques et cassettes sont tous reproduits pour être conservés dans une banque de données numériques et des copies compressées sont réalisées pour la diffusion. De plus, le site internet de l'organisme contient un choix d'enregistrements accessibles en ligne. Ce centre est financé par une importante organisation bouddhiste nord-américaine dont le siège social est à Halifax.

Cette présentation de l'état chaotique des archives sonores dans la région de l'Atlantique m'amène à faire quelques réflexions sur les nombreux problèmes constatés, ainsi que sur des solutions possibles. Les trente institutions considérées ici représentent toute la gamme des situations possibles. À certains endroits, on ne sait même pas par où commencer pour envisager la préservation à long terme des documents sonores. On procède souvent par tâtonnements, sauf dans les rares centres archivistiques qui possèdent des stratégies de préservation bien structurées visant les collections sonores. Le financement est un problème partout (sauf semble-t-il dans les archives bouddhistes), et les efforts pour obtenir de l'appui financier vont dans plusieurs directions. Si un fait évident ressort de ma recherche auprès des détenteurs de collections sonores, c'est que les centres reliés à des universités ont beaucoup plus de succès à faire financer leurs efforts de numérisation que les autres archives.

Les universités de l'Atlantique ont obtenu des subventions importantes du gouvernement fédéral à travers les programmes de Patrimoine canadien. Le principal programme à mentionner est celui de *Culture canadienne en ligne*, mais divers autres programmes offerts en partenariat ont aussi financé des projets de numérisation. En 2007, par exemple, j'ai obtenu, pour des fins de recherche, une subvention du Programme de diffusion lié aux langues officielles administré conjointement par Patrimoine canadien et le Conseil de recherche en sciences humaines (CRSH), ce qui m'a permis de faire numériser un total de 120 entrevues menées auprès de membres de la communauté franco-terreneuvienne et qui sont déposées au Memorial University Folklore and Language Archive. Malheureusement, certains programmes de subvention fédéraux permettant la numérisation disparaissent aujourd'hui, les autorités gouvernementales considérant qu'ils ont essentiellement atteint leur but, soit d'assurer une présence plus importante de la culture canadienne sur l'internet.

Les universités accomplissent des travaux dans le domaine de l'archivistique non seulement à l'aide de fonds publics mais en ayant aussi accès à des programmes de financement privés, comme la Fondation McCain, le Trust pour la préservation de l'audio-visuel au Canada et le *Inukshuk Wireless Learning Plan*. Les fondations privées peuvent aussi financer des organismes non-universitaires, mais les centres d'archives indépendants n'ont souvent pas les ressources de base nécessaires à la préparation et à l'administration d'un important projet de subvention. Ils dépendent en général du modeste financement que leur accorde leur conseil provincial des archives ou encore leur musée provincial.

J'ai été surpris de constater que le Programme Jeunesse Canada au travail offert aux établissements du patrimoine a rarement été cité comme une source de financement des travaux de numérisation. Bien que ce programme permette l'embauche d'équipes d'étudiants, il faut aussi que les employeurs puissent leur fournir l'équipement nécessaire au travail, en plus d'assurer la formation et la surveillance, ce qui n'est pas possible dans bien des cas. Comme la numérisation de photographies et de documents écrits pose moins de défis techniques que le son, les efforts sont souvent concentrés dans ce sens.

Une solution aux nombreux défis que pose la numérisation des collections sonores serait l'établissement d'un service commun qui conseillerait les centres régionaux dans l'acquisition d'équipement technique, dans la préparation de demandes de subventions et dans la gestion des projets. Le programme de numérisation offert par les Archives provinciales du Nouveau-Brunswick fournit un excellent exemple d'une initiative peu coûteuse qui produit de bons résultats.

En Nouvelle-Écosse et à l'Île-du-Prince-Édouard, où les musées régionaux font partie de réseaux financés directement par leurs gouvernements provinciaux, il est surprenant de constater qu'aucun programme de préservation concerté ne vise les archives sonores. On comprend toutefois que ces institutions doivent concentrer leurs efforts à l'élaboration d'expositions et de programmes éducatifs. Il leur est donc difficile d'accorder une priorité à la conservation de leurs archives. Un autre problème à résoudre est le manque d'information en matière de droits de propriété. Au Conseil de conservation du Nouveau-Brunswick, par exemple, beaucoup d'entrevues réalisées dans le passé n'ont pas été numérisées parce que les personnes interviewées avaient seulement donné leur accord pour l'utilisation de l'information dans le cadre de projets spécifiques. Ailleurs aussi, on hésite parfois à reproduire des collections sonores, faute de renseignements sur leur propriété intellectuelle. Les questions reliées au droit d'auteur nécessiteraient donc l'accès à un service de conseils qui n'existe pas présentement dans la région de l'Atlantique.

Enfin, la numérisation et la préservation de fonds sonores posent des défis techniques importants pour les responsables des centres d'archives un peu partout dans la région. Le grand intérêt qu'a suscité mon sondage téléphonique me permet de constater qu'il existe beaucoup de bonne volonté chez les organismes contactés. Mais les efforts sont peu coordonnés et il y a un manque flagrant d'expertise technique dans le domaine des archives sonores. Je suppose qu'une situation semblable existe aussi dans d'autres régions du Canada. Souhaitons que le Conseil canadien des archives se penche sur le problème. On pourrait aussi souhaiter que les nombreuses nouvelles initiatives de partenariat entre les universités et les organismes communautaires amènent des résultats positifs.

Note

1. Mes remerciements s'adressent à toutes les personnes qui ont participé au sondage téléphonique et qui m'ont ainsi permis de réaliser cette étude. L'anonymat des répondants est respecté ici.

References

Fortier, Normand. 1993. "Guide to Oral History Collections in Canada — Guide des fonds d'histoire orale au Canada." *Canadian Oral History Association Journal* 13. Available at <http://www.canoha.ca/guide> (accessed on May 2, 2009).

Gael Stream / Sruth nan Gaidheal. Available at <http://gaelstream.stfx.ca> (accessed on May 29, 2009).

Shambhala Archives. Available at <http://www.shambhalashop.com/archives> (accessed on June 1, 2009).

Money Is Time
Case Studies in Small Canadian Regional Archives

Grant Hurley

It would be a daunting task to assemble a full account of the rich and varied assortment of small regional archives located in cities and communities across Canada. From historical societies, municipal archives and local museums to religious orders, medical associations and ethnic organizations, small archives in Canada are hardly homogenous. The diverse nature of small institutions involves both positive and negative aspects. On one hand, their unique characteristics make small archives highly valuable resources by ensuring that important records are preserved at a local level, an area often beyond the reach of larger institutions. On the other hand, their heterogeneity has caused the ongoing plight of local archives to be ignored in terms of policy study, scholarly attention and government funding. As an amorphous group, small regional archives have the unfortunate tendency to fade into the background of discussions on Canadian archives in favour of larger, more easily definable institutions.

Despite the sparse attention they have received, small archives nevertheless constitute the backbone of Canadian archival holdings. Taken together, the sum of their collections would far surpass the proportion of holdings shared by federal, provincial/territorial, corporate and other large archives (Taylor 1994: 142). Without the bottom-up histories small archives offer, "original research on the development of our society, institutions, and culture... would be entirely impossible" (Symons 1983: 58). In a 1977 paper, Kent Haworth noted that the "greatest challenge facing Canada's archival profession [is] the preservation of local records" (28). Today the challenge remains much the same, as the existence of small institutions is continuously under threat on multiple fronts. This essay uses a case study approach to examine the status of two institutions in New Brunswick to capture the shared challenges that small archives face. It focuses on three general topics that encapsulate the issues facing them: lack of adequate time for archivists to fulfil necessary tasks in the face of increased demands and responsibilities; finding stable sources of funding; and dealing with the demands of digitization, digital records and the Internet. I argue that while small regional archives are integral to maintaining the histories of Canada, they are under constant threat. I conclude with general recommendations for improving the condition of small archives in Canada.

The terms "local archives," "regional archives" and "small archives" are used synonymously throughout this essay to denote any physically "small" institution containing a strictly limited group of holdings. Limits apply not only to the size of a repository's archival holdings, but to the interests small institutions represent, staffing procedures and operating budgets. It should be noted that available resources on small archives consulted do not explicitly delineate what constitutes a "small" institution, a symptom of the present dearth of knowledge in the field. It is hoped that the features outlined here move towards an acceptable outline of the characteristics that distinguish small regional archives, elements substantially different from larger repositories in Canada. Small archives collect fonds restricted to a specific geographical area, organization or subject. Their stated mandates designate exactly what kinds of acquisitions fall under their jurisdictions (Canadian Council of Archives [CCA] 2001: 2). The terms "regional," "local" and "community" signify the primary audiences these archives serve. An archival institution's holdings reflect the needs of those who founded it, its location and audience, and the specific goals and mandate the archive fulfils. Rooted in their originating spaces and defined by geography, small archives create intimate bonds with the communities they serve by allowing users to gain greater self knowledge through their collections, affirming individual and group identities through narratives offered by local and family history, photographs and other records. In the words of noted archivist Hugh Taylor, small archives are "valued by an increasing number of people… not for reasons of nostalgia, and not for their great wealth of research material, but for a sense of place in a constantly moving society" (1994: 142). Due to their physical location, small archives perform integral roles in ensuring the preservation of local history across Canada. The unique character of small Canadian archives provides an important advantage in the construction of Canadian narratives. The holdings of regional institutions such as the Jewish Historical Society of British Columbia, the Sisters of the Order of St. Benedict in Winnipeg, Manitoba, or the Cupids Historical Society of Cupids, Newfoundland and Labrador, differ widely, but all occupy an important place in the Canadian archival system by virtue of the particular archival spaces they fulfil.

Aside from the restrictions of size and mandates, small archival institutions typically share other common characteristics: they are accessible to the general public, hire few or no staff and operate on limited budgets. For the purposes of this essay, the archival holdings of a small institution must be readily available to the public; a personal collection or group of private papers held in an individual's home does not constitute an archive (CCA 2001: 1). The facility where the archive is located must provide a minimum level of protection and allotted space for its holdings, whether that consists of a room containing boxes of acid-free folders or a climate-controlled space (Archives Association of British Columbia 1994: 2). Finally, a small archive requires formal organization, with an active board of directors or other management body, and regular staff to ensure its operation (CCA 2001: 1–2). The limitation of hired staff is an important measure of a small archive. A large proportion of small archives lack the funds for a full-time archivist and resort to hiring a part-time archivist who typically works several hours per week, a position known in the field as the "lone arranger" (Pevar 2005: 52). Labour is often supplemented by local volunteers and historians, and if grants are available, through student work. Many small institutions do not hire professional staff at all, instead relying exclusively on knowledgeable volunteers, primarily the result of limited operating budgets and funding sources. The Canadian Conservation Institute categorizes "small" institutions as organizations "with an operating budget of less than $100,000" (CCI: 2010). The budgets of many small archives in Canada likely fall far below this figure. At present, Canada lacks any consistent funding structure for small archives, meaning that many repositories rely on a wide array of income sources from federal, provincial and archives council grants to fundraising initiatives and donations unless they fall under the jurisdiction of larger institutions such as universities or museums.

The exact number of small archives in Canada is difficult to determine due to an ongoing need for consistent listings and readily available data. Using data supplied by provincial and territorial archives councils from their membership lists and survey reports kept at the Canadian Council of Archives, Louise Charlebois, manager of the Advisory Services Program at the CCA, estimates that there are 614 small archives in Canada. She notes that this figure remains an estimate, as not all small archives in Canada are members of federal or provincial archives councils, especially in the case of local museums and libraries that contain an "archives room" but do not extend their responsibilities beyond informal archival practices. According to Charlebois, the CCA has determined that there are over 800 archives in Canada, a number that reinforces the claim that small archives represent the bulk of the Canadian archival community (CCA 2010). This figure is further supported by the online database of records on the Archives Canada (Canadian Archival Information Network) website, which notes that it provides access to approximately 800 institutions, many of which are small archives (Archives Canada: 2010). Regardless of the exact number of small archives in Canada, it is safe to say that their numbers overwhelm those of larger institutions such as government-operated federal and provincial archives. Hugh Taylor's 1994 observation that "in Canada today … there are hundreds of small archives for every large one" remains accurate (142). The difficulty in obtaining accurate statistics for the number of small archival repositories in Canada reflects the blank space small institutions occupy on the map of the Canadian archival system, with its tendency to focus on "macrocosmic dimensions" rather than the numerous small institutions that populate the archival landscape (Taylor 1994: 142). One step towards increasing their profile is to begin the sustained process of gathering accurate data on the number and character of small institutions in Canada, an initiative that could be mounted with the aid of provincial and territorial archives associations, which tend to maintain closer affiliations with the local institutions under their jurisdictions.

Some might argue that small community-based archives should not exist at all. Their collections could easily be placed in central provincial or federal institutions, which are typically in a better situation to ensure adequate preservation. This position ignores the view that communities have a right to retain records that emerge from their particular contexts and serve their particular concerns (Haworth 1977: 33). Local records are chiefly accessed by their primary users: local people, and best preserved by those who are most knowledgeable about them: local archivists. As Carol Couture has argued, archival appraisal is "necessarily based on a thorough knowledge of the creating institution or person" (2005: 84). Local archivists are in a better position than an archivist on a provincial or federal level to assess records from their own community. Furthermore, local archivists have the opportunity to be in direct contact with members of the community, to be involved in their community and to conduct valuable research about their community. This local presence provides a greater chance to identify and acquire important community records and increases the connection between the archive and the population it serves (Haworth 1977: 33). Thus, the existence of local archives allows for greater numbers of records to be preserved, which in the long term can only benefit the preservation of Canadian history and culture. If T.H.B. Symons's 1982–83 claim that "archival records are an endangered species" holds true today, then local archives are in an excellent position to rectify the problem (59). Few people are likely to travel the distance to a provincial institution to deposit a diary, book of photographs, map or any other kind of record they have discovered unless they understand the value of their donation and see the trip as worth the time and effort. However, if an archival repository is present in their community, community members are more likely to know the archivist, think of the archive and feel assured that their donation will be cared for by someone they trust.

Despite their comparatively small size, local archives are hardly passive depositories. Archives are spaces that hold an enormous amount of power over "memory and identity" and "the fundamental ways in which society seeks evidence of what its core values are and have been, where it has come from, and where it is going" (Schwartz 2006: 3). In selecting what records to include and exclude, archivists have the power to construct specific narratives of their communities. While an archive can be viewed as a simple repository of facts, it is at the same time "constituted [of] webs of power relations that work to make the archive central to social, political, economic, and cultural reproduction" (Schein 2006: 91–92). As such, "memory is not something found or collected in archives, but something that is made and continually re-made" by an archivist (Schwartz 2006: 3). In holding such power, community archivists are in an ideal position to be sensitive to the need of representing a variety of voices of the community because they live and work in that community. Thus, holdings of local archives are better situated to contain records from all aspects of community life.

To examine the particularities of small archives in detail, I chose to study two regional repositories in New Brunswick: the Charlotte County Archives in St. Andrews and the Mount Allison University Archives in Sackville. These institutions were selected for several reasons. First, the location of both of the institutions in the same province ensures some consistency in the case studies. The regulations for archives to receive membership in provincial archives councils differ markedly from province to province, which could skew comparisons in terms of policy. Furthermore, New Brunswick is an old province, having been carved out of Nova Scotia in 1784 following the mass immigration of Loyalists fleeing the American Revolution. With a long history of documentary records, New Brunswick provides a fascinating opportunity for case studies in the field. Of the approximately forty small archives present in the province, the Charlotte County Archives and Mount Allison University Archives are positioned to offer significant historical narratives, both local and national (Council of Archives New Brunswick: 2010). The institutions studied here are both individual in character and representative of the wider concerns archives face: the discussion following these case studies attempts to address both of these interests.

In December 2008 and January 2009 I visited the Charlotte County Archives and the Mount Allison University Archives and interviewed the archivists of these institutions, Janice Fairney and Rhianna Edwards, respectively. The area covered by the Charlotte County Archives includes the towns of St. Andrews, St. Stephen and St. George, all of which were settled in the late eighteenth century by separate groups of Loyalist immigrants from New England. The two latter towns were sites of vigorous industrial activity until recent times, and St. Andrews transformed itself from early days of trade and shipbuilding into a tourist mecca for well-heeled New Englanders and Upper Canadians. The Mount Allison University Archives, though dedicated to collecting records relevant to the university community, is also responsible for records from the surrounding Chignecto area, a prominent site of early Acadian and English occupation and conflict during the Seven Years War and the American Revolution. Both archives regularly serve family historians as well as academic, professional and amateur historical researchers.

I selected an archival fonds from each of the institutions visited as examples of the variety of important contributions to Canadian narratives that small regional archives make. The Charlotte County Archives contain the Grace Helen Mowat Collection, which includes the business records, correspondence and literary manuscripts of author and businesswoman Grace Helen Mowat (1875–1964). In 1914 Mowat founded Charlotte County Cottage Craft, an enterprise selling knitted goods in St. Andrews, New Brunswick. The store sourced its products from the work of local women who possessed valuable knowledge of the arts of rug hooking, weaving and knitting. Mowat provided a central location from which these products could be sold while maintaining the creative freedom of the farm women producing its wares. Their earnings provided a measure of economic independence for rural women, whom Mowat knew "lived difficult and restricted lives… house-bound and sometimes isolated" on rural farms (Rees and Rees 2009: 72). Cited as part of the Canadian handicraft revival movement, Charlotte County Cottage Craft drew its products and inspiration directly from "native skill, native materials, and the natural beauty of the area," making it worthy of study for historians of Canadian culture, identity and regionalism (Vance 2009: 272; Rees and Rees 2009: 75). Mowat contributed to Canadian culture in other ways; she wrote poetry, plays and prose throughout her life, including *A Diverting History of a Loyalist Town* (1932) based on knowledge obtained from her Loyalist ancestry, and a historical novel titled *Broken Barrier* (1951). Her literary efforts gained her the acclaim and friendship of Canadian poet Bliss Carman. Letters contained in the fonds show an extended correspondence between Mowat and Carman, including Carman's praise for her collection of poems for children, *Funny Fables of Fundy* (1928), as having "ease and felicity, fine humour, and a very sound content good for grownups as well as children."[1] Canadian author Charles G.D. Roberts offered similar support to Mowat in a letter appreciating the volume's "flashes of essential poetry."[2] In 1951 Mowat received an honorary degree from the University of New Brunswick in recognition of her contributions to the province. The large collection of manuscripts that makes up a section of the fonds would be an invaluable asset to a researcher investigating Mowat's literary career, which awaits close scholarly attention.[3]

The Mount Allison University Archives contain fonds from the Department of English comprised of papers removed from the office of Canadian poet John Thompson shortly after his death in 1976. Thompson

(b. 1938) had a short literary career, but it was one that would have a lasting influence on Canadian literature. Arriving at Mount Allison as a professor in 1966, Thompson published one book of poetry during his lifetime, *At the Edge of the Chopping There Are No Secrets* (1973), and *Stilt Jack* posthumously in 1978. Thompson's work was admired by such authors as Margaret Atwood, Michael Ondaatje and Alden Nowlan and is notable for pioneering the ghazal form in Canadian literature (Sanger 1995: 15, 105). Though his work was "underappreciated in its time," according to critic James Polk, "partially because he was working on a more ambitious level than many Canadian critics of the time could recognize," Thompson is slowly being rediscovered as a radical contributor to the modernization of Canadian literature (Polk 1997: 1115). The Mount Allison Thompson fonds include correspondence between Thompson and important contemporary poets, between Thompson and the university (including the famous 1970 letter in which he is denied tenure), personal letters, records of the courses he offered and other private papers. This collection would provide valuable evidence for biographical and critical research on Thompson, which is yet to be undertaken on a large scale.[4]

The Charlotte County Archives is contained within the thick granite walls of a nineteenth-century prison that closed its doors in 1979. While the upper floor has been converted into a climate-controlled vault for the holdings, the lower cells have been maintained as they were, making the site a point of interest for the numerous tourists who visit St. Andrews each year. The archives was originally a branch of the Charlotte County Historical Society and now is independently maintained by a board of directors. On a daily basis it is managed under the supervision of Janice Fairney, who looks after a revolving roster of volunteers and summer students during the year. Because of tight funds, Fairney is only able to work ten hours per week on wages paid by the archives. Additionally, she provides volunteer hours as a service to the institution. Maintaining the daily operation of the archives takes the majority of her limited time. As she explained in interview, her week is spent "mainly [in] administration work, unfortunately," though she added, "I do try to keep three hours where I am doing nothing but archival work, whether it's accessioning, sorting or just looking at our collections." Administration duties include maintaining relationships with the Provincial Archives of New Brunswick and the Council of Archives New Brunswick (CANB), looking after the Archives' double role as a tourist destination, coordinating volunteer and student work, filling out grant applications for special projects, balancing the financial books and responding to the variety of genealogical, historical and photographic requests the Archives regularly receives. In short, there is little time in the few hours per week she works to do what she would like to do most: "looking after the collections a lot better: accessioning, sorting [and] cataloguing." While the genealogical resources available at the archives are significant, control of the holdings is in dire need of attention, as there are few finding aids, catalogues or computer databases detailing what the archives contain. Locating items in the storage vault is an exercise in patience. There is no simple way of searching for records, except by browsing through a general and outdated guide, or hundreds of accession sheets, some of them illegible or missing. Volunteers and students had not contributed to archival work until Fairney was hired, leaving a significant portion of tasks to the limited time of archivists. The result has been a steadily growing backlog of unsorted records, some in urgent need of preservation. The collection at the archives is strong, but tragically underused: access is simply too time consuming for the average researcher.

Further issues resulting from lack of time concern policy and outreach. Despite its incorporation as an independent institution, the archives has no written plan for the future, official mandate or operating policy. The lack of policy is a major obstacle for the archives if it seeks to represent itself as a responsible, accountable organization. Indeed, Fairney noted that lack of policy may have contributed to the recent failure to receive some government grants. Educational and outreach initiatives to encourage community awareness of the archives' presence are sporadic, though responses to them from the community are often positive, according to Fairney. Efforts include a seasonal lecture series, tours for schools and summer camps, haunted prison sleepovers for local children and historical articles printed in the local newspaper. Summer students are primarily responsible for these endeavours, only because they have a full-time work week to administer these projects. Student positions at the archives are funded by a combination of federal and provincial government summer student work programs.

The Charlotte County Archives relies for its funding on the cumulative income from a $4,000 operational grant from the Province of New Brunswick, individual grants for specific projects and a wide variety of fundraising efforts and miscellaneous sources of income. These include a letter campaign to solicit donations, yard sales, a lecture series, a gift shop, the sale of scanned photographs and charges for conducting research. The archives also receives voluntary donations from visitors. Income from all of these sources is unstable. As Fairney noted, "our funding is not secure," and "income from donations this year is down." At the same time, funding for summer students, who keep the archives open on a daily basis during the busiest time of year (and the greatest window for revenue) remains unstable due to recent government cuts. According to Fairney, the archives board of directors, whose role is to take primary responsibility for fundraising initiatives, is "burnt out" and contributes little more than the time volunteered to meet on a regular basis. There is hope that with the retirement of several longstanding members, newer members will provide fresh approaches to increase the variety of fundraising projects and the visibility of the institution in the community. The archives is lucky to be making use of the old prison as a rent-free facility courtesy of the Province of New Brunswick, without which Fairney is "not certain how we would survive." If the archives were suddenly charged for the use of the facility or moved out at the whim of the province, the institution could not possibly be maintained.

Despite increasing demands for digital services, the Charlotte County Archives is not able offer more than an email address for requests. Greatest effort in this area is currently being focused on digitizing the Archives photograph collection. Fairney noted that the collection dates from the mid-nineteenth century and encompasses "every aspect of life in Charlotte County," making it an extremely valuable resource for social historians and the public alike. The eventual plan is to put a large selection of the photographs onto a website for the use of the public through a government grant, with the hope of using the site to attract greater use of the archives' holdings as a whole. While digitization is proceeding remarkably quickly due to sustained volunteer work, the lack of policy and guidelines in this area remains a stumbling block. Efforts have been initiated by Fairney to ensure that standards for digitization, database meta-data and backup systems meet RAD and National Archives requirements. Unless these standards are enforced by an explicit policy there is no guarantee they will be maintained or followed consistently in the future. Other than photograph services, there are no plans for making finding aids or catalogues of holdings available on the Internet, as these resources do not exist in any great number in the first place. If the archives does manage to increase its Internet presence, it must expect greater demands on its holdings. If access to holdings descriptions and the physical records themselves remains a struggle, the present situation will only worsen, especially considering that the archives cannot afford to hire additional staff to meet a potential increase in public demand for its services.

In summary, the Charlotte County Archives is in a precarious position. The intricate balance the archives has come to depend upon is built atop a multiplicity of insecure income sources, student work and volunteer contributions that could be fatally tipped at any moment by the volatile winds of the economy and politics. In its specific case, the most pressing issue is that of money. With an increased and stable operating grant from government, equally assured grants for summer student employment and a guarantee that the facility in which it is currently located can continue to be used long into the future, the archives would have a stable basis upon which to build a more efficient organization. If the institution had the income to provide Fairney and a second archivist with a full-time (or even part-time) wage, the kinds of organizational and policy work urgently required could be undertaken. The combined problem of lack of money and time has created serious issues concerning policy and the actual purpose of the Archives: to preserve local records. With adequate and stable funds to ensure the archivist is able to do the kinds of accessioning, organizing, and outreach work that is expected of her, further issues such as policy and digitization could be adequately addressed.

The Mount Allison University Archives is located in the R.P. Bell Library on the Mount Allison campus, divided between offices on the third floor and storage in the basement. The Archives is a department within the university's library system and is run under the direction of Rhianna Edwards. As Edwards noted in interview, it is a "one-person archives," meaning that the majority of her time is spent "managing the archives, keeping it running, [and] keeping projects going." This consists of daily administrative work, which includes grant applications, working with researchers and supervising staff and projects. Walk-in researchers average 300 per year, with a greater number of email and telephone requests. In addition to her work in the archives itself, the nature of Edwards' position as a university faculty member requires her to spend time sitting on boards and committees within the university and the greater New Brunswick archives community. Edwards admits that "very little, if no arrangement and description gets done by me." This kind of work is generally completed through the help of grants that employ other staff and students, and as a result, the backlog at the archives is large but not unmanageable. The greatest hurdle in this area lies in increasing efficient access to records descriptions, which is taking place by converting the archives' outdated card catalogue system for indexing the contents of fonds to a digital descriptions database.

According to Edwards, the most pressing challenge that cannot be properly addressed because of the shortage of time is the development of a policy for the archives. She notes that the archives has "grown without a solid plan. What I would really like to have time to do would be to sit down and map out a strategy about how it should evolve over the next five years." The last policy was a mandate passed by the University Senate in 1984, now obsolete in light of the Internet and digital records. Related to policy, the institution is presently supposed to be gathering complete institutional records for the university. According to Edwards, this activity is conducted on an "ad hoc basis" because of the absence of a consistent records management program on campus. As institutional records become increasingly electronic, the task of gathering records will only become more difficult to manage. This is an issue that the university archivist must be given time to address with the cooperation of the Mount Allison administration.

While the Mount Allison University Archives has the advantage of an established facility and a permanent full-time salary for one university archivist, there is only a very small discretionary budget. It is funded by a $1,000 supply budget from the university and grants for summer student staff and special projects such as digitization. Little revenue is derived from donations or users of the institution. Grant applications occupy a great deal of Edwards' time, as she notes that some "grant applications are just wild in terms of what you have to answer and what you have to try to prove." Any activities that the archives wishes to conduct outside of daily administration and core work, which includes the arrangement and description of fonds, requires external financial support. Grant applications keep the archives working on more diverse projects, such as its 2008 web exhibition on the history of sport at Mount Allison, "Three Cheers for Old Mount A!" Grants are also integral to ensuring vital employment for summer students. Though the archives is secure in terms of its status within the university community, it is limited in terms of what it can do for the greater Chignecto area, which forms part of its jurisdiction. Edwards noted that if she had more time, she "would be out in the community a lot more… beating the bushes and letting people know I'm here" in order to acquire valuable local records that might otherwise disappear. In terms of funding, the archives is in a stable position, though stability does not ensure adequate growth or development.

Plans for digitization at the Mount Allison Archives are in full swing. A descriptions database, in its preliminary stages, was launched online in April 2009, in addition to an existing general catalogue of holdings and some special exhibitions. Further descriptions will be added to the online database as time for the project allows. The digitization of photographs is proceeding at a steady pace. Funding was received two years ago for 500 photographs and further funding was received last year for another 500. Along with digitization, the archives is taking the opportunity to appraise its photograph collection by assessing duplicates, negatives and transparencies and entering their meta-data into one comprehensive descriptive system. It also has an established standard for the digitization of photographs.[5] The eventual plan is to provide access to the majority of the photographs on the Internet, barring copyright and privacy hurdles. The Mount Allison Archives is in a good position in terms of its management of digitization projects.

In comparing the archives with the Charlotte County Archives, the difference between a full-time and part-time archivist is clear: much more core archival work is completed in the run of a day. Nevertheless, a great deal of accession and description work still needs to be done. This would be helped by a second part-time or full-time archivist in addition to Edwards, who would be responsible for more core archival activities. The university should provide funding for such a staff member, ideally someone from the local community, who must possess adequate training. Edwards noted frequently that the archives has always been "under-resourced" and an additional permanent staff member would be invaluable. The problems of policy development and campus records preservation are issues that will not disappear unless the archivist has the time to deal with them. Furthermore, the Archives cannot expand, grow and provide adequate services unless there are stable sources of funding for summer students and specific projects, not to mention time to expand its presence in the community, which is its mandate to serve.

The challenges shared between the Charlotte County Archives and the Mount Allison University Archives require resolutions on a greater scale than their individual institutions are equipped to provide. The first requirement is for adequate funding for enough staff to ensure that proper management, accessioning, arrangement, description and digitization work is completed in a timely, accurate fashion. A backlog of material is a constant and unavoidable reality for all archives, but when the backlog represents the majority of an archival institution's holdings, a solution must be sought. In the case of the Charlotte County Archives, a continued, stable operational grant from government sufficient for the salaries of two archivists is required for the archives to move beyond a hand-to-mouth existence. For the Mount Allison Archives, the university should provide funds for a second archivist. With money provided for salaries, the archivists would have time to address the specific problems that face their institutions. Policy issues are foremost in importance after increasing time spent on accessioning and description. As Edwards has noted, the Council of Archives New Brunswick does not require archives to have developed policies for their institutions to become members, while in comparison, the Council of Nova Scotia Archives does. If the CANB were to implement a regulation ensuring that archives have adequate policies and helping those without policies to develop them, potentially dangerous issues concerning policy could be averted. This is particularly true of digital records management, where clear policy is essential to ensure the careful long term maintenance of secure digital backup systems. The CANB and other archives councils should provide mandatory assistance in drafting policies and administer workshops on managing digital records effectively. Concerning other staff, the importance of summer students was emphasized by both archivists. That funding for summer students each year remains difficult to obtain is a problem that must be rectified by provincial and federal governments. Student employment at archival institutions has the added benefit of increasing interest in archives among youth, thus providing the opportunity to refresh the profession with new approaches and an increased familiarity with aspects of digital archives.

The greatest dilemma affecting all small archives is facilitating access to their holdings. Small archival institutions cannot hope to survive in an increasingly Internet-based archival universe if their records descriptions, finding aids and databases are not easily accessible. In a survey of academic historical researchers, "half of the respondents… had experienced problems because access to sources was limited by their geographic location, while

47 percent of respondents identified the lack of a finding aid as a barrier to access" (Duff, Craig and Cherry 2004: 63). The majority of respondents reported using university, municipal, historical society and museum archives as sources for their research (60). However, the study concluded that "respondents want better and faster access to finding aids" (71), which small archives are not always in a position to host on their own websites, if they are available digitally or available at all. The solution may be in the national archival database project, Archives Canada (formerly known as the Canadian Archival Information Network), which is administered by the Canadian Council of Archives. While T.H.B. Symons's vision of a collaborative network of archives has been a longstanding and widely shared one (Symons 1975: 82), it has not become a feasible reality until the Internet facilitated these new kinds of connections. With the online database as a centre from which researchers can view holdings descriptions from a wide variety of archives across Canada, access will be significantly increased, making for greater use of archival records, even across long distances, and a strengthened archival community as a whole. In order for a true system of archives with a central, searchable database of holdings to become a reality, governments and institutions need to recognize the importance of local archives and fund them accordingly. In an archival environment where local archivists can afford to take time doing what they have been trained to do regarding the proper arrangement, description, conservation and preservation of their materials, greater numbers of descriptions can be added to the national database in a shorter period of time. That small archives are able to implement procedures for digital records and digitization projects is clear from the kinds of small scale work completed by the institutions discussed. As projects inevitably increase in scale, small archives will have to be given resources to cope with the kinds of storage, organization and maintenance hurdles that are involved in managing large amounts of data. In order for the necessary step to digital access to take place, it is essential that the groundwork of records organization, accessioning, arrangement and description be completed first.

Many of the difficulties experienced by small archives such as the two investigated in this essay could be observed at all levels of the Canadian archival community: all archives share the same basic roadblocks in their daily operations. However, small archives stand to lose the most if Canada's archives are perceived solely from a top-down perspective. Though an archive may be small in size, it must be acknowledged that its holdings may contribute as much to narratives of Canadian history and culture as those of a large archive. The failure to recognize small archives as legitimate members of the archival system ensures that they are prevented from voicing their particular and pressing concerns in the shadow of larger archives. While serious problems exist across all sizes of archives, such difficulties can mean the difference between life and death for a small archive. Funding is an obvious example in this regard. For a small archive, a $1,000 cut to its operational grant may mean its doors would stay permanently closed, while for a larger institution such a reduction in income might present a problem, but would not prove ultimately lethal. That present government funding continues to remain precarious for all archives is a given: it should not become a given that funding should remain precarious evermore. Greater recognition that small archives have a large part to play in the system as a whole can go a long way towards encouraging budgets and policies that favour archives generally. The vast and colourful network of archives in communities across Canada has the potential to present a voice for change. Given their particular grassroots connections to the communities they serve, a comprehensive system of archives with the ability to effectively lobby government is not out of reach.

The challenges that the Charlotte County Archives and the Mount Allison University Archives face are surmountable. The continued existence of these archives, despite various obstacles, speaks to the interests and endurance of the archivists, communities and users that support them and to an existing archival environment that supports record preservation at the local level in theory, if not in practice. However, it would be unrealistic and irresponsible to expect these archives to battle the forces of the economy and policies that often do not work in their favour. With a commitment of stable and adequate governmental and institutional support for local archives, combined with further efforts on the part of archives councils, much can be accomplished in creating a sustainable, accessible archival universe. Small regional archives represent the foundation upon which narratives of Canadian history are constructed. Their diverse collections inform the daily realities of Canadians through intimate connections to a localized past, providing access to the people and events that have formed the communities in which they are situated. If the narratives which define Canada are to be accurate and complete, small regional archives must be appropriately acknowledged and supported in an environment that genuinely values their contributions to Canadian life.

Notes

I wish to sincerely thank Janice Fairney and Rhianna Edwards for their kind cooperation and feedback in the preparation of this essay. I am grateful for the assistance of Louise Charlebois at the CCA in establishing an estimate of the number of small archives in Canada.

All quotes from the interviews included in this essay are excerpted from the transcripts of interviews with Janice Fairney on December 19, 2008, and with Rhianna Edwards on January 19, 2009. Interviews were conducted with the approval of the Mount Allison Research Ethics Board, and both archivists had the opportunity to comment on the essay.

1. Charlotte County Archives, MC92, Grace Helen Mowat Collection, MS 7/360, "Letter: Bliss Carman to Grace Helen Mowat, August 28, 1928."
2. Charlotte County Archives, MC92, Grace Helen Mowat Collection, MS 7/362, "Letter: Charles G.D. Roberts to Grace Helen Mowat, September 16, 1928."
3. Diana and Ron Rees's biography of Mowat, *Grace Helen Mowat and the Making of Cottage Craft* contains a useful section on Mowat's literary accomplishments.
4. Peter Sanger's introduction to *John Thompson: Collected Poems and Translations* contains excellent biographical information on Thompson.
5. The Mount Allison Archives digitize all photographs as TIFF files at 300 dpi or greater and ensure multiple backup copies reside both within the Archives and on a secondary hard drive located outside the university campus.

References

Archives Association of British Columbia. 1994. *A Manual for Small Archives*. Vancouver: Archives Association of British Columbia. Available at <http://aabc.ca/msa> (accessed on March 20, 2010).

Archives Canada. 2010. "About Us." Available at <http://www.archivescanada.ca/english/about.html> (accessed on March 20, 2010).

Canadian Conservation Institute. 2010. "Services." Available at <http://www.cci-icc.gc.ca/services/clients-eng.aspx> (accessed on March 20, 2010).

Canadian Council of Archives. 2001. "Institutional Guidelines for Small Archives." Available at <www.cdncouncilarchives.ca/GuideSmallArchives_EN.pdf> (accessed on March 20, 2010).

Charlebois, Louise. 2010. "Estimate of 'Small Archival Institutions' in Canada." Personal communication.

Charlotte County Archives. "Grace Helen Mowat Collection." Finding Aid, MC92,

Council of Archives New Brunswick. 2010. "List of Current Membership." Available at <http://canbarchives.ca/canb/595/List-of-Current-Membership> (Accessed on March 20, 2010).

Couture, Carol. 2005. "Archival Appraisal: A Status Report." *Archivaria* 59 (Spring): 83–107.

Duff, Wendy, B. Craig and J. Cherry. 2004. "Finding and Using Archival Resources: A Cross-Canada Survey of Historians Studying Canadian History." *Archivaria* 58 (Fall): 51–80.

Haworth, Kent M. 1977. "Local Archives: Responsibilities and Challenges for Archivists." *Archivaria* 3 (Winter): 28–39.

Mount Allison University Archives. "Department of English Fonds: 1965–76." Finding Aid, Accession 7661.

Pevar, Susan. 2005. "Success as a Lone Arranger: Setting Priorities and Getting the Job Done." *Journal of Archival Organization* 3, 1 (Spring): 51–60.

Polk, James. 1997. "John Thompson." In E. Benson and W. Toye (eds.), *The Oxford Companion to English Literature*, 2nd ed. Don Mills: Oxford University Press. 1115–16.

Rees, Diana, and Ron Rees. 2009. *Grace Helen Mowat and the Making of Cottage Craft*. Fredericton: Goose Lane.

Sanger, Peter (ed.). 1995. *John Thompson: Collected Poems and Translations*. Fredericton: Goose Lane.

Schein, Richard. 2006. "Digging in Your Own Backyard." *Archivaria* 61 (Spring): 91–104

Schwartz, Joan M. 2006. "'Having New Eyes': Spaces of Archives, Landscapes of Power." *Archivaria* 61 (Spring): 1–25.

Symons, T.H.B. 1975. *To Know Ourselves: The Report of the Commission on Canadian Studies*. Vol. 2. Ottawa: Association of Universities and Colleges of Canada.

———. 1982–1983. "Archives and Canadian Studies." *Archivaria* 15 (Winter): 58–69.

Taylor, Hugh. 1994. "Some Concluding Thoughts." *American Archivist* 57 (Winter): 138–43.

Vance, Jonathan F. 2009. *A History of Canadian Culture*. Don Mills: Oxford University Press.

Section III

Re-Producing, Re-Presenting the Archival Narrative — Mapping the Virtual World

Marshland Memories
Constructing Narrative in an Online Archival Exhibition

Robert Summerby-Murray

In 2003, an archival digitization project was initiated in conjunction with Canadian Heritage, the National Archives of Canada, the Canadian Council of Archives and Mount Allison University. By mid 2004 when the digitization project was made available as a virtual exhibition on the Internet, over a thousand images had been scanned, drawn from several dozen fonds in the Mount Allison University Archives. In addition, new scholarly text had been developed to interpret these images and to place them in their historical, geographical, social, political and archival contexts. This essay reflects on some of the theoretical issues raised within this digitization project, particularly on the creation of narrative within an online archival exhibition.

This project began with two objectives: first, to make archival resources available in digital form for researchers and second, to tell the critical stories of the peoples, economies and societies of the Tantramar marshlands in southeastern New Brunswick. Colleagues across many disciplines had toiled in the rich resources of the Mount Allison University Archives, exploring genealogy, economic change, artistic expression, political history and environmental change, to name only a small subset of research topics. For all of us, it was clear that these archives held a depth of material that no one researcher could plumb; equally clear was the sense of responsibility on the part of researchers, archivists and librarians to increase the accessibility of this material so that further questions could be asked (and perhaps even answered). The concept of a digital archive offered the possibility of enhancing access to materials hidden deeply in manila folders and tattered ledgers, in sepia-tone photographs and hand-written diaries. In other words, the digital archive could overcome the physical limitations of the fonds, replacing white archival gloves with the click of a mouse and reducing damage to the physical materials themselves. An unexpected side effect of digitization of many of the resources was a dramatic improvement in legibility. For example, scanning at high resolution uncovered detail that had been overlooked previously. Similarly, the ability to manipulate the document (even by such obvious tools as zooming into an enlarged image) prompted a depth of analysis not available with the documents in their original form.

By broadening access through electronic means, a digital archive also offered the prospect of democratizing interpretation, removing elements of the gatekeeper function that both limits and, paradoxically, assists researchers in their quest. Using a web interface on the Internet provided a constantly open electronic door to the archival resource, with no finding aids, no delayed requests for materials and the potential for a stronger user-driven perspective on the records. Conversely, wider access created a dramatic reduction in formal control over the resource. With substantial primary material placed on the web in public view, archivists and researchers were encouraged to consider copyright concerns early in the project.

The most significant point for the purposes of this discussion, however, was the second objective of creating an appropriate critical narrative, both in the selection and arrangement of archival materials and in the scholarly interpretation of these materials. Constructing narrative (from a disparate and frequently incomplete or non-systematic archival resource) raised numerous problems, most of which were not apparent when we began the project. With the intention of telling the story of the marsh environments, successive occupying peoples and consequent economies, cultures and politics, the project took "place" as its unifying principle, with concomitant concern for the land and the human construction of landscape. As historical geographers, this was a natural starting point for us; the three researchers had done considerable earlier work on local histories, environmental change, cultural attributes of place and settlement geographies as well as more specific studies (using many of these same archival resources) on international trade, business histories, agricultural systems and local politics. A retrospective view, however, suggests that our unifying (but unstated) principle in situating the place of the Tantramar marshlands was heavily influenced by a political economy of liberal capitalism. By this, we mean the political, economic and social systems that encouraged the exploitation of the natural resources of the region, the accumulation of wealth from these resources in the hands of the owners of venture capital and a spirit of free enterprise and modernist progress that encouraged all participants in the local economy to improve their economic and social standing. The retrospective view taken in this essay suggests that this implicit ideology acted as a modernist impulse that shaped original acquisition of the archival materials themselves, their sense of provenance and *respect des fonds*, and our own selection and interpretive processes as scholars. In some specific cases of archival resources we were able to make this explicit (particularly in interpretations of farm records and business histories), but in general we paid less attention to this unstated agenda. Inevitably, this approach shaped the creation of our narrative in the virtual exhibition, which resources we chose for the project, how we chose to present and interpret them, and what sort of overall coherence we sought from the final digital result.

In this essay, I provide a retrospective view, not intended to be unfairly critical of our work at the time in constructing the virtual exhibition but rather to underscore several issues that were just under the surface and which have been amplified subsequently through more direct engagement with the archives, library science and museum studies literatures. As with any project of this type and magnitude, a key challenge was navigating through the diversity of possibilities and options. The technical elements of the narrative process were frequently uppermost in our minds but in what follows I focus less on the technical issues we faced in carrying out the project and more on the question of narrative construction within this digital archive resource. I engage several questions we faced in selecting materials, working within the bounds of the fonds available to us and in constructing a sense of narrative. My goal is to raise awareness of both the possibilities and perils of creating an apparently seamless narrative, or what I describe as false coherence within narrative, to the unintentional exclusion of other voices, somewhat akin to Light and Hyry's "aura of objectivity" (2002: 221). Finally, I posit a series of alternative positions for the creation of a digital archive resource. How might multiple and alternative narratives be framed? What are our roles as researchers, as archivists, librarians and museum professionals, all with shared responsibilities for the creation of narrative, in shaping new approaches for digital archival resources, and in reviewing and critiquing the final product as active scholarship?

Approaching Archival Narrative

The construction of narrative (and multiple, competing and contested narratives) in the archival record has been keenly debated in the theoretical literature over the past decade. There are, however, relatively few examples of researchers applying these theoretical positions to a set of archival resources. Particularly important in framing the theoretical debate has been the contribution of Cook (2001), notably his positioning of alternative narratives of postmodernity within archival practices. Rather than rebelling against alternative uses and interpretations (the "fashionable nonsense" of the title of his 2001 article), Cook challenges key archival concepts of *respect des fonds*, provenance and order, suggesting that other, more fluid interpretations are possible — particularly when archival documents are placed in the hands of end-users rather than archivists trained with important perspectives of accountability and context. Miller (2002) and Dirks (2004) expand this point, arguing for greater understanding of archival context and suggesting room for new "synthesized strands" (Dirks 2004: 29). Deodato's discussion (2006) is particularly useful in that it connects the implications of postmodern archival practices to changing information technologies that produce "information fragmentation into hundreds of channels, thousands of niche markets, and millions of Web pages" (Cook 2001: 23, in Deodato 2006: 52). Deodato is (perhaps overly) critical of the "established orthodoxies" of archival practice, arguing that there has been an abdication of social responsibility by not addressing the multiple narratives suggested by new technologies, new arrangements of archival resources and more creative (including digital) finding aids. Instead, the implication is that archival practices (and by extension interpretations on the part of researchers) have reinforced the modernist project of positivism, "rationality, objectivity and universal Truth" that seeks to "subject subordinate social groups to hegemonic ideologies" (Deodato 2006: 53). Instead, drawing heavily on Cook (2001), Deodato calls for a "postmodern archival paradigm" (2006: 53) that notes explicitly that records are not neutral representations but are constructed; that archivists are not passive and impartial but are mediators of the record; and that provenance is about more than original source and has a created and constructed context. Duff and Harris make a similar point, noting that each "new layer or generation of use adds to the provenance and changes the context of the record" (2002: 271). By ignoring this, the archival record is presented as monolithic, speaking only to a dominant meta-narrative rather than allowing the "fluid, polysemic and multi-relational" opportunities that might be engaged by new information technologies such as the digital archive or web-based virtual exhibition (Deodato 2006: 58).

Fragmentation, multiple narratives and seemingly limitless ways of rearranging the archival record through digital means challenge a modernist sense of organization, order and accountability. Given that it is often these last three characteristics that define the "aura of objectivity" (Light and Hyry 2002: 221), the "landscapes of power" or "illusion of control" (Schwartz 2006: 1; Schwartz 2000: 1) within the archival record, Duff and Harris (2002) suggest that new forms of archival description are required that force a reassessment of order, organization and accountability. They argue that "No approach to archival description, no descriptive system or architecture, can escape the reality that it is a way of constructing knowledge through processes of inscription, mediation and narration" (275). In noting that archival description and representation run the danger of telling only the meta-narrative, they draw upon Hayden White's argument that meta-narrative steals from history by marginalizing the small stories and imposing implicit ideological power (White 1987: 72). I argue also that this applies not just with reference to the meta-narratives of archival descriptive practices but also to the subsequent interpretation of these archival records by the researcher. Indeed, the interpretation of meta-narrative is the main preoccupation of this discussion.

Duff and Harris (2002) suggest a normative framework for assessing archival descriptive standards that might be applied to the new organizational and interpretive possibilities of digital archives. Deodato (2006) develops these points more explicitly, noting that the standards (and by implication, the archival record itself) should not be presented as natural and should indicate the biases of its creators; acknowledge a process of transparent making and remaking of the record; allow for diverse means of searching, organizing and interpreting records; engage marginalized groups and allow for multiple sub-narratives; and, in addition, "seek ways of troubling its own status as a meta-narrative" (63) by embracing "a politics of ambiguity and multiplicity" (Duff and Harris 2002: 285).

Several authors have explored these issues in relation to particular records, raising important points about the authority of the archival record and its power status. For example, in interpreting the photographic record, Charbonneau (2005: 137) expresses concern for the "transformation of the archive into mere image bank," where the value of the document, photograph or record in the context of the fond is diminished. Also in relation to archival photographs, Schwartz (2000: 1) questions the "illusion of control" resulting from the arrangement, order and presentation of records, formulating this point into a more recent discussion of the spaces of the archives as a "landscape of power" (Schwartz 2006: 1). Similarly, Tyacke (2001) posits the tension between the preservation function of archival records and the importance of a new politics of greater access and narration. MacNeil (2008) argues for a rethinking of the concept of original order in archival documents, actively questioning whose order is being engaged, empowered and privileged anyway. Of considerable relevance to the problematizing of our *Marshland* project, Senechal (2005: 139) explores the impact of the worldwide web on archives, raising questions of authorship and narrative in the creation of "new" archival fonds. Similarly, Withers and Grout (2006) have addressed these issues with regard to digital maps.

The literature on museum studies offers an additional perspective, particularly as museums develop virtual exhibitions of artifacts and archival materials, engage new types of visitors with multiple motives and are forced to negotiate sometimes explicitly corporatist agendas. Some of this literature draws heavily on new conceptions of museum visitors as consumers with multiple motivations. The works of Falk and Dierking (1992) and Falk and Sheppard (2006) are especially valuable here as they argue for the need for multiple narratives. As a result, Corsane (2005) argues that museums (and by extension, archives) can no longer be places of absolute knowledge and authority; instead, "They can only provide representations and interpretations of the world. There is no one fixed message to be transmitted and no single voice" (9). As a result, if the consumer is given more power (through curatorial and archival practices that create contingency of narrative, fluid digital access and user-manipulated artifacts or records), as Sack (1992) has suggested, the relationship between meta-narrative and multiple (even individual) interpretation becomes ever more problematic. In reviewing trends in museum studies in the 1990s, Harrison (2005) quotes Weil's criticism that museums have projected a false ideological neutrality through their "seemingly value-free work of collecting, preserving and displaying" (Weil 1990: 46, quoted in Harrison 2005: 38). MacDonald (1998:1) is more explicit in referring to a "politics of display" particularly in regard to the presentation of science and technology (as dominant paradigms of late twentieth-century liberal capitalism). Similarly, Lavine and Karp (1991) argue for a greater understanding of multicultural politics in the creation and representation of museum narrative, a point reinforced by Bradshaw's (2009) analysis of the issues confronting the curators of the Canadian Museum for Human Rights.

The parallels with archival practice are significant in terms of the projecting of an "overwhelming cultural authority" (Karp and Kratz 1991: 23) although there is, as yet, little explicit evidence of public archives becoming themselves "monuments to the representation of late capitalism" as Duncan and Wallach (1978: 28) suggest, cynically, for museums and art galleries. (Private archives may be a different story, and we might point to the significant resources of the Hudson's Bay Archives as worthy of further study in this light.) Of particular relevance to our present discussion, the literature on museum studies points to a "new museology" that draws on a stronger presence of social history and vernacular and material culture (especially as conditioned by the Annales school of French historians and social theorists such as Vidal de la Blache, Braudel and Ladurie, as well as social historians in Britain such as Wrigley) (Stam 2005: 54). Of note here is the argument that museums are social institutions with political roles, shaping multiple narratives to address varied consumers. The same arguments apply to archives — and to our construction of narrative in the *Marshland* project, whether or not these were explicit motives on the part of the creators or authors.

In the second part of this essay I argue that our digital archives project, incorporating both textual and graphical archival materials as well as subsequent scholarly interpretation, demonstrates many of the issues currently being debated in the archives, library science and museum studies literatures. By considering a case study, I suggest that a meta-narrative of liberal capitalism framed a potentially false coherence in our interpretation. Alternative narratives might usefully be considered but were for the most part subsumed by the dominating paradigm. Finally, the normative framework outlined by Duff and Harris (2002) provides a benchmark for evaluating the project, especially in the absence of more formal peer review processes of new digital media and virtual exhibitions.

Creating *Marshland*

In 2003, my former colleagues (Peter Ennals, Professor of Geography, and Cheryl Ennals, University Archivist) and I received funding from the Canadian Culture Online Program of Canadian Heritage, the National Archives of Canada and the Canadian Council of Archives to "research, select, digitize, describe and interpret" resources that would achieve the twin objectives of accessibility and narrative construction for some of the remarkable stories of the Tantramar marshlands. From the outset, this was a significant partnership, not simply from the three external agencies that provided funding but also internal to the university. In addition to the partnership of the three academics and a research assistant, the project was developed with the intention of producing a teaching resource and was supported internally by contributions from the Mount Allison Libraries and Archives and the Purdy Crawford Teaching Centre. The project was carried out under the supervision of the university librarian and involved significant in-kind support from the university's Department of Computing Services.

The sources available to us were many and varied, demonstrating the richness of the archival resource at Mount Allison. One of the requirements of our mandate was that we restrict ourselves to materials available in the Mount Allison University Library and Archives, focusing on the extent to which these allowed us to tell several intersecting stories about this place called Tantramar, at the edge of marsh and sea.[1] (Figure 1).

Relying solely on our own archival materials was a challenge, not because of their paucity but because of their abundance. Framing narratives within this selection process required us to weight some stories more heavily than others, reflecting concentrations within the archival resource and our own implicit narratives. As an example (and as we note on our website), most of the materials in the Mount Allison Archives relating to the Tantramar marshlands are English language documents. For this reason, the virtual exhibition treads very lightly on the presence in the area of First Nations peoples and Acadian settlement. Some significant historical topics that might be expected to be included in a virtual exhibition of the Tantramar marshlands, such as the 1755 Siege of Fort Beauséjour, the Eddy Rebellion of the 1770s and the Chignecto Ship Railway project of the 1890s, were omitted not only because little documentary or interpretive evidence resides in this archive, but also because we chose to focus our efforts on the nature of agricultural life in this remarkable environment (reflecting our unstated narrative of economic and spatial change within liberal capitalism rather than narratives of political history). Of course, documentary records on many of these other topics are available, and we took pains at the beginning of the exhibit to point readers/viewers to other archives such as the Centre d'études acadiennes at l'Université de Moncton, the New Brunswick Museum

Archives, the Provincial Archives of New Brunswick and the University of New Brunswick Special Collections and Archives.[2]

We first created a broad outline of topics (see more detailed discussion below) and then set about working through the various archival records, selecting materials that contributed to these topics. Drawn from twenty-seven different fonds and collections,[3] these archival documents were scanned, creating a digital resource of over 1000 images (comprising almost 25 GB of data).[4] These materials were arranged into a story board, with each researcher being responsible for writing short pieces of interpretive accompanying text, particularly at upper levels of the site. Appropriate meta-data was collected to aid in identification and cross-referencing, and all of the digitized resources (graphical and textual) were then arranged into a series of web pages within the architecture of the site.[5] To the narratives were added other interpretive pieces such as bibliographic references, online sources, statements of copyright, a very useful listing of family names present in the documentary materials themselves (particularly important given that many of the materials came from specific family fonds), location maps, a timeline with links to topics and documents contained in the virtual exhibition and sponsor acknowledgements. Design of the virtual exhibition was initiated by one of the researchers but was coordinated by the university's web designer and carried out by the student research assistant, who had the technical skill to upload images and text as well as ensure effective navigation through the virtual exhibition.

By the end of the project in late summer 2004, the virtual exhibition was mounted on the Mount Allison website and opened to the public. The final result, we believe, was coherent and extensive, demonstrating the broad chronological sweep of human habitation on this marsh environment over a millennium and bringing to light significant archival sources that would otherwise have been more difficult to access. On this latter point, the construction of the digital archive demonstrated a constant but healthy tension between our desire to make archival documents more easily available and the need to protect and conserve documents and access. This included consideration of copyright issues and a recognition that the virtual exhibition was itself publishing archival records on the web and making these records more vulnerable to unauthorized use. In addition, the exhibition demonstrated the production of a particular narrative concerning the evolution of the marsh economy, its relationship to agricultural production and commodity markets, and some of the institutional structures that conditioned development in the Tantramar region. In short, this liberal capitalist ethos was just under the surface in our narrative but certainly present in the journals of farmers (and our choice of documentary evidence of agricultural change), our interpretations of patterns of settlement, the evolution of transport systems which provided the means of exporting agricultural goods, and our choices of photographs and maps of farms. Even our choice of a final "Marsh as Muse" topic raised questions about artistic and community expression as a contrast (even antidote) to the everyday economic exploitation of the marsh environment and the accumulation of capital wealth in the hands of producers.

Significantly, we made choices and thus constructed narrative. For the most part, we joined with an already well-established narrative on the impress of liberal capitalism on the marsh environment (Wynn 1985), the impact of technological changes (such as dyking and draining advances) (Summerby-Murray 2003), the forms of connection to external markets (both through demand for particular goods and the physical connections of road, rail and shipping), and the shifting roles of governments at federal, provincial, municipal and sub-municipal levels. Along the way, although somewhat tangentially, we engaged with narratives more heavily influenced by social histories such as the changing roles of farm women (Summerby-Murray 2010), representations of the worker (particularly vis-à-vis local capitalists) and the plight of the small farmer. These latter narratives were not developed in great depth; indeed, they form alternate narratives that might be constructed if the archival sources were arranged in different (and competing) ways, including taking more advantage of digital technologies to query and rearrange the archival documents and resources. More discussion of this aspect follows later.

Our set of linked topics framed the focus on the marsh environments, their settlement history and political economy. In effect, these topics were chapter headings in a grander narrative, a narrative which set out to understand change in the landscape and the various ways individuals and groups had influenced this change. For historical geographers and an archivist, this was a traditional and familiar approach to telling the story of the marsh environments, the influence of land on life and life on land. This approach was highly empirical and, while not deliberately a-theoretical, was not explicitly driven by a theoretical or ideological viewpoint. The narrative sought to create a general chronological overview, covering the generally accepted periods of settlement and human occupation on the Tantramar marshlands as developed by earlier scholars (Bezanson and Summerby-Murray 1996; Hamilton 2004; Summerby-Murray 1999; Wynn 1985). The eight topic headings were Natural Environment, First Peoples and the Marsh, European Contact and Mapping, Acadian Settlement, Occupation by English-Speaking Settlers, Agricultural Improvement, Marsh Economy & Society in the 20th Century and Marsh as Muse.

Particular consideration was given to the development of a marsh hay economy in the mid-nineteenth to mid-twentieth centuries, reflecting the researchers' assessment of this topic's significance as well as the greater availability of documentary and related sources in the archives. The general architecture of each topic is best illustrated through the example of Agricultural Improvement — although a similar analysis might be done for any of the other major themes. The opening page[6] provides an introductory summary of agricultural improvement in the Tantramar marshlands between 1760 and the early twentieth century, framing what various authors have described as the growth of the "hay economy." The summary immediately gets to grips with patterns of land ownership established in 1761 following the 1755 deportation of the Acadian population and subsequent resettlement by British settlers from New England, drawing on relevant archival documents presented in an earlier section, such as the 1791 land grant map (Figure 1). The significance of the formal system of property allocation in framing an economically diversified landscape (with access to forested uplands, marsh lots and town lots) is noted as is the increased consolidation and concentration of land in the early nineteenth century. The latter processes had an important impact on the organization and financing of processes of drainage and dyking. The summary introduces the work of the Commissioners of Sewers, the sub-municipal political system that managed the collection of taxes for drainage and dyke work and, through the Commissioners themselves, hired the labour, purchased equipment and materials, and supervised the work.

In noting the significance of these political, economic and social struc-

Figure 1. Sackville Land Grant Map, 1791–1808. Mount Allison Archives. R McLeod Fonds, 2004.15.

tures, the summary contends that the Tantramar marshlands were transformed during the nineteenth century into an increasingly export-oriented agricultural system, supported by a complex set of relationships: between farmer and worker, buyer and seller, capital and labour. The implication of this was that the landscape was shaped progressively and was being improved with a liberal modernist impulse that would benefit all participants — but particularly those who held land and other forms of capital and who managed access to markets (both locally for labour and inputs and more regionally). This was seen in myriad ways, from increased urban markets for hay (and demand for improved road and rail transport), to increased technical specialization on the part of Commissioners of Sewers, to increasingly capital-intensive dyking projects, including some that required significant amounts of capital and in at least one case the creation of a drainage and dyking company, the Missiguash Marsh Company. The summary includes an inset map as an example of the engineering and cartographic work required to manage the complex enterprise of individual property owners somehow to be united in common cause. In terms of the organization of the topic, four subthemes explore "Extending the Reclaimed Area of the Marsh," "Management of the Marshes — the Commissioners of Sewers," "Transportation Systems," and "Agricultural Production."

Each subtheme is illustrated by a representative image of an archival document (a map, photograph or text) from which the viewer is led to an even deeper and more complex exploration of the archival record. Each thumbnail image opens to a higher resolution view of the specific document, frequently with multiple pages. Generally, a representative sample of pages was chosen, but in some cases the virtual exhibition takes the viewer deep inside the archival record, creating a detailed research resource for future study. In the case of the "Extending the reclaimed area..." subtheme, a further interpretive text situates the Tantramar marshlands developments in relation to increased demand for hay and connects the five selected archival documents. While one of these documents is a little esoteric (the listing of marks made by farmers on their sheep and cattle grazing the common pasture on the marsh), the other documents include mortgages, land transfers and wills, crucial evidence of the concentration of land into fewer, more powerful farmers' hands and a vital link between the realities of marsh farming and the significance of this work to local and regional capitalist economies.

In building a coherent narrative around agricultural intensification and the increasing capital intensity of marsh agriculture in the nineteenth and twentieth centuries, the "Managing the Marsh" subtheme follows a similar pattern in its presentation of eighteen archival documents. These documents range from detailed maps of landholdings, to account books of rates levied for drainage work, to legislative documents establishing new political and economic relationships or requirements (Figure 2), through to an image of a humble dyking spade, a technology derived from Acadian practices of the early eighteenth century. In presenting and interpreting these archival documents and images, we constructed a coherent narrative of the importance

Figure 2. Letter to D. Harper from J.A. Roberts, Chair of the Maritime Marshland Reclamation Commission, Fredericton, N.B., September 13, 1949. Mount Allison University Archives, Harper Family Fonds, 7740/2/31.

of farming, the external demand for hay (especially in relation to competing crops such as grains, potatoes and turnips) and the evolution of an increasingly capital-intensive economy, dominated by large landholders, mostly male, and with strong connections to the industries and financial service providers established in the town of Sackville. (Key examples of these connections are the role of industrialists and lawyers in holding mortgages that supported the development of the hay economy and the development of corporations to manage and market hay exports — such as the Sackville Hay and Feed Company, which eventually became Eastern Hay and Feed and was the forerunner of the Atlantic Wholesalers grocery company and the present-day Atlantic Superstores chain.)

Similarly, in presenting "Agricultural Production" as a subtheme, the exhibition celebrates successful farming operations as evidenced by a "property at death" assessment ordered by a probate court, several sets of financial records (such as a farm daybook recording accounts and other transactions) and farmers' diaries. The trappings of successful agricultural capitalism are present also in archival evidence of the Sackville and Westmoreland Agricultural Society and the minutes of the Point de Bute Grange 1881–86. In order to facilitate access for students and later researchers, large portions of many of these minute books (as well as the various diaries) were scanned.

At this point in the exhibition we began to encounter some competing voices, not sufficient to disrupt the dominant narrative of liberal capitalist material progress but enough to suggest the potential for alternate constructions of power in the Tantramar economy and society. For example, in this subtheme we included "An account of the expenditure of 45 pounds for the purchase of seed potatoes for the destitute and other inhabitants of the Parish of Sackville, Charles F. Allison, May 13, 1846" as an example of the socio-economic issues appearing as successful farmers (and merchants and manufacturers) gained wealth ahead of labouring families. Similarly in this subtheme, we included a selection of pages from the diary of Alice Etter Bulmer, a farm wife whose detailed comments provide insights on the Tantramar economy and society of the 1920s and 1930s, especially in terms of the transition to mixed farming following the end of the "hay days." Bulmer's diary demonstrates the male-dominated discourse of farm life and the restrictions faced by rural women on their mobility. These archival records provide a glimpse of alternate ways of viewing the marshlands — and provocatively suggest alternate ways in which the virtual exhibition could have been organized to re-purpose or upset the implicit power relationships of the dominant meta-narrative of increasingly intensive capitalist agriculture. At the very least, these alternative views provide a potential means of "troubling" the status of the dominant narrative, as Deodato suggests (Deodato 2006: 63).

The brief example of this portion of the virtual exhibition focusing on

"Agricultural Improvement" demonstrates several concerns with the construction of narrative in the archival record. Most importantly, the largely linear architecture of our virtual exhibition suggests a progressive and generally increasingly successful view of historical change on the marshlands. Local economies, society and politics reflected this success, and there were clear links between agricultural success and the success of merchants, manufacturers, bankers, mortgagors and other institutional players, many of these links being demonstrated through the preservation, subsequent availability and selection of archival documents in that the records of those with economic, social and political power have a greater tendency to survive. We know that the selection of our documents played a large role in the creation of this narrative itself. It is clear also that the presentation of these documents, with their associated interpretive texts, has created an authoritative voice, perhaps even weighted heavily (if unintentionally) with Light and Hyry's "aura of objectivity" (2002: 221), despite the selection of documents from the various fonds being obviously partial and not purporting to provide a complete and comprehensive evidentiary story.

While we stand by the research behind the selection of documents and the associated interpretive texts, the narrative constructed in the virtual exhibition has a strong coherence, perhaps even a false coherence in that it suggests a certain historic-economic inevitability. One of our important objectives was to create a dynamic and remarkable teaching, learning and research resource. The last thing we wanted to do as researchers was suggest that the exhibition somehow answered all the questions and told all of the stories. There are many more narratives that deserve to be told — and in this we delight in the potential of the exhibition to generate new questions and arrangements of materials in the hands of other researchers and viewers with multiple motivations.

Conceiving of these new multiple narratives would be aided by the meta-data collected for each archival record, allowing for new arrangements, searching and re-presentation. For example, drawing particularly on social history components, an exhibition could be created from the existing digital archive to highlight the role of women or labour. Rather than following the principles of *respect des fonds*, dynamic searching of meta-tags could call up components of the archival record into a new arrangement — constructing an alternative narrative. Such an exhibition, perhaps designed dynamically on demand by the viewer, would challenge the liberal capitalist ethos behind the current exhibition's selection and narration processes and would usefully problematize the exhibition's assumptions, including the implicit assumptions surrounding the "landscapes of power" in the Tantramar region (Schwartz 2006: 1).

This returns us to the normative framework suggested by Duff and Harris

(2002). In large part, our virtual exhibition presented as "normal" its selection and arrangement of archival sources, reinforcing key archival principles of order, accountability and *respect des fonds*. The archival record itself was seen to be "made," in that there was no opportunity to remake these records into new or alternative arrangements, a process that might be engaged by using the meta-data tags on each item as suggested above. The exhibition took the reasonable and standard approach of following a loose chronological scheme which highlighted the progressive development of marsh agriculture, especially in the nineteenth and early twentieth centuries but perhaps unwittingly (and in response to the comparative lack of archival material) played down later conceptions of the marshland as a source of artistic inspiration, as a site of ecotourism or a place of enhanced species diversity. Finally, the virtual exhibition engaged only tangentially with marginalized "othered" voices; building connections to these voices (particularly of women, labour, First Nations and youth) was limited by the silence of the archival record. In the absence of these connections in a formal setting (such as a university or public archive) it becomes particularly difficult for the coherent story to "trouble its own status as a meta-narrative" or embrace "a politics of ambiguity and multiplicity," as Duff and Harris suggest (2002: 285).

Challenging these issues in the context of a virtual exhibition is also difficult; this environment is quite different from a peer-reviewed publication in a scholarly journal — and yet it could be subject to similar critique regarding the use of sources, the methodologies of interpretation, unconscious bias and the like. Compounding the problem of appropriate critique is the "aura of objectivity" (Light and Hyry 2002: 221) lent by the realities of the archival record itself: the overwhelming strength of the virtual exhibition is its presentation and re-presentation of primary materials; its more subtle weakness is the paradoxically authoritative voice of the archival record itself and the concomitant potential to create false coherence.

Marshland achieved its twin objectives of making accessible a vast array of primary data to researchers and the general public and of creating a coherent narrative interpretation of the lands, economies and social issues of the Tantramar region. The digitization project made excellent use of a diverse set of archival resources and incorporated a high level of original interpretation, which was well supported by appropriate scholarly works. The disjuncture between the use of partial sources from the archival record and the sense of coherent narrative remains problematic, particularly when set against current scholarship in library and archive science and museum studies, which provide fundamental critiques of the construction of narrative. Further work might consider digital means of assisting the creation of multiple narratives, even to the point of using technologies to completely customize user queries so that multiple and contested narratives can be framed and tested. This involves a fundamental reassessment of concepts of order, accountability and *respect des fonds*, of the sort suggested by Cook (2001) and the work of several related scholars explored earlier in this discussion. While *Marshland* may suffer from several unstated assumptions and the reinforcement of meta-narratives of liberal capitalism, it also points the way to possible new interpretations that will be the object of the next generation of digitization projects in libraries, museums and archives.

Notes

I acknowledge with gratitude the work of Peter Ennals, Cheryl Ennals and Gerry Watson in working with archival sources, creating interpretive text and constructing the *Marshland* website. Particular thanks is due to Rhianna Edwards, University Archivist, for assistance with copyright issues and image reproductions. In all of our efforts, we were supported by Bruno Gnassi, University Librarian, and the staff of Mount Allison University's Computing Services Department. I acknowledge also the funding which made this project possible and provided a fertile ground for subsequent critique of archival digitization as a scholarly process.

1. *Marshland: Records of Life on the Tantramar* <www.mta.ca/marshland>.
2. See <http://www.mta.ca/marshland/pages/links.htm> for a complete list of links to other related libraries and archives.
3. See the complete listing at http://www.mta.ca/marshland/pages/archivalsrc.htm
4. Technical information on scanning equipment and processes such as data compression are found at <http://www.mta.ca/marshland/pages/techinfo.htm>.
5. More details on meta-data capture, the use of audio files, original cartography produced for the exhibition from archival records and web design are found at <http://www.mta.ca/marshland/pages/techinfo.htm>.
6. <www.mta.ca/marshland/topic6_agriculture/agriculture.htm>.

References

Bezanson, N., and R. Summerby-Murray. 1996. *Background Report: An Historical Geography of Tantramar's Heritage Landscapes*. Fredericton: Province of New Brunswick.

Bradshaw, J. 2009. "It Takes a Lot of Wrongs to Make a Museum of Rights." *Globe and Mail*, December 12: F1 and F6.

Charbonneau, N. 2005. "The Selection of Photographs." *Archivaria* 59 (Spring): 119–38.

Cook, T. 2001. "Fashionable Nonsense or Professional Rebirth: Postmodernism and the Practice of Archives." *Archivaria* 51 (Spring): 14–35.

Corsane, Gerard (ed.). 2005. *Heritage, Museums and Galleries: An Introductory Reader*. London and New York: Routledge.

———. 2005. "Issues in Heritage, Museums and Galleries: A Brief Introduction." Ch. 1 in Gerard Corsane (ed.), *Heritage, Museums and Galleries: An Introductory Reader*. London and New York: Routledge: 1–12.

Deodato, J. 2006. "Becoming Responsible Mediators: The Application of Postmodern Perspectives to Archival Arrangement and Description." *Progressive Librarian* Summer 2006: 52–65.

Dirks, J. 2004. "Accountability, History, and Archives: Conflicting Priorities or Synthesized Strands?" *Archivaria* 57 (Spring): 29–49.

Duff, W., and V. Harris. 2002. "Stories and Names: Archival Description as Narrating Records and Constructing Meanings." *Archival Science* 2 (3): 263–85.

Duncan, C., and A. Wallach. 1978. "The Museum of Modern Art as Late Capitalist Ritual: An Iconographic Analysis." *Marxist Perspectives* Winter: 28–51.

Falk, J.H., and L.D. Dierking. 1992. *The Museum Experience.* Washington, DC: Whalesback Books.

Falk, J.H., and B. Sheppard. 2006. *Thriving in the Knowledge Age: New Business Models for Museums and Other Cultural Institutions.* Lanham, MD: AltaMira Press, Rowman & Littlefield.

Hamilton, W. 2004. *At the Crossroads: A History of Sackville, New Brunswick.* Kentville, N.S.: Gaspereau Press.

Harrison, J. 2005. "Ideas of Museums in the 1990s." In G. Corsane (ed.), *Heritage, Museums and Galleries: An Introductory Reader.* London and New York: Routledge: 38–53.

Karp, I., and C. Kratz. 1991. *The Fate of Tippoo's Tiger: A Critical Account of Ethnographic Display.* Los Angeles: Getty Centre.

Ketelaar, E. 2001. "Tacit Narratives: The Meanings of Archives." *Archives & Museum Informatics* 1 (2): 131–41.

Lavine, S., and I. Karp. 1991. "Introduction: Museums and Multiculturalism." In I. Karp and S. Lavine (eds.), *Exhibiting Cultures: The Politics and Poetics of Museum Display.* Washington and London: Smithsonian Institution Press: 1–9.

Light, M., and T. Hyry. 2002. "Colophons and Annotations: New Directions for the Finding Aid." *American Archivist* 65: 216–30.

Macdonald, S. 1998. "Exhibitions of Power and Powers of Exhibition: An Introduction to the Politics of Display." Ch. 1 in S. Macdonald (ed.), *The Politics of Display: Museums, Science, Culture.* London and New York: Routledge: 1–24.

MacNeil, H. 2008. "Archivalterity: Rethinking Original Order." *Archivaria* 66. Available at <http://journals.sfu.ca/archivar/index.php/archivaria/article/view/13190> (accessed on May 20, 2010).

Marshland: Records of Life on the Tantramar, virtual exhibition website, Mount Allison University Library and Archives <http://www.mta.ca/marshland/index.htm> (accessed January 11, 2010).

Miller, L. 2002. "The Death of the Fonds and the Resurrection of Provenance: Archival Control in Space and Time." *Archivaria* 53 (Spring): 1–15.

Sack, R. 1992. *Place, Modernity and the Consumer's World.* Baltimore: Johns Hopkins University Press.

Schwartz, J. 2000. "'Records of Simple Truth and Precision': Photography, Archives and the Illusion of Control." *Archivaria* 50 (Fall): 1–40.

_____. 2002. "Coming to Terms with Photographs: Descriptive Standards, Linguistic Othering and the Margins of Archivy." *Archivaria* 54 (Fall): 142–71.

_____. 2006. "Having New Eyes: Spaces of Archives, Landscapes of Power." *Archivaria* 61. Available at <http://journals.sfu.ca/archivar/index.php/archivaria/article/

view/12532> (accessed on May 20, 2010).
Senechal, S. 2005. "The Effect of the Web on Archives," *Archivaria* 59 (Spring): 139–52.
Stam, D. 2005. "The Informed Muse: The Implications of 'The New Museology.'" In G. Corsane (ed.), *Heritage, Museums and Galleries: An Introductory Reader.* London and New York: Routledge: 54–70.
Summerby-Murray, R. 1999. "Interpreting Cultural Landscapes: A Historical Geography of Human Settlement on the Tantramar Marshes, New Brunswick." In C. Stadel (ed.), *Themes and Issues of Canadian Geography III.* Salzburger Geographische Arbeiten, 34 (Salzburg, Austria: Institute of Geography and Geoinformation, University of Salzburg): 157–74.
_____. 2003. "Commissioners of Sewers and the Intensification of Agriculture in the Tantramar Marshlands of New Brunswick." *The North American Geographer* 5 (1 & 2): 183–204.
_____. 2010. "Eggs, Raspberries and Domestic Space: The Spatial Construction of Family in 1930s New Brunswick." Ch. 5 in B. Hallman (ed.), *Family Geographies: The Spatiality of Families and Family Life.* Oxford and Toronto: Oxford University Press: 88–107.
Tyacke, S. 2001. "Archives in a Wider World: The Culture and Politics of Archives." *Archivaria* 52 (Fall): 1–25.
Weil, S. 1990. *Rethinking the Museum.* Washington, DC: Smithsonian Institution Press.
White, H. 1987. *The Content of the Form: Narrative Discourse and Historical Representation.* Baltimore and London: Johns Hopkins University Press.
Withers, C., and A. Grout. 2006. "Authority in Space? Creating a Digital Web-Based Map Archive." *Archivaria* 61. Available at <http://journals.sfu.ca/archivar/index.php/archivaria/article/view/12533> (accessed on May 20, 2010).
Wynn, G. 1985. "Late Eighteenth Century Agriculture on the Bay of Fundy Marshlands." In P. Buckner and D. Frank (eds.), *The Acadiensis Reader: Volume 1: Atlantic Canada before Confederation.* Fredericton: Acadiensis Press: 44–53.

Connected Constructions, Constructing Connections
Materiality of Archival Records as Historical Evidence

Ala Rekrut

Canadian archivist-philosopher Hugh Taylor suggests that archives are

> a branch of our heritage that is so often taken for granted, perhaps, because we see the documents we handle as simply providing reliable information in support of other material culture, and therefore materially "invisible".… Because literacy objectifies and detaches us from what we read, information becomes almost rootless, floating away from the artifact in which it was anchored. (1995: 9)

Challenging historians to study the mass media as important sources for history, Mary Vipond, in her 2003 Presidential Address to the Canadian Historical Association, noted that her colleagues "continue too often to assume that the media by which [cultural] meanings are often transmitted need not to be factored into the analysis of cultural practices" (2003: 8).

Both archivists and users of archives can benefit from a greater awareness of materiality — to develop "material literacy" skills, akin to media literacy or visual literacy skills. Awareness of the range of communication pathways present in records opens both archivists and users to different ways of identifying, experiencing and interpreting evidence in records and in representations of records. Interaction with records, through sight, sound, smell and touch, imparts firsthand knowledge of historic technologies and puts the researcher into the place of the creator and previous users of records. Access to archival records in their original forms enables gathering of primary evidence of how the records were created and continue to be used, through observation of the physical materials, their construction and condition.

"Material culture" is a term used mainly by anthropologists for objects which have been made or modified by human beings. Since this is also a definition of "artifacts," the difference is one of emphasis. "Artifacts" stresses individual objects, often privileging the objects in isolation from their cultural contexts. Material culture study emphasizes the meanings, which can be derived from the interrelationships of objects within their cultural contexts or, in the case of archaeology, within their physical contexts. "Materiality" is another closely related term, which implies a higher level of agency for the objects in current as well as past interactions and is more frequently used outside anthropology.

In traditional archival theory, the materiality of records has usually been assumed to be incidental to, and largely disconnected from, their "intellectual" or "informational" value, but over the last three decades archival theory has been re-oriented around the concept of records as evidence of the dynamic contextual milieux of their creation.[1] This contextualist shift in understanding records supports an increased and overt acknowledgement of materiality as integral to archival value: materiality is integral to context, content and structure, which together define records as records and records as evidence.

While the material "turn" has been considered in areas of the humanities such as anthropology and cultural studies, it has received little attention in either archival or historical studies. However, the organizers of the First International Conference on the History of Records and Archives in 2005 indicated that material history and material culture are an

> integral part of records history that had received scant attention in the past… [and that] the fruits of this research should be unapologetically situated to the core of archival interest.… Materiality, machines, people, presumptions, and multiple layers of culture are part of the essential dimensions of any record — the intellectual challenge is to seek out and identify these intersections and to explore them as part of the process of archival management from appraisal to description to reference. (Craig, Eppard and McNeill 2005: 7)

This essay describes how materiality is considered in historical and related disciplines, and provides as a case study example, an examination of two versions of the content of Hudson's Bay Company (HBC) post journals from the Moose Fort trade post. These documents are used to foreground the materiality of records, suggesting some ways in which researchers can use materiality as historical evidence and highlighting how reproduction of records may result in compromises or losses to this evidence, negatively influencing both the questions that can be asked of records and the stories they can tell.

The materiality of records is anchored in the social circumstances surrounding their physical creation and is manifest in at least two ways: the physical "background" upon which the written text or images appear and the successive interactions between records and their multiple users across time. Materiality is therefore perhaps the most primary of sources regarding the conditions of the records' own creation.

Forensic examination of the physical composition of records (e.g., paper, photographic emulsions, ink, fasteners, folds, broken sprockets, fingerprints and other stains) is perhaps the most obvious way in which materiality is used as evidence. Prior to the 1970s, analysis of physical evidence was a common historical practice, although the emphasis was on determining the authenticity of written documents using tools from "auxiliary disciplines" such as linguistics, palaeography, sigillography, codicology, heraldry and diplomatics (Shafer 1969: 111–18; Howell and Prevenier 2001: 56).

These tools were mainly developed for analysis of Western legal, judicial and Church-created documents and, therefore, are of limited relevance to the much broader and diverse records underpinning the developing field of social history. In *A Guide to Historical Method*, published in 1969, R.J. Shafer indicated that additional tools from anthropology might be used by historians for analysis of "mute" physical remains, but he appears not to consider the possibility that written documents, also, might "speak" about both their creators and their past users through their materiality as well as their written text (47–57). Guides to historical methods published in the past thirty years have generally taken less technical/physical and more theoretical and interdisciplinary approaches to analyzing sources.[2] This shift appears to have distanced historians from records as physical phenomena and neglects consideration that material artifacts are intellectual as well as physical constructions. Discussion of the materiality of source records rarely appears in academic history journals although other fields have indicated considerable interest in materiality, especially anthropology, sociology and cultural studies.

In spite of this reduced attention to physical evidence, a survey of 173 Canadian historians indicated that 92 percent preferred to use archival records in their original forms (Duff, Craig and Cherry 2004). In unprompted narrative responses to the question of why they preferred this format, thirty-one of the respondents cited ease of legibility; twenty-five cited authenticity, accuracy or reliability; twenty-three cited completeness. The authors also reported:

> Fourteen respondents noted a physical connection with the past or a greater sense of context when using the original format…. [One] noted "Contextual features (condition, type of paper) that contribute to one's understanding (that is, aside from content as such), is [sic] missed often or masked in copying." The importance the physical or spacial [sic] attributes of the original was highlighted by four respondents. One stated that "It provides the actual 'texture' as well as the actual 'text'! This allows the user to reconstruct the full 'sense' of the document." (66)

The physical interactions with records as described by these survey respondents have little to do with the technical analyses of "traditional" historical methods noted earlier but speak to a sensory engagement with the records as historical communications. Thus, in addition to conveying evidence through a technical, or forensic, analysis of tangible evidence (i.e., record materials, construction and condition), materiality can convey evidence through observation of personal sensory interactions and the responses it prompts.

The materiality of archival records is occasionally described by historians in more personal accounts of the research process and in more interdisciplinary academic work. In her introduction to *Archive Stories: Facts, Fictions, and the Writing of History*, Antoinette Burton indicates her project stemmed from a "conviction that history is not merely a project of fact-retrieval… but also a set of complex processes of selection, interpretation, and even invention — processes set in motion by, among other things, one's personal encounter with the archive" (2005: 7–8). She notes that historians rarely speak or write of "such contingencies… though they are quite ready and even eager to tell their archive stories when asked" (8). Burton feels these "archive stories" pose a risk to "the claims of objectivity which continue to underwrite the production of history" (9). Responding to results of a *Journal of American History* survey of historians, George H. Roeder noted: "None mentioned, and doubtless few received, guidance as to how to use non-written, non-numeric sources, often essential for research on sensory experience" (Roeder 1994: 1120). He felt that the sensory dimensions of history have also been overlooked in the past because they may not have seemed relevant to traditional political, military and intellectual history (1116).

Museums, which deal explicitly with objects and their interpretation, have developed a substantial body of literature related to communication and learning theory, which may shed some light on interactions between researchers and records. Among satisfying experiences identified by museum visitors are those that can be categorized as object, cognitive and introspective. Object experiences include "seeing rare things" and "seeing 'the real thing'." Cognitive experiences include "gaining information or knowledge"; and introspective experiences include "imagining other times or places" and "feeling a spiritual connection" (Black 2005: 285). These types of experiences may correspond to those felt by researchers working with original records. It is likely that archives' researchers mainly seek cognitive experiences and therefore privilege those, while taking their object and introspective experiences for granted. However, their object experience would likely be intensified by their direct physical contact with the material.

Another approach to understanding the variety of ways in which individuals may engage with records is to consider human learning styles. Learning styles or preferences may be categorized as visual (seeing), aural (hearing), reading or writing (processing text) and kinesthetic (doing) (VARK n.d.). Western business and education cultures favour written presentations of information, so it is not surprising that most archival and historical research practices assume written records and text-oriented tools as the norm. Archivists and historians are increasingly aware of a need for literacy in visual and oral sources, but kinetic and tactile experiences have not been given the same attention. Book conservator and educator Gary Frost has suggested that although readers are rarely conscious of book action, a reader using a physical book is engaged in "a haptic process in which the hands prompt the mind to provide an ergonomic relation to the content" (Frost n.d.) and that "dexterity itself is a medium of information" (Frost 2005). In other words, not just the record but also the sensory encounter shared by its users over time provides historical evidence. Historian Mark M. Smith suggests that, in the West, sensory perception is considered a physical rather than a cultural act, and he advocates development of a sensate habit "because it pricks consciousness and questions assumptions about what to examine and how to examine it" (Smith 2007: 3, 5, 100).[3] Greater attention to the materiality of records, therefore, enables development of fuller, richer historical understandings from the embodied traces remaining in archival records.

Why do records look, feel, sound, smell and move the way they do? Creators select those which meet their communication and recordkeeping needs from the materials and techniques available to them and under the influence of the contemporary social, political and cultural climate and of other individuals and organizations, as represented in Figure 1a.[4]

The term "creator" can be understood to include all those who have contributed to the way a record has looked or acted from its conception to the present. Following the model shown in Figure 1b, a letter between two individuals could later be recreated by other individuals either by physically adding or removing material components or by recontextualizing that letter,

Figure 1a A Simplified View of Initial Events in a Record's Creation

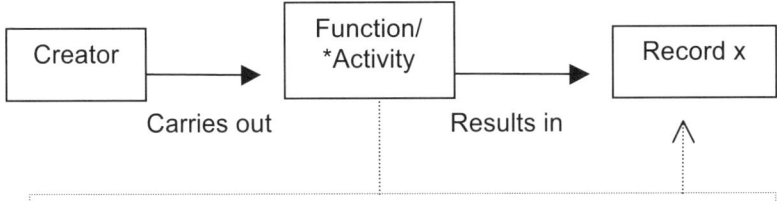

*Procedures related to activity will include:
- Selection of communication audiences and technologies
- Selection of record keeping technologies (e.g. records management systems, forms, layouts, recording media)

These choices will be manifest in the record or its metadata

Figure 1b A Simplified View of Subsequent Events in a Record's Existence

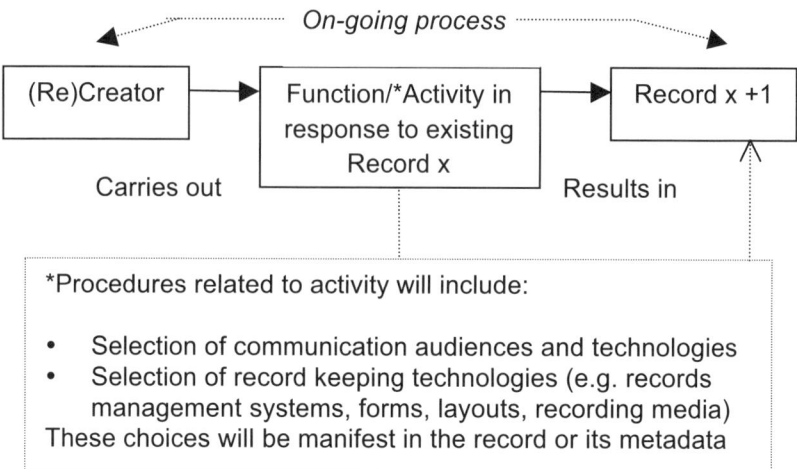

for instance, as an example of penmanship or an example of conventions of social discourse, as evidence of an event described in the letter or through representation in archival descriptions and visual images.

Records can also be physically altered through additions and deletions by the creator or by subsequent custodians. A knowledge of all the materials and technologies present may be required to assist in recognizing later additions, in recognizing missing components (such as seals, ribbons or postage stamps), in establishing the sequence and relative dates of the changes and in distinguishing the "original" from copies. Once created, a record also starts changing as a result of the deterioration generally attributed to "time" — the combination of light, pollution, heat and humidity. Since these agents of deterioration can usually be decelerated or accelerated through human intervention (or lack thereof), the type and level of deterioration present in the record provides evidence of previous care and use by its past and current custodians.

In 2002 the Hudson's Bay Company Archives (HBCA) acquired a journal for Moose Fort[5] which had clearly served as the rough copy for the 1789–91 entries of the official post journals. This is the only case in which the archives has both the official post journals and an earlier iteration of substantially the same written content, and therefore it serves as an ideal example of the role materiality can play in understanding and interpreting the two versions of the text. The person in charge of each of the HBC's posts was responsible for recording daily events and transactions in a journal, which was sent to London at the end of each trading season. Since these journals were prepared in compliance with the HBC's requirements, the HBC is considered the

Figure 2 Covers of Moose Factory Journals, 1789–1791. On left: Archives of Manitoba, HBCA, E.372/1. "Rough journal." On right: Archives of Manitoba, HBCA, B.135/a/76. "Official journal."

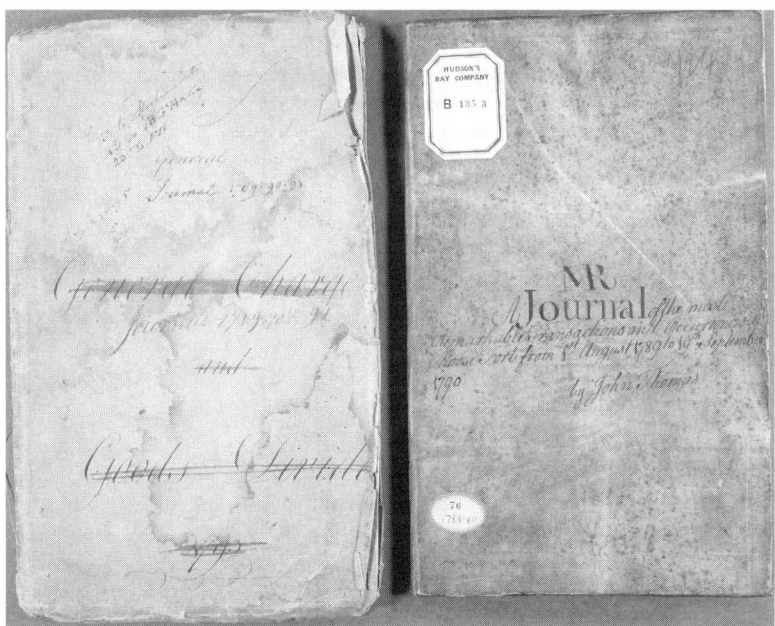

creator of the records, with the post's chief trader or his delegate writing the entries. While the two journals are almost identical in written content, there are substantial and meaningful differences in their physical materials and construction, as can be seen in Figures 2–4.

Four pages of thick paper act as the cover of the rough journal. These pages are clearly identified as accounts for 1793, although this title has been crossed out and the journal title added in smaller letters. The existence of these rough accounts pages and the rough journal entries is primary evidence of a practice of making rough drafts from which the official records of the HBC would be copied. The account pages have been cut down but still extend beyond the text pages. This journal must normally have been stored flat after the covers were attached, since it could not stand upright supported by these cover papers alone. The size, thickness, coarse fibres and uneven fibre distribution identify this cover paper as wrapping paper rather than writing paper. The reuse of the account paper as a protective covering for the text suggests that at this post and at this time there was a scarcity of, or unwillingness to use, new or more conventional covering materials for this purpose. The reuse of wrapping paper for the rough copy of the accounts may suggest either a scarcity of paper large enough to accommodate the

Figure 3 Journals Open to First Journal Entry. Accounts are visible on the inside of the "cover," opposite the first entry of rough journal, at left. At right, the text of the official journal begins on the back of the first page. Note also the Hudson's Bay Company stamp on the second page of text.

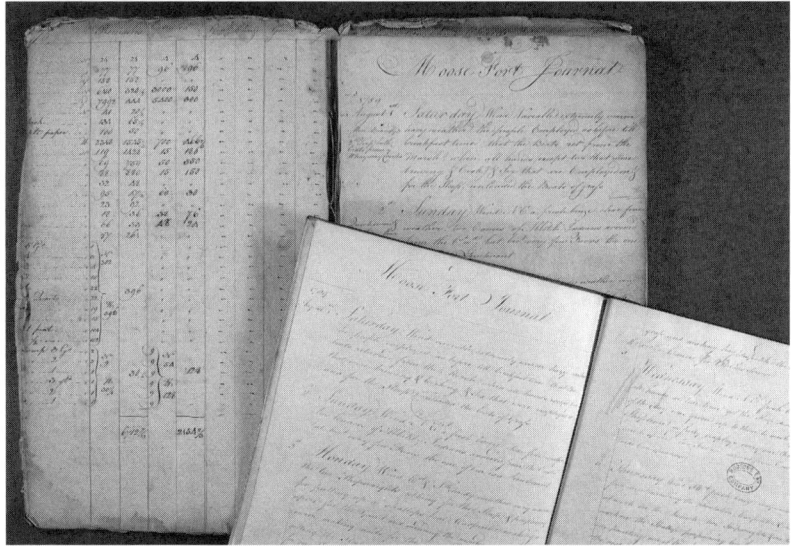

layout of the accounts or a general scarcity of writing paper. These scarcities might be connected to inadequate supplies requested from, or supplied by, the HBC, or to problems with the timing of the arrival of the supply ships due to weather, damage or loss at sea.

Stains on the inner pages may suggest incidents that occurred while reading or writing the text, and a chemical analysis of these stains might indicate they are from candle wax or lamp oil used as a light source, or are drips from food being consumed, or similar residues on the fingers. Large but superficial liquid stains are visible on the front cover and bottom edges of the pages. The shape of the main stain on the cover indicates something dripped on it from above; the fact that it does not penetrate through the cover paper suggests the excess liquid was mopped up. The degree of colour contrast at the wet-dry boundary, or "tideline," suggests that the cover paper had already undergone some deterioration prior to the wetting event, so this event probably occurred well after the journal had been written and assembled. The relatively light colour of the stain also suggests that it was from a relatively clear liquid, such as seawater. Yellow-brown discolouration along the edges of the paper is best seen in Figure 3; this is the result of air pollution, which could not penetrate far through the closed volume and is commonly seen in books from industrially polluted areas, often, as in this case, coupled with

Figure 4 Journals Open to Page 11. Note the margin notations and additions between the lines of the rough journal (at top left) and the clean orderly uniformity of the official journal (at bottom right).

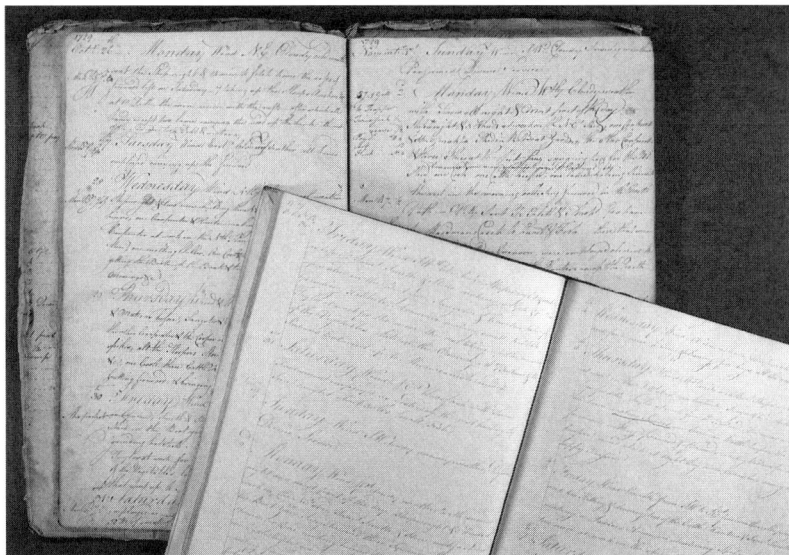

fine soot. Unless the rough journal was stored in a furnace room or similar localized polluted area, it must have spent some of its post-Moose Fort life in an industrial centre, most likely in Great Britain.[6]

The text block of the rough journal has been assembled from three folded sections of pages, as seen in Figure 6.[7] The first of these sections is made up of high quality white writing paper (now discoloured to yellowish). The lighter weight papers of the last two sections would be less expensive than that used for the first section. It is possible that this inferior quality paper was issued by the HBC specifically for day-to-day post business use.

At least three distinct formulations of brown writing ink appear to have been used for the text of the "rough" journal, and at least two are alternated within the same period of time. Ink powder was available by this time and would have been most practical for storage and transport; water, beer or similar liquids would be mixed with the powder to make ink. Variations in the colour, thickness and glossiness of the ink are therefore understandable, given that new ink must have been made periodically. Ink viscosity and thickness would also change as the liquid evaporated from the ink bottle or as the ink was diluted with fresh liquid, and the ink would have flowed smoothly in the warmth of summer or well-heated rooms, and poorly in conditions closer to freezing. Visual characteristics of the inked words can therefore be interpreted to reflect physical conditions when and where the entries were

Figure 5 Detail of rough journal, Page 1. Note visual characteristics of writing and the sewing thread and holes in and near spine edge.

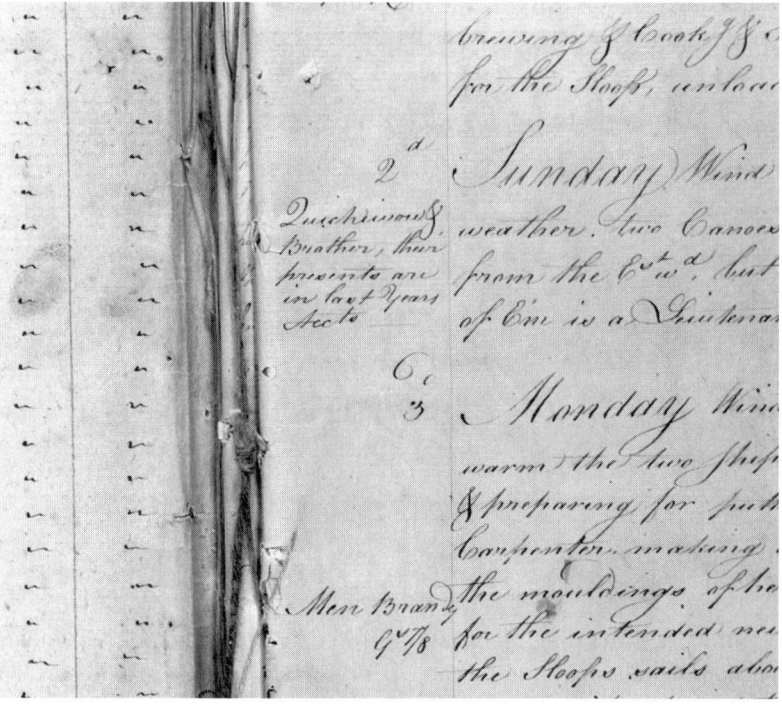

made. Based on the way the written lines swell and diminish and the minimal impression left on the hard surface of the paper, the ink was applied with a quill pen. Again, variations are expected as the quill tip wore down and needed to be re-cut periodically.

The original sewing that secured the cover to the three sections of the "rough" journal is difficult to understand, especially since many threads have broken. The volume appears to have been assembled by someone with little knowledge of standard bookbinding techniques. The first two sections appear to have additional sewing holes at their spines, suggesting they may have been separate booklets at one time. Two sets of side-stab sewing holes extend through all four sections, indicating they may have been part of a larger structure at one time, possibly with other similar records.

The official journal for 1789–90 is sewn through the centre in a single section with a limp vellum cover. This journal has a more formal presentation, with a simple impressed decoration around its edges, end-leaves and a title page. Blank books likely would have been made in bulk by a stationary bookbinder in accordance with the HBC's specifications and sent to all their posts for creation of their official records. The cover is flush with the textblock,

Figure 6 Detail of official journal, Page 11. Note visual characteristics of writing.

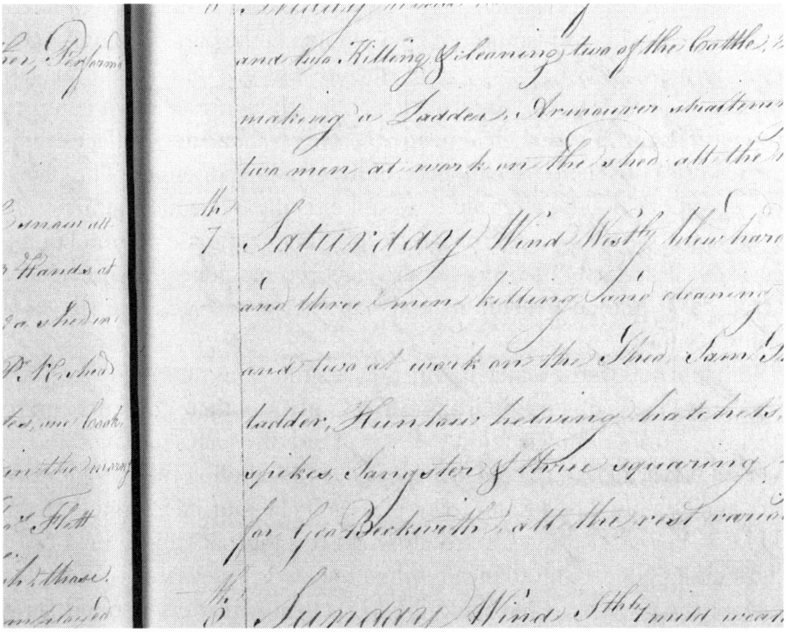

and two Killing & cleaning two of the Cattle
making a Ladder, Armourer straitening
two men at work on the shed all the
7 Saturday Wind Westly blew hard
and three men killing and cleaning
and two at work on the Shed Sam S
ladder, Hunter helving hatchets,
spikes, Sangster & three squaring
for Geo Beckwith all the rest vario
8 Sunday Wind Sthly mild wea

and wear on the bottom edge suggests a history of being shelved upright. Black ink stamps and paper labels with HBCA cataloguing information are also later additions, applied after the archives was established in 1920 but before the records were transferred to the Archives of Manitoba in 1974. These signs assert the ownership and classification schemes of the HBCA over previous ordering systems for the records. They also suggest that the spines and covers of the journals were not considered as intrinsically valuable as the text inside and therefore that the HBCA followed library-based models of stewardship rather than museum or gallery models.

The text pages of the official journal have few stains, but bear the sooty and yellow-brown edge discolouration described above and which is common to the HBC records, which were stored in London through its most industrial coal-burning period. Further evidence of storage is present in the ground-in soot and mould spots on the cover of the journal: these do not extend to the back cover, suggesting that the mould attacked only the exposed surface and that, at that time, the journal was located at the top or edge of a pile, bundle or shelf. The paper used in this journal appears to be the same as in the first section of the "rough" journal, and the brown ink used in the "official" journal appears relatively consistent throughout, suggesting it was written over a short period.

A simple visual analysis of the materials and construction of the records has been offered here, but microscopic, instrumental and chemical analyses could be carried out on components of the journals to identify their composition more precisely; for instance, the plant fibres in the paper might suggest where the paper was made, or impurities in the graphite might suggest where it was mined. Every physical element of the journals has a complex socio-cultural and technological history; between them they reflect events in the histories of science, technology, industry and economics. The physical composition of the paper alone would encompass textile manufacture and recycling (the main source of paper fibres before the use of wood pulp), mining and industrial chemistry (chalk, coloured pigments and other filler materials) and animal husbandry and slaughterhouses (gelatine size as a glue and coating).

Both journals were created to function as simple business recordkeeping systems: the covers of both journals serve to identify their contents and to protect them from damage, and the sewing holds the pages together and in sequence. Nevertheless, the tactile experience of handling the two journals differs significantly. The vellum cover of the official journal is smooth, hard and glossy. Vellum is quite stiff, so although this journal can be held open easily, it closes almost automatically when released. The writing is thin, the surface of the pages feels hard and the pages turn with a crisp sound. This journal's construction is efficient and robust, and it has suffered only superficial damage over more than 200 years. The structure of the rough journal is much less formal. The cover function is served by several pieces of soft and absorbent paper. The sewing has held the sections together in order, but the sewing holes have worn at the cover and the sections are loose and detaching. The pages stay open easily since the structure provides no tension to pull it closed. While this recordkeeping system follows general bookbinding principles, its makeshift construction appears not to have been designed with consideration for aesthetics, long-term storage or frequent use.

In addition to serving as a draft of the official journal, the rough journal appears to be a document intended for internal use at the post. Since the accounts pages used for the covers are dated 1793, the journal as we see it now was clearly not assembled until after the individual sections had completed their function as drafts of the official records. Instead of being discarded or used as scrap paper (as the account pages were), the three sections were bound together, clearly signalling the intention of longer term use in some other capacity.

The variations in the appearance of the rough journal entries and the crudeness of its construction can bring the modern researcher closer to fur trade post life and practices, as well as provide a sense of events in its history. In contrast, the official version, intended for the eyes of the company officers, has been smoothed into a neat and continuous narrative, with the same standardized appearance as every other HBC post journal from that time and place.

Most researchers first become aware of particular records through their archival descriptions. These follow the archival principle of provenance, which foregrounds the relationship between the records and their creator or donor. These written descriptions represent the records in a uniform format intended to provide context for the records and to help a researcher decide which records may best serve their needs. Wendy Duff and Verne Harris observe: "The power to describe is the power to make and remake records and to determine how they will be used and remade in the future.... For the form of narrativity — like all forms — is not merely a neutral container. It shapes, even determines, the narrative content in significant ways" (2002: 272, 276). In creating these narratives, archives and archivists determine what researchers can know about the records, as represented visually in Figure 7.

The Canadian standard, *Rules for Archival Description (RAD)*, follows the "traditional" description model and has been widely adopted by archives across Canada. RAD specifies description of physical aspects of records only within the Physical Description area (1.5) (Canadian Council of Archives 2008). The "Extent of descriptive unit including specific material designation" (1.5B) is the only mandatory element, so a RAD-compliant physical description of each of the Moose Fort journals might be as brief as "textual records: 1 volume." An optional element is provided for "other physical details" (3.5C1), but in the chapter for textual records the examples are limited to supports "other than paper, the presence of seals, illustrations, maps, or the

Figure 7 Levels of Mediation: Archival Description of Original

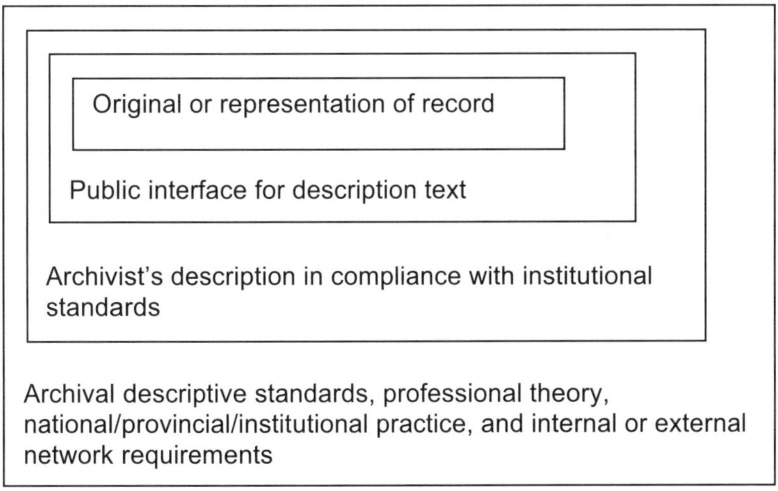

Original or representation of record

Public interface for description text

Archivist's description in compliance with institutional standards

Archival descriptive standards, professional theory, national/provincial/institutional practice, and internal or external network requirements type of binding"; a paper support is not itself significant enough for notice, and no mention is made of the writing medium. These directions and the related examples could shape the official Moose Fort Journal description to read "textual records: 1 volume: watermarks; pamphlet-bound; 32cm x 20 cm approx."

The Physical Description of records is separated from the "Archival Description area" (1.7), which includes elements for the administrative and custodial history of the records' creator. No part of the physical description field calls for systematic identification of the material composition and technologies involved in the creation or of evidence of physical changes to the state of the records since their creation (other than damages still present).[8] While the inclusion of seals and bindings in the examples above suggests this is the place to record their presence, their context as integral organizational — let alone functional — devices is lost. There is also no requirement to identify how the unit being described participated in recordkeeping systems.

The 195 Moose Factory post journals, dated 1730–1941, are described together in a 1955 HBCA catalogue[9] through a list of reference numbers, post locations and dates. The description of the rough journal, which was prepared after its acquisition, indicates its writers as well as physical details such as the missing pages, and it highlights the unusual binding construction. The 1955 catalogue and the 2002 description are only available as hard copies in the archives' research room. The *RAD*-compliant physical description of the Moose Fort post journals in the Archives Descriptive Database is limited to the total number of items in this series. No indication is given that these "journals" for 1789–91 are a single bound structure with continuous entries, that it was not physically constructed as a unit until sometime after 1793 or that it physically differs from the official journals in any way. The materiality of the records is not represented in this description, yet it is important to understanding the different roles the official and rough journals played in the life of the fort and of the HBC.

At the Archives of Manitoba, researchers and staff are encouraged to use the online descriptions, which also serve as the entry point for off-site access to surrogate representations of the records, such as interlibrary loan of microfilm and, in future, for digital images of the records. By relegating materiality to mainly optional fields and by separating physical description from description of the records' contexts of creation and use, *RAD* represents the physical qualities of records as distinct from and of less significance than their "archival" nature. The physical manifestations of the histories of creation, use and care of the records are excluded from the core elements of standard archival description.

Time, travel and financial constraints may prevent researchers from physically entering an archives to consult records, and not every archives allows access to records in their original forms, usually citing restrictions due to preservation or security concerns. In these cases researchers may be limited to visual surrogate representations of the original records and may not be aware of how these surrogates themselves shape what can be known about the records they represent.[10]

Microfilm was developed to sequentially capture and store small-scale photographic representations of records. Microfilm is limited in its ability to capture the colours and to differentiate details of source records, but it is easily reproducible and easy to sell or loan to research facilities or to individual researchers with access to microfilm readers. It can also be converted to digital images to facilitate use of these images in electronic publications and websites. While microfilm has been relatively undisputed as a tool to broaden access to records, as digitized representations of original analogue records become increasingly available, a few critical voices have drawn attention to what is lost in this translation from the source record, represented visually in Figure 8.

Archivist Joanna Sassoon suggests that while mechanical reproduction technologies can be seen as democratic because they are used to improve access, these technologies can also be repressive because they control "what

Figure 8 Levels of Mediation: Interaction with Microfilm of Original Record

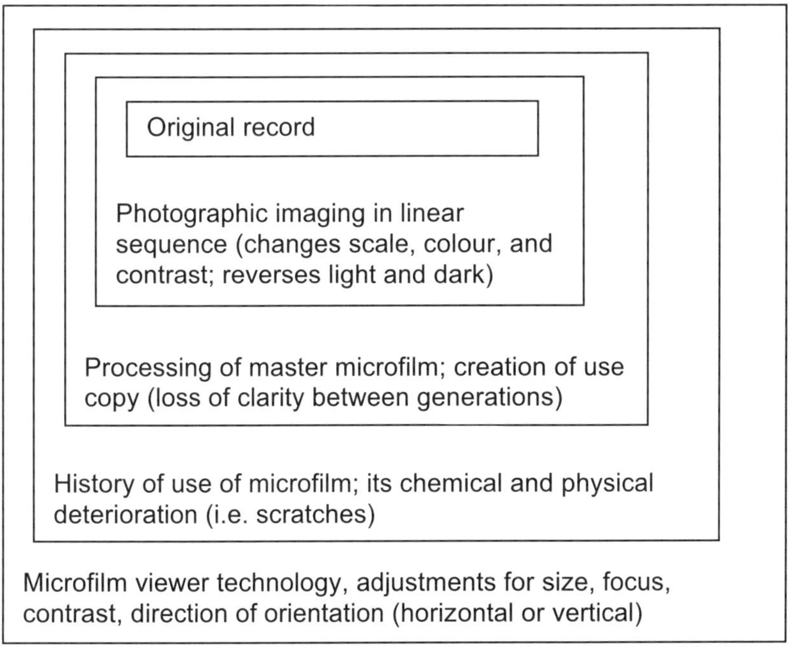

```
┌─────────────────────────────────────────────────────────────┐
│ ┌─────────────────────────────────────────────────────────┐ │
│ │ ┌─────────────────────────────────────────────────────┐ │ │
│ │ │ ┌───────────────────────────┐                       │ │ │
│ │ │ │ Original record           │                       │ │ │
│ │ │ └───────────────────────────┘                       │ │ │
│ │ │                                                     │ │ │
│ │ │ Photographic imaging in linear                      │ │ │
│ │ │ sequence (changes scale, colour, and                │ │ │
│ │ │ contrast; reverses light and dark)                  │ │ │
│ │ └─────────────────────────────────────────────────────┘ │ │
│ │                                                         │ │
│ │ Processing of master microfilm; creation of use         │ │
│ │ copy (loss of clarity between generations)              │ │
│ └─────────────────────────────────────────────────────────┘ │
│                                                             │
│ History of use of microfilm; its chemical and physical      │
│ deterioration (i.e. scratches)                              │
└─────────────────────────────────────────────────────────────┘
Microfilm viewer technology, adjustments for size, focus,
contrast, direction of orientation (horizontal or vertical)
```

is made accessible, and with criteria as to what is appropriate to be made public through digitising rarely being discussed" (1998: 9). The mediations between the original document and the microfilm image observed by the researcher also obscure the materiality of the source records.

HBCA records have been systematically microfilmed since the 1950s, but the rough journal has not yet been microfilmed. A single reel of microfilm,

Figure 9 Cover of B.135/a/76 as it appears on Microfilm 1M89. Note the appearance of the film sprocket holes in the image. Archives of Manitoba, HBCA, 1M89.

1M89, carries images of the official Moose Factory journals from 1785 to 1796. The continuous tone black and white images have been filmed in high contrast. The thickness of the journal is not captured in this imaging, and no information regarding the administrative or technical processes and standards which informed the microfilming appears either on the film or in the related archival description.

The cover of the official Moose Fort post journal, shown in Figure 9, was photographed as a single page while the open journal pages have been photographed as double-page images, so while the page-to-page relationships are retained, the pages are reduced in size on the screen. At the Archives of Manitoba microfilmed images can be printed from a reader/printer, or they can be scanned as digital files and saved or printed. Digital scanning and printing further increase the contrast between the light and dark areas of the image, and the thinnest pen strokes have all but disappeared. Stains and shadows appear darker in the microfilm image, creating a different visual balance. Horizontal scratches on the surface of the film appear as lines and can be seen in Figure 10. Because these are black like the background and they appear in the same compressed visual plane as the image, some of these lines may be interpreted as marks on, or folds in, the pages of the journal. These create additional sources of uncertainty and potential error in interpreting

Figure 10 First Page of Journal Entries in B.135/a/76 as it appears on Microfilm 1M89. Note fingertip of camera operator holding the journal open at bottom left.

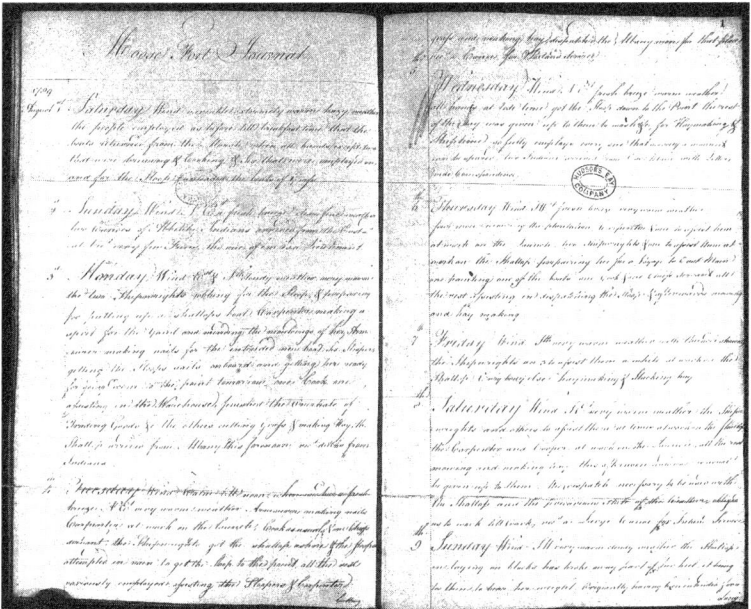

the reproduced images. When reading the text of original documents, the human mind can give higher priority to the colour and orientation of the writing and lower priority to other information, such as stains and shadows. The mind can also shift attention between different characteristics of the object, such as the contrasting hues and tones of colours, texture of pages, appearance of the stains and other non-text phenomena, the crisp sound of the turning pages and the smell of the materials.

The new materiality of the microfilm form displaces the materiality — and especially the mechanical action — of the original journals. The action of loading and viewing a microfilm involves threading the plastic film onto the metal and glass apparatus and cranking a handle to pull the film through the machine. The image appears backlit on a flat glass screen. To find a page on a microfilm one must scroll though all the open pages, pausing periodically to verify one's current location. The scrolling action of the microfilm is more analogous to a long electronic document than to a book. The microfilm technology enhances the linear sequencing of the post journals as a standardized corporate narrative, but obscures the communication functionality more directly manifest in the materiality of the original journals. The flat, static, microfilmed and scanned images of the pages are fundamentally different in character from the physical qualities of the journal, and dynamic interaction with the three-dimensional journal is replaced by the microfilm reader or computer interface.

Digital images made from original records, rather than from microfilm of the records, have more potential for accurate visual representation of some qualities of archival records, such as colour. There is, however, equal potential for misrepresenting these qualities (whether intentionally or not) at the points of image capture, editing, printing or screen rendering, as represented visually in Figure 11. Researchers working with less mediated or more transparently mediated records can be informed by a broader and more reliable range of observations and experiences than if they are limited to surrogate images, which are the byproducts of endless combinations of technical and physical limitations of the technology and the human operator.

Archivists working with visual images have looked to art history, anthropology and other interdisciplinary sources to develop a better understanding of how non-textual records communicate. Joanna Sassoon advises that significant meaning is lost or distorted in the process of digitizing archival photographs: the change in format creates "new discursive systems which may obliterate previous meanings," resulting in the "dematerialising, de-historicising and decontexualising" of the historic photographs as they are conflated with their digital images (1998: 13). Sassoon limits herself to discussing photographs in this article, but it appears clear that the context and materiality of source documents in any medium will always be different from

Figure 11 Levels of Mediation: Interaction with Digital Image of Original (speculative)

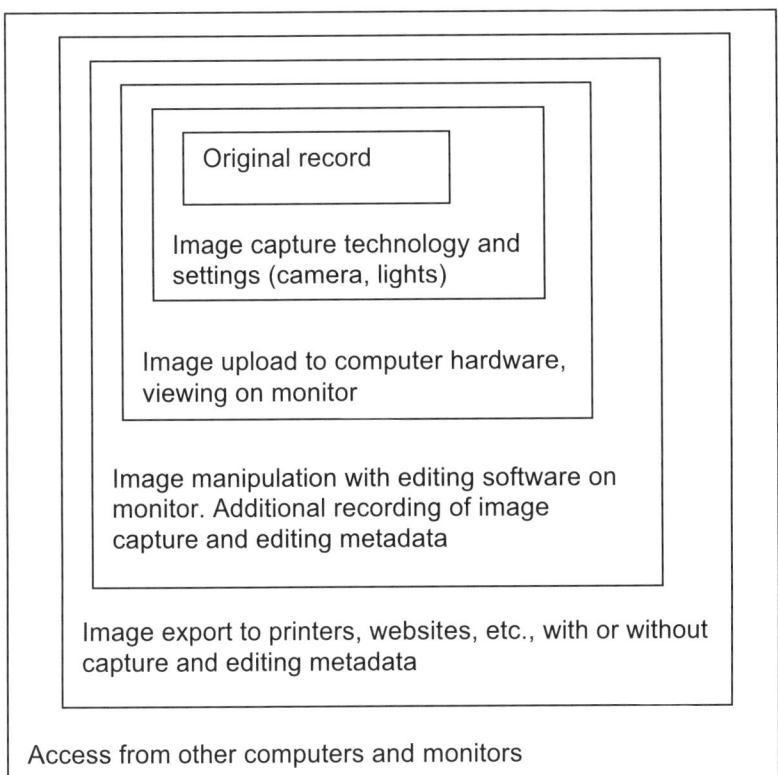

the context and materiality of the representations of those documents. More recently, Sassoon cautioned archives to consider the implications of digitization of archival records for the evidential value of those records (2007a: n.p.). Additionally, she has called for archives to expose, and for historians to call archives to make evident, their roles in "pre-cooking the raw materials of history" (2007b: n.p.).

The mediations or interventions of standard archives practice profoundly shape access to and understanding of archival records. There is meaning in the way the two Moose Fort journals are physically constructed, in the way they look and feel and in the performance of their functions. The structural and visual differences between the journals become readily apparent when one personally engages with these records. The materiality of the microfilm, and of the grayscale digital images reproduced for this publication differ profoundly from the appearance and performance of the source journals. Records in their original forms compress the past and present without the mediating element of written descriptions, photography, a computer screen or another book. They remain participants in present human activity and act as a sensory connection to past human activity.

Archival practice considers textual records and text-oriented tools such as *Rules for Archival Description* as the norm, even though text-oriented, reading/writing-based access services and tools clearly do not serve all members of society equally well. Archivists can better serve a wider variety of clients and research interests by developing access tools which address a wider variety of learning behaviours and actively highlight the many ways in which records can perform their communication functions. Archives can review policies of limiting access to original records to verify whether the risks of damage or theft truly outweigh the loss of materiality for researchers, or if these risks could be mitigated though stabilization of fragile records, improved training and procedures for handling by staff and researchers, or improved security training for staff supervising research rooms. Where original records cannot be made available, archives could also offer "discovery" or "touch" collections of records with no archival value to simulate or contextualize the archival records' technologies. Those who have access only to an image of a record have access to significantly less materially manifested evidence than those who can use the original records.

Nevertheless, access to the evidence lost in microfilming, digitization or other imaging methods can be at least partially restored through improved tools for documentation and dissemination of records, for instance, by adding the capacity to zoom in on high-resolution images of records or by displaying the images next to versions enhanced to highlight or "restore" aspects of their materiality, such as yellowing or fading. Surrogate representations can thus be used as a strategy for enhancing access to and documentation of records' materiality, as long as archives reveal both the context for creation of those representations and the limitations of the representations as an access, a documentation or a preservation tool.[11] Outreach programming could actively draw attention to the mind behind the matter and offer opportunities to increase sensitivity to why records look, smell, feel and move the way the do. Reading records more deeply and more broadly increases the possibilities of telling richer stories and engaging wider audiences with the same limited archival resources.

The materiality of records is anchored in the social circumstances surrounding their physical creation and is manifest in at least two ways: the physical "background" upon which the written text or images appear, and the successive interactions between records and their multiple users across time. The materiality of records is, therefore, primary evidence of the societies that created, preserved and used them. Archives' users can apply "material literacy" skills to recognize and interpret meaning from beyond surface text or image in order to more fully understand the societal context which produced a record (or representation of a record) and to more critically consider how these different iterations shape both the questions that can be asked of records and the stories they can tell.

Notes

1. See for instance the work of Tom Nesmith, Terry Cook, Verne Harris, Joan Schwartz, Laura Millar and Brien Brothman.
2. Howell and Prevenier (2001), cited above, is a relatively recent exception in that it includes the traditional tools as well as the newer interdisciplinary approaches, but it does not explicitly discuss materiality of archival records as evidence.
3. Olga Belova described how, by privileging sight over the other senses, René Descartes sought "objective" knowledge. "This passive intellectual engagement with the object of study complemented by a physical detachment from it gave rationale to a clear-cut distinction between the body and the outside world, the seer and the seen" (Belova 2006: 95).
4. As Joan Schwartz notes, documents are "created by a will, for a purpose, to convey a message to an audience. To understand them as the product of actions and transactions, either bureaucratic or socio-cultural, we must return them to the action in which they participated. It is their functional context that transforms [them] into archival documents" (1995: 42).
5. Archives of Manitoba, HBCA, Moose Factory post journals, E.372/1. Moose Fort, located in northern Ontario on the shore of James Bay, was later renamed Moose Factory.
6. The donor of this journal, a resident of Mississippi, did not know how his family acquired it.
7. Several sheets of paper placed on top of one another and then folded make up a section (also called a quire or signature). Sections are generally attached to one another by sewing through the folded centres of the pages. A single section with a wrapped cover and sewn through the middle is a pamphlet binding. The majority of HBC post journals are pamphlet bound.
8. An optional Notes area (1.8) includes elements for Physical Condition and Conservation. The Physical Condition element (1.8B9a) is only to be used if "that condition materially affects the clarity of legibility of the records." The Conservation element (1.8B9b) is only for indicating the nature of any "conservation treatment" the unit has received; since these terms are not defined, it is difficult to determine whether the scope is limited to conservation treatments carried out by a professional conservator or to all repairs by custodians over time (including those which have since failed or caused additional damage), or if it should include the common interventions carried out during arrangement and processing, such as flattening or rehousing.
9. HBC Catalogue of Archives, Section B, vol. 1, Post Journals 1701–1870, 76.
10. Martha Howell and Walter Prevenier caution that the historian must understand the context in which copies of records have been created and that it is the responsibility of a text editor to identify any differences from the original text (2001: 63–64). They refer only to differences in the written text, however, and

do not discuss changes in materiality between originals and copies of records, nor do they mention any other means of representing records.

11. The Library of Congress includes descriptions of the sources for digital images and the technical set-ups and processing for each segment of their "digital collections. See for instance: <http://memory.loc.gov/ammem/arendthtml/arendthome.html> and <http://memory.loc.gov/ammem/doughtml/doughome.html>.

References

Belova, Olga. 2006. "The Event of Seeing: A Phenomenological Perspective on Visual Sense-Making." *Culture and Organization* 12: 93–107.

Black, Graham. 2005. *The Engaging Museum: Developing Museums for Visitor Involvement*. London and New York: Routledge.

Burton, Antoinette (ed.). 2005. *Archive Stories: Facts, Fictions, and the Writing of History*. Durban and London: Duke University Press.

Canadian Council of Archives. 2008. *Rules for Archival Description*, revised version July 2008. Available at <http://www.cdncouncilarchives.ca/archdesrules.html> (accessed August 9, 2009).

Craig, Barbara, Philip B. Eppard and Heather McNeil. 2005. "Exploring Perspectives and Themes for Histories of Records and Archives." The First International Conference on the History of Records and Archives, *Archivaria* 60 (Fall): 1–10.

Duff, Wendy, Barbara Craig and Joan Cherry. 2004. "Finding and Using Archival Resources: A Cross-Canada Survey of Historians Studying Canadian History." *Archivaria* 58 (Fall): 51–80.

Duff, Wendy, and Verne Harris. 2002. "Stories and Names: Archival Description as Narrating Records and Constructing Meanings." *Archival Science* 2: 263–85.

Frost, Gary. 2005. "Haptic Evaluation of Books." Available at <http://futureofthebook.com/haptic-evaluation-of-books/> (accessed August 9, 2009).

_____. N.d. "Reader's Guide to Book Action." Available at <http://futureofthebook.com/readers-guide-to-book-action/> (accessed August 9, 2009).

Howell, Martha, and Walter Prevenier. 2001. *From Reliable Sources: An Introduction to Historical Methods*. Ithaca, NY and London: Cornell University Press.

Roeder, George H., Jr. 1994. "Coming to Our Senses." *The Journal of American History* 81: 1112–22.

Sassoon, Joanna. 1998. "Photographic Meaning in the Age of Digital Reproduction." *LASIE (Library Automated Systems Information Exchange)* December: 5–15.

_____. 2007a. "If Digitization of Archival Records is the Answer, What on Earth Is/Are the Questions?" Lecture sponsored by the Association for Manitoba Archives, 2 October, 2007, Archives of Manitoba, Winnipeg, Manitoba.

_____. 2007b. "Beyond Phantoms of Remembrance." Paper presented as part of the University of Manitoba Department of History colloquium series, October 3, 2007, University of Manitoba, Winnipeg, Manitoba.

Schwartz, Joan. 1995. "We Make Our Tools and Our Tools Make Us: Lessons for Photographs for the Practice, Politics, and Poetics of Diplomatics." *Archivaria* 40 (Fall): 40–74.

Shafer, Robert Jones. 1969. *A Guide to Historical Method*. Homewood, IL: The Dorsey Press.

Smith, Mark M. 2007. *Sensing the Past: Seeing, Hearing, Smelling, Tasting, and Touching in History*. Berkeley and Los Angeles: University of California Press.

Taylor, Hugh. 1995. "'Heritage' Revisited: Documents as Artifacts in the Context of Museums and Material Culture." *Archivaria* 40 (Fall): 8–20.

"VARK: A Guide to Learning Styles." N.d. Available at <http://www.vark-learn.com/english/> (accessed August 9, 2009).

Vipond, Mary. 2003. "The Mass Media in Canadian History: The Empire Day Broadcast of 1939." *Journal of the Canadian Historical Association* 14: 1–21.

Physicality as Apotheosis
The Changing Roles of Atoms and Bits in the Digital Age

Melissa McCarthy

One of the pharaohs of ancient Egypt, it is said, was dining one day with the god Theuth, a prolific inventor. Theuth presented many of his inventions to the pharaoh for approval, including such things as mathematics. On this day he proudly presented his newest creation, hieroglyphic writing, which he touted as of great benefit for the memory and wisdom of the Egyptians. As we are so accustomed to reading and writing, it would seem obvious that the pharaoh would be delighted, both with the positive effects of the new technology on society and, more cynically, with the possibility of memorializing his own kingly achievements in a tangible form. But the pharaoh was wise and farseeing, and he had some reservations about the new technology. He told Theuth that people who learned to write would become dependent on it and would, in essence, forget how to remember. As for wisdom, the pharaoh foresaw that people would gain instead a great deal of superficial knowledge while actually remaining quite ignorant (Plato 2008: 69). It is worth noting that he did not, however, ban writing.

There are, I think, two lessons that we can draw from this. The first is that we, as the first generations of people to use the Internet and to digitize materials, may not be the best judges of the possibilities of the technology, both good and bad. The second, to mix ancient metaphors, is that once the technology is out of Pandora's Box, it is going to be widely adopted and it is going to change society, and the best thing we can and should do is to adopt it with the enthusiasm of Theuth and an attempt at the wisdom of the pharaoh.

A survey of the current literature dealing with archival holdings, particularly photographs, the most common component of a virtual exhibit, suggests that the issue has been approached from two primary points of view: first, the purely practical, concerned with issues such as scanner resolution, website design and ways of tracking usage statistics; and second, the postmodern philosophical, concerned with issues such as the creation of new forms of otherness. I intend to steer a middle course between these two approaches. Immediate practicalities such as the best scanner vary greatly depending on the particular institution's needs, and any general statements on these issues are likely to be too broad to be useful. The indepth philosophical approach, on the other hand, while doubtless important and, to some, fascinating, is complex and theoretical and is generally descriptive rather than prescriptive. I intend to focus mainly on the practical lessons which can be gleaned from these.

The one generalization I will make at the outset, because it is a vital one, is that too many institutions (as can be seen by a quick Google search) put up hastily created virtual exhibits with no plan for maintaining them, often simply because money was available for a virtual exhibit. Images are often put up before they have been properly described at the item level, leaving the viewer with a collection of lovely images and no way of knowing what they represent, what their significance is or why they are being displayed together. These poorly planned exhibits often do not meet the needs of the archives or of its users and often do not survive for more than a few years. Their creation has been little more than a waste of time and money, and they are a disappointment to those who find their digital traces online with no way of gaining access to the content which was once there.

In recent years, the funding for such projects has begun to dry up as more people become aware of these issues, and remaining funding stresses the planning process. The guidelines for the 2009–10 iteration of the Archival Community Digitization Program, operated by Library and Archives Canada, include the following criteria:

> Projects should take the form of thematic, narrative web exhibitions of digitized archival material. Successful projects will tell a compelling story based on one or more specific themes, time periods, or locations. Digitized content will be portrayed within a well-developed context and in such a way that it will be easily understood by the target audience....
>
> The project must be well-planned and include a realistic project timeline demonstrating efficient use of resources (i.e., human, financial, and technological)....
>
> The proposal must demonstrate that the resources required to maintain the project during a minimum of five (5) years after the launch of the project will be covered by the applicant and its partners. The proposal must also demonstrate that there will be a content owner who will ensure that the content is maintained and appropriate changes and updates are incorporated. (2008: 4)

As these guidelines indicate, it is crucial to have a well-thought-out plan for any virtual exhibit, including its goal, its intended audience and, vitally, its maintenance. The goal, which seems like the easiest part of this plan to address, is actually a very tricky question. Many archives intend for their virtual exhibits to increase access to their photographic collections, perhaps even creating a new user base, while helping to preserve their photographic prints and negatives by reducing researchers' need to handle them. This is all very well and good, but there is at present a debate as to whether a scanned photographic collection is, should be or even can be equivalent to a collection confined to paper.

This question is in large part an extension of a broader debate on "bits versus atoms," which has been raging since the Internet began to form part of people's daily lives. We are increasingly faced with choices between the two worlds: the highly technological world of bits, which promises (but does not necessarily deliver) 24/7 convenience, ease of use and instant gratification (for instance, banking online) versus the less technological world of atoms, the "real" world (for instance, going to the bank to complete all your transactions). I and my contemporaries in the developed world — members of what author Don Tapscott calls the Net Generation, who in 2010 are between the ages of thirteen and thirty-three — are, for the most part, seeing most of our lives slide into the world of bits, sometimes without even noticing it — not only online banking, but Flickr and Facebook and Twitter and YouTube and blogs and text messages and all the rest of the Web 2.0 world (Tapscott 2008). A telling instance of this occurred when I was in library school, and one of our assigned readings was not available online. A group of librarians-in-training immediately began complaining about the inconvenience of having to walk to the university library, which was right across the street, go through the stacks and get a paper book down from the shelf, instead of having instant access to it from the computer lab in our own building — and it wasn't even a rainy day. Ironically, in another class the week before, we had been passionately defending the continuing relevance of the library's role as repository of the very same paper books which we now found it such a chore to use.

The arguments for and against the increasing place of online technologies in our daily lives closely mirror arguments used at other times and relating to other technologies. Examples include the Egyptian pharaoh's arguments against writing; worries about radio technology; worries about early telephones and, much later, cell phones; the famous concern about television adapted from the work of Marshall McLuhan, that the medium was the message and that the message would destroy children's attention spans, among other things; the recent concern over calculators in schools lessening students' ability to do math independently from a machine (WikEd 2009); and the pervasive and continuing fear that workers will be replaced by machinery and that remaining workers are becoming deskilled and dependent on machines to perform even simple tasks. It is easy to ridicule the earliest of these concerns. Who today condemns writing in favour of trying to remember every piece of information he or she is likely to need? The oldest concerns relating to technology have long since ceased to be concerns, and the technologies in question — writing, radio, television — have become largely non-controversial parts of our society. But the more recent concerns are still vital; these technologies — video games, calculators, the Internet and computerized technologies in general — have yet to become so much a part of our minds that we cease to think about them. The result today is yet another worry over the impact of increasing technology on our lives, which in turn leads to the conception of physicality as an apotheosis. Multiple websites (perhaps somewhat ironically) urge us to return to letter writing; a Google search for "art of letter writing" returns hundreds of laments on the death of this art, of which a typical one equates the loss of letter writing with a loss of emotional connection (Pimm 2001). One man has gone so far as to compose a violin concerto in mourning (Boosey and Hawkes 2009). Afraid that the current emphasis on computerization, the Internet, ebooks, ecommerce, e-everything is devaluing physical objects and our physical lives, we respond by clinging ever more tightly to the physical object and to the idea of physicality, believing that true authenticity lies only in the realm of the physical. What is physical becomes real, what is virtual becomes fake, and with increasing incursions of the virtual upon the physical — such as Photoshopped images — we become ever more obsessed with what is real.

We tend to think of this desperate attachment to the "real thing" as a twenty-first-century phenomenon, but a remarkably cogent expression of it was written in 1936 by the German cultural critic Walter Benjamin. His essay "The Work of Art in the Age of Mechanical Reproduction" could, with a few terminological changes, be easily mistaken for a study of the effects on art and on archival materials of our own new technologies such as Photoshop. As Benjamin points out, "Even the most perfect reproduction of a work of art is lacking in one element: its presence in time and space, its unique existence at the place where it happens to be" (Benjamin 1936: 20). How much more relevant is this to the scanned photograph in a virtual exhibit than to Benjamin's examples of manuscripts and bronze statuary? A copy of a manuscript or of a statue, however lacking in original presence, is at least a tangible and potentially perfect copy. A virtual copy, on the other hand, is necessarily an entirely separate creation, an intangible object with its own history, completely divorced from the original physical artifact. Benjamin drives this point home as he continues:

> This unique existence of the work of art determined the history to which it was subject throughout the time of its existence. This

includes the changes which it may have suffered in physical condition over the years as well as the various changes in its ownership. The traces of the first can be revealed only by chemical or physical analyses which it is impossible to perform on a reproduction; changes of ownership are subject to a tradition which must be traced from the situation of the original. (20)

This statement applies to photographs as much as to works of art, and as archivists know, it can also apply to documents. Archival description includes the changes in physical condition and ownership as vital aspects of the history and meaning of archival collections. For Benjamin:

> The presence of the original is the prerequisite to the concept of authenticity.... The whole sphere of authenticity is outside technical — and, of course, not only technical — reproducibility. Confronted with its manual reproduction..., the original preserved all its authority; not so vis à vis technical reproduction. (20)

Again, the technical reproduction in the twenty-first-century sense is even farther removed from the original than what Benjamin has in mind. "The situations into which the product of mechanical reproduction can be brought" — Benjamin is thinking of easily distributed photographs of art objects and phonograph records of musical performances — "may not touch the actual work of art, yet the quality of its presence is always depreciated" (21). Furthermore, "Since the historical testimony rests on the authenticity, the former, too, is jeopardized by reproduction.... And what is really jeopardized when the historical testimony is affected is the authority of the object" (21). In other words, in creating virtual exhibits, we are allowing many more people to see our holdings than would otherwise be the case, but at the same time, we are harming the authenticity and authority of the objects we are reproducing.

Benjamin also points out that "the technique of reproduction detaches the reproduced object from the domain of tradition. By making many reproductions it substitutes a plurality of copies for a unique existence" (21). Writing in 1936, he could not have dreamed of present forms of digital reproduction, in which no quantifiable change occurs between the original digital item and its copies. Items which have been "born digital," then, may not suffer from the same loss of authenticity and authority when they are copied and recopied. But for those items which began life in the world of atoms, we must bear in mind the changes which we inflict upon them in turning them into objects made up of bits.

A related issue, one which is seen both in our current tenacious attachment to physicality and in some previously mentioned concerns about technology, is connected to popularization. Perhaps the best example is the printed book. When the movable-type printing press became popular in the fifteenth century, it entered a market which had seen only handwritten books for centuries. As anyone who has seen the Book of Kells or a medieval Book of Hours can attest, these were not clumsy, amateurish creations but, in many cases, exquisite creations. They were handwritten in beautiful, elaborate, standardized fonts, many of which were copied by the early printers. Some text was highlighted in red. Illustrations were meticulous, brilliantly executed, vividly coloured and prevalent — indeed, in the case of the Books of Hours, the beauty of these lavish illustrations could be as important as the devotional purpose of the work (Thorpe 1976). The best and most prized books were written on pure white vellum, into which the ink was absorbed. There was a vibrant, thriving set of technologies associated with book production (Eisenstein 1983: 20).

Then, in the early modern era, the movable-type press was introduced into the established world of handwritten works. Over time, this meant that books could become vastly cheaper and therefore available to a much broader audience. The bookseller Vespasiano, whose clients were the wealthy people who were the traditional audience for books, responded with indignation. He scorned the new, cheap, mass-produced books (although his clients were happy to invest in the better-made and more decorative printed books and appreciated the new books' quicker availability) and gloried ever more in his own stock of handwritten texts. While this reaction was atypical and was shaped by Vespasiano's professional prejudice, it is not difficult to see behind such complaints the fear that the "common people" were acquiring books and that this would devalue books and learning in general (Eisenstein 1983: 18).

I suspect that a similar process is at work today. Those who criticize virtual exhibits tend to frame their complaints in terms of the banality and questionable usefulness of many of the exhibits and the use of scarce resources on virtual exhibits to the exclusion of other, perhaps more important archival activities. These are certainly valid criticisms, which should prompt archives to create better, more useful virtual exhibits and to ensure that time and money spent on these exhibits are not being taken away from other activities. But beneath the surface, is there another complaint lurking?

Archives used to be reserved exclusively for serious researchers, who would have to sign registers and fill out request slips for the materials they wished to see and submit to careful observation as they used the delicate materials. To use a photograph (particularly a colour print — black-and-white photographs are more chemically stable and more damage-resistant) is, in a very real sense, to use it up; handling a photograph and exposing it to the light creates and accelerates damage, so that each photograph can be used only so many times before it disintegrates. Even textual records can easily be damaged by improper handling. Archives and their contents were therefore unimaginably precious, watched over by an archival priesthood, doled out in the archival sanctuary with great precautions to the faithful few.

Now, with online exhibits, the great unwashed masses can find archival materials, sometimes even on file-sharing sites such as Flickr and YouTube. There is no register to sign. The endless stream of call slips has been replaced by a search box. There is no hovering archivist ensuring that materials are not mishandled. There is no need for a visit to the sanctuary; materials can be accessed from anywhere. Perhaps most importantly, a scanned image cannot be used up. Each time it is loaded, it is exactly the same as it was before. The delicate, ephemeral photograph made of atoms has become a sturdy set of bits. Anyone, from serious researchers to casual web searchers, can see and use online photographs for any reason they choose, from anywhere, at any time. Is this, in the eyes of some archivists and of some of the traditional users of archives, devaluing the archival photograph by making it accessible to all, in the same way that the mass-produced printed book seemed to some owners of libraries of handwritten volumes to devalue the book?

I do not know the answer to this question. Certainly a great many archivists and a great many patrons of archives are adopting the new technologies with glee and perhaps in some cases with more of the enthusiasm of Theuth than the wisdom of the pharaoh. There is no denying the fact that we are living through a period of great change in technological possibilities and in society and that the utility of some of the more outré-seeming experiments (such as archives in Second Life, "a virtual world where more than 15 million users have created avatars–or online personas–enabling them to… interact with others… in real time" [Theimer 2009a]) has yet to be determined. These will, if they prove useful applications of technology to archives, become the norm or, if not useful for our purposes, be quietly discarded. The difficulty for archivists today is in determining which experiments to try for ourselves in an environment of limited time and money.

In the Middle Ages, there was an evolving tension between words and images (Starkey 2004: 15); in the early modern era, between handwritten and printed words. We are now negotiating the interface between atoms and bits, perhaps an even more fundamental change. Because it is impossible for those living through such a paradigm shift to envision the ultimate results, the best one can do is to establish a working compromise between the elements in tension. Thus the medieval text incorporated images as a vital part of its meaning. In the earliest surviving illustrated manuscript of Wolfram von Eschenbach's popular saga *Willehalm* (compiled circa 1270), the images directed the presenter of the text in how to dramatize the story for his listeners (Starkey 2004: 15). This collaboration between the word and the image to create the meaning gradually, in later manuscripts, gave way to the familiar dominance of the word as it became more common for people to read individually and silently than to view a performance of a text. In the same way, the early modern printed text emulated the handwritten text as closely as possible. In both cases, the creators of the texts seized upon aspects of the new paradigm — in the Middle Ages, the rise of secular copyists, the subsequent spread of literacy and book buying and the accompanying societal shift to individual reading led writers to use and then gradually to eliminate images directing the use of their texts; in the early modern period, with the rise of printing and the corresponding broader diffusion of texts, such conveniences as page numbers and standard editions were quickly adopted (Eisenstein 1983: 21). Similarly, we are aware of some of the new possibilities of virtual exhibits, such as collaborative exhibits involving two or more institutions without the complex issues of borrowing physical objects from another institution's collection and the "far greater opportunities [in a virtual rather than a physical exhibit] for exploring documents in a multitude of choice-led, interactive experiences" (Lester 2006: 96), and we would do well to take advantage of these possibilities. It is important to remember, however, that there is no established best way to create such an exhibit, simply because we are still living through this paradigm shift and cannot yet see how the changes will evolve.

In the current wave of technological enthusiasm, we must keep in mind that the difference between the physical item and the virtual item is not just a question of semantics and beliefs. There is a basic difference between a physical item — particularly a photograph — and its virtual counterpart. As has been mentioned, people are increasingly aware of the difference, both physical and emotional, between a copy and the "real thing." In a physical exhibit, visitors can see a real photograph and experience it as a three-dimensional object; it gives them a sense of participating in the reconstruction of the past, of interacting with an important object. A physical copy, and still more a virtual copy, constitutes a "transformation of the record to a mere artifact [which] denies the archival integrity of the record, based as it is in nearly all cases on its content" (Lester 2006: 88). Traditional physical exhibits, explains Peter Lester, can be based on the archival content and context of the items on display, in which case "the exhibition loses its significance, as a form of advocacy, because the content message can still be conveyed if the originals were replaced by copies" (88); or they can be based on the iconic resonance of the items on display rather than on the archival content and context, in which case their full meaning is lost. "It is this abiding struggle at the heart of the 'archival exhibition' which distinguishes it from other types of display, and it is this struggle which overshadows the development of the virtual exhibition," all of whose digitized photographs are not the "real thing" (Lester 2006: 88–89). Although the virtual exhibit is capable of reaching a much broader audience with less wear and tear on the documents, the experience is necessarily a step removed from the physical and so is less significant and less memorable.

A properly designed exhibit with sufficient description and meta-data to clarify each item's informational content can offer enough information to most researchers, but some researchers may need to examine the physical object to gain, for instance, clues as to its method of production. We must also remember that in a virtual-only exhibit, some of the experience of interacting with the original is lost. A March 2009 report by the Association of Research Libraries points out in a discussion of the overall value of physical exhibits in libraries, archives and museums: "A published descriptive catalog or a virtual version of the exhibition online ideally provides longevity and greater access to the exhibition" (20) rather than replacing the traditional physical exhibition. The comparison of the virtual exhibit with the published catalogue is telling: neither of these extensions of the physical exhibit can or should replace the experience of visiting and interacting with the primary physical exhibit. The experience of the catalogue or of the virtual exhibit is intended to be complementary to the experience of the physical exhibit.

On the other hand, with certain fragile items, the virtual exhibit may be the only practical option. Trinity College, Dublin, which holds the Book of Kells, has created an authorized reproduction of it in both physical and DVD-ROM format. As the Book itself has become too fragile to be put on display, these reproductions are the only opportunity anyone outside of the College archives can have to examine it. The digital copy has an additional advantage over the "analogue" physical copy, in that the book can be browsed by theme. The Book is famous for its whimsical illustrations of animals, which is one of the available themes; the user can find all the images of, for instance, rabbits with one click of the mouse (Board of Trinity College Dublin 2004). This is a creative and useful implementation of digital technology. We must keep in mind, however, that for most items, digitization is not the only practical choice for providing access. Few items are as famous or as in demand as the Book of Kells, and few are as fragile. Even if we can use digital technology to provide innovative means of access to items in our holdings, we must always remember the differences between the original item and a copy.

We need also to be careful of what we are digitizing. We are privileging certain items over others in choosing which items in our collections to digitize, which items to put before the public eye. This is inevitable, as there are unlikely to be any institutions with the budget, the time or, frankly, the level of physical and intellectual control over their records required to digitize their entire holdings all at once. But we should be careful that we are not selecting only eye-catching items that we hope will get us a lot of hits on Flickr, rather than the "workhorse" series that researchers tend to request. (If many users visiting the archives request a given series, that series is likely to be among the most used online as well.) It has been suggested on the basis of Zipf's Law[1] that "by digitizing representative portions of 20% of our collections, we could adequately serve 70% of our users" (Hurst-Wahl 2009a). Even if this mathematical digression is inaccurate, it certainly suggests that there is more of a need to digitize representative samples of our archival collections than to hurry everything onto the Internet as swiftly as possible.

As an example of the lack of consensus among archivists on the issue of digitization, however, another archivist uses the famous 80/20 rule — whereby 80 percent of requests to an archives are for only 20 percent of its holdings — to argue that it is instead the less-used items which should be put online; otherwise, he says, they may disappear (Crawford 2001). This leads digitization consultant Jill Hurst-Wahl to ask, "Do you want to satisfy the most user requests or provide access to important obscure items in your collection?" (Hurst-Wahl 2009b). Archivists hoping to create a virtual exhibit are thus left with one more important question to answer with very little definitive guidance from the broader archival community.

An issue related to that of which items we will privilege through digitization is that we are necessarily privileging certain types of users over others. One virtual exhibit cannot meet the needs of all users. Are we targeting, for instance, a school-age audience, genealogists or people interested in local history? Does our target audience expect all the bells and whistles possible with the latest technology, or will they find that confusing and prefer a more bare-bones, easier-to-navigate approach? It will be difficult if not impossible to create one exhibit that allows every possible target group to have a satisfying experience. So who are we trying to serve first? This is another question to which every archives is likely to have a different answer based on their own situation and immediate priorities. But it also raises another question: To whom are we accountable? To our board of directors? To our users? To our budget? This is a more difficult question to answer, and my own answer is that we are primarily accountable to the records under our care. Regardless of which audience we are targeting and what sort of exhibit we are creating, we need to ensure that we are maintaining the integrity of the records as best we can.

A further challenge with maintaining this integrity arises in Web 2.0. This much-used and misused buzzword refers to the new technology which "is characterized as facilitating communication, information sharing, interoperability, user-centered design and collaboration on the World Wide Web." In other words, Web 1.0, the first iteration of the Web, was read-only; users could read webpages but not interact with them. Web 2.0, by contrast, is read/write, meaning that users can interact with sites in meaningful ways.

The most commonly adduced example of Web 2.0 technology is blogging. On a blogging site such as LiveJournal.com, all of the content is created by users, and each post on most blogs is open for public comment. While most blogs are of interest only to the blogger and their friends, in the aggregate this adds up to a great deal of content which is of use to someone. Another example is the famous Wikipedia, the open encyclopedia where all of the entries are created and managed by the users.

There are intriguing possibilities for archives whose websites offer Web 2.0 functionality. Perhaps the most useful, particularly for an exhibit of photographs, is tagging — attaching pieces of searchable meta-data to each item. For instance, a photograph of a covered bridge in New Brunswick might be tagged "covered bridge," "New Brunswick," "Vaughn Creek" (the specific location) and "lighthouse" (if a lighthouse is also visible in the photograph). A user clicking on any of these tags will be taken to a dynamically generated page containing all of the photographs that have been given that tag. The American National Archives and Records Administration (NARA) is creating a new Web 2.0 site and is considering allowing users to tag its photographs. They explain, "Our current online catalog, the Archival Research Catalog (ARC), does not allow for tagging. Staff archivists can add subject terms from our authority list of approved subject headings (based on the Library of Congress Subject Authority Headings), but in many cases there is not enough time to index the descriptions. People using the catalog would be able to add whatever tags or keywords to the catalog descriptions" (National Archives and Records Administration 2004).

That non-archivists might provide useful identifying information is more than wishful thinking. Photograph collectors Jack and Beverly Wilgus posted to their Flickr account a photograph of an unknown man with a conjectural story about him. A history buff suggested that the photograph could be of Phineas Gage, who is important in the history of neuroscience for his survival of a brain injury in 1848. No photographs had previously been known of Gage. The identification of the photograph subject with Gage has since been confirmed (Wilgus and Wilgus 2009). Kate Theimer, of the blog ArchivesNext, comments:

> It's a fantastic story, and as good an example as I've found of the power Flickr has to connect people with images to people interested to helping learn more about those images. Not every archives will end up with results as dramatic as the Wilguses, but if you don't share your images, you have very little chance of making identifications like this one. The world can now see the face of Phineas Gage, thanks to people willing to share their images, people willing to share their knowledge, and a service that brought them together. (2009b)

No one seems to be suggesting that archivists do away with formal archival description — indeed, I would suggest that a good archival description will become even more vital in locating and using photographs as more and more of them are made available online — but it is possible that allowing the public to add tags to properly described photographs will make them even easier to use and possibly turn up connections that the archivist had not noticed.[2]

One intriguing possibility for user-supplied content is in use by the U.K. National Archives. It is called Your Archives, and it allows users to "contribute [their] knowledge of archival sources held by The National Archives and by other archives throughout the UK." It explains, "The content on these pages has mainly been contributed by users and is designed to offer information additional to [the professionally created information] available in the Catalogue, Research Guides, DocumentsOnline and the National Register of Archives. The National Archives does not vouch for the accuracy of the information held within Your Archives" (National Archives 2009). This solution allows the public to contribute useful information while ensuring that this user-provided information, which has not been verified, is not confused with the authoritative description provided by the archivists.

It is truly exciting to be living at a time when these developments are arising. The judicious use of new technology, combined with careful adherence to archival standards, could potentially help to compile and create access to the stories of Canada and of Canadians. Not only can the Internet enable archives to make their materials more accessible, developing knowledge of and stimulating interest in Canadian history, but it can also allow non-archivists and non-historians to contribute their knowledge and their own stories. Top-down, formal history written by professional historians can thus combine with bottom-up history contributed by all interested Canadians. There is no better place for this to occur than on the websites of archives, where the primary documents are posted to allow both types of history to be written and discussed. Virtual exhibits could be of incalculable value to those who are interested in telling Canada's stories.

But, of course, all of this innovation does not mean that the old Web 1.0 has been swept away and replaced by the shiny new Web 2.0; a great many sites in the style of Web 1.0 continue to exist. Indeed, the site of my own organization, the Council of Archives New Brunswick,[3] is an old-style, read-only Web 1.0 site. We invite feedback through a form on the site and through email, but we do not have facilities for public interaction on the site itself. While it would be possible to add such features, I feel that the site's target users are best served by having it remain a place to get information rather than a place to provide it. On the other hand, it has been said, "Nobody hangs around in the 'publish and browse' Internet [of Web 1.0] anymore. Increasingly people prefer to participate in a new generation of user-fabricated communities where users engage and co-create with their peers" (Tapscott and Williams 2006: 38). With more and more people becoming familiar with advanced web functions, this is certainly something to consider; people may well be more inclined to revisit a site to which they can add and to which they feel that they are useful contributors.

Which style should a virtual exhibit follow, then? Should it be a more didactic Web 1.0 site which provides information, or should it be a more freewheeling Web 2.0 site with a greater focus on interaction and user participation? As with so many questions about virtual exhibits, the answer can only be that it depends on the plan and goals for the site. It is true that some users will inevitably misuse Web 2.0 functionality, posting spam messages and obscenities, but such messages can be deleted by staff. A Web 2.0 site is not a democracy, allowing uncontrolled freedom of expression to all; it is a benevolent dictatorship, welcoming user input but providing no guarantee that objectionable content will not be removed. Still, a Web 2.0 site will be more work than a Web 1.0 site in that it will require monitoring. If part of the goal of your exhibit is to gain information from your users, for instance by having them identify unknown people in photographs, it would probably be best and easiest to allow them to post directly to the site. For a site whose purpose is to present information rather than to request it and for an understaffed and overworked institution, it may be best and easiest not to include such functionality. For all its benefits, Web 2.0 necessarily involves giving up more of your time in monitoring the site and some amount of control over the site's contents.

We have — and will probably always have — more control over paper than bits. In some ways, that is a good thing. We must never forget that the world of bits is still an uncertain one: digital preservation is a great deal of work and can be very expensive, files can become corrupted, servers can go down, computer viruses can strike, file formats can become obsolete, not all users will be able to access all online files (for reasons of incompatible hardware/software or simply because they lack computer or Internet access or are uncomfortable with computers), it is unlikely that the fabled day will ever come when everything is online, and at any rate there are sufficient differences between the physical object and its virtual "ghost" to make reference to the paper original a continuing necessity. Whatever may happen in the world of bits, we know that the world of atoms is fairly stable. The great benefit of paper-based documents — both written documents and photographs — is that they do not require mechanical intervention to use them. All of the information contained within them is available to the naked eye. Barring catastrophe, the originals of all our collections — at least those that weren't born digital — will be there in our archives, waiting to perform the tasks that only they, and not their digital ghosts, can do. These are all reasons to go forward into the digital universe with our eyes open, to enjoy it and to use it as best we can, including making virtual exhibits, while continuing to love paper, as I do, for its own sake.

So what does all of this mean for the small archives hoping to create a virtual exhibit? The process can seem daunting, but it is not that difficult to produce an exhibit which will be of value to its audience. But it is vital to examine closely the goals of the virtual exhibit. Each virtual exhibit is an entry into the competition between bits and atoms, between the virtual and the physical. Its goals should take this competition into account. At best, perhaps we can use both virtual and physical exhibits to begin a collaboration, rather than a competition, between these two worlds.

Notes

1. Briefly, Zipf's Law states that the frequency of use of any item is inversely proportional to its rank on a table of frequency; in other words, the most frequently used item will be used twice as often as the second most frequently used item, which in turn will be used twice as often as the fourth most frequently used item, and so forth (Adamic).
2. The pros and cons of tagging, as well as some of the controls which might usefully be applied to the process, are well laid out in a *D-Lib Magazine* article, "Folksonomies: Tidying Up Tags?" (Guy and Tomplin 2006), which I would recommend to any archivist interested in the issue.
3. <canbarchives.ca>.

References

Adamic, Lada A. "Zipf, Power-laws, and Pareto — a ranking tutorial." Available at <http://www.hpl.hp.com/research/idl/papers/ranking/ranking.html> (accessed August 23, 2009).

Association of Research Libraries. 2009. *Special Collections in ARL Libraries: A Discussion Report from the ARL Working Group on Special Collections*. Washington, DC: Association of Research Libraries.

Benjamin, Walter. 1936. "The Work of Art in the Age of Mechanical Reproduction." In Meenakshi Gigi Durham and Douglas Kellner (eds.), *Media and Cultural Studies: Keyworks*. Second edition. Maldon MA: Blackwell Publishing.

Board of Trinity College Dublin. 2004. *The Book of Kells, Trinity College Library Dublin* CD-ROM.

Boosey and Hawkes. 2009. "Dean, Brett: The Lost Art of Letter Writing (2006) 38' for Violin and Orchestra." Available at <http://www.boosey.com/cr/music/Brett-Dean-The-Lost-Art-of-Letter-Writing/51444> (accessed December 1, 2009).

Crawford, Walt. 2001. "Exceptional Institutions: Libraries and the Pareto Principle." *American Libraries* 32, 6: 72–74.

Eisenstein, Elizabeth L. 1983. *The Printing Revolution in Early Modern Europe*. New York:

Cambridge University Press.

Guy, Marieke, and Emma Tomkin. 2006. "Folksonomies: Tidying Up Tags?" Available at <http://www.dlib.org/dlib/january06/guy/01guy.html> (accessed August 23, 2009).

Hurst-Wahl, Jill. 2009a. August 19. "Can You Use Zipf's Law to Determine What to Digitize?" Available at <http://hurstassociates.blogspot.com/2009/08/can-you-use-zipfs-law-to-determine-what.html> (accessed August 23, 2009).

———. 2009b. August 21. "Selection Criteria, Zipf's Law and the Pareto Principle." Available at <http://hurstassociates.blogspot.com/2009/08/selection-criteria-zipfs-law-and-pareto.html> (accessed August 23, 2009).

Lester, Peter. 2006. "Is the Virtual Exhibition the Natural Successor to the Physical?" *Journal of the Society of Archivists* 27, 1: 85-101.

Library and Archives Canada. 2008. "Archival Community Digitization Program (ACDP) Financial Assistance Application Guidelines 2009–2010." Available at <http://www.cdncouncilarchives.ca/ACDP0910/ACDP09-10_Guidelines_EN.pdf> (accessed August 23, 2009).

National Archives. 2009. "Home Page — Your Archives." Available at <http://yourarchives.nationalarchives.gov.uk/index.php?title=Home_page> (accessed August 23, 2009).

National Archives and Records Administration. 2009. "Question: Should We Allow the Public to Tag Descriptions in Our Online Catalog? Why or Why Not?" Available at <http://blogs.archives.gov/online-public-access/?p=49> (accessed August 23, 2009).

Pimm, Bobbie Ann. 2001. "The Lost Art of Letter Writing." Available at <http://www.bobbieann.net/LetterWriting.html> (accessed December 1, 2009).

Plato. 2008. *Phaedrus*. Translated by Benjamin Jowett. Charleston, SC: Forgotten Books.

Starkey, Kathryn. 2004. *Reading the Medieval Book: Word, Image, and Performance in Wolfram von Eschenbach's Willehalm*. Notre Dame, IN: Notre Dame University Press.

Tapscott, Don. 2008. *Grown Up Digital: How the Net Generation Is Changing Your World*. New York: McGraw-Hill.

Tapscott, Don, and Anthony D. Williams. 2006. *Wikinomics: How Mass Collaboration Changes Everything*. New York: Portfolio.

Theimer, Kate M. 2009a. July 27. "Open House at Stanford's Virtual Archives in Second Life." Available at <http://www.archivesnext.com/?p=317> (accessed August 23, 2009).

———. 2009b. July 30. "An Amazing Flickr Success Story: 'Maybe You Found a Photo of Phineas Gage? If So, It Would Be the Only One Known.'" Available at <http://www.archivesnext.com/?p=320> (accessed August 23, 2009).

Thorpe, James. 1976. *Book of Hours: Illuminations by Simon Marmion*. San Marino, CA: Henry E. Huntington Library and Art Gallery.

WikEd. 2009. "Calculators in the Classroom." Available at <http://wik.ed.uiuc.edu/index.php/Calculators_in_the_Classroom> (accessed December 1, 2009).

Wilgus, Jack, and Beverly Wilgus. 2009. "Meet Phineas Gage." Available at <http://brightbytes.com/phineasgage/index.html> (accessed August 23, 2009).

A New Build
Digital Tools for Archives, Commons, and Collaboration

Dean Irvine and Meagan Timney

As the ecologies of archives adapt to the environments of new media, so do the toolkits necessary to create and maintain them. Nowhere has this been more apparent than for the creation of a digital media commons for the Editing Modernism in Canada project (EMiC). Funded by the Social Sciences and Humanities Research Council of Canada's Strategic Knowledge Cluster grant program, EMiC includes over fifty participants, with representatives from regions across Canada and from France, England, Belgium, New Zealand and the United States. EMiC's mandate focuses on collaborative research, networking and training initiatives that contribute to public literary culture and ensure that Canadian modernism becomes an ongoing part of literary discourse in Canada. To this end, our project facilitates collaboration among a transnational network of researchers and institutions to produce new print and digital editions of Canadian modernist texts from the early to mid-twentieth century.

In June 2009, a group of graduate students, postdoctoral fellows and faculty affiliated with EMiC trekked out to the University of Victoria to attend the Digital Humanities Summer Institute (DHSI). There were a dozen of us; some came with computing skills and digital editing projects in the works; others were standing at the bottom of the learning curve staring straight up. Most enrolled in one of the two introductory courses in text encoding or digitization fundamentals. We selected Susan Brown and Stan Ruecker's seminar on Digital Tools for Literary History. They introduced us to a whole range of text-analysis and visualization tools from which we started to pick and choose ones that we thought might be useful for the EMiC kit. These tools have been principally intended for the analysis of text datasets, either simple transcriptions of the kind that one finds on Project Gutenberg or enriched transcriptions marked up in Extensible Mark-up Language (XML). The common denominator is obvious enough: these tools are designed to work with *transcribed* texts. But what if we wanted tools to work with texts rendered as digital images? What if we did not want to read transcribed texts but instead use tools that could read encoded digital images of remediated textual objects? What kinds of tools are being developed for linking marked-up transcriptions to images? How can these tools be employed by scholarly editors?

When we started in 2007 to assemble the people involved in the EMiC project, few of us could have imagined asking — never mind answering — these questions. At best we had thought that some of the more intrepid among us might produce hypertext or hypermedia editions that provided digital facsimiles of manuscript and print materials along with transcribed and encoded texts that we edited. We thought that we would mostly be working in print media, especially since so few of us possessed the coding skills necessary to produce much more than rudimentary electronic editions that did not really do anything more sophisticated than what we already could do in print. Our project funding lasts for seven years, but, absurd as it may seem, we had already started to worry that it might not be long enough for any of us to master the skills we needed. More to the point: the researchers affiliated with the project are, for the most part, humanities scholars who come from institutions without year-round access to the kinds of digital humanities training and expertise available at the University of Victoria, McMaster University or the University of Alberta and elsewhere. If the idea was to train EMiC participants so that they could work on their own or in collaboration with others on digital editions, it became staggeringly obvious that one week a year at DHSI was not going to get many of us very far up the learning curve. Brown and Ruecker already showed us that we did not all need to invent the wheel: that is what tools are for — collaboration. And, given the EMiC community-building mandate, that is exactly what we needed for our project: collaborative editing tools.

Libraries, Archives and Commons

What is EMiC going to feed into these tools? EMiC collaborates with archives and libraries committed to large-scale digitization projects. In partnership with Library and Archives Canada (LAC), EMiC is undertaking the digitization of the LAC's fonds of modernist authors, beginning with the literary papers of P.K. Page (to be followed by those of Elizabeth Smart, F.R. Scott, Marion Dale Scott, Miriam Waddington, Patrick Anderson and John Glassco, among other modernists). This EMiC partner project allows us to link to manuscript and typescript versions of published texts as well as previously unpublished texts, correspondence and other archival materials. With Paul Hjartarson and his cohort of graduate-student collaborators at the University of Alberta, we are also working toward a project that will see the digitization of the Sheila Watson and Wilfred Watson fonds located at archives in Toronto and Edmonton.

None of the materials being processed by the EMiC or its partners has been made available through current mass-digitization projects, including those undertaken by Google Books, Canadiana.org and the Open Content Alliance's Internet Archive. Nor are these texts available in transcription on Project Gutenberg. One of the decisive methodological differences between the digitization and transcription of literary texts under the mandate of these mass-digitization projects and that of EMiC is our attention to the bibliographic and codicological particularities of texts. While the library-driven preservationist program of Canadiana.org — which now includes the digitization of the Canadian Institute for Historical Microreproductions microfiche catalogue and which includes multiple editions of texts — comes closest to the digitization program of EMiC, neither the image quality nor the file formats of any current national or international mass digitization projects is suitable to editorial projects that require high-resolution scans of original materials. Even though mass digitization resources are complementary to the work of producing digital editions and archives, these projects cannot really be expected to meet the particular and specialized requirements of scholarly editors. To take full advantage of the collaborative editing tools under development by EMiC and its partners, and in conjunction with the digitization of archival materials, we assume responsibility for the production and storage of a digital commons which will be accessible to members of the project for their editorial work, to researchers who cannot otherwise consult physical copies and to the general reading public. This is the developmental work that two EMiC postdoctoral fellows (Meagan Timney and Matt Huculak) are in the process of prototyping using Omeka, a platform that supports Dublin Core Metadata.

From these archival and library collections EMiC generates not digital versions of the same but a different kind of repository, a digital commons. Among the key differences between archives and commons are the collective social production and distribution of the resources included in the commons. Rather than an archive (or fonds) of material attributed to a single creator, the commons is collectively produced by and distributed among those who contribute their labour to the project. Material deposited in the EMiC digital commons cannot be restricted for exclusive access or reproduction by one individual scholar; it is available at any time for use by any and all of the project's participants. This notion of a digital commons as a "social product" and as a "source of innovation and creativity" is one key to the conception of the common as variously and expansively defined by Michael Hardt and Antonio Negri (2009: 112). For the authors of the *Empire* (2000), *Multitude* (2004) and *Commonwealth* (2009) trilogy, the common is recognized not just as natural resources but as social phenomena such as "ideas, affects, codes, knowledges, information, and images" (2009: 299). Predicated on the sociality of the common and the production of social goods, the practices of scholarly collaboration undertaken in the creation of the EMiC digital commons are by no means biopolitical in the sense of an anti-capitalist insurrection against biopower — that is, the political subjection of human life by governments that allows for the control of entire populations — as theorized over the past decade by Hardt and Negri in response to and as elaboration on the concepts introduced by Michel Foucault. Materials from the commons may be appropriated and transformed by the labour of project participants to become their intellectual property and, in turn, protected either by copyright or registered under the terms of a Creative Commons licence. While the digitization of printed and archival materials is being undertaken with the permission of authors and their estates, project participants are responsible for securing permissions to reproduce materials from the commons for public dissemination if those materials are not already in the public domain. EMiC's digital commons is not intended to replace the need for critically edited versions of modernist texts, nor is it designed to reproduce texts currently in print; it is, rather, a digital supplement to the corpus of critical editions already in production by EMiC editors and a repository of raw materials for the production of print and digital editions.

Digital Tools

The history of digital text-editing tools dates from the late 1990s. According to our most recent count, there are as many as twenty-eight different tools in various states, some long orphaned and others still at alpha and beta stages. Even narrowing our selection down to tools or collections of tools that allow users to edit or display images within the context of textual environments or editions, there are as many as ten such open-source resources. These range from tools that simply display an image alongside a text to software suites that support the development of complete image-based environments with substantial functionality beyond text-to-image mapping.

A number of projects are in the process of developing tools that point towards an acceptance of collaborative editing as a method of edition production. These tools offer mechanisms for the creation of editions that combine XML/TEI markup, image manipulation and collation, visualization software and knowledge representation. Many rely upon the specifically *social* nature of current web technologies and find their footing in crowd-sourcing as the primary mechanism for markup and annotation. What follows is a non-exhaustive list of some of the current work that has been or is being done in these areas. The tools discussed below fall into one or more of the following categories:

1. Text-based (XML) Markup
2. Image Manipulation, Annotation and Markup

3. Tagging
4. Visualization
5. Aggregators, Collections Builders and Knowledge Repositories

Text-based (XML) Markup Tools

Text-based tools allow for the collaborative markup of documents, most often in XML/TEI. They range from legacy software such as the Analytical System Tools and SGML/XML Integration Applications (Anastasia) and Editing Digital Interactive Texts in an Online Network (EDITION), to more recent projects such as eLaborate, TextGrid and TEXTvre. TextGrid uses a collaborative document markup interface, as well as a project and user management system to facilitate the markup of texts. TEXTvre, which will be modelled on TextGrid, has been described as a "a working exemplar VRE for textual scholarship."

Image Manipulation, Annotation, Markup Tools

Tools in this category aid, primarily, in the analysis and annotation of digital images (sometimes in conjunction with text documents). The Agrippa Files/Virtual Lightbox, a "browser-based Java tool for studying, juxtaposing, comparing, and resizing multiple images as if arranging slides on a 'lightbox,'" serves as a prime example of an image comparison tool (Liu n.d.). The lightbox "workspace" allows the user to study multiple images from William Gibson's *Agrippa (A Book of the Dead)* through a combination of functions, including zoom in and out, increase and decrease contrast, convert images to grayscale, as well as invert images. Beyond image manipulation and comparison, recent tools serve as a link between encoded texts, images of texts and image annotation. The Ajax XML Encoder (AXE) is a web-based tool that facilitates tagging text, video, audio and image files in a collaborative environment. According to the whitepaper, AXE "is a web-based annotation tool capable of identifying 'regions of interest' in video, audio, and image files located anywhere on the Internet, and encoding these regions in an XML file. It can also be used to generate XML documents from texts located on the web." The Edition Production and Presentation Technology (EPPT) editing tools also allow for the integration of images and texts through XML encoding. More recent tools (currently in the process of development) include the Text-Image Linking Environment (TILE) (Reside, Porter and Walsh n.d.) and the updated Image Markup Tool (IMT) (Holmes, Timney, and Joyce n.d.); both projects are partnered with EMiC. The former will offer a web-based platform that will "provide output in TEI (any flavour, including the EpiDoc customization), using facsimile or SVG for the image-linking mechanism, and in the IMT flavour of TEI, as well as in METS" (Reside, Porter and Walsh n.d.). The latter will build on the current iteration of the software to provide a cross-platform desktop application that will encode XML documents based on the TEI P5 schema. The Image Markup Tool will allow for the loading and display of a wide variety of image formats, and some of the basic features of the desktop editor will include syntax highlighting, and colour-coded categories for sorting annotations into groups. EMiC, which will be the flagship for the IMT, will also create a publication platform that will house the editions created using the tool.

Because TILE is being designed to be interoperable with IMT, the key difference being that the former is web-based and the later desktop-based, the EMiC project will be able to take advantage of both web and desktop environments. The obvious advantage of TILE is that it offers an environment for real-time collaborative editing, which is certainly something that EMiC could use to its advantage as a research and pedagogical tool to facilitate long-distance collaborations across our distributed network of researchers and institutions. That TILE is designed to be interoperable with IMT is crucial, since our publication engine will be designed to work interchangeably with both of these web-based and desktop-based tools.

Tagging Tools

Collaborative or social tagging is "the process by which many users add metadata in the form of keywords to shared content" (Golder and Huberman 2006). We now use the term "folksonomy" to describe this type of user-generated cataloguing. The Collaborative Tagging Tool (CATT) aims to build a proof-of-concept, or prototype, for an open-source collaborative tagging environment, with which to "aggregate, link or cross-reference, edit, and share vetted primary documentary texts — along with their scholarly enhancements, analyses, and commentaries, in the form of markup, annotation, keyword tagging, [and] linking." The final product will serve to identify the key needs for such an environment and the use of crowd-source tagging in digital humanities projects.

Visualization Tools

Visualization tools present large amounts of information in graphical format. The collaborative creation of information visualizations will broaden our conceptual understanding of the primary digital object. For the Collaboratory for Humanities, Art, and Technology (CHAT), the primary object comprises a database of popular poetry written between 1700 and 1900, which will be visualized "in various aspects determined through coding as well as data-mining that is both directed by and productive of ontological categories" (Mandell, Gannod and Greenberg n.d.). The poetry visualization tool will encode and visualize the metrical, tropological and phonic systems of poetry through a system including, but not limited to, colour wheels, elocutionary diagrams and word fountains. The Knowledge Cartography project offers "a cartographic approach to the representation of knowledge in its present configurations." According to Quaggiotto (n.d.), the "collaborative ATLAS lets the user list his [sic] bio-bibliographic resources in a shared environment and access them through many different maps and representations. The interface becomes therefore an Atlas of knowledge cartographies, designed to show a complex environment through the overlapping of different images." Also, the Networked Infrastructure for Nineteenth-Century Electronic Scholarship (NINES) game, Ivanhoe, offers a truly collaborative environment (game) that privileges digital visualization as a method of knowledge representation. Ivanhoe is a "formalized digital space where" players, actions, and documents "dynamically interact."[1]

Rather than following past practices of transcribing texts and marking up transcriptions in the creation of electronic texts, EMiC and its partners will pioneer image-based editing, semantic markup, analysis and visualization of texts in a field of emergent practices in digital-humanities scholarship. Instead of producing reading environments based on linear-discursive transcriptions of texts, EMiC will produce, in collaboration with its partners, techniques and technologies for encoding and interpreting the complex relations among large collections of visual and audial objects in non-linear reading environments.[2]

For example, consider the series of textual visualizations by Stefanie Posavec done in collaboration with Greg McInerny of Microsoft Research. They include textual variants among and revisions to six versions of Charles Darwin's *Origin of Species*. Consider also another visualization of the multiple editions of Darwin's *Origin*, "The Preservation of Favoured Traces," by one of the creators of the Processing visualization environment, Ben Fry. The potential of these Origin projects for the kinds of editorial, text-analysis and visualization work that EMiC and its partners are undertaking has only just started to be explored. What these particular projects lack, however, is any significant element of interactivity. It will be invaluable to create interactive visualization tools available to render in ecological structures the relationships among different versions of texts as well as the masses of linear lists of textual variants and revisions that editions typically relegate to the apparatus of the text. That is what these two *Origin* projects already do: they produce aesthetic objects as such, instead of what many consider an unreadable apparatus of textual lists. This represents a major transformation in the way in which editors could imagine constructing the apparatuses of digital editions.

High-performance visualization environments for mass-digitized corpora (e.g., digital books, archives and libraries) are just now emerging as the next evolutionary stage in the technologies and practices of image-based digital editing in the humanities. Recent developments in information-visualization theory and technology are modelled on ecosystems; see, for instance, the

Mandala rich prospect browser developed by Stéfan Sinclair of McMaster University and Stan Ruecker of the University of Alberta.

As emergent practices, these projects have yet to develop fully elaborated technologies and practices of producing image-based editing ecosystems, generating editions and archives as ecological structures and reading the ecologies of archives and editions. If humanities scholars follow the work of the natural sciences in using algorithmic techniques to visualize ways of reading the environment, we can in turn develop technologies in which the environment "reads" text-based visual objects.

Not only can we design and adapt tools to visualize our digital editions, but we can extend the compass of these tools to read across multiple editions and across the whole of our digital commons. Examples of these kinds of analytic tools have been developed as part of the Visible Archive project, designed by Mitchell Whitelaw for the National Archives of Australia. Demonstration videos of the A1 Explorer and the Series Browser are available for viewing, and the programs can be downloaded and launched as Java executable files on the Visible Archive Project Blog.

Aggregators, Collections Builders and Knowledge Repositories

The tools in this final category represent the broader spectrum of collaborative work through their functionality: knowledge aggregation. The NINES Collex, an "online collecting and authoring space in which researchers can create and publish their own work," facilitates the collection of digital "exhibits" and allows scholars to search and collect materials from across a broad number of peer-reviewed federated digital sites. These exhibits can be tagged, analyzed and annotated, as well as shared with other users. Like Collex, the Canadiana.org Digital Collections Builder (DCB) aggregates larger collections. It includes support for multiple collections, XML import and export functions, Dublin Core, MODS and EAD meta-data, and the OAI meta-data harvesting protocol. While Collex and the DCB serve to aggregate larger collections, tools such as Just in Time Research (JiTR) (Rockwell n.d.) and the Transliteracies' Research-oriented Social Environment Tools (Rose n.d.) offer knowledge creation tools that take advantage of Web 2.0 technologies. JiTR allows for "mashups" of online texts through the creation of collections that can be organized, labelled, annotated and shared among users; this is one of a suite of tools developed under the umbrella of TAPoRware at the Universities of Alberta and McMaster. Rose Tools is "a research-oriented social environment for tracking and integrating relations between authors and documents in a combined 'social-document graph.' It allows users to learn about an author or idea from the evolving relationships between people-and-documents, people-and-people, and documents-and-documents." Digital humanists are also taking advantage of specifically tailored knowledge management systems, especially Omeka. The Public Knowledge Project, with both its Open Journal Systems and Open Monograph Press (see, for example, its section on exhibitions and archives, with catalogue and monograph capacities), will privilege knowledge sharing and collaborative knowledge creation. Most recently, EEBO Interactions offers "social networking for Early English Books Online," in which users can create knowledge repositories, ask questions, annotate and collaborate.

Many of the tools mentioned above, and especially those mentioned in the final category, draw upon the meme of the *social* web, including media sharing, blogs, bibliographic and bookmarking tools, aggregators, collaborative (scholarly) editing, project management software and wide-scope content management systems. With a project such as EMiC the social web is constituted in one way by the collaborations among its participants in the production of its digital commons. That our editorial project has now evolved from its own network of collaboration to a much larger-scale partnership with the Canadian Writing Research Collaboratory (CWRC), directed by Susan Brown at the Universities of Guelph and Alberta, speaks to the extensibility of EMiC's commons. EMiC is helping with the development of CWRC's innovative web-based service-oriented platform that features (a) a database to house born-digital and newly digitized materials (Online Research Canada, ORCA) marked up with meta-data (indices, annotations, cross-references) and (b) a toolkit for facilitating new collaborative modes of scholarly writing and editing online. EMiC's involvement in the creation of the CWRC toolkit hinges on our project's partnerships with the IMT and TILE markup tools and their interoperability in web-based and desktop-based environments. Porting an image-based markup tool such as TILE into the CWRC toolkit and by making it interoperable with the desktop-based IMT and the EMiC publication engine will exponentially increase the functionality and sociality of the platform for the scholarly editing community and, consequently, the productivity of our project.

The principal reason why we know any of this is because we have become part of the digital humanities community that makes the pilgrimage each June to attend the Digital Humanities Summer Institute. There we met and started to collaborate with digital humanists who have been instrumental in the transformation of EMiC from a predominantly print-based editing project to one that is increasingly invested in the implementation of computing tools in the construction of online reading environments. As EMiC and its partner projects work toward the digitization of Canadian modernist literary archives and the formation of our digital commons, it will be crucial for us to continue our training as digital humanists so that our collaborations with libraries and archives across Canada continue to produce raw resources for the production of new editions.

Notes

1. For more on Ivanhoe, see the special issue of *Text Technology* 12.2 (2003), especially Nowviskie, who writes that Ivanhoe is a "game that takes full advantage of the graphic and interactive possibilities of a spatialized and subjective discourse field, and which permits players to navigate, contribute, and respond to changes in that field using the same visual vocabulary that constitutes it."
2. EMiC's development of visualization tools will be undertaken in partnership and collaboration with programmers affiliated with the Canadian Writing Research Collaboratory at the University of Alberta, as well as Digital Infrastructure group of the Network in Canadian History and the Environment (NiCHE) at the University of Western Ontario.

References

"Ajax XML Encoder" [AXE]. n.d. <http://mith.info/AXE/>.
"Analytical System Tools and SGML/XML Integration Applications" [Anastasia]. n.d. ITSEE, University of Birmingham. <http://www.sd-editions.com/anastasia/index.html>.
"Collaborative Tagging Tool" [CATT]. n.d. <http://text.etl.luc.edu/HRIT_CaTT/index.php>.
"Collex." n.d. <http://www.collex.org/>.
"Digital Collections Builder" [DCB]. n.d. <http://dcb-gcn.canadiana.org/>.
"Early English Books Online Interactions." n.d. <http://eebo-interactions.chadwyck.com/guidelines>.
"Editing Digital Interactive Texts in an Online Network" [EDITION]. n.d. <http://www.sd-editions.com/EDITION/>.
"Editing Modernism in Canada" [EMiC]. n.d. <http://editingmodernism.ca>.
"eLaborate." n.d. Huygens Instituut KNAW, Royal Netherlands Academy of Arts and Sciences. <http://www.e-laborate.nl/en/>.
Fry, Ben. n.d. "The Preservation of Favoured Traces." <http://benfry.com/traces/>.
Golder, Scott and Bernardo A. Huberman. 2006. "Usage Patterns of Collaborative Tagging Systems." *Journal of Information Science* 32.2: 198–208.
Hardt, Michael and Antonio Negri. 2009. *Commonwealth*. Boston: Harvard University Press.
Holmes, Martin, Michael Joyce, and Meagan Timney. n.d. "Image Markup Tool" [IMT]. <http://tapor.uvic.ca/~mholmes/image_markup/>.
Irvine, Dean. 2006. "Editing Archives] Archiving Editions." *Journal of Canadian Studies* 40.2 (Spring): 183–211.
"Ivanhoe." n.d. Networked Infrastructure for Nineteenth-Century Electronic Scholarship. <http://www.nines.org/about/software/ivanhoe.html>.
Liu, Alan. n.d. "The Agrippa Files/Virtual Lightbox." University of California, Santa Barbara. <http://agrippa.english.ucsb.edu/>.
Mandell, Laura, Jerry Gannod, and Ira Greenberg. n.d. "Collaboratory for Humanities, Art, and Technology." <http://www.orgs.muohio.edu/chat/index.html>.

Nowviskie, Bethany. 2003. "Subjectivity in the Ivanhoe Game: Visual and Computational Strategies." *Text Technology* 12.2.

"Omeka." n.d. Center for History and New Media. George Mason University. <http://omeka.org/>.

Posavec, Stefanie, and Greg McInerny. n.d. "Entangled Word Bank." <http://www.itsbeenreal.co.uk/>.

"Public Knowledge Project." n.d. <http://pkp.sfu.ca>.

Quaggiotto, Marco. n.d. "Knowledge Cartography." <http://www.knowledgecartography.org/>.

Reside, Doug, Dot Porter, and John A. Walsh. n.d. "Text-Image Linking Environment" [TILE]. <http://mith.info/tile/>.

Rockwell, Geoffrey. n.d. "Just in Time Research" [JiTR]. <http://ra.tapor.ualberta.ca/~jitr/>.

Rose Tools. n.d. "Research-oriented Social Environment." <http://transliteracies.english.ucsb.edu/category/research-project/rose>.

Sheila Watson Archives. n.d. Kelly Library, St. Michael's College, University of Toronto. <http://www.utoronto.ca/stmikes/kelly/special_collections/sw_finding/index.html>.

Sinclair, Stéfan, and Stan Ruecker. n.d. "Mandala." <http://mandala.humviz.org/>.

"TextGrid." n.d. <http://www.textgrid.de/>.

"TEXTvre." n.d. <http://textvre.cerch.kcl.ac.uk/>.

Whitelaw, Mitchell. n.d. "The Visible Archive." <http://visiblearchive.blogspot.com/>.

Wilfred Watson Fonds. n.d. University of Alberta Archives. <http://archive1.macs.ualberta.ca/FindingAids/WilfredWatson/WWatson.html>.

Respect des fonds and the Digital Page

Emily Ballantyne and Zailig Pollock

Like many such projects conceived in the digital age, *The Collected Works of P.K. Page* is a many-headed monster — combining text and image, markup and stylesheet, database and edition, page and screen — which would literally have been inconceivable a few years ago. But like most of its predecessors in pre-digital days gone by, the *Collected Works* has at its foundation that somewhat mysterious and highly contested archival entity, the fonds. Although the authors of this essay are utterly dependent in their research on the work of archivists, our firsthand knowledge of archival theory, especially with regards to fonds, is relatively limited. In the comments that follow we write very much from the point of view of eavesdroppers on the conversations of our colleagues in the archival world, conversations which have stimulated us to think more deeply about what we are trying to accomplish as editors and, especially, as digital editors.[1] We have been especially struck by the work of Terry Cook on the concept of the fonds in a post-custodial, postmodernist era, and by his observation that "behind the text there are many other texts being concealed" (2001: 27). In the spirit of this proposition we conduct, in what follows, a kind of archaeological investigation of the *Collected Works* as a series of layered texts, each of which conceals as much as it reveals. If the *Collected Works* is to succeed in its aims, its designers and developers, as well as its users, must have a well-informed respect for each of these layers, beginning at the beginning with *respect des fonds*.

Respect des fonds

The fonds is the "entire body of records of an organization, family, or individual that have been created and accumulated as the result of an organic process reflecting the functions of the creator" and is "the chief Archive Unit" in most modern archival systems (Jenkinson 1966: 101). The fonds is distinguished from the collection: "the first is the result of a natural process, the product of clearly defined activities, whereas the latter is an artificial construct" (Couture and Rousseau 1987: 161; cited in Cook 1992: 27). Collections follow some "'ideological' concept of sorting… without preserving [individual items] in the context of their discovery" (Duchein 1983: 65). It is the emphasis on the context, on the "dirt" and "scribbles" which "archivists need to be careful not to clean up… [or] erase" (Millar 2002: 15) that distinguishes the fonds from collection; collections are "anti-fonds" (Cook 1992: 27). This distinction is crucial to an understanding of the relationship between archives and so-called digital archives, which are, are, in effect, anti-archives.

Respect des fonds, a formulation of French archival theorists of the early nineteenth century, consists of respect for provenance ("keeping archival records clearly segregated by their office of creation and accumulation") and for original order ("the logical structure and internal arrangement of the records of each creator") (Cook 1992: 25). But although this is "the basic principle of archival science" (Duchein 1983: 64), the concepts of *respect des fonds* and of the fonds itself have been the subject of much debate in the post-custodial era "with its conceptual paradigm of logical or virtual realities" (Cook 1992: 26). From this perspective, the fonds is as much a "conceptual principle" as a "physical entity" (Cook 1992: 33). Citing Lyotard's definition of postmodernism as "incredulity towards meta-narratives," Cook argues:

> Archival principles, such as *respect des fonds*, are… historically contingent, not universal or absolute. The record is now perceived as… reflecting the narrative intentions of its author and the receptivity of its contemporary audience as much as its actual informational content…. This does not mean that nothing is true, or that everything is adrift in a sea of meaningless relativism…. It does mean that meaning is *relative* to the context of the creation of the record, that behind the text there are many other texts being concealed. (2001: 27)

Cook's emphasis on the "narrative intentions" of fonds is particularly relevant to personal fonds. Catherine Hobbs has explored the particular challenges of personal fonds in a number of essays, where she argues for "embracing storytelling rather than narrow records-as-evidence formulations" (2009: 218). Personal fonds always constitute narratives:

> The creation of the individual life is also the struggle with the self, with seeking consistency and meaning in a life sometimes chaotic and idiosyncratic. Certain viewpoints, relationships, and activities therefore get filtered out, suppressed, marginalized, or, conversely, highlighted, made central, part of the meaningful narrative of self-definition that human psychology demands of the self. There is a tension in the writing of private documents between controlled "public" action and the unconscious seeping of the "inner" personal-

ity onto the page.... In my view, the personal record should not be treated as if it contained only straightforward evidence, but as the site of multiple constructs — of a person upholding and struggling with ideas, of self and of others, while simultaneously contradicting, convincing, and contriving. (Hobbs 2001: 131–32)

In a self-reflective note, Hobbs comments on this passage: "It may be that, in dealing with poets and fiction writers, I see this tension between intention and the unintentional/revision and spontaneous expression in a more extreme way, since these creators create with a conscious mind to creating" (132, note 7). Be that as it may, these comments seem to us particularly germane to P.K. Page's narrative of self-definition in her fonds.

In her published work, P.K. Page (1916–2010) was deeply concerned with constructing a "meaningful narrative of self-definition," especially in the latter half of her long creative life. The collection of largely autobiographical essays, *The Filled Pen*, which appeared in 2007, was her own initiative, and, as the editor of the volume (Pollock, co-author of this essay) can testify, she played a very active role at all stages of selection, organization and annotation. Her long autobiographical poem, *Hand Luggage* (2006), on which she was working at the same time as *The Filled Pen* (2007), is another deliberate attempt to shape the public narrative of her life and work. Finally, and, most significantly for this essay, *Brazilian Journal* (1987), published some thirty years after the events it recounts, comprises a retrospective reworking of the narrative of her crucial years in Brazil, as recorded in the diaries of that period, recently added to the Page fonds. In this last instance, as well as in many others, it is only when we turn to the fonds in a spirit of respect for its provenance and its original order, that we can see clear evidence of the "tension in the writing of private documents between controlled 'public' action and the unconscious seeping of the 'inner' personality onto the page."

All of the records currently in the fonds were deposited by Page herself. Although there has been some reordering of the material for the convenience of researchers, Page's own filing system has been respected as much as possible; any reorganization that has taken place is indicated in "Notes on the Arrangement of the P.K. Page Fonds" by Ann Goddard, archivist at the time the fonds was accessioned.[2] It seems fair to assume, then, that the narrative embedded in the Page fonds has been shaped at least as much by Page herself as by the interventions of the archivists which are discussed in the "Notes" and that if, "behind the text there are many other texts being concealed," Page herself has played a major role in this process.

As Hobbs notes, "It is through a long acquaintance with the records... that the characteristic habits of mind and rationales become palpable strains of the individual's self-narrative" (2001: 132). What strains of Page's self-narrative are palpable in these records? There are two "concealed" texts that stand out, precisely because of the almost total lack of evidence of their existence in the fonds. These are the records of the two crucial experiences of the first half and the second half of Page's life, respectively: her passionate love affair with F.R. Scott and her engagement with Sufism. Of the over 2500 files which comprise the fonds, there is one file of correspondence with Scott (container 8, file 60). This file dates from many years after the end of the affair, and there are no direct references to the relationship in it or anywhere else in the fonds. The situation is similar with respect to Sufism. There are three pages of general comments on Sufism in one file (container 69, file 4), but nothing to indicate how central Sufism was to Page in her later years.

In the fonds, then, there is evidence that Page has retrospectively "filtered out, suppressed, marginalized" major aspects of her personal life, in the interests of creating a certain kind of public narrative. Scholars may make what they will of these key exclusions from the Page fonds, but they are clearly as much a part of Page's self-narrative as what she chooses to reveal.

The foregoing account of Page's self-narrative is somewhat misleading since it ignores the fact that the Page fonds was not static but evolved during her lifetime. The nature of this evolution is suggested by the history of the acquisition of the fonds, beginning in 1984. After a series of smaller acquisitions in the following decades, the fonds doubled in size in 2008, going from 58 containers to 116. Much of the material in this latest accession has been recently created, but a substantial proportion dates back to well before the time of the initial accession, in some cases back to the 1940s. Why had Page waited so long before deciding to deposit this material in the archives? The question arises as well with a group of files which the authors are currently in the process of preparing for the archives. We first became aware that there might be a substantial amount of material that Page had held back when Pollock received the following email from her on September 1, 2009:

> Let me not give you a fit but I have a lot of old or half written poems still in my files here. I've just never managed to send them to the archives. What would you like me to do with them? Send them to you? If I send them to the archives it's unlikely they'll get round to them in a hurry. Or shall I just scrap them?

"Or shall I just scrap them" is a typically mischievous example of Page's tendency to pull the leg of her editor, whom she sometimes viewed as a harmless drudge whose obsession with minutiae amused her no end. As she knew he would, Pollock immediately responded with a vigorously worded message instructing her to scrap nothing but to send the material to him without delay. When we went through the material in the files, we began to suspect that her explanation that she "just never managed to send them to the archives" did not tell the whole story, since some of it is quite different from anything in the archives — more personal. There are some very frank love poems for example, and one that seems to deal with a miscarriage. In other words, we suspect that Page's decision to finally add this material to her fonds, fifty years or more after some of it was written, reflects a shift in her self-narrative, a shift which is already hinted at in the mass of documents which she deposited in the archives in 2008. Much of that material, like the files sent to Pollock, is of a very personal nature: most notably the diaries from her years in Australia, Brazil and Mexico. Our sense is that after having crafted and published her narrative of self-definition in *The Filled Pen* and *Hand Luggage* — after having set the public record straight — she now felt easier about allowing public access to private material even if it complicated this public narrative.

A further complication is that in June of 2010, approximately six months after Page's death, Pollock, in his role as her literary executor, went through material still remaining in Page's home, with the assistance of Ballantyne, to prepare it for deposit in the archives. It is clear from Page's correspondence with Pollock that she intended at least some of this material for the archives. For example, two days before her death, she asked him to recommend a student at the University of Victoria to help her prepare material for the archives (email, January 12, 2010). However, the fact remains that the final decision concerning this material, unlike all the other material in the fonds, will have been made by Page's literary executor, without her specific authorization. This, of course, raises an interesting question of provenance. Geoffrey Yeo argues that "the fonds grows during the lifetime of its creator, but its conceptual boundaries are stabilized when the creator dies" (2009: 60). However the Page fonds will have been "stabilized" after Page's death, not "when the creator dies." This is not a trivial point, since the new material will substantially alter Page's self-narrative currently implicit in the fonds. Although we were unable to find anything on Page's relationship with F.R. Scott — we must assume that Page destroyed any such material if it ever existed — we found a wealth of material on Sufism, in the form of correspondence, study notes, diary entries and so forth. Pollock has decided that this material should be added to the fonds, even though Page had chosen to hold it back in the past. Would Page have approved of this decision, which Pollock made in light of his understanding of the ongoing evolution of the fonds? We will never know. But it is crucial for researchers to be aware of the unique provenance of the latest additions to the fonds and what it tells us of their relationship to Page's self-narrative.

What relevance does this all have to the *Collected Works of P.K. Page*? At the heart of the *Collected Works* will be a database whose data will be largely (though not exclusively) drawn from the Page fonds. The relationship between the *Collected Works* and the fonds will need to be carefully thought through and articulated. In particular, the editors will need to be cognizant of the fact that although the database has its ultimate origins in the fonds, it is not simply a digital version of it; that just as the fonds is "the site of multiple constructs," to recall Hobbs's phrase, so is the database — and the difference between them is at least as important as their similarity.

One of the most extended recent discussions of the relationship between database and fonds is "Database as Genre: The Epic Transformation of Archives" by Ed Folsom, co-editor of the online Walt Whitman Archive, and a series of responses to this essay, most notably by Jerome McGann, creator of the online Rossetti Archive. The word "fonds," which is not in common use by American archivists, does not actually appear in Folsom's essay, but for the purposes of our discussion Folsom's use of the term "archives" is the equivalent of "fonds" when he is referring to the actual physical records maintained by archivists rather than the representation of those records in electronic databases.

As the phrase "epic transformation" in his title suggests, Folsom sees databases as a new and improved version of archives, doing what archives do but doing it better. He does grudgingly grant archives a special role because of their "physicality," but the purple and strangely sexualized prose in which he characterizes this role, suggests fetishization rather than respect:

> Archives are all about physicality, and such is their charm and their allure for researchers.... Real archives may well produce something pathological in the researcher.... They contain not only the records of a period but its artefacts as well, their dust the debris of toxins and chemicals and disease that went into making the paper and glue and inks, that went into processing the animal skins that wrap the books we open and, in the dusty light, read and inhale. When we emerge from an archive, we are physically and mentally altered. We emerge with notes — photocopies if we're allowed — but never with the archive, which remains behind.... Many of our books (and virtually all our biographies) are tales of archive survival. (Folsom 2007: 1577)

Against this feminized image of the archives as a fallen woman, threatening to allure us with her toxic charms in the dusty light, Folsom posits the database as a decidedly masculine "epic" hero ever on the "attack" (1574) and engaged in "battle" (1575). For Folsom this battle is "between database and narrative" (1575): both archives and databases are non-narrative, but databases alone recognize narrative for what it really is, the "enemy" who must be defeated (1577). What Folsom's rather overheated rhetoric conceals is the fact that databases, like archives, inevitably embody narratives.

As McGann points out in his reply to Folsom, there are three ways in which any database will be shaped by the narrative intentions of its creators. First, the records in a database consist of fields, which must be defined before the database can be constructed: "databases and all digital instruments require the most severe kinds of categorical forms. The power of database — of digital instruments in general — rests in its ability to draw sharp, disambiguated distinctions" (2007: 1590). In the very act of choosing these fields, making these distinctions, the creator of the database is imposing a set of values which inevitably reflect a particular narrative about the records. There is a precise parallel to the "mediation by the archivist in setting standards,… imposing orders of arrangement, creating logical descriptions" (Cook 2001: 27). Second, databases require an interface: "No database can function without a user interface, and in the case of cultural materials the interface is an especially crucial element of these kinds of digital instruments" (McGann 2007: 1588). But every interface "embeds, implicitly and explicitly, many kinds of hierarchical and narrativized organizations" (1588). Finally, databases do not contain documents: they contain *representations* of documents, which are inevitably selective: "We are interested in documentary evidence because it encodes, however cryptically at times, the evidence of the agents who were involved in making and transmitting the document.… Scholars… reconstruct a complex documentary record of textual makings and remakings, in which their own scholarly investments directly participate" (1592).

This final point is worth pursuing since it is so often elided in discussions of databases and of digital representation in general. Folsom, himself, is repeatedly guilty of this elision. For example, he argues that the superiority of databases over archives is that they provide much greater access: "Where before scholars had to travel to many individual archives to examine Whitman's poetry manuscripts, they are now able to access all those manuscripts from a single integrated finding guide" (1575). While the ability to access digital representation of manuscripts is a great boon to scholars, the only way to access the manuscripts themselves is to visit the archives in which they are stored. This is not a trivial point. Folsom's argument implies that a complete digital reproduction of every significant feature of a document is possible. Once this has been accomplished, scholars have "access" to the thing itself, or as close to it as to make no difference. Therefore there is no longer any reason to visit the archives apart from their somewhat louche "charm and allure." Folsom's "desire for completeness" (1575), for "the unknown hovering beyond the brink of what can be classified and enumerated" (Hayles 2007: 1607), is reminiscent of Del Jordan's "crazy" ambition in *Lives of Girls and Women*:

> I would try to make lists. A list of all the stores and businesses going up and down the main street and who owned them, a list of family

> names, names on the tombstones in the Cemetery and any inscriptions underneath. A list of the titles of movies that played at the Lyceum Theatre from 1938 to 1950, roughly speaking. Names on the Cenotaph (more for the First World War than for the second). Names of the streets and the pattern they lay in.
>
> The hope of accuracy we bring to such tasks is crazy, heartbreaking.
>
> And no list could hold what I wanted, for what I wanted was every last thing, every layer of speech and thought, stroke of light on bark or walls, every smell, pothole, pain, crack, delusion, held still and held together-radiant, everlasting. (Munro 1983: 210)

It recalls as well, the equally crazy ambition of Borges's Chinese College of Cartographers who

> evolved a Map of the Empire that was of the same Scale as the Empire and that coincided with it point for point. Less attentive to the Study of Cartography, succeeding Generations came to judge a map of such Magnitude cumbersome, and, not without Irreverence, they abandoned it to the Rigours of Sun and Rain. In the western Deserts, tattered Fragments of the Map are still to be found, Sheltering an occasional Beast or Beggar; in the whole Nation, no other relic is left of the Discipline of Geography. (141)

If it is true that the map is not the territory, it is equally true that the database is not the archive. Folsom is the first to admit that his use of the term "archive" is very loose indeed: "We call it *The Walt Whitman Archive*, but that's a metaphor, meant to evoke the dust and texture and smell of the old books and documents themselves. The Whitman archive is, in actuality or virtuality, a database"[3] (Folsom 2007: 1575). But this metaphor conceals the fact that rather than being a new and improved version of the archive for the postmodern age, the "digital archive" is conceptually no different from the premodern archive-as-collection, superseded in archival theory and practice nearly two centuries ago by the archives-as-fonds. Prior to this,

> neither administrators nor archivists felt the slightest scruple, in any country, to separate and dispose of documents of the same origin, or to regroup and mix documents of different origins whenever the need made itself felt for practical or intellectual reasons of convenience. (Duchein 1983: 65)

Collections, especially in digital form, are of course extremely useful, but they serve a very different function from fonds, which contain real physical objects with spatial and, by implication, temporal relationships to each other — all of which are inevitably lost in a digital representation, which must by its nature be highly selective in how it represents what it chooses to represent. It is only by keeping the distinction between database and fonds absolutely clear that we can acknowledge what each conceals and reveals. How, then, do we intend to do this in the Digital Page?

The Digital Page: Edition and Database

The Digital Page, which is currently in the planning stage, will consist of two distinct layers, the edition and the database. The edition, which is the first thing the user will see, acts as a portal to the database, or rather to the interface that provides access to the database. For simplicity's sake, in what follows we focus on the poems, though the Digital Page will also contain prose fiction and nonfiction, memoirs, children's literature, paintings and correspondence.

The first layer will consist of an edited version of each work included in the *Collected Works* arranged in three ways: alphabetically, chronologically and by collection. Users will also be able to further narrow their choices to published poems, collected and/or uncollected, and unpublished poems, complete and/or incomplete. The works will be presented in the form of clean reading-texts, edited, emended and regularized according to criteria laid out by the editors. The date of initial composition of the work and of the copy-text being used in the edition will be indicated, and, where appropriate, there will be links to lists of regularizations (in conformance with the "house style" of the edition) and emendations, and to explanatory notes. Each work will also be linked to the second layer of the Digital Page, the database. The database will consist of transcriptions and digitized images of every *text* which constitutes the *work*, to use a distinction commonly drawn in genetic textual theory (McGann 2006), making up a complete representation of the genesis of the text from beginning to end.[4]

The most important component of the interface will be a table of texts organized chronologically by date of composition, each entry of which will be linked to a timeline for the Digital Page as a whole, incorporating information about Page's life, every work included in the Digital Page and Page's milieu. This timeline will initially be based on the research of Sandra Djwa, Page's biographer, but it will grow along with the Digital Page and will be an invaluable resource for exploring the genesis and socialization of all of Page's texts.

Each entry in the table will also be linked to a genetic transcription whose aim is to provide a narrative of the process of revision, not a verbal description of the appearance of the page (see Pollock 1993). The genetic transcription will be encoded in machine-readable TEI, the most widely used

XML-based markup system for literary texts. It will be up to the editors to choose from among the hundreds of tags available to highlight the structural and semantic aspects of the texts which they consider most important. These will include a tag set currently being developed for genetic editions by the TEI Consortium. XSLT style sheets will be designed by the editors to generate not only the genetic transcription in which the process of revision is fully displayed, but also a clean reading-text, displaying only final revisions. A case study presenting an example of the genetic and reading-texts of a single poem is discussed below.

Where there are variant texts, each point where a text varies from others in the series will be marked as a "revision site" (Bryant 2002: 97–8). Each revision site will be linked to a listing of all the variant versions of this site, enabling the user to see at a glance the genesis of the passage in question, without the need for complex coded representations as, for example, in the Hans Gabler print edition of Joyce's *Ulysses*.

Each genetic transcription will also be linked to an image of the page or pages on which it is based, either printed texts or texts in the Page fonds. Pollock is currently supervising the selection and page identification of the literary manuscripts in the Page fonds, as the first stage of a joint project of Library and Archives Canada and EMiC (Editing Modernism in Canada) to digitize all modernist literary manuscripts in the archives. To link transcription to image we will be using the Image Markup Tool currently being developed at the University of Victoria in collaboration with the *Collected Works*. This tool will allow users to link passages in the transcription to the relevant sections of the image and to associate them with a wide range of annotations.

In addition to the table of texts there will be the following, where appropriate:

- a history and physical description of the texts;
- a collation check, allowing the user to call up an image of any two versions side by side; and
- audio and video recordings.

The editors of the *Collected Works* will, of course, strive to put forward as complete and balanced a presentation of Page's artistic achievement as possible. But as should be clear from this very brief overview of its structure and interface, the Digital Page, to recall McGann's statement, "embeds, implicitly and explicitly, many kinds of hierarchical and narrativized organizations." Inevitably the editors' choice of texts to include will reflect their sense of what is artistically and biographically significant, and their focus on genesis and social context will highlight certain aspects of the texts at the expense of others. In any case, the narrativized organizations embedded in the Digital

Page will be very different indeed from Page's own self-narrative embedded in her fonds. It will be the responsibility of the editors to keep this distinction as clear as possible: by discussing it explicitly; by providing access to images of each text in the context of the original order of the fonds; and by never using the term "digital archives."

At the very top layer of the *Collected Works of P.K. Page* is a series of printed volumes, to be published by the Porcupine's Quill, which will complement the Digital Page. These inexpensive and attractively designed volumes will be intended for general readers and students, rather than as primary scholarly resources. They will not contain an extensive textual apparatus, which will be more effectively presented digitally, but they will contain critical introductions, in which the editors present their own narratives concerning the works and glosses which will highlight aspects of the works which the editors consider important. And in keeping with the genetic basis of the *Collected Works*, the works will be arranged chronologically, rather than, say, by published collections or by theme. In this way, one final layer of narrative will be added. To paraphrase the passage quoted earlier from Cook, in the interplay of narratives which make up the *Collected Works of P.K. Page*, meaning is relative to the context of the creation of the edition as well as of the fonds on which it is based.

A Case Study

The following case study, based on an edition by Ballantyne of a file of Brazilian poems in the Page fonds, is intended to provide a practical demonstration, within the limits of print, of the genetic/social editing approach of the editors of the Digital Page and of the *respect des fonds*, which is central to their practice.

During Page's time in Brazil (1957–1959), she came up against an unexpected obstacle: "Brazil pelted with images" (2007: 35). Page's pen could no longer keep up with the stimuli overwhelming her. She chooses a violent metaphor, of being "pelted," to describe her relationship with her new environment. Brazil physically abuses her with its magnitude and its power over her creative psyche. Simultaneously, Page loses her grasp on a previously mastered medium: poetry. An established poet, Page had published widely in both *Preview* and *Contemporary Verse*. She had also published a novel, *The Sun and the Moon*, in 1944, under the pseudonym Judith Cape, as well as a book of poetry, *As Ten as Twenty*, in 1946. Her poetry had gained widespread acclaim after her second collection, *The Metal and the Flower*, won the Governor General's Award for Poetry in 1954. Page was set up for a career as a successful poet. And then, with a quick succession of "pelts," this proven poet was left voiceless by the Brazilian landscape.

"Natural History Museum" is located in a file folder prepared by Page (container 27, file 5) containing material from the transitional months of 1957 that mark the beginning of her time in Brazil and her abandonment of poetry for painting. The twenty-seven poems, most of them fragmentary and all unpublished, shed new light on Page's process, both of losing old identities and gaining new ones. As she moves from fragment to fragment, Page continually re-examines her sense of self in relation to the immensely attractive but alien environment in which she finds herself.

The edition which Ballantyne has produced of the entire file traces a narrative of Page's movement into poetic silence. Its genetic framework emphasizes the process of composition: intervening blanks and deletions create a more complete picture of Page's struggle against silence. Unlike the *Brazilian Journal*, these poems have not been retrospectively "worked up" as part of the social process of negotiation leading to a published work; they therefore offer a more direct access to the Brazilian period as it was initially experienced, illuminating and complementing the *Brazilian Journal* as well as the many paintings coming out of this period. However useful the *Brazilian Journal* is in recreating the process of Page's turn to visual media, it is a highly wrought text, purposefully created for publication. It presents a controlled portrait of Page's poetic silence as a stage in a more or less seamless transition to her emergence as a visual artist.

The poems in the fonds reveal a less smooth and much more painful process. They allow us to re-evaluate the tensions underplayed in the *Brazilian Journal*, shifting the focus back to the original moment of poetic crisis. The poems are transitional, moving constantly between positive negotiations with the environment and an intensive exclusion from it. They are largely dark, negative, isolating, while at the same time their colours and images are vivid, bright, often breath-taking. In the rawness of their form, their almost obsessive reworking of a small number of basic motifs and their restlessly shifting attitudes to these motifs, they illustrate the "tension in the writing of private documents between controlled 'public' action and the unconscious seeping of the 'inner' personality onto the page," to refer back to the previously cited passage from Hobbs.

This tension is particularly evident in one of the dominant motifs of the poems: animals as viewed objects, forcibly relocated to foreign zoos and museum spaces. Implicitly comparing herself to these creatures forced into an oppressive environment they cannot escape, Page scrutinizes her own relationship to the Brazilian landscape. The largest group of fragments exploring this concept centre on a poem which, in its most complete version, is entitled "Natural History Museum." Each of the fragments in this group presents animals on display, either imprisoned or dead. The fragments vary widely, in length and in degree of completion, although certain motifs recur throughout. Page focuses on animals unfamiliar to someone of her Canadian background: sloths, marmosets, tropical birds and golden spiders. There is a clear juxtaposition between containing and controlling the foreign, and the spectacular display of oddity and difference. In the Digital Page the genesis of the various fragmentary versions of "Natural History Museum" will be traced through the use of hyperlinked "revision sites" as noted above. However, since this form of presentation is difficult to reproduce in print form, in what follows we focus on only one, substantially revised, version of the work. Before doing so, we provide a few words about the method of transcription used.

Each line of the genetic text is numbered. Variants of a line are arranged chronologically and identified by a number in parentheses following the line number: e.g., 2(1), 2(2), 2(3) indicates 3 successive revisions of line 2. The last in a series of revisions is the one that appears in the clean reading-text.

When a revision extends over more than one line, the lines making up each version are grouped together: e.g., 1(1), 2(1), 3(1) followed by 1(2), 2(2), 3(2). "Nested" revisions occur when there are line-level changes within grouped changes. For example, if, in the middle of a three-line group, Page decided to change a word in one of the lines, the change needs to be marked within the larger group. Such changes are marked by letters, to keep them separate from the larger group changes. For example, 1(2), 2(2a), 2(2b), 3(2) means that Page replaced an initial group of lines with a second group — lines 1–3 — but within this group she further revised line 2.

To make the revised portions of the text stand out from the rest of the text, revisions are marked using angled brackets <> and square brackets []. The angled brackets mark a passage that was altered *from* by addition, deletion or relocation. The square brackets mark the passage that it was altered *to*. Thus, <x> means that x was changed to something, and [y] means that something was changed to y. The smallest unit marked off by the brackets is a single word or punctuation mark. Every set of angled brackets has a corresponding set of square brackets. That is, every change "from" must be completed by a change "to."

In the Digital Page, the following colour coding is used:

- <> and [] are red
- The parenthetical numbering of the lines in a series of revisions are red, except for the final one, making it immediately obvious where a series of revisions ends. The line with the parenthetical number in black is the one that appears in the clean text.
- For revisions of layout, indications of the aspect of layout being revised — line spacing, indentation, forced line breaks, etc. — are indicated in blue.

Genetic Text

1	I saw a baleen in his bones
2	long-fingered hands close to his ribs
3	I saw him swim in the air like a stone
4	I saw through the holes in his face
5(1)	<>
6(1)	astraddle a painted tree in the crook of its wood
7(1a)	the sloths<> in <their> loofah fur
7(1b)	the sloths <[cretinous faced> suited] in[] loofah fur
7(1c)	the sloths [union] suited in loofah fur
8(1)	the zebras long spine
9(1)	& the coral snake pretty in brine—
10(1a)	<in> a coffin of glass all the pretty singers
10(1b)	<>a coffin of glass all the pretty singers
11(1)	<dead on sticks, heads cocked>
5(2)	[in a coffin of glass all the pretty singers]
6(2)	[dead on sticks, heads cocked]
7(2)	astraddle a painted tree in the crook of its wood
8(2)	the sloths union suited in loofah fur
9(2)	the zebras long spine
10(2)	& the coral snake pretty in brine—
11(2)	[]
11	A gold splotched spider guards /his golden web—
12	the marmosets grow stamens out of their ears
13	& their fingers feel like the stems of /violets
14(1)	yet a face the size of the top point of <inner> thumb
14(2)	yet a face the size of the top point of [your] thumb
15	looks at you with frustration

This text, like many others in the file, consists of an apparently random list of images. Lists and the unsatisfactoriness of lists are repeated motifs throughout the file, which ends with a list of birds of Brazil and their characteristics. At one point Page writes:

> the list is still a list
> not dissimilar to the laundry slip

Her poetic silence looms in front of her, demanding a new aesthetic response to the world she is confronted with. Eventually, Page's struggles to make sense of a landscape that both excites and terrifies her lead to a stronger relationship to the purely visual image and to her temporary abandonment of poetry for painting. But for now she is still groping for some overarching pattern to embody her conflicted response to Brazil. Her discontent with her attempts to impose form on her experience is reflected in the large number of fragmentary versions of "Natural History Museum," as well as in the internal revisions to the text reprinted here, which suggests an indeterminacy in her attitude to the animals she describes.

The sloths, for example, are described in several different ways. The image begins quite stripped down: "The sloths in their loofah fur" (7[1a]). Page then elaborates, describing the sloths as "cretinous faced" and "suited in loofah fur" (7[1b]). Her sympathies appear confused. While she anthropomorphizes the sloths, marking their fur as clothing, her intention is unclear: does the adjective "cretinous" suggest that the sloths are a dwarfed and mentally challenged kin, somehow comparable to herself, or is this term simply derogatory, ridiculing and distancing the sloths? Page finally chooses to remove the reference all together. Her final revision is to make the sloths "union suited in loofah fur" (7[1c]). Since a union suit, a one-piece set of long underwear, is worn only by human beings, this somewhat comical image retains the humanization of the sloth which was suggested by "cretinous" but does so without the negative connotations of the earlier version. And perhaps one may even see in the word "union" a further suggestion of the link between human and animal. By emphasizing qualities in the sloth that are positive and human-like, Page balances her own negative reactions to the more absurd features of the creatures she presents with the sympathetic tone, which the catalogue as a whole seems to reflect. It is only in the genetic version of the text that Page's conflicted attitude to the sloths, and by extension to her own situation, can be fully appreciated.

The stanza describing the sloths begins, in the final version:

> in a coffin of glass all the pretty singers
> dead on sticks, heads cocked
> astraddle a painted tree in the crook of its wood

Originally, though, these lines came later. By moving them forward in revision, Page emphasizes the darkness of what is being described: the museum as a showcase of death and suffering. The animals' environment is an artificial structure that is a caricature of their natural environment.

The poem ends with an account of animals which are not actually dead and mounted, but which are entrapped and consumed with impotent "frustration," the word with which the poem ends. The revision in line 14

            14(1)   yet a face the size of the top point of <inner> thumb
            14(2)   yet a face the size of the top point of [your] thumb

serves to strengthen the parallel between human and animal, observer and observed, a parallel Page draws in a passage in the *Brazilian Journal* which is clearly related to these lines: "The impotence of a marmoset in a rage, pitting itself against me, its fingers like the stems of violets, unable to break the skin of my hand. How quickly one learns about scale with a marmoset for comparison" (37). In the futility with which the marmosets fight to break out of their confines, Page recognizes her own troubled relationship to Brazil.

Without the genetic transcription of the poem, the narrative of Page's struggle with her Brazilian experience, which is evident in the process of revision, is unavailable. It is concealed in the clean reading-text, which presents only the final stage of revision. The genetic text is meant to work in conversation with the reading-text, providing various sites for interpreting meaning.

Reading-text

             Natural History Museum
             I saw a baleen in his bones
             long-fingered hands close to his ribs
             I saw him swim in the air like a stone
             I saw through the holes in his face
      5   in a coffin of glass all the pretty singers
             dead on sticks, heads cocked
             astraddle a painted tree in the crook of its wood
             the sloths union suited in loofah fur
             the zebra's long spine
      10   and the coral snake pretty in brine—
             A gold splotched spider guards his golden web—
             the marmosets grow stamens out of their ears
             and their fingers feel like the stems of violets
             yet a face the size of the top point of your thumb
      15   looks at you with frustration

This reading-text of the poem, not the genetic text, is, of course, the one that will appear in the print edition of the poems. And although the Digital Page will trace the genesis of the poem, the poem's relationship to all of the other Brazilian material in the file and in the fonds as a whole will be difficult to unravel from the elaborate digital showcase we are lovingly constructing to display Page's work. Showcase or coffin? Perhaps in this context the poem can best be read as the poet's warning about constricting her work in a "coffin of glass," which can offer only an artificial representation of it, much as a digital "archive" can offer only an artificial representation of the archive itself. In other words, perhaps "Natural History Museum" is a prophetic message to the Digital Page: *respect des fonds*.

Notes

1. We would like especially to acknowledge the help provided by Catherine Hobbs, Literary Archivist (English), Library and Archives Canada.
2. The Page fonds provides less information on provenance and original order than more recently accessioned fonds. The Alistair MacLeod fonds is a case in point. The finding aid for this fonds presents a much fuller description of the original state of the records it contains and a detailed rationale for whatever reorganization was deemed necessary. In the case of the Page fonds, there is a one-page "Notes on the Arrangement of the P.K. Page Fonds"; for the MacLeod fonds there is an "Arrangement Note" followed by detailed comments on virtually every folder in the fonds. For a discussion of *respect des fonds* and the MacLeod fonds, see Hobbs 2009: 228–29.
3. Folsom is not alone in his loose usage of the term "archives." For example, in *The Fluid Text*, John Bryant uses the terms "electronic archive" and "electronic library" interchangeably (149) as equivalents of "electronic database." It may seem pedantic to criticize the loose use of the term "archives" by Folsom and Bryant, for, as Marlene Manoff points out, the term "has become a kind of loose signifier for a disparate set of concepts" (10). However, in discussions of the differences between digital representations of physical objects and the objects themselves, it makes sense to use different terms to register the differences.
4. We are currently defining the "end" as the last authorized text, but there is no reason why this could not eventually be extended to include adaptations of Page's works after her death. See Bryant's discussion of "cultural revision" (108–11).

References

Borges, Jorge Luis, and Adolfo Bioy Casares. 1972. "Of Exactitude in Science." *A Universal History of Infamy*. Trans. Norman Thomas di Giovanni. Harmondsworth: Penguin.

Bryant, John. 2002. *The Fluid Text: A Theory of Revision and Editing for Book and Screen*. Ann Arbor, MI: University of Michigan Press.

Cook, Terry. 1992. "The Concept of the Archival Fonds in the Post-Custodial Era: Theory, Problems and Solutions." *Archivaria* [Online] 35.

———. 2002. "Fashionable Nonsense or Professional Rebirth: Postmodernism and the Practice of Archives." *Archivaria* [Online] 51.

Couture, Carol, and Jean-Yves Rousseau. 1987. *The Life of a Document: A Global Approach to Archives and Records Management*. Translated by David Homel. Montreal: Véhicule Press.

Duchein, Michel. 1983. "Theoretical Principles and Practical Problems of *Respect des fonds* in Archival Science." *Archivaria* [Online] 16.

Folsom, Ed. 2007. "Database as Genre: The Epic Transformation of Archives." *PMLA* (October) 122.5: 1571–79.

Hayles, N. Katherine. 2007. "Narrative and Database: Natural Symbionts." *PMLA* (October) 122.5: 1603–08.

Hobbs, Catherine. 2001. "The Character of Personal Archives: Reflections on the Value of Records of Individuals." *Archivaria* [Online] 52.

———. 2009. "Reenvisioning the Personal: Reframing Traces of Individual Life." In Terry Eastwood and Heather MacNeil (eds.), *Currents of Archival Thinking*. Santa Barbara, CA: Libraries Unlimited.

Jenkinson, Hilary. 1966. *A Manual of Archive Administration*. London: Percy Lund, Humphries.

Joyce, James. *Ulysses*. 1984. Edited Hans Gabler. New York: Garland.

Library and Archives Canada. 2006. Finding Aid: Alistair Macleod fonds LMS-0263 Acc. 2005-01, March.

———. Finding Aid: P.K. Page fonds R2411-0-2-E.

Manoff, Marlene. 2004. "Theories of the Archive from Across the Disciplines." *Portal: Libraries and the Academy* 4: 9–25.

McGann, Jerome. 2007. "Database, Interface, and Archival Fever." *PMLA* (October) 122.5: 1580–92.

———. 2006. "From Text to Work: Digital Tools and the Emergence of the Social Text." *Text: An Interdisciplinary Annual of Textual Studies* 16: 49–62.

Millar, Laura. 2002. "The Death of the Fonds and the Resurrection of Provenance: Archival Context in Space and Time." *Archivaria* [Online] 53.

Munro, Alice. 1983. *Lives of Girls and Women*. New York: New American Library.

Page, P.K. 1987. *Brazilian Journal*. Toronto: Lester & Orpen Dennys.

———. 2006. *Hand Luggage: A Memoir in Verse*. Erin, ON: Porcupine's Quill.

———. 2007. *The Filled Pen: Selected Non-Fiction of P.K.* Zailig Pollock, editor. Toronto: University of Toronto Press.

Pearce-Moses, Richard. 2005. *A Glossary of Archival and Records Terminology* [Online].

Pollock, Zailig. 1993. "The Editor as Storyteller." *Challenges, Projects, Texts: Canadian Editing. Twenty-fifth Conference on Editorial Problems,* University of Toronto, November 17–18, 1989. AMS P: 54–69.

Yeo, Geoffrey. 2009. "Custodial History, Provenance, and the Description of Personal Records." *Libraries & the Cultural Record: Exploring the History of Collections of Recorded Knowledge* 44 (1): 50–64.

Section IV

Case Studies in Archives and the Canadian Narrative

Titling *He Drown She in the Sea*
The Archive as Paratext

Jocelyn Hallman

The literary archive is a space of transaction. In this space, the producers, arrangers, describers and interpreters of texts exchange ideas about words and collaborate in the production of literary meaning. As they perform these tasks, authors, archivists and readers transact in an archival space that is at once physical and discursive. The materiality of the archive works alongside the discourses that surround and inhabit it, and the spatial relationship between the physical and the discursive within this space is characterized by extremes of proximity and distance to a literary text. Both types of archival content assist literary scholars in the explication of texts and the circumstances surrounding their production, but many scholars also approach the archive as a revelatory space, one in which the intentions, opinions, personalities or biographical details of an author surface and engender more accurate or "authentic" readings of her texts.

  This reading strategy flattens the complex spatial and discursive potential of the archive. The term "fonds" calls to mind the word "fount," and many readers are indeed quick to consider the archive as a fount, a source, of information about an author and his or her intentions. This leads to readings of texts that are more informed, certainly, but that may ignore the ways in which the archive as a space of transaction also acts paratextually. Like the archive, the paratext is characterized by a complex relationship between physical and discursive space, and both aid us in contextualizing the contents of literary works while simultaneously reflecting many of their narrative and thematic concerns. We might think of the archive as a paratext, a space of transaction that acts as a mediating device, rather than as a fount of authorial revelation. Paratexts are characterized spatially by their proximity or distance from the words on a page; the title of a literary work, for example, mediates our reading of that work from a close physical relationship to the text, but the archive constitutes a more discursive paratext, one physically distant from the literary work. Nevertheless, both types of transactional spaces facilitate the construction of narratives and of interpretive contexts for reading, and they also reflect the thematic qualities of literature that take issues of place and space in particular as central concerns. This conception of the archive as paratext is particularly useful in studies of literary and academic narratives that interrogate the relationships between physical and discursive place.

Gérard Genette, who has produced sustained critical attention to the paratext, characterizes it as a "threshold of interpretation," an entry point into a text that governs its reception and interpretation. This threshold is "a zone not only of transition but also of *transaction*" (1997: 2, emphasis in original) between an author and the interpreter of his or her work, and Genette identifies spatial distinctions between transactional zones — between paratexts — based on their physical closeness to that work. He explains that a paratext "necessarily has a *location* that can be situated in relation to the location of the text itself: around the text and either within the same volume or at a... distance" (4, emphasis in original). Those that are part of the physical work — titles, title pages, dedications, prefaces, forewords and afterwords, to name a few — comprise what Genette calls the "peritext." The peritext, which is characterized by its proximity to the work, is spatially distinct from the ""epitext": "any paratextual element not materially appended to the text within the same volume but circulating, as it were, freely, in a virtually limitless physical and social space" (344). These spaces are mostly discursive; they contain journals and diaries, for example, along with media references to authors or texts, writers' professional or personal communications, and both implicit and explicit contextual information (5). The epitext is more fluid than the peritext; it "consists of a group of discourses whose function is not always basically paratextual (that is, to present and comment on the text), whereas the more or less unchanging regime of the peritext is constitutively and exclusively inseparable from its paratextual function" (345). Titles, for instance, are almost always appended to texts — few titles exist without a textual object to describe — and almost always serve to present and comment on them. They therefore reside in the space of the peritext. An archive, on the other hand, does not exist solely as an appendage to literary texts; it has many functions and contributes to various discourses, only one of which is literary interpretation. It might therefore be considered to reside and act in the spatial category of epitext.

Genette simplifies the relationship between these two paratextual categories by proposing a formula: "*peritext + epitext = paratext*" (5, emphasis in original). However, reading the archive as epitext reveals a more fraught relationship between peritext and epitext than this equation suggests. As we read, we negotiate the spaces between the distant archive and the various peritexts of a literary work, and in some cases this archival material mediates not only our interpretation of the text itself, but of its peritexts as well. For example, materials such as drafts, manuscripts, letters and private journals might shed light on the way in which a work's title was conceived and constructed, offering the reader not an absolute truth about authorial intention, but rather a secondary lens through which to read the peritext appended to the work. At a simple constitutive level, it may be true that peritext + epitext = paratext, but in the process of navigating between these spatially distinct categories, we also see epitext — what Genette describes as the "fringe of the fringe" (346) — altering peritext, working inwards from the outer discursive fringe to mediate the inner, materially connected threshold of interpretation. Reading the archive as paratext, then, requires that we attempt to map the spatial and discursive levels of paratext, questioning how they function in relationship to one another and in relationship to the literary work.

This process of sorting out the relationships between levels of paratextual mediation resembles the creation of narratives that take place and space, centre and margins, and the nature of interpretation itself as central concerns. The term "narratives" here includes both the literary and, perhaps more provisionally, the processes of archival acquisition, selection and appraisal. What parallels might we draw between the paratextual character of archives, the thematic concerns of the literature they mediate, and the very process of (and narratives created by) archival construction?

Such questions are particularly apt for interrogating the archive in the Canadian context, characterized as it is by a history of immigration, vast distances between urban centres and rural margins, and its preoccupation with its own marginalization in relation to Britain and the United States. A substantial amount of recent Canadian archival literature has focused on the archiving of historically marginalized literatures: those of women, immigrants, Aboriginal peoples and queer writers.[1] This work, and its counterparts in literary criticism, tends to deal, even if implicitly, with the mapping of physical and discursive spaces in relation to authors, their archives and their narratives.

These issues come to a head in a consideration of the Shani Mootoo fonds, located in the Special Collections at the Simon Fraser University Library in Burnaby, British Columbia. The fonds was acquired from Mootoo by Eric Swanick, Head of Special Collections, in 2005, and it contains 2.65 metres of textual records, including typescripts, drafts and working papers for all of her published works; drafts of unpublished works; professional correspondence; lecture notes; notebooks and sketchbooks; interviews; book reviews and announcements. It also contains material related to Mootoo's art works, including video and audio cassettes, photographs, slides and paintings (Burger 2008: 2). Swanick's acquisition of the material was driven by his collection development strategy, which focused on acquiring the manuscripts of younger, emerging Canadian literary talent. At the time, Mootoo was living in Vancouver, and while York University also expressed interest in her papers, she opted to place them at Simon Fraser (Swanick 2010). Mootoo selected an institution near Vancouver for the placement of her papers, and the archivist in turn placed Mootoo in a Canadian literary collection. Mootoo, a woman of Indian ancestry, born in Ireland and raised in Trinidad, has studied, taught, resided, and written professionally in Canada for many years. Many of her essays, short stories, poems and novels take as their subject the experience of the transnational subject, and this, alongside Mootoo's sexuality and issues of queer identity in her literature, has been the focus of much of the literary criticism on her work produced thus far. However, this placement of her literary papers, both by Mootoo and by Swanick, in a Canadian institution — and a West Coast institution specifically — has not been addressed in this criticism. What narratives about place, nationality and the Canadian literary canon are shaped and retold by this archival process? How do both the archival process and the resultant fonds, acting as paratexts, disrupt or otherwise intervene in the academic and literary discourses that repeatedly place Mootoo and her work into categories of Caribbeanness, of Indianness and of diasporic literature? And how is this archival intervention into the placement of Mootoo's work reflected in or troubled by her own fictional narratives?

Among the drafts and working papers of her fictional works, the fonds at Simon Fraser University contains numerous drafts of Mootoo's novel *He Drown She in the Sea* and several files worth of correspondence related to its genesis and publication between the author, her agent and her editors at Grove/Atlantic and McClelland and Stewart. Like most of Mootoo's works, *He Drown She* interrogates issues of diaspora, ethnicity, the complex connections between geographical and imagined spaces, and the location of the individual within social and cultural place. It is set partially on the fictional Caribbean island of Guanagaspar, partially in Vancouver and Squamish, British Columbia, and partially in a dreamscape of ambiguous location. Issues surrounding geographical, imaginary and social place in the novel reflect those surrounding the placement of Mootoo's papers at Simon Fraser University; the ways in which Mootoo is placed geographically and discursively in the academic and literary fields are as problematic as the placement of characters in the novel, especially its central characters, Harry and Rose. In *He Drown She*, Harry, the son of a fisherman and a maid, falls in love with Rose, the daughter of his mother's employer. What appears to be a simple case of love unrequited on the bases of race and social and economic class is in fact more tenuous; Harry occupies various places — in his coastal village, at the school he attends with Rose and, later, in his own home in British Columbia — and so does Rose. Both inhabit several physical, cultural and narrative spaces as the novel takes the reader from the present day to the characters' childhoods in Guanagaspar, and at no point does either fully comprehend the ways in which these places shape their relationships or the drowning that Rose will later stage. This drowning becomes the crux upon which both the narrative and Mootoo's placing of the characters hinges.

It also shapes the titling of the novel. However, an investigation of the Mootoo fonds reveals that Mootoo and her editors used various titles during the writing process to reflect different elements of Harry and Rose's traversal of geographic and social spaces. This illuminates not exclusively what Mootoo's intentions were as a writer but also how readers of *He Drown She* might interpret the narrative. As epitext, the archive thus shapes our understanding of both the novel's peritext and its contents. The series of drafts and working papers for the novel and the correspondence between Mootoo and her agent and editors reveal that during its five-year production, *He Drown She* went by at least thirteen titles — most of which concern specific moments in Harry and Rose's narratives and evoke particular locales. For a user of the archive, this range of titles triggers the reader to imagine Mootoo's constructions of place differently, altering the interpretive process. The archive contextualizes the title, brings its own paratextuality into focus and reflects the pull between proximity and distance that characterizes the novel — and its own paratextual relationships. Here we do not see a simple equation of peritext + epitext = paratext; instead, the epitext shapes our reading of the peritext, altering its role in interpretation.

Collectively, the Mootoo fonds narrates the creative progress of *He Drown She* — especially its titling — and yet there are many holes in this narrative. The chronology of titles is not clear, and because the manuscripts and correspondence in the collection were received by Simon Fraser University in indeterminate order, the timeline has been pieced together by the archivist. Mootoo's correspondence with her agent Maria Massie, her editor Elisabeth Schmitz at Grove/Atlantic and her editors Jennifer Lambert and Ellen Seligman at McClelland and Stewart takes the form of printed emails which reveal that some of the novel's working titles were suggested by Mootoo herself, while others were offered up by the editors. However, these emails too construct a patchy narrative, as they appear to have been printed only sporadically, and so the origin of each title is uncertain. The thirteen titles used from 1999–2005 include *Presents of an Egg-Man*; *Roshini* (evidently an early name for the character Rose); *Harry the Egg-Man*; *A Guanagaspar Story*; *The Servant's Son*; *The Summer of Rose*; *Rip Tide*; *The Merciful Sea*; *A House by the Sea*; *Rhododendron in the Sea*; *The Boy from Timbano Trace*; *The Fish Vase*; *Once, a Raleigh Man*; *The Woman Who Gave Love Birds for a Present*; and finally, *He Drown She in the Sea*.

Genette's discussion of the title as paratext emphasizes its position as a constructed object, one that eludes definition and requires special critical attention. It is part of the peritext and is not only located in close proximity to the text, but it is often placed and repeated in various locales on the body of the book itself — the front and back covers, the spine, title page, half title page, running heads and dust jacket, among others (1997: 66), acting as a tool for the author and publisher to reaffirm the novel's thematic concerns. In the McClelland and Stewart 2005 hardcover edition of *He Drown She in the Sea*, the title is located in various places: the spine, the dust jacket, on three title pages and in the running head. The archive does not reveal who first suggested the title — Mootoo or one of her editors — but it was a very late addition to the work. The title acknowledges a moment in the novel when Piyari, Rose's servant, tells Harry what she suspects Rose's husband to have done to his wife, and the act of titling the novel grants thematic significance to this moment. On the spine, dust jacket and title pages of the novel, the title is presented typographically with the word *Drown* dropped a half-line below the rest of the text, perhaps spatially representing Rose's submersion. However, on the dust jacket colour is also used to distinguish the words of the title; *He*, *She* and *Sea* are depicted in orange, while the remainder of the words, including *Drown*, are in blue. This visual grouping of rhyming words, paired with the off-set and thematically crucial word *Drown*, offers a structured representation of Piyari's narration and conveys the lyrical quality of her English. Here, we see the peritext performing multiple possible functions at the levels of both plot and language — typographically, visually and thematically.

In this McClelland and Stewart edition, the title is also accompanied by a small graphic icon of a palm tree and a thatch-roofed house. This image, which appears on one of the novel's title pages, also appears throughout the novel alongside the titles of chapters primarily set in the Caribbean. For those set in Canada, another icon appears, featuring a large evergreen tree in the foreground, several smaller evergreen and deciduous trees and a craggy mountain range in the background. Genette uses the term "intertitles" to describe chapter headings, and in this case Mootoo's intertitles are both textual and graphical. The textual components often hint at the contents of each individual chapter, further delineating Mootoo's thematic aims, but sometimes they are ambiguous — like the dream sequences that frame the narrative — and sometimes they are identical to the titles that Mootoo or one of her editors proposed for the novel, such as "A House by the Sea" or "Rip Tide." Each textual intertitle is also accompanied by one of the place-specific icons. Certainly, the graphical and stylistic features of *He Drown She*'s titling and intertitling were probably not designed by Mootoo at all; as Genette explains, an author is only ever a co-sender of a peritext's illocutionary message, sharing responsibility for its construction and meaning with publishers, editors, and the public (1997: 74). For this reason, the title and other peritexts of a novel should always be understood as products of the editorial, publishing and critical processes. In addition, Genette explains that any written or verbal commentaries on a novel's title, including authorial complaints or comments about it and lists of titles conceived but not chosen for a book (66–68), should be considered as valuable as paratextual material as the published title. Most importantly for our discussion, Genette emphasizes the paratextual role of lists of working titles: "they stress various thematic aspects unavoidably sacrificed by the definitive title" and are "a wholly legitimate part" of the paratext of a given work (66). As components of the epitext, they have the power to change our interpretation of the peritext as we interact with the materials in the discursive and physical space of the archive. The definitive title of *He Drown She*, drawn from Piyari's narrative of Rose's supposed death, causes the "unavoidable sacrifice" of other thematic aspects of the novel. However, the full range of titles revealed by the archive reflects Mootoo's concern with a broad spectrum of issues, many of which are similar to those associated with the spatial distribution of paratexts: questions of where thresholds of interpretation lie, the proximity and distance of mediating factors in a narrative, and the connections between social, cultural and discursive "place."

Not surprisingly, these issues of place and proximity are prominent in critical treatments of *He Drown She in the Sea*. None of these treatments discuss Mootoo's archival material at Simon Fraser University, but almost all consider the role of place — and the role of the novel's title — in the narrative. Diana Brydon, for example, reads Mootoo's novel in the context of "emotional geographies," interrogating the way in which it adopts narrative strategies "to chart reimagined relations to place," namely through reconstructions of its characters' pasts (2006: 95). The novel remaps the "emotional geography" of the Trinidadian diaspora as well as the subjectivities of its members — African and Indian — questioning what kinds of narrative structures might be adequate for addressing both issues of diasporic subjectivity and the relationship between Canada and the Caribbean (94–95). For Brydon, two of the novel's formal features contribute to this questioning: its title and its oneiric narrative frame. The dream, she claims, "connects the emotional seascape of exile in Vancouver to the emotional landscape of [Harry's] island home in Guanagaspar" and "remaps the meaning of the novel's title, 'he drown she in the sea,' from its narrative of male violence against women to provide instead an image of freedom for both 'he' and 'she' through immersion in a desire that proves stronger than social convention" (97–98). This immersion is represented in the novel's closing dream sequence, in which Harry and Rose cling to the ocean floor until two tidal waves, "like opposing armies," crash above them (Mootoo 2005: 346). The two waves might stand in for any number of opposing forces in the novel, but the dream suggests that Harry and Rose have survived the push and pull of conflicting conventions, social classes and places, and even of conflicting histories. Brydon suggests that Piyari's narrative represents a form of unofficial history, "history from below," a version of events that allows Rose and Harry to make their escape undetected, fully aware of their own role in shaping this version of history (108).

In a similar way, the archive — a collection of cultural histories and narratives, in addition to an author's papers — contributes to the shaping of different versions of history, both "official" and "unofficial." However, it frequently relies on the classification of texts and writers, and Mootoo herself is often discursively located as a Trinidadian writer rather than a Canadian writer, which creates a specific version of her history and influences readings of her texts. Brydon troubles this process, writing, "Neither Trinidad, Canada, nor diaspora provides an adequate context for understanding these fictions. Rather than seek a suitable classification to pin them down, this essay reads them as implicitly in dialogue with a range of theoretical discussions located at the cusp between feminism, postcolonial, and globalization studies" (94). As a paratextual aid to reading, the archive also acts as a "dialogue" between author, publisher, editor, archivist, scholar, reader and any number of agents involved in textual production, but the placement of a manuscript collection also depends upon classification along institutional and cultural lines. We ought to consider the ways in which the archive might truly act as a "dialogue" or as a mediator between various theoretical discussions, especially when it comes to issues of place and ethnicity.

The vocabulary of mapping, place and ethnicity has entered into many theoretical discussions of the archive. Pamela Banting, for example, conceives of the archive as a site in which archivists and scholars exercise interpretive control over materials, causing a dispersal of authorial control; the author is said to disappear in the archive, which paradoxically "poses as a collection while creating in actuality a diaspora" (1986–87: 120). Brydon conceives of *He Drown She* as a "dialogue," which, like "diaspora," is a dynamic term, suggesting that both literature and literary archiving are in motion, in process, as sites of intersection and of scattering. Place and placement are central to both terms, as a dialogue relies on the proximity of two subjects; a diaspora, on the other hand, is characterized by the separation or distance between them. Here, again, we see the spatial relationship between the near and the far, the peritext and the epitext, and the ways in which paratextual information is gathered in the body of a text and scattered in wider discursive contexts such as the archive. However, unlike Genette, Banting sees the archive as residing in the present, with no possibility of the author having preceded it (121). The issue of presentness in the archive, as opposed to history, and the use of dynamic vocabulary such as "dialogue" and "diaspora" to describe the archive lead to questions about how the archive functions in connection to a text such as *He Drown She*. Place and placement are crucial here: does it matter that Mootoo's fonds were placed at a Vancouver institution, in a Canadian collection, rather than in a Trinidadian or diasporic context; does this alter or insert the archive into the dialogue about an author and her "place" according to literary discourse?

The language used by Catherine Hobbs of Library and Archives Canada also brings such considerations to bear on the nature of archival work. Hobbs speaks of the archivist's responsibility to source as many records of an "event" from as many different "locations" as possible; ideally, the archivist should "render the full dynamics of the literary scene, its archival record, and the scholarly analysis of that record" (Hobbs 2006: 112). This involves following literary scholarship on the authors whose collections reside in the archive, but also endeavouring "to map developments more widely, seeing and predicting the effects of the ever-changing literary scene on writers," working through acquisitions strategies akin to processes of "mapping" and "reorienting" (112). This language of process, of mapping, of geographic creation and classification in the archive emphasizes the dynamic nature of archiving and its reliance on specific events, but it also speaks to the archival creation of a version of events, much like the unofficial version of Rose's "death" that Piyari narrates in *He Drown She*. Hobbs's vocabulary here frames the archive as a dynamic space, capable of both raising and addressing questions of place and placement.

This dynamism also characterizes the language of archiving used by Michael O'Driscoll and Edward Bishop. They use the term "intervening archive" to describe the function they see archives performing in the circuit of textual production and reception, and this is closely related to the mediating function of the paratext. They contend that archives function not as merely physical institutional caches but as "spatial-temporal processes" and that the importance of archiving lies not solely in its physicality but in its construction as "an historical, material, and ideological set of practices" (2004: 3). Like the ideas of "dialogue" and "diaspora," these conceptions of archives and archiving emphasize movement and change; as both a "process" and a "practice," the archive is concerned with — and archiving always resides in — the present. Archiving might be described as intervening, O'Driscoll and Bishop claim, because it "operates as a form of mediation at every stage of cultural circulation" (4) — it intervenes into the ways in which we understand, write about and teach cultural history, much like Genette's conception of the paratext. However, this conception of the archive as in motion, in the present, intervening, also relates to its mediation of cultural memory. Brydon reminds us that *He Drown She* is characterized by its "invocations of diasporic memories and longings" (94), and like Hobbs, O'Driscoll and Bishop refer to the archive as an "event" in which the archival transfer of private history and narrative into the public sphere resembles the revelation of an anecdote, which facilitates both the remembering and forgetting of information. This remembering and forgetting — "moments of enunciation, iteration, inscription, or performance" (O'Driscoll and Bishop 2004: 3) through which such narratives become public and enter into cultural memory — characterize not only the archive but the major thematic concerns of *He Drown She* as well. The processes of both telling and archiving stories alter the retention or the loss of cultural memory, particularly for diasporic communities. This is important because it links the generic qualities of the archive with Mootoo's novel on a thematic level — *He Drown She* is also concerned with movement, diaspora, the past and the present, and language, both dialogue and narrative. In this link, O'Driscoll and Bishop's intervening archive can be said to mediate not only textual circulation but also literary interpretation.

Because of the seemingly personal nature of Mootoo's concerns with diaspora, migration and language, many readings of Mootoo's works, and of *He Drown She in the Sea* specifically, link her transnational and specifically Trinidadian identities to those of her characters. Even asking what place Mootoo's fonds occupies in a Canadian institution — how this placement intervenes into discourse surrounding the author and her work — suggests that her connection to Trinidad is somehow troubled by the archival process, in turn implying that she possesses an "authentic" or "essential" connection to Trinidad to begin with. However, the connections between place and identity are fraught both for Mootoo as a writer and in the narrative of *He Drown She*.

Mootoo complicates notions of place and belonging, for example, in her nonfiction prose. "On Becoming an Indian Starboy" is a semi-autobiographical essay in which Mootoo recounts the stories of her own ancestors and of the transformations in identity she has undergone as an immigrant to Canada. In this essay, she speaks of "breaking" and "braiding" identities together as a transnational subject, and she describes this activity as "the way of the Trinidadian living abroad" (2008: 83). As a "tourist" in her own country, not fully conforming to social conventions and strictures, Mootoo claims to have met her "First Real Indian" only after having travelled to Canada (87). Several other moments of national and cultural ambiguity also followed her immigration; she tells the tale of a visit to Trinidad shortly after gaining Canadian citizenship and discovering that she has lost her status as Trinidadian; having been born in Ireland and having acquired a Canadian passport, she had unwittingly relinquished her citizenship (88-9). In another anecdote, Mootoo recalls being "claimed" as Irish at a writers' festival in Ottawa; despite considering her Irish birth to be an inconvenient footnote to her own life, she is discursively located in a given literary context, challenging her sense of cultural identity (89). The purpose of Mootoo's anecdotes does not seem to be the retention of any definable identity, however. She tells these stories in order to trouble the very concepts of place and belonging, of ethnic and literary classification and categorization. "As a writer," she says, "I beg for longer notions of who we are, rather than the shorthand ones, such as South Asian. Longer definitions take more time to express" (94).

A similar sentiment is discernible in *He Drown She*. Kristina Kyser argues that Mootoo challenges the idea of an essential connection between culture and self, and culture and text, by using alternative sources for the construction of identity in the novel. Mootoo dismisses metaphors that describe ethnicity and culture as "portable units" that can be carried to multiple places by a diasporic subject or distributed uniformly among many (Kyser 2008: 72-3). According to Kyser, she uses the spatial metaphor of the sea to destabilize this essential relationship between self and culture that many critics and readers imagine grants the writer insider authority on (and insider access to) a given ethnic or cultural identity (73). Kyser performs a psychoanalytic reading of the novel's dream sequences, demonstrating that Mootoo's depiction of Harry's ambiguous dreamscapes "throws into question both Harry's status as a cultural representative and the efficacy of narrative in conveying an essential connection between self and ethnicity" (75). In addition to these dreamscapes, which I previously identified as one of the novel's three central settings, Mootoo creates a Caribbean world more through her characters' memories, desires and imaginations than she does through the presentation of factual events, realistic places or even real place names, keeping both physical and psychological distance between her self and this culture. In this way, Kyser believes, Mootoo problematizes the idea that she speaks from some kind of authority about place and culture and the idea that readers can gain access to this "insider" information through her texts (82). This reconfiguration of what Kyser calls the "autoethnographic paradigm" compels us to "reassess how insider authority is assigned and valued, how ethnic texts are classified — particularly in relation to the social and political realities they are deemed to reflect — and what kind of access to this reality is granted to 'outside' audiences by autoethnographic writing" (73). The issue of how ethnic texts are classified in the face of this reconfiguration is pertinent to our discussion of the archive, particularly to how the archival placement of an author's manuscripts affects literary and scholarly narratives about her. This classification constitutes one form of epitext, controlled in Mootoo's case not only by archival selection and arrangement but by her own decision to place her fonds at a Canadian educational institution.

Given Mootoo's reluctance to accept singular notions of cultural identity, it may be possible to view the placement of her fonds at Simon Fraser University as an act of paratextual importance: altering the discursive epitexts attached to her work and to her public persona offers a new way of perceiving Mootoo outside of the usual categories of Indian, Trinidadian, Caribbean and diasporic. Through the processes of selection, acquisition, appraisal and description, the archivist participates in this recontextualization, disrupting narratives about Mootoo currently in circulation. The archive as a space of transaction, dialogue, diaspora and intervention plays a mediating role in this process, and in the case of *He Drown She* we also witness the alteration of epitext by peritext. The Mootoo fonds reveals the complexity of its titling, and our reading of the narrative changes. Just as the application of a definitive title to a literary work necessarily marginalizes its other thematic concerns, Mootoo explores the ways in which the categorization and labelling of cultural experience in *He Drown She* contribute to social marginalization, both close to and at a distance from "home." In this, the epitextual archive and the peritextual title together inform Harry's and Rose's struggles with internalized social expectations about geographic and social place, and the ambiguity of the novel's title reflects their lack of belonging in either.

The various working titles that the Mootoo manuscripts reveal, which were connected to the novel throughout its production, reflect the importance of these spaces and places, of cross-cultural and cross-continental movement, and of narrative constructions in *He Drown She in the Sea*. We might consider Mootoo's fonds, then, as a paratextual aid to reading her fiction based not only on the nature of the archive but on its content as well. Knowledge of the numerous titles that were attributed to *He Drown She* during the drafting process compels the reader to reinterpret the novel based on their evocations of meaningful locales, spatial displacements and narratives within the story. This complicates the novel's depictions of place in all its manifestations. Two titles specifically — *The Summer of Rose* and *Once, a Raleigh Man* — capture in different ways the narrative force and ambiguity of place that characterize the novel, shifting the reader's focus from Squamish to the fictional Caribbean island of Guanagaspar, from oneiric or imaginary narratives of place to physical locales, and from impositions of social place to reconsiderations of what constitutes "proper" place.

The novel opens with an extended narrative by a character we know only as "Madam" to her servant Piyari. "Madam" is, of course, Rose, and her narrative — and later, Harry's memories of the same events — details *The Summer of Rose*. This title was adopted and discarded several times, although it is not clear who first suggested it; it first appears in an email from Seligman to Mootoo dated June 31, 2001 (MsC 76.7.9), was later changed, and was again referred to as the working title on January 22, 2002, in an email from Schmitz to Mootoo (MsC 76.7.10). By July 2003 the novel was titled *Rip Tide*, but Mootoo again suggested *The Summer of Rose* on September 12, 2003, in an email to her agent Massie (MsC 76.7.8). Clearly, this title characterized the book well for Mootoo and represents a strong paratextual lens for interpretation. The narrative that it recalls is wholly set in Squamish and Vancouver — although Rose narrates her memories from Guanagaspar

— and Mootoo emphasizes the British Columbian landscape and social order throughout, in addition to the question of Harry's place within them. As a landscaper by trade, Harry feels at home in his environment, but he is also able to control the land, shape it and alter its contours, much as he alters his social place in his migration from Guanagaspar to Squamish. Mootoo evokes the sensual qualities of this space in order to contrast Harry's new home and his old; the "odour of the sea, its floor churned and spat up by winter storms, saturates the air" (Mootoo 2005: 21) of the cold, wet and green space he comes to inhabit. This depiction of the sea, which Rose will later call "ice water" (57) and which Harry thinks of as "that frigid salt water crammed with mountain-slide debris and logs escaped from booms" (24), contrasts starkly with the warm Caribbean water of Guanagaspar. Harry's house on Howe Sound is framed by "a curtain of mist and clouds, hanging in the fjord … [which] blots out the shore on the far side" (21), and his senses of place and pride are tied to this weather and the landscape. On an outing with Kay, he marvels at the picture-postcard quality of the surrounds: "Ahead loomed range beyond range of ice-capped mountains. Here and there were bursts of lavender, clumps of mustard goldenrod. Pride coursed through him; he had become an insider" (42). Harry shares his sense of belonging, his pride and the landscape with Rose, taking her sightseeing during "the summer of Rose"; she tells Piyari that "he tell me he wanted to show me, that same day self, a fishery where you could stand up and watch salmon try to climb up a wall in a river. And a canyon" (52). This rugged environment becomes the backdrop for their affair, and Rose even takes part in Harry's landscaping projects, digging, weeding, planting and watering (56), a fact her servant Piyari puzzles at, given her high station in Guanagaspar.

Indeed, the narratives evoked by the title *The Summer of Rose* also focus largely on Harry's social station in Canada. Rose remarks that "you could still hear that a little bit of this place remain in him, but he sound Canadian" (17). His speech, almost dialect-free, represents for Rose his migration and social climb. Yet, in the context of his new environment and nation, she sees this as appropriate. "He give up some of his Guanagasparian ways, though, you know," she tells Piyari. "He used to be so quiet here — almost frighten-frighten to come in our neighbourhood — but he is a man of his own making now, you know. He has his own business, and he employs people. He really come up good, and with not one bit of help from anybody. If you see where he was born, where he and his mother used to live when he was a child" (15). Rose is awed by Harry's sense of ownership over his new land (both his seaside home and the surrounding area) and by the ease with which he navigates it. Yet, as she narrates her summer to Piyari, she complicates the importance of narrative and history in the construction of place: "and as I telling you, everywhere he went, he had some story to tell. He tell me the history of this and a story about that — but this history business is of no interest to me, in truth, yes… I mean, what is the point in knowing so much detail about a place you are not from?" (15). This troubles not only notions of place in the novel but what it means to remember, to narrate and to historicize. The Mootoo fonds and this paratextual detail it offers the reader by way of title thus change how we read the novel. *The Summer of Rose*, along with two other working titles drawn from this narrative stream — *The Fish Vase* and *The Woman Who Gave Love Birds for a Present* — evoke thematic concerns and interpretations distinct from those garnered from the title *He Drown She in the Sea*. Piyari's tale of Rose's death, in contrast, situates us firmly in Guanagaspar, in a servant's home in the sticky tropical heat, grounded in a specific moment of narrative ambiguity.

Another of Mootoo's working titles, *Once, a Raleigh Man*, was adopted as early as January 2000 (MsC 76.1.51) and again from October 2001 to at least January 2002 (MsC 76.1.50-1). This title situates the story at Harry's childhood home on the beach, which is spatially distinct from and provides a sharp contrast to Squamish in climate, landscape and social environment. Raleigh is presented in an ambiguous dream sequence at the beginning of the novel, in which Harry imagines a tidal wave engulfing the village. Mootoo's description of the flood is vivid: "The sea begins to swell, swelling until its surface is smooth and shiny, like a taut plastic bag on the verge of bursting … if the sea continues to grow like that, it is bound to split its plastic-like surface, emptying it of its intestines and all that it has swallowed" (1–2). After the impact, "the shattered remains of houses are strewn, and in the ocean, now settled back in its place, are floating bodies and wood chips the size of matchsticks: the remains of boats, houses, and furniture" (4). The title *Once, A Raleigh Man* draws the reader to Harry's childhood home, and this space is associated with the destructive force of the ocean — a force that destroys indiscriminately. The novel's second section, which narrates the history of Harry's parents (a narrative whose own plausibility is suspect due to the ambiguity of its speaker), recalls this dream in its description of the death of Harry's father. A storm rips through Raleigh: "the sea chopped and boomed … each wave that shattered rolled high up the beach, scattering chip-chip, pebbles, sea cockroaches, and starfish, spitting fringes of dense, ochre-coloured froth laced with seaweed, tangled fishing lines, bits of old net, and cork floaters" (105). In this, Mootoo portrays the ocean spitting back on to land that which it does not wish to consume, or that for which, having been consumed, it has no more use. In both semi-fantastical narratives — the dream sequence and Harry's pre-history — she confuses real and imaginary place in the novel and, because neither narrative possesses realistic integrity, she emphasizes the possibility of fallible narration, one which makes connections between dreams and history, faulty memories and real places.

If the novel were titled *Once, a Raleigh Man*, these tensions might be more prominent upon first reading. So too would Mootoo's portrayal of a memory-trigger — scent — in connection with Raleigh. After the storm that brews on the day of Seudath's death, the odours of flotsam and trash permeate the village — "air that blew in from across the ocean was heavy with the scent of things from the ocean's bed ripped up and churned" (105) — and Raleigh itself is associated not only with this scent but with others that Harry has archived in his memory. His mother Dolly, for instance, runs to catch the taxi to work, conscious "with each breath [of] the odour of the sea: crab, fish bones, seaweed, and chip-chip" (108). Later, in Squamish, Harry returns to Raleigh in his memory after detecting similar scents in a sip of wine. He tastes "ocean wind, seaweed, oysters, crab, and at the back of his throat, more an odour than a taste, a low-tide mangrove swamp. A tide of longing washes over him. Longing for Raleigh, a place he has not been to in years" (67). This place is, for Harry, a completely different sensory experience than Squamish; its rice paddies, cane fields, fish markets and "the coconut tree whose trunk was shaped like a Z" (103) characterize his childhood, and to imagine this as the central image of the novel, as we would do if Mootoo had indeed titled it *Once, a Raleigh Man* — or *The Boy from Timbano Trace*, or *The Servant's Son*, both of which are drawn from this portion of the narrative — would be to alter the primary thematic concerns of the work. The archive thus presents the reader with alternate interpretive frames through which to read, informing both our understanding of the novel's peritexts and its constructions of memory, history, narrative and the forces that threaten all geographic and social constructions of place equally.

Moving between the physical and discursive spaces that characterize each level of paratext, from the archive to the titles of *He Drown She in the Sea* to the literature itself, we see how the archive intervenes not only in the construction of literary interpretation but in the narratives that accompany the categorization and classification of texts and authors. As epitext, it alters our understanding of the novel's peritexts but also our understanding of Mootoo's role in the Canadian literary canon. The discourses that locate her as an Indian, Trinidadian, Caribbean or diasporic writer are disrupted by the archival process as much as are our readings of her work.

As noted, the Mootoo fonds came to be held at Simon Fraser University as a result of both Mootoo's own decision to place her papers there and Eric Swanick's process of archival selection. Amy Tector writes on the role of archival selection in constructing the Canadian literary canon, suggesting that the institutional placement of the papers of lesser-known writers offers "a counter-discourse to narrow views of Canadian canonicity" (2006: 105). While Tector refers specifically to the works of Magdalena Eggleston at Library and Archives Canada as an example of a virtually unknown writer whose papers contribute to reconsiderations of Canadian literary canonicity, I suggest that the placement of Mootoo's fonds at Simon Fraser performs similar work, offering a counter-discourse to those currently circulating in the literature — and doing so from the archival epitext, the "fringe of the fringe." As the archive initiates dialogue and shifts narrowly defined relationships between discursive categories and the physical text, so too does Mootoo's novel. Diana Brydon views *He Drown She in the Sea* as a work that shifts our understanding from a simple centre-periphery model to one of global interconnectivity. "Where once Canada and the Caribbean could be placed within the dynamics of centre-periphery models," she writes, "in which places like Guanagaspar were mostly invisible, these models have yielded to globalization models in which particular places, such as global cities and the Caribbean itself, are being reconceptualized as crossroads of the world" (2006: 101). Narratives like Mootoo's therefore "burst the bonds of area studies, encouraging readers to think globally about their local contexts" (103). In this, I see novels such as *He Drown She* interrogating conceptions of space and place, centre and margin, and proximity and distance in much the same way as the archive. Read as epitext, the archive has the potential to alter not only peritexts but the relationships between the material text, the discourses surrounding it and literary interpretation.

Contrary to conceptions of the archive as founts of authorial revelation, this reading relies upon the shared responsibility of the author, the archivist, the reader and others involved in textual production. The archive as paratext serves as more than an author's construction of meaning in his or her own work; it functions as "narrative," as "dialogue," as "diaspora," as "practice" and as a "process" that intervenes, mediates and shapes literary interpretation while readers, in turn, shape it. Issues of memory, history, narration and interpretation are as vital to the literary archive as they are to Mootoo's *He Drown She in the Sea*. In Piyari's narrative, Mootoo releases history and memory into the public sphere and participates in the act of archiving culture, as do authors, archivists and readers when they construct narratives in the literary archive. These narratives mediate how we read fictional texts and, I would argue, how we read geographical, imaginary and social place within them. The story that a literary archive narrates is provocative, offering up details that allow us to make new meaning from texts and to reconsider our conceptions of place. How does place figure in a work of fiction? What place does a writer like Mootoo occupy in a Canadian archive? Can the literary archive effectively deal with issues such as globalization, cross-cultural exchange and diaspora? As paratext, the literary archive is characterized by proximity and distance, physicality and discursivity, and it is a space in which various levels of paratextuality shape interpretation. This is a space of transaction, a threshold of interpretation — one that will need to be further mapped if it is to be made useful in literary criticism. An examination of Mootoo's *He Drown She in the Sea* reveals that there is no simple equation for the solution to the problems of titling, categorizing, narrating or archiving. Similarly, the equation of peritext + epitext = paratext begs reconsideration. The literary archive as paratext navigates complex physical and discursive spaces, and its role in the interpretive process — and in the construction of Canadianness in literature — is anything but simple.

Note

1. See, for example, *Archivaria* 68 (Fall) (2009), Special Section on Queer Archives; Laszlo 2006; Shilton and Srinivasan 2007; and Tector 2006.

References

Banting, Pamela. 1986–7. "The Archive as Literary Genre: Some Theoretical Speculations." *Archivaria* 23 (Winter): 119–22.

Brydon, Diana. 2006. "'A Place on the Map of the World': Locating Hope in Shani Mootoo's *He Drown She in the Sea* and Dionne Brand's *What We All Long For*." *MaComère: Journal of the Association of Caribbean Women Writers and Scholars* 8: 94–111.

Burger, Karine. 2008. "Shani Mootoo Fonds MsC 76." Simon Fraser University Special Collections and Rare Books.

Genette, Gérard. 1997. *Paratexts: Thresholds of Interpretation*. Trans. Jane E. Lewin. Cambridge: Cambridge University Press.

Hobbs, Catherine. 2006. "New Approaches to Canadian Literary Archives." *Journal of Canadian Studies* 40, 2: 109–19.

Kyser, Kristina. 2008. "Tides of Belonging: Reconfiguring the Autoethnographic Paradigm in Shani Mootoo's *He Drown She in the Sea*." In Eleanor Ty and Christl Verduyn (eds.), *Asian Canadian Writing Beyond Autoethnography*. Waterloo: Wilfrid Laurier University Press: 71–84.

Laszlo, Krisztina. 2006. "Ethnographic Archival Records and Cultural Property." *Archivaria* 61 (Spring): 299–307.

Mootoo, Shani. 2005. *He Drown She in the Sea*. Toronto: McClelland and Stewart.

———. 2008. "On Becoming an Indian Starboy." *Canadian Literature* 196: 83–94.

O'Driscoll, Michael, and Edward Bishop. 2004. "Archiving 'Archiving.'" *English Studies in Canada* 30, 1: 1–16.

Shani Mootoo Fonds. Special Collections and Rare Books. Simon Fraser University Library. MsC 76.

Shilton, Katie, and Ramesh Srinivasan. 2007. "Participatory Appraisal and Arrangement for Multicultural Archival Collections." *Archivaria* 63 (Spring): 87–101.

Special Section on Queer Archives. 2009. *Archivaria* 68 (Fall).

Swanick, Eric. 2010. February 22. Personal email.

Tector, Amy. 2006. "The Almost Accidental Archive and its Impact on Literary Subjects and Canonicity." *Journal of Canadian Studies* 40, 2 (Spring): 96–108.

The Letters of Frances Stewart
Two Centuries of Layered Representation

Jodi Aoki

On the morning of June 1, 1822, and three years before Peter Robinson was to direct the first mass emigration of Irish working-class families to the Peterborough area, Frances Browne Stewart, along with her husband, Thomas Alexander Stewart, their daughters, Anna, Ellen and Bessy and their two servants left Belfast aboard the brigantine *George* for Upper Canada. In tow were their French poodle, Cartouche, and a cargo of farm implements and nails, china and cutlery, candlesticks, mattresses and blankets, and several boxes of books, including Tom's complete set of Shakespeare's plays.[1] Upon arrival in the New World, the family lived in Cobourg while Tom arranged for a grant of land in Douro Township, and on the evening of February 11, 1823, they settled at last into their new log house along the shore of the Otonabee River at the present-day site of Peterborough.

Frances's legacy of immigrant letters provides an extraordinary opportunity to examine a first-person narrative of one of the earliest European settlers to the Peterborough area. Spanning three-quarters of a century and numbering almost 400, including the letters Frances received from family and friends, they are a remarkable testament to female immigrant experience in the colony. Available in original, transcribed and digitized format, the letters are located in a number of depositories. Most are housed at Trent University Archives and have been fully transcribed and made available on the archives website. A few dozen additional letters, exchanged between Frances and her friend, Catharine Parr Traill, are located at Library and Archives Canada, and transcriptions are available on a web exhibit dedicated to Catharine and her sister, Susanna Moodie. Other letters are located at the Baldwin Room of the Toronto Reference Library and at the Huntington Library. Of all these holdings, approximately a hundred items are attributed to Frances. The letters reveal aspects of her early years in Ireland and her voyage across the Atlantic en route to a life easily discerned to have been a stark contrast to her pre-emigration experience; they speak to class and gender and reveal that memory, myth and nostalgia figured prominently in Frances's perception of her experience in the New World.

The letters, which ended only upon her death, suggest that Frances placed a far higher value on a cultured life than on one that merely guaranteed physical survival. They provide detail of her day-to-day experiences: her tasks and responsibilities in the home; her relationship with her husband, children and servants; her encounters with Aboriginals; her impressions of her natural physical surroundings; and her struggles to retain the semblance of genteel order in a vastly different social and physical environment. Uprooted and living in isolation without the direct support of loved ones in the homeland, Frances developed a strength and tenacity that figured in her ability to nurture a despondent husband ill-suited to life in the Canadian bush, to educate their children and, couched within the parameters of humble feminine demeanor, to exert influence in the community, all while experiencing intense feelings of loneliness and despair. For Frances, giving up was not an option; she felt a deep inherent responsibility to ensure that their family survived, and the values she placed on religion, on her relationships with female friends and on letters received from the homeland, as well as her pride in her children and in mastering new domestic tasks, albeit through necessity, all facilitated her rise to a position of agency within the family and of some prominence within the wider community.

Born in Ireland in 1794, Frances had been raised by a loving cousin, who tutored her in the Bible, French and Italian, music, chemistry, botany, mathematics and classical and contemporary literature. Her elitist upbringing among the likes of Sir Francis Beaufort, after whom the Beaufort Sea is named, and Maria Edgeworth, who was to become a widely published author, is revealed in the exchange of correspondence. Although she was to live apart from her family and friends for almost fifty years, the genteel Anglo-Irish protestant sensibilities of her protective extended family were to influence Frances's immigrant experience and perspective through her entire life. Her correspondents devotedly continued to support and encourage her through the regular exchange of letters and by frequently arranging transatlantic shipments of books, journals and newspapers to her. With such backing, Frances endeavoured to educate her brood of children (ten in all) in the wilderness and to raise them in Church of England doctrine, their upbringing to her standards made difficult especially in the early years by the absence of schools and churches.

Though a historical treasure, the archival letters of Frances Stewart also pose a conundrum. They have undergone tremendous transformation through the two centuries since she wrote them and are represented in a complex multilayered legacy. Close inspection reveals, for instance, that some of the so-called *originals* are actually hand-copied variants; they are signed as though by Frances but are not in her hand. Others are extracts lacking salutation or attribution. Many of the letters were copied in full or in part upon receipt in Ireland and circulated to other acquaintances, thus accounting in part for the multiple layers. The archival holdings also include manuscript copies of the letters edited for the purpose of publication in the book, *Our Forest Home: Being Extracts from the Correspondence of the Late Frances Stewart*, compiled by Frances's daughter, Ellen Dunlop. Both editions of *Our Forest Home*, published in 1889 and 1902, which until recently were only available in hard copy in private Stewart family collections or in rare book library depositories, are now also available digitally, the first edition as a facsimile copy on the Early Canadiana Online website, and the second, as both a facsimile copy on the Our Roots: Canada's Local Histories On-Line website and a typed transcription on the Trent University Archives website.[2]

Ellen and her brother Charles were both active in gathering their mother's letters from Ireland, Ellen acquiring some from relatives during a visit there in 1852, long before her mother's death, and later through the post, and Charles some, probably in 1859, on a visit to Ireland while he was living in England. There is evidence that by 1871 Charles had begun to compile a manuscript and that Frances had added supplementary notations and corrections to it just a few months before she died, on February 24, 1872.[3] The complexity of the added notations suggests that Frances may have had a hand in the preliminary editing of the publication.

Archival holdings reveal that, although Ellen's and Frances's lives were intertwined in an indubitably loving way, their relationship was often turbulent. Frances writes to Ellen:

> Why should you always wish your life was only beginning — I think you have had in general as happy a life as anyone can have — for who is there that can say they never have had a sorrow or felt a regret — no not one! — but I think our family have *uncommon* reason for happiness & thankfulness for few profess so many real & true blessings — & the true sources of happiness as we do — and one of the greatest is the strong & warm union & attachment which exists amongst us… You need not think with sorrow of any trouble or pain you have given me my dearest Ellen for there is no young person in the world who does not give some trouble to those who have the care of them — & I am sure you have not given me more than the others tho' I may have oftener had occasion to call to you or find fault with you for trifles — because your natural character was of that *rapid* giddy impatient nature, which required to be constantly controlled — just like our own poor horse Johnny — who is good & useful & valuable — but he has now suffered by the same failing of thoughtless eagerness & quickness which you have sometimes suffered from — but which is very much abated lately — So my dear

> Ellen do not any more think you have given me too much pain, for there are few days I do not return thanks to God for having given you to me — for tho' you may have faults — which it is my duty (often a painful one) to point out & correct — yet you have also many many amiable & truly valuable qualities which are far beyond your faults — I never can remember faults — or quarrels or offences — & I wish you were the same, for it saves one much misery.[4]

Notwithstanding the apparent tensions between Ellen and Frances that continued into Ellen's adulthood, they visited each other regularly after her marriage to Charles Dunlop in 1845, and several endearing letters from Frances to Ellen exist in archival holdings. One could speculate that in the maturity of her later years, Ellen was sorry for the misery they shared.

Ellen's correspondence with her uncle and his son, her cousin Alexander, both of whom she had come to know in 1852 on her visit to Ireland, convey crucial details about her motives in publishing the letters. Upon receiving confirmation in 1888 that her uncle had some letters in his possession, she writes:

> I am so glad to hear you have some of my mothers valued letters so wonderful now to read & cull through as I have been doing, many a time a tear comes while I go over this deeply interesting pleasure. Could you spare all to me, how truly obliged I would feel to add the aged relics to those I have crumbling away which caused me to feel the need to copy from them what will otherwise never be known to our next generation of who they sprang from, & what my loved parents went through.[5]

This passage sheds light on her objective in pursuing the letters and reveals the heavy sense of responsibility she felt to commit the memory of her mother's life to a publication for family descendents. In another letter, she affirms, "I am doing all this for my mother's children, grandchildren, & great g children — it will be of great interest."[6] Even though claiming that the first edition of *Our Forest Home* was for a private audience, she strived to make it marketable for Victorian public audiences by limiting personal references, as another passage reveals:

> I cull from each letter the advance of the country — description of work done by whom, country opening her mind on difficult subjects — the increase of family duties — & above all her own inward expression of Gods dealing with her soul… expressions of love to those she wrote to, & the outpouring of her soul in her beautiful religious feelings — these have to be preserved, yet slightly left out.[7]

The above extract is revealing in its explanation of the methods that Ellen planned to employ as editor. Religion would figure less prominently than the originals allowed, and the trials and tribulations of Frances's pioneer experience would predominate. Elaborating, Ellen adds, "I am leaving out all the *endearing* expressions, merely the thread of interest running through about the advance of the settlement & the family incidents, so well & graphically told, so true to life."[8]

While Ellen's revelations help to understand her editing decisions in the published layers, it is important to be cognizant of the fact that much of the unpublished material, too, was edited in small or substantial ways at least once and sometimes more often and by several people. The archival conundrum would be easier to unravel if the passages generally duplicated each other across the various layers. However, there is often new material in subsequent layers, and it is obvious that many of the published passages cannot be measured against primary counterparts. It is apparent that Ellen had access to primary documents that are not available in known archival depositories today, a factor that lends importance to the published compilations in *Our Forest Home*. Where cross-referencing is possible, however, it is evident that several passages are omitted, and sections of disparate letters are frequently included as one and subsequently misdated.

While any analysis of past lives and meaning is already complex and conditional, the divergent layers of text in Frances's writings complicate the effort to reconstruct her life. Because the aberrations across the layers comprise divergences from the original texts, they may represent alternate intentions and meanings. How does one analyze these layers of narrativity? This is a question that has implications for the re-description of Frances's life but a question that is impossible to fully answer.

The *Our Forest Home* layers, for example, while largely reflecting the sensibilities of a loving and protective daughter, also emulate the tradition of popular Canadian writing during the late nineteenth century. Philip Davis explains that "facts, statistics, information, and explanation were all part of the Victorian effort to achieve explicit understanding, in bringing to the forefront of consciousness their own underlying background of social and philosophical changes" (2002: 404). While conforming to publishing conventions and guidelines, Ellen's portrayal of Frances also facilitated the telling of her own life story, her commentary adding new material and alternate perspectives. No doubt, there was prestige attached to this project, Ellen being the daughter of one of Peterborough's earliest settler families and, indeed, an immigrant, herself.

Ellen received research and editing assistance from several people: two of her brothers; a sister; a nephew; two nieces; her younger friend, author and editor Arnold Haultain, who helped to secure a publisher for *Our Forest*

Home; and, most importantly, her beloved friend and friend of her mother's, Catharine Parr Traill. All of these people would have been immersed in their own discursive locations, hence presenting different foci and emphases vis-à-vis Frances's life and experiences. Through her association with Catharine, for example, Ellen had gained a perspective of the colonial context within which her mother's life could be viewed. She had seen firsthand that Catharine, who had learned much about survival in the wilderness from Frances, had received unprecedented fame through her literary expression of her pioneer experience, a fact that may have served to heighten Ellen's sense of responsibility to commit her mother's writings, too, to publication. Unlike Catharine's works, however, which were written during the period of actual pioneering and viewed as valuable sources of information for prospective immigrants to Upper Canada, *Our Forest Home*, given its date of publication, would have had little influence on women of Frances's own generation.

Catharine Parr Traill's role in the execution of *Our Forest Home* was considerable, although circuitous. As early as 1882, she wrote to Ellen seeking Ellen's and her siblings' approval of her plan to write a biography of Frances for a publisher in Toronto:

> I wish to know if you and your family would object to my making use of the memoir I wrote with your dear brother C's [Charles's] references — of your beloved Mother, and also if you would make a few extracts from her early letters…. Some one of the family could have undertaken it better than myself if they were so willing; yourself or one — or one of your brothers — So if on consideration you should *so decide*, let me know as soon as you can do so conveniently. (Ballstadt, Hopkins and Petermen 1996: 221)

Catharine mentions her interest in writing about the family again in 1884, this time using unspecified material that had been compiled by Ellen's brother Henry. Although detail is sketchy, it appears that she planned to use Henry's manuscript in a book of articles by various authors called "Prairie Homes" and to reimburse him if the work was published, although her expectations for remuneration were minimal.[9] A year later, in 1885, another related reference appears. Without elaborating, she writes, "I have finished the extracts from your dear mothers letters, and will return the original papers."[10] This passage indicates that Catharine copied extracts from Frances's letters, and another letter, written at about the same time, affirms her interest in seeing the letters published. She says, "I have read the memorial papers; Your dear mothers letters with great interest — they would make a charming volume with the additional matter that you possess."[11] Although Ellen's letters to Catharine have not survived, it is apparent from Catharine's communications that there was an ongoing dialogue about the possible publication of the letters. In late 1886, Catharine wrote to Ellen again on the subject, saying:

> I have often thought how interesting to the old folks in Peterboro and Douro would be portions of your own dear Mother's MS. writings appear in the *Review* — I have you know made most interesting selections from the original document. Would you like to have my MS to make use of?[12]

The following comment reiterates Catharine's desire for Ellen to use her manuscript material and, conceivably, could be viewed as a carefully worded proposal that she become a ghostwriter or at the very least, an editor for her friend. She writes:

> I send you the MS. collated from your old record and some passages in old letters, that you let me make extracts from — Now dear friend just use it as seems best to your own judgment. I thought it better just to let you have it without taking any passage of interest from it myself. I think you may find it useful, and it is fairly written out which will save your eyes as copying from MS. is often tiresome unless pretty plainly written.[13]

By her own assertion, it appears that Catharine had already *edited* the letters loaned to her by Ellen, choosing excerpts that she deemed publishable. While it is impossible to verify whether Ellen's final rendition was largely influenced by her friend, it can be verified that many of the published inclusions are substantively different from the corresponding archival record, making them thereby questionable as faithful representations of the original texts.

A further problem arises in distinguishing Ellen's voice from that of Frances when reading the publication. Ellen unobtrusively weaves her own commentary in and out of the principal text, sometimes without distinguishing punctuation, an effect that contributes to the re-description of her mother's life. People view Frances's life and experience depending on which narrative they have read, and it is reasonable to question whether the Frances Stewart whom most know through reading Ellen's Victorian compilation is the same Frances Stewart whose purpose in writing her letters was to communicate her feelings to an intended audience of reciprocating loved ones who were painfully and forever missed. Frances is very clear about her audience, remarking in one letter, "I am always happy when I can write my letters at night for then I am with my friends."[14] That Ellen understood the importance of the exchange of letters in her mother's life is evident:

> How often I saw my mother read her Home letters & *weep* as if her heart would break — yet her letters were written in such a brilliant

tone — & hope contentment & gratitude to God for her *blessings* which many would call crosses.[15]

Despite Ellen's memory of her mother's unhappiness, however, she nevertheless grievously underrepresented the loneliness that defined Frances's immigrant experience in *Our Forest Home*.

Because most readers generally view Frances from their impressions derived from having read her published letters, one might conclude that Ellen's editing choices and the resultant imbalance have sometimes contributed in adverse ways to her mother's persona. While Frances's elitist class sensibilities are certainly interwoven into much of the archival literary evidence, the emphases employed by Ellen in the publication skew the interpretation of these writings. To illustrate, Ellen appears to have incorporated several fictions in order to elevate the family name. For example, she draws on the compelling images related to the visit in 1826 to Douro Township of the Lieutenant-Governor of Upper Canada, Sir Peregrine Maitland, the Hon. Zaccheus Burnham and the Commissioner of Crown Lands and Surveyor General of Upper Canada, Peter Robinson. She allegedly quotes from one of the letters, saying, "T- [Tom, Frances's husband] says Mr. Robinson shook his hand almost off" (Dunlop 1889: 50), and in the same letter, "he [Sir Peregrine Maitland] talked to me a good deal both before and after dinner, as he thought proper that I should take precedence, and consequently I sat between him and Mr. Robinson" (Dunlop 1889: 53). Unfortunately, there is no extant account of this visit in Frances's original letters. Quotations such as the above may reflect actual letters that no longer exist and that did indeed make such claims, or they may be constructed events and indicative of the heightened sense of class-consciousness that was instilled by Frances in her children. Ellen was cognizant of a societal position that she held as a member of one of Peterborough's earliest pioneer and genteel families.

The difference in emphasis between the extracts that Ellen chose to publish and the original letters is striking. In *Our Forest Home*, Ellen emphasizes the upper echelons of society connected with her family and minimizes her mother's personal feelings. Frances, on the other hand, as the original letters reveal, emphasizes kinship connections that, by happenstance, included people of social prominence, and she repeatedly wrote of her loneliness. The original writings, too, include not only the upper echelons of society, as one might believe by reading *Our Forest Home*, but also several references to Frances's servants; according to one original account about an accident that Betty Delaney, a servant who immigrated with the Stewarts, had during the winter of 1823, she and Tom lovingly attended to her needs while she convalesced. Frances writes:

> One night my poor little maid Betty slipped on the ice at the back

door, fell & broke one of her ribs in two places as her side came against the handle of a tub. Tom & I laid her on a Matrass in our room & had her bled, & early next morning had the Doctor to see her, who ordered low diet, saline draughts & quiet — so she lay there for some days.[16]

Ellen, however, marginalizes Betty in her version of the event, saying, "the servant fell, while carrying a tub of water, on the icy steps and broke some of her ribs. So my mother had her hands full" (Dunlop 1889: 17). In referring to Ellen's account in *Our Forest Home*, Elizabeth Jane Birch writes, "here is one example of how an Irish servant is marginalized on the fringe of a story and the reader never hears her voice or her impression of this unfortunate experience" (1997: 32). Birch has precisely identified an example whereby Frances was re-described by Ellen through later editing. By emphasizing events relating to powerful and well-known people and by marginalizing experiences that involve the lower classes, Ellen effectively creates an image in line with her own sharpened class sensibilities. This example reflects a difference in the attitudes of the two women towards the servant class. Frances depended on her servants and worked alongside them; she needed their help in ensuring the family's survival and valued their companionship, especially in the early years after immigrating to the isolated township. Ellen, on the other hand, did not live in isolation as a married woman, separated from family and friends. Unlike her mother, who had raised ten children plus a few others, she had gained prosperity through marriage and had only a few dependents at any one time. Her financial status ensured that she could distinguish herself from the labouring class through the types of work that she was required to do, and the latest commodities of the burgeoning industrial revolution would have been within financial reach.

Since its publication more than a century ago, *Our Forest Home* has been referenced in dozens of historical accounts of Upper Canada and Peterborough and in a number of academic studies of pioneer colonial women. Histories by Edwin Guillet (*Pioneer Days in Upper Canada*, 1933) and (*The Valley of the Trent*, 1957), The City and County of Peterborough (*Peterborough: Land of Shining Water*, 1967), Alex Edmison (*Through the Years in Douro*, 1967) and Martin, McGillis and Milne (*Gore's Landing and the Rice Lake Plains*, 1986), as examples, all have used *Our Forest Home* as a major source for accessing information about immigrant experience in the Peterborough area during the early part of the nineteenth century and all portray Frances most favourably and with utmost respect. Other writers, too, have accorded Frances the status that Ellen so determinedly strove to portray. Robertson Davies in his epilogue to the two plays, *At My Heart's Core* and *Overlaid* cites *Our Forest Home* as one of his sources for the first play. He writes:

> Mrs. Stewart, gentlest and most humorous of the three [Frances Stewart, Catharine Parr Traill and Susanna Moodie], never ceased to be an Irish lady of the upper class in her attitude toward other people; it was not that she constantly insisted on her rank — she was much too real a lady for that — but that it never occurred to her to think that in a new land social values might be different. (1966: 112)

Charlotte Gray, too, citing *Our Forest Home* in *Sisters in the Wilderness* (1999), uses Frances as one of her primary accesses to Catharine and her life and, like Davies, portrays Frances as a genteel woman who was regarded with the greatest respect by those who knew her. Ellen was very successful in presenting Frances as an honourable and upright woman of the genteel class.

However, Ellen's compilation, as with all historical reconstructions, is also viewed with some skepticism. Quoting verbatim from *Our Forest Home* is now seen to be risky as it is evident in several instances that Frances is not necessarily represented accurately. Ellen's claim that her mother named Peterborough as a compliment to Peter Robinson (Dunlop 1889: 58), for example, is one assertion that has been called into question. Unsupported by an original letter, it appears that the claim represents more than an embellishment or post-facto reconstruction — it appears to be an actual fabrication. Although there is no concrete documentation that identifies just how Peterborough was named, historian Elwood Jones attributes the name to the Hon. Zaccheus Burnham (2004: 5). Born in New Hampshire near a town named Peterborough, Burnham was a land surveyor and member of the Family Compact and also a large-scale entrepreneur whose interests included promoting the Newcastle District in government circles. Jones asserts that the name of choice, "Peterborough," was political, saying, "The name was special, and no government would forget that this was a town founded on promises of continuing support" (8).

Amid the controversy, no one questions that Frances was present at the 1826 meeting at Government House with Maitland, Burnham and Robinson when the name "Peterborough" was chosen. Because of the lack of documentation to support Ellen's claim that her mother chose the name, however, her version of the naming is cast in doubt. It is possible that as the years passed, Stewart family oral tradition skewed particular aspects of the event, and Ellen's version may simply represent her own childhood memory of a story that she had no reason to doubt, and one that reflected a desire to enhance the family's good name. It is also possible that she did have access to a no-longer-available original account in one of Frances's letters. Jones's findings, on the other hand, speak to the *official* naming procedure, an analytical determination derived at through research conducted at a vantage of more than a hundred years. Unfortunately, there seems to be no absolute, concrete proof in the matter; it is conceivable that the two ideas converged and seemed serendipitous to those assembled, to name "Peterborough" in honour of both Peter Robinson and Zaccheus Burnham.

Perhaps the trade-off for the heavy editing in *Our Forest Home* is Ellen's own commentary, which at times provides information about the history of Peterborough that is not found anywhere in the available archival letters written by her mother. She gives her own firsthand depiction, for instance, of Scott's Plains before it was named Peterborough (Dunlop 1889: 43–44) and describes the turmoil in the area at the time of the 1837 Rebellion (95). Frances's extant letters, surprisingly, seldom mention events of historical significance. By interjecting elements of her own lived experience, Ellen gives readers access to historically important material. As editor, she felt some obligation to provide an enriched historical context for change and evolution, especially when Frances's letters were lacking in this respect. She devotes almost four consecutive pages to her childhood memory of Aboriginals, for example, recounting fascinating detail about early Christian conversion efforts (58–61). As might be expected, the Natives in Ellen's depictions are stereotyped and, though both Frances and Ellen regarded them as "other," Frances's observations, while sketchy, are less qualitative than Ellen's. Ellen's Natives were "strange wild savages of the forest" (58), from a position of some sixty years after their early encounters, and she recalls feeling terror as they approached through the woods:

> Oh, what a terror to us children to see these strange people coming through the trees from the river, rolled up in a blanket, red leggings, moccasins on their feet, long black hair matted and hanging loose over their face and shoulders, red eyes always turning about, looking at us with great curiosity, trying to bargain for their articles. (58)

Such an interjection by Ellen has implications for the reader's perception of Frances. The extent to which Ellen unobtrusively interjects her own commentary facilitates this effect and contributes to the re-description of her mother.

While Frances's letters have been compromised through editing over the centuries, it remains impossible to fully know, even from an analysis of the original documents, her intentions when she wrote them. Several variables complicate the ability to analyze their meaning. David Gerber in his examination of immigrant writings has found that immigrants purposefully interchanged fact and fiction in their accounts of their new lives. Such findings underscore any analysis of past lives, indicating that meaning is complex and conditional and that words which are already fraught with ambiguity and nuance must be examined from the perspective of the past, as far as possible. Gerber, in his argument that "Immigrants have always risked a radical rupture of the self, a break in their understandings of who they are"

(2006: 3), points to an important dynamic that influenced the composition of the pioneer immigrant letter, the period of instability that most immigrants faced upon settling:

> Emigration puts a singular strain on personal identity, because it is a radical challenge to continuity. It may set individuals adrift by sundering their relationships to places, things, and people. Not only does it remove, if only for a time, practical, material, and psychological sources of support, but it also disrupts the emigrant's own self-awareness, for it is through this continuous relationship to places, things, and above all, to other people, that we know ourselves. (67)

Elizabeth Jane Errington furthers this argument, stressing the importance of the sense of continuity and shared community that immigrants derived from the transatlantic exchange of letters with family and friends. According to Errington, the exchange of letters helped to affirm one's place in the world and provided a critical reminder of one's past life while helping to ease the transition to a new:

> Letters were also a means of integrating the Old World and the New, of tying the familiar domestic landscapes, people, and relationships of home into the new and increasingly familiar world of a face-to-face colonial community. On both sides of the Atlantic, receiving or sending even one brief letter reaffirmed who one was and where one fitted into the world. (2007: 138)

It is important in light of the above to appreciate and understand that letters and diaries and journals are self-conscious autobiographical writings, serving to create and anchor the identity of the writer. Anthony Giddens believes that such writings assist in keeping one's narrative coherent and more profoundly, that "a person's identity is [found]... in the capacity *to keep a particular narrative going*" (1991: 54). In order to survive, Upper Canadian immigrants needed to keep their narrative going. Physical contact no longer possible, the letters exchanged with the home country provided a tangible medium through which they could continue their narrative. Not only did letters provide the sole outlet for the expression of sentiments, worries and ambitions, they served to create and affirm a personal narrative and facilitate the construction of self — or a re-construction of self after the "rupture."

Contemporary theorists such as Duncan Bell, who work with concepts of landscape, memory and national myths, have much to contribute to how one views the formative years of an immigrant society and, subsequently, how one interprets the intentions and meanings behind the literary representations. In the case of Frances and Ellen, the complications for interpretation are manifold because the intentions and meanings of the several layers, from the original texts to the published compilations, can never be stated with certainty. Frances meant her words to have certain meaning when she used them however they were received and interpreted. Ellen interpreted them within the context of her own life and represented them in *Our Forest Home* according to her own principles and convictions. It is evident that, through the medium of the extracted segments from her mother's letters and the reworded compilations in *Our Forest Home,* Ellen created a new set of intentions and meanings, the letters arguably reconceived and represented to tell her own immigrant story.

Bernadine Dodge has observed that, "Reconstructing the past from memory, text, or image, requires a narrative — a reconceptualizing of events and experiences to make them sensible, rational, coherent, and frequently, to make past events serve a contemporary moralizing purpose" (2002: 19). In the case of both Frances, in her original letters, and Ellen, in her edited renditions of them, the tenuous connections between past and present are revealed. Bell, arguing that memory "is what keeps the past — or a highly selective image of it — alive in the present" (2006: 2), expounds upon the idea that *perceptions* of the past are what shape the stories that people tell about themselves. Narrativity is a process comprised of more than the constructive elements of a text; meaning and context are key, and the narrator's socio-cultural experiences and intentions and the period in which they live are enmeshed in it. Frances's original letters comprise the first layer(s) of her narrative, while the edited letters fashioned by Ellen in *Our Forest Home* comprise new layers with alternate meanings. Ellen's representation of her mother's letters reflects a desire to reconstruct them for her audience, in the first edition for family, or so she claims, and in the second, for a marketplace still rife with Victorian attitudes and tastes. The nature of the editing, especially in the second edition, for example, falls in line with commercial attractiveness and leads away from the day-to-day life that Frances wrote about. The layers of narrativity all have different purposes and have implications for the analysis of Frances's life.

For over a hundred years, researchers have had access to the letters of one of Peterborough's earliest British immigrants through Ellen Dunlop's *Our Forest Home*. During the last quarter century, some of the original letters have become available also, thanks to family descendents who have donated these historical documents to public archives for permanent preservation. Comparative analyses reveal that many of *Our Forest Home's* letters have no original counterparts, and this lends particular importance to it, as it includes firsthand accounts available nowhere else. From the perspective of the twenty-first century, however, it has become popular to devalue the publication in light of the obvious editing imposed upon the letters by Ellen. One must realize that it is by the fortuitous circumstance that many letters have been saved, that researchers are able to make comparative analyses and measure the textual anomalies. It is the availability of the comparative documentation that has enabled researchers to identify the fact that Ellen's compilation hinged heavily on her own experiences and her own socio-cultural framework. We can, therefore, begin to appreciate the work for the textual artifact that it is.

The issues surrounding the archival sources are important to understand, as the deviations tell a story. They provide alternate glimpses into Frances's life — and Ellen's life — and reflect changing perspectives over time. Such extensive textual evidence affords researchers the opportunity to study the life of one of Canada's earliest European settlers. Undeniably, itemization and demarcation of the many layers is a meticulous undertaking. Notwithstanding all the problems, however, in the end, the layers are all grounded in historical reality. While the retelling of Frances's life in carefully manipulated text by a loving and protective daughter is provocative, it provides a fascinating record made at a particular time and place and is a link to a real past life. Through enhanced accessibility to the letters via the Internet, researchers have the opportunity to compare the multifarious texts and to raise new questions about the possibilities of purpose and meaning across the centuries.

Notes

1. Trent University Archives (hereafter TUA), 02-017, Thomas Alexander Stewart collection, Box 1.
2. Early Canadiana Online website <http://www.canadiana.org/cgi-bin/ECO/mtq?doc=13970>, Our Roots: Canada's Local Histories On-Line website <http://www.ourroots.ca/toc.aspx?id=11325&qryID=a31c5377-8205-43c0-ac1c-f7da9880c63a>, Trent University Archives <http://www.trentu.ca/admin/library/archives/ourforesthome.htm>.
3. TUA, 97-023, Frances Stewart fonds, Folder 3, [manuscript], 1871-1872.
4. TUA, 94-007, Stewart-Dunlop fonds, Box 1 Folder 7 Letter #1, Frances Stewart to Ellen Dunlop, n.d. This letter may have been written a year or two before Thomas Alexander Stewart's death in 1847.
5. Public Record Office of Northern Ireland (hereafter PRONI), D 1424/3/47, Kirkpatrick papers, Ellen Dunlop to George Kirkpatrick, 26 June 1888.
6. PRONI, D 1424/3/49, Kirkpatrick papers, Ellen Dunlop to George Kirkpatrick, 29 October 1888.
7. PRONI, D 1424/3/47, Kirkpatrick papers, Ellen Dunlop to George Kirkpatrick, 26 June 1888.
8. PRONI, D 1424/3/49, Kirkpatrick papers, Ellen Dunlop to George Kirkpatrick, 29 October 1888.
9. Library and Archives Canada (hereafter LAC), M 29 D 81, Traill family collection, Catharine Parr Traill to Ellen Dunlop, 3 February 1884.
10. LAC, M 29 D 81, Traill family collection, Volume 2 File 11, Catharine Parr Traill to Ellen Dunlop, 28 April 1885.

11 LAC, M 29 D 81, Traill family collection, Catharine Parr Traill to Ellen Dunlop, fragment, [Autumn 1885].
12 LAC, M 29 D 81, Traill family collection, Volume 2 File 11, Catharine Parr Traill to Ellen Dunlop, 20 November 1886.
13 LAC, M 29 D 81, Traill family collection, Volume 14 File 6, Catharine Parr Traill to Ellen Dunlop, [1887].
14 TUA, 78-008, Frances Stewart fonds, Letter #269, Frances Stewart [excerpts, bound with ribbon], 27 May 1826.
15 PRONI, D 1424/3/49, Kirkpatrick papers, Ellen Dunlop to George Kirkpatrick, 29 October 1888.
16 TUA, 78-008, Frances Stewart fonds, Letter #98, Frances Stewart to Maria Noble, 24 February 1823.

References

Primary Sources

Huntington Library, Sir Francis Beaufort collection.
Library and Archives Canada, Traill family collection.
Public Record Office of Northern Ireland, Kirkpatrick papers.
Toronto Reference Library, Baldwin Room, Frances Stewart correspondence.
Trent University Archives, Frances Stewart fonds.
_____, Stewart-Dunlop fonds.
_____, Thomas Alexander Stewart collection.

Secondary Sources

Ballstadt, Carl, Elizabeth Hopkins and Michael Peterman (ed.). 1996. *I Bless You in My Heart: Selected Correspondence of Catharine Parr Traill*. Toronto: University of Toronto Press.

Bell, Duncan. 2006. "Introduction: Memory, Trauma and World Politics." In Duncan Bell (ed.), *Memory, Trauma, and World Politics: Reflections on the Relationship Between Past and Present*. Basingstoke: Palgrave MacMillan: 1–32.

Birch, Elizabeth Jane. 1998, c.1997. "Picking Up New Threads for Kathleen Mavourneen: The Irish Female Presence in Nineteenth-Century Ontario." Master's thesis, Trent University.

Davies, Robertson. 1966. *At My Heart's Core* and *Overlaid*. Toronto: Clark, Irwin.

Davis, Philip. 2002. *The Victorians*. The Oxford English Literary History, Volume 8, 1830–1880. New York: Oxford University Press.

Dodge, Bernadine. 2002. "Across the Great Divide: Archival Discourse and the (Re)presentations of the Past in Late-Modern Society." *Archivaria* 53 (Spring): 16–30.

Dunlop, E.S. (ed.). 1889. *Our Forest Home: Being Extracts from the Correspondence of the late Frances Stewart*. Toronto: Printed by the Presbyterian Printing and Publishing Co. Available at <www.canadiana.org/cgi-bin/ECO/mtq?doc=13970 (accessed September 7, 2010).

_____. 1902. *Our Forest Home: Being Extracts from the Correspondence of the Late Frances Stewart*. Second edition. Montreal: Gazette Printing and Publishing Co. Available at <www.ourroots.ca/toc.aspx?id=11325&qryID=a31c5377-820543c0-

ac1c-f7da9880c63a> (accessed September 7, 2010) and <www.trentu.ca/admin/library/archives/ourforesthome.htm> (accessed September 7, 2010).

Edmison, John Alexander (ed.). 1967. *Through the Years in Douro (Peterborough, Ontario), 1822–1967.* Peterborough: A.D. Newson.

Errington, Elizabeth Jane. 2007. *Emigrant Worlds and Transatlantic Communities: Migration to Upper Canada in the First Half of the Nineteenth Century.* McGill-Queen's Studies in Ethnic History. Series 2; 24. Montreal: McGill-Queen's University Press.

Gerber, David. 2006. *Authors of Their Lives: The Personal Correspondence of British Immigrants to North America in the Nineteenth Century.* New York: New York University Press.

Giddens, Anthony. 1991. *Modernity and Self-Identity: Self and Society in the Late Modern Age.* Stanford: Stanford University Press.

Gray, Charlotte. 1999. *Sisters in the Wilderness: The Lives of Susanna Moodie and Catharine Parr Traill.* Toronto: Viking.

Guillet, Edwin C. 1933. *Pioneer Days in Upper Canada.* Toronto: University of Toronto Press.

―――― (ed.). 1957. *The Valley of the Trent.* Toronto: The Champlain Society for the Government of Ontario.

Jones, Elwood. 2004. "The Naming of Peterborough." *Heritage Gazette of the Trent Valley* 8, 4 (February): 5–8.

Martin, Norma, Donna S. McGillis, and Catherine Milne. 1986. *Gore's Landing and the Rice Lakes Plains.* Cobourg: Hayne's Printing.

Peterborough, Land of Shining Water: An Anthology. 1967. Peterborough: City and County of Peterborough.

Shearman Hall, Elizabeth, and Jean Shearman. 1993. *A Sense of Continuity: The Stewarts of Douro.* Revised edition. Toronto: Pro Familia.

From Bath to Birchbark
The Peregrinations of a Marriage Poem

Gwendolyn Davies and Carole Gerson

In 1752, an anonymous witty poem entitled "Advice to a Young Lady Lately Married" was printed in England in the *Bath Journal*.[1] Thirty-seven years later, its authorship was definitively confirmed when it reappeared in Esther (Lewis) Clark's *Poems Moral and Entertaining*, issued in Bath in 1789. By that date, Clark's piece had long since assumed multiple identities as it journeyed through Britain and across the Atlantic, with stops in Pennsylvania, Boston, New York, New Brunswick and Quebec. It proved so appealing that it was frequently reprinted in periodicals and hand-copied for friends. During the eighteenth and nineteenth centuries, its preservation in newspapers, in writers' papers and in commonplace books led to its inclusion in posthumous publications prepared by families and friends of deceased poets who assumed that this poem belonged among their loved one's literary remains (Matthews 2004). In the twentieth and twenty-first centuries, many scholars have likewise assumed that the poem was composed by the person whose hand held the pen that had transcribed it, or at least that it originated in the region where the manuscript version was stored. Hence, it has been identified as American or Canadian by North American scholars, seeking to establish their country's early literary history, who have been unaware of the ease with which such texts traversed the Atlantic.

    Reconstructing the history of this poem has literally taken us from graveyards to Google, plunging us, on one hand, into traditional archival research in the Duke Humfrey's Library at the Bodleian and, on the other, into recently digitized eighteenth- and nineteenth-century printed volumes, newspapers and magazines. Databases such as ECCO (Eighteenth-Century Collections On-line) and APS (American Periodical Series) have created expansive electronic archives by making available many scarce publications whose few surviving copies reside in restricted libraries and by providing sophisticated search engines that make it possible to search an entire digital corpus for a single phrase from a specific poem. As well, Google Books enables one to find textual citations in a wide array of twentieth- and twenty-first-century publications, including scholarly works and local histories. Their notes can then lead to additional print and manuscript sources. The result is that research on an obscure eighteenth-century poem can benefit not only from traditional archival sleuthing but also from what John Teskey has described as an electronic "research infrastructure for scholars" that looks "at how things have evolved, how writers have influenced one another in Canadian literature, or any number of questions that researchers can start putting to a file" (Woods 2009: 25).

In the early 1990s, we were busily scanning library shelves, old newspapers, magazine collections and archival holdings looking for interesting, well-crafted poems to include in our collection, *Canadian Poetry: From the Beginnings Through the First World War*, published by McClelland and Stewart in 1994. Among the texts found, first in Grace Helen Mowat's *The Diverting History of a Loyalist Town*, and then in typescript form in the Mowat Papers in the Charlotte County Archives in St. Andrews, New Brunswick,[2] was a lively marriage poem, "Advice to Mrs. Mowat," originally written on birchbark to celebrate the November 14, 1786, wedding of Loyalist Mehetable Caleff in Saint John, New Brunswick, to Captain David Mowat, a Loyalist mariner from Massachusetts (Mowat 1976: 56–58; Jack 1908). Thus began a saga that has become a two-continent search for the origin and history of the Mowat marriage poem, which, as a verse letter, opens with the epistolary address, "Dear Hetty," and concludes with the signature of bridesmaid and ostensible author, "Anne Hecht." Just before the last eight lines, a portion of the birchbark had apparently disintegrated, so that the poem published in *Canadian Poetry: From the Beginnings Through the First World War*, using Grace Helen Mowat's book version as copytext, was missing several lines. (David S. Shields also reprinted this version in his 2007 *American Poetry: The Seventeenth and Eighteenth Centuries*). An accompanying letter from bridesmaid Anne Hecht, also written on birchbark, had likewise partially crumbled. Enough of it had survived, however, to explain that, because of an intervening ball and the bridesmaid's sensitivity to Hetty's new domestic preoccupations, the epistolary poetic "advice" regarding the marriage had arrived somewhat after the event (Mowat 1976: 58; Jack 1908: 313).

Some information can be found about the players in the 1786 birchbark version of the poem. Anne Hecht, its assumed author, was the daughter of a German-born Loyalist army officer from New York who had lost major property holdings in New York and St. Augustine during the American Revolution. Evacuating his family to England at the conclusion of the war, he was appointed assistant commissary in New Brunswick in November 1783, to oversee the distribution of fuel and food to ten thousand Loyalist refugees scattered along the Saint John River (Wright 1972: 97). Still too financially embarrassed in 1785 to bring his family from England to Saint

John, he clearly had been able to do so by November 1786, when Anne Hecht acted as bridesmaid to Mehetable Caleff at an Anglican wedding ceremony conducted by the Reverend Mr. William Bisset (Jack 1908: 313; Mowat 1976: 55). Anne herself then faded into the shadows, following her family to Digby, Nova Scotia, where her father died in 1804[3] and where, in her mature years, she married Loyalist Colonel Isaac Hatfield, Commandant of the Loyal Corps of Westchester Refugees, on September 15, 1813 (Punch 1978: 13, #129). Her husband died nine years later at the age of seventy-four (Punch 1978, 100, #2534).

Of the recipient of the poem, Mehetable Caleff, somewhat more is known. Born in Ipswich, Massachusetts, in 1768, she was the daughter of Dr. John Caleff, a surgeon at the siege of Louisbourg in 1745, a member of the Massachusetts legislature at the outbreak of the American Revolution and a man of learning.[4] As the representative for the Penobscot Loyalists for two years in London while the boundary lines between Massachusetts and British North America were being resolved, Dr. Caleff had left his wife, Dorothy Jewett Caleff, the granddaughter of colonial Governor William Dummer of Massachusetts, in Ipswich to defend their property from confiscation. Described by contemporaries as a "vigorous and resourceful woman,"[5] Mehetable Caleff's mother sensed the moment when persecution of the Loyalists threatened the safety of her children and the preservation of her personal property. She secretly chartered a sloop in 1783 to wait in the creek below their home so that she and her children could nightly move selected household effects to the boat under cover of darkness, and then sailed with her young family to the Bay of Fundy. In the midst of a blinding snowstorm, the sloop ran ashore near Red Head/Mispec, New Brunswick, whereupon mother and children, including Mehetable, trudged nine miles through the storm until they reached habitation.[6] Following her marriage to Captain David Mowat, a family friend who had helped to save her father from capture (Jack 1908: 312–13), Mehetable seems to have remained in Saint John for two years. During that time, two of her children were buried in the Loyalist Graveyard on Sydney Street (313). Moving to St. Andrews, New Brunswick, circa 1790, when her parents retired there, Mehetable Caleff Mowat replicated her mother's wartime initiative by serving as public executrix of the wills of both her father and her husband and by overseeing the lives of her twelve children after the death of her husband at sea in 1810 (Robinson 1980: 105).[7] She died in St. Andrews on December 19, 1860, at the age of ninety-two.[8] Nothing is known of the fate of her birchbark wedding memorabilia, nor when the poem and letter were transcribed by her descendant Grace Helen Mowat, as the items themselves seem to be no longer extant, either in private hands or in the Mowat family papers in the Charlotte County Archives in St. Andrews.

We cite these examples of the initiative of Mehetable and her mother because their "lived" lives, their politicization during the American Revolution and their independent resourcefulness stand dramatically at odds with the public sentiments of the marriage poem, "Advice to Mrs. Mowat." Susan Branson noted in *These Fiery Frenchified Dames: Women and Political Culture in Early National Philadelphia* that whether women had been "eager patriots, besieged loyalists, or reluctant nonpartisans," they had emerged from the war having "developed a collective consciousness of women's talents, interests, and potential" (2001: 10). The American newspaper and magazine world was not hesitant in picking up on the interests of this constituency, often engaging its readership in debates on women's education, gender roles in marriage and women's contribution to domesticity and/or society. Some articles, noted Branson, recognized "that women did have a certain degree of power within their domestic relationships, and the strategies they offered to wives for getting what they wanted involved not a challenge to the traditional patriarchal role of husband as a wife's superior, but rather suggested that a wife might cajole her husband, in the most demure manner, to achieve her ends. Delicacy and domestic diplomacy, rather than direct rebellion, were advocated as the methods of attaining a woman's goals" (29).

The poem, "Advice to Mrs. Mowat," stands as a good illustration of this approach. Organized as a series of iambic tetrameter couplets that energetically sustain the movement of a relatively long poem of ninety-six lines, the verse epistle begins by suggesting that it is the bride who has had the autonomy to leave the "single state" and to "choose yourself a mate." That being said, successive couplets undercut any suggestion of female agency, arguing that it is a wife's role "To make her husband bless the day/ He gave his liberty away" (18–19) and that "Heaven gave to man unquestioned sway./ Then Heaven and man at once obey" (52–53). The poem moves through a series of marriage manual recommendations ranging from advice on housekeeping to personal deportment, particularly stressing the importance of tactful diplomacy and accommodation as agents of marital success ("And always keep the golden mean" (27) and "In all things there's a proper mean" (33)). However, the key lines of the poem for modern and, presumably, many eighteenth-century readers are undoubtedly 78–81: "Then shun, O shun that hated self,/ Still think him wiser than yourself./ And if you otherwise believe/Ne'er let him such a thought perceive." This subversive directive, in a society where "once married, a woman became, in the eyes of the common law inherited from England, a *feme covert,* one whose legal person was subsumed or 'covered' by that of her husband" (Yalom 2001: 147, 158), may well suggest the confidence that companionate relationships began to give women in the eighteenth century. What is appealing here is the elasticity of this poem's applicability – traditional for the conservative and impishly ironic for the iconoclastic – especially in its disclaiming conclusion:

> But now, methinks, I hear you cry,
> Shall she pretend, O vanity!
> To lay down rules for wedded life,
> Who never was herself a wife?
>
> I own you've ample cause to chide,
> And blushing throw the pen aside.

The modern reader, schooled to read women's apparently compliant writing for subversive undercurrents, could easily take these lines to suggest that much of the preceding content should be viewed ironically, with women giving each other knowing winks as they laid out the rules for submission to patriarchy. And, as we were soon to find out, although this poem may have been addressed to Mehetable Caleff, it had a far wider applicability than we could ever have anticipated when we decided to include it in our anthology.

It was after the publication of *Canadian Poetry: From the Beginnings Through World War 1* that we discovered an advertisement in the *Quebec Herald*, April 12, 1790, for the printing by subscription of two poems by the late William McMurray, one entitled "Labrador" (which is actually by George Cartwright) and the other, "Advice To A New Married Lady" (with lines identical to those in our 1786 "Advice to Mrs. Mowat") (Tremaine 1952: 299–300). We were puzzled. Then, in 2000, in Karin Wulf's *Not All Wives: Women of Colonial Philadelphia*, we encountered in her discussion of perceived domestic responsibilities several lines identical to those in the Mowat marriage poem. Wulf's lines, however, were attributed to an unnamed suitor rejected by Clementina Cruikshank in Philadelphia in 1768 (2000: 89). We now went on "red alert" to solve the mystery of the Mowat marriage poem and its antecedents.

The breakthrough came in the spring of 2009, when, through the research and collegial generosity of Roger Lonsdale, now retired from the English Department at Balliol, we were able to identify the origin of our 1786 marriage poem, written on birchbark in Saint John, New Brunswick. Lonsdale had first researched the poem, and its author, Esther Lewis Clark (fl. 1747–89) (pseudonym "Sylvia") of Holt, Wiltshire, while working on his 1989 edition, *Eighteenth Century Women Poets: An Oxford Anthology*, where the poem appears as "Advice to a Young Lady lately married." Lonsdale's research on the immediate publishing history of Lewis's poem as it moved from the *Bath Journal* on May 25, 1752, to the *Gentleman's Magazine* in May 1752, to the *London Magazine: Or, Gentleman's Monthly Intelligencer*, in June 1752, has contextualized its early history for us. Lonsdale noted in his introduction to Lewis in *Eighteenth Century Women Poets* that "Advice to a Young Lady lately married" was "often reprinted in periodicals in the following decades" and was also to be "found in common-place books of the period" (1989: 226) and very kindly shared with us an example of the poem in a commonplace book in the Bodleian Library.[9] This particular volume was reputed to be from the library of John Graham Clarke, grandfather of poet Elizabeth Barrett Browning. Such highly portable venues as commonplace books and periodicals could explain how the poem moved from its initial beginnings in the *Bath Journal* to North America.

Our efforts to track this poem's peregrinations raise interesting questions about the ways that popular literature journeyed through the English-speaking world in the decades from 1752 to 1833, the period during which it can be found through searches of digitized texts and selected archival sources. While one might expect that tracking textual variants would be a reliable way to trace the poem's travels and genealogy, this proves not to be the case. Instead, two different versions turned up in England almost at the moment of the poem's birth, followed by a third some twelve years later. All three found their way to the New World.

In the same month that the poem first appeared in the *Bath Journal*, on May 25, 1752, it was also published in the *Gentleman's Magazine*.[10] Both versions are marked Holt, Wiltshire, May 15, 1752, but their titles and their texts are not identical. The *Bath Journal* text, which we shall call version A, differs from the 1752 *Gentleman's* text (version B) in two key places (in addition to the title): line 23 of A is "But daily those affairs inspect," whereas the same line of B is "But matters ev'ry day inspect." Line 89 of A is "From rising Morn, 'till setting Night," whereas the same line of B is "From morn to noon, from noon to night." Neither of these changes significantly affects meaning; what is intriguing is their consistency in subsequent appearances of the two versions. Whether either can be viewed as authoritative is uncertain; the version that appears in 1789 in Clark's book, *Poems Moral and Entertaining*, follows A for lines 23 and 51, but differs otherwise in many respects from both A and B (hence we call it version D).

Version A, the first to turn up in the New World, was on the front page of the *Pennsylvania Gazette* of October 26, 1752,[11] just five months after its initial publication in the *Bath Journal*. A variant of this text (A2, which drops four lines [27–30] from the middle of A), is preserved in manuscript in the Plumsted papers held by the Pennsylvania Historical Society. Addressed to "Dear Clemy" (Clementina Cruikshank) and dated December 8, 1768, this poem is frequently cited by American historians, including Karin Wulf, as an illustration of the limited position of women in eighteenth-century American society (Daniell 1981: 166; Wulf 2000: 162; Eustace 2008: 62). One might assume that the source for "Dear Clemy" was the *Pennsylvania*

Gazette – if it were not the case that version A2, lacking the same four lines, had previously appeared in the *London Magazine* in October 1756.[12] This second appearance of her poem in the *London Magazine* caught the attention of the author, who lost no time in publishing a vehement response, signed "E. L."[13] Hence, it would seem that each of these variants travelled independently to Pennsylvania: version A from Bath to the editor of the *Pennsylvania Gazette*, and version A2 from London to Clemy's unnamed friend. Version A's next known appearance in North America was in the *Boston Magazine* in 1784.[14] To further complicate the picture, version A appeared in the *Gentleman's Magazine* in December 1763, ten years after that periodical had published version B.[15]

Version B also travelled extensively, which is perhaps less surprising because one would expect the enduring London-based *Gentleman's Magazine* to have reached a broader audience than the *Bath Journal*. Within a month, this version appeared in the *London Magazine* and in the *Scots Magazine* of Edinburgh.[16] Six years later it turned up in a London miscellany entitled *The Muse in a Moral Humour*.[17] It, too, crossed the Atlantic, to be written on birchbark in New Brunswick in 1786. Now titled "Advice to Mrs. Mowat," this poem was gleefully picked up by researchers such as ourselves as a distinctive Canadian/Loyalist text.

This is not the whole story. There is yet another version to take into account. While versions A, A2 and B continued to circulate in London serials and miscellanies, someone created a version C by cutting the end of version A and replacing the six concluding lines that give the poem its ironic kick with the moralistic couplet, "These rules observed by a wife / Will make her happy for her life." Version C first appeared in 1764 in a London series entitled *Miscellaneous Correspondence*[18] and was printed in the *Gentleman's Magazine* in December 1775[19] — making this the poem's third appearance in that magazine. Crossing to the New World, version C turned up in the *New York Weekly Museum* in 1788,[20] and entered British North America in 1790, when it was cited in the *Quebec Herald* as a poem forthcoming in a pamphlet that seems never to have advanced from advertisement to publication.[21] Reprints of version C appeared in the *Philadelphia Minerva* in 1796 under the title "Instructions for Conjugal Happiness"[22] and in the *Richmond Enquirer* in 1817, the title changed to "Advice to a Young Wife" (Kierner 1988: 267, n. 55).

While these versions of her poem swirled through the English-speaking portions of the northern hemisphere,[23] Esther Lewis Clark published her book, *Poems Moral and Entertaining* (1789) containing a version with so many further alterations that it requires a new letter and is therefore designated as version D. Although definitive in representing the poet's final intentions, this version seems to have travelled nowhere.[24] All subsequent incarnations of the poem found in Britain and North America reproduce versions A, A2, B or C, sometimes with additional changes to these base texts. For example, Mrs.

Pickering's adaptation of version B, entitled "Verses Addrest to my Niece, Miss. S. B. of Chester, upon Her Marriage," was published in her volume of *Poems*.[25] Most creative was the anonymous author of a gender-reversed imitation, entitled "Advice from a Young Gentleman to his Male Acquaintance, lately Married."[26] While clever, this version invites a less ironic interpretation.

Because the poem circulated anonymously, those who found hand written versions assigned authorship somewhat too easily. Putative authors include the presumably American young woman who wrote it out for "Dear Clemy" in 1768; Anne Hecht, who copied it onto birchbark for Mehetable Calef in 1786; William Murray, a sailor who drowned in Labrador and left a copy which his friends included in a pamphlet they hoped to publish by subscription in Quebec in 1790 to raise money for his widow and children; Mrs. Pickering, who personalized version B; and Patricia Darling Rolland, whose relatives included version B in her *Poetical Pieces* (1817), issued in Edinburgh three years after her death in 1814.[27]

Indeed, what the different versions and wide-ranging distribution of Clark's marriage poem illustrate are the porous boundaries of the Atlantic world in the eighteenth century and the importance of careful archival research. Nor is the repetition of Philadelphia in this story surprising. During the eighteenth century, notes historian Esther Clark Wright, "Philadelphia was the principal receiving and distributing centre of population for the Atlantic seaboard, and it was only slowly, and with much difficulty, that New York forged ahead to supremacy in the nineteenth century" (Wright 1988: 36). Ships from Bristol and London brought the latest periodicals to the city, and a perusal of the *London Magazine* for the critical year of 1752, when the poem first appeared there, shows evidence of an American reading clientele. Not only was a copy of Clark's marriage poem published in June 1752, but so also were news items picked up from the Annapolis, Maryland, *Monthly Chronologer*, in October 1752 and letters from Charles-Town, South Carolina, reprinted in December 1752. A fold-out map of Pennsylvania appeared in December 1756 as part of a series on "British Plantations in America." Most tellingly, the Bodleian Library's copy of Esther Lewis Clark's 1789 *Poems Moral and Entertaining*, which contains her final text, was originally owned in the eighteenth century by one of her local townspeople, A.C. Sandiforde, of Bath.[28] Somehow this copy crossed the Atlantic to Pennsylvania, where, in 1958, using funds from the "Bodley's American Friends," the Bodleian purchased this same copy from a rare books dealer in Philadelphia for its collection. So, clearly, in addition to the circulation of the poem in periodicals and private correspondence, and probably through commonplace books as well, it also entered Philadelphia in book form.

In an article in *The Chronicle Review*, Johanna Drucker, 2009 Digital Humanities Fellow at the Stanford Humanities Center, noted that "Scholars no longer only visit archives in person; they access library material with immediacy (and increased mediation) online" (2009: B6). Our online experiences in exploring the peregrinations of Esther Lewis's 1752 marriage poem reinforce Drucker's observations, for without the searchable electronic archives for newspapers and periodicals from eighteenth and early nineteenth-century Britain and North America, we would never have been able to deduce the circulation history informing Anne Hecht's birchbark poem. Nonetheless, one also cannot throw out the baby with the bathwater. Digitization projects, as Stuart Woods has observed in "History, bit by bit," are often selective, still driving scholars back to "the physical archives" if they "really want to access the source material" (2009: 25). Our research on the origins of "Advice to Mrs. Mowat" demonstrates the applicability of both Drucker's and Woods's comments. Searchable online newspapers have yielded more versions of the poem than we could ever have conjectured and have opened up a fascinating and layered series of questions about literary dissemination in the eighteenth-century Atlantic world that continue to remain a challenge as every new database brings new examples to light.[29] But, ultimately, it was the traditional archival research done by Roger Lonsdale for his book *Eighteenth Century Women Poets* and his generous sharing of his research with us that identified the author of the birchbark marriage poem to be Esther (Lewis) Clark. Reading Clark's final version of the poem in her 1789 *Poems Moral and Entertaining* in the Duke Humfrey's Library at the Bodleian in Oxford — admiring the binding, feeling the texture of the paper and appreciating the typesetting — has made the contrast between the original British context of the poem and its birchbark British North American incarnation truly palpable. Google and our university libraries' electronic resources allowed us to crawl through many online archives to achieve insights denied to us when we first encountered "Advice to Mrs. Mowat" in the early 1990s. But the hushed tones of the Duke Humfrey's Library also reminded us of the magic of traditional archives and their special collections.

A young Lady's Advice to one lately married
First printed in the *Bath Journal*

Gentleman's Magazine 22 (May 1752), 234
[Version B]

[Poem to Clementina, 8 Dec 1768]

Plumsted papers, Historical Society of Pennsylvania
[Version A2]

Dear Peggy! since the single state	Dear Clemy since the Single State
You've left, and chose yourself a mate;	You've left, and Chose yourself a mate,
Since metamorphos'd to a wife,	Since Metamorphosed to a Wife
And bliss or woe's ensured for life,	And Bliss or woe insured for Life.
A friendly muse the way would shew	A Friendly Muse the way would Shew
To gain the bliss, and miss the woe.	To gain the Bliss and Miss the Woe
But first of all, I must suppose	But first of all I must supose
You've with mature reflection chose;	You've with mature Reflection Chose,
And, this premis'd, I think you may	And this premised, I think you may
Here find to marry'd bliss the way.	Here find to married Bliss, the way,
Small is the province of a wife,	Small is the Province of a Wife
And narrow is her sphere in life;	And narrow is her sphere of Life,
Within that sphere to move aright	Within that sphere to move aright
Should be her principal delight:	Should be her principal Delight
To guide the house with prudent care,	To guide her House with prudent Care
And properly to spend and spare;	And properly to spend and spare
To make her husband bless the day	To make her Husband bless the day
He gave his liberty away;	He give his Liberty away ~
To form the tender infant mind:	To form the Infants' tender minds
These are the tasks to wives assign'd;	These are the tasks to wives assigned
Then never think domestic care	Then never think Domestic Care
Beneath the notice of the fair;	Beneath the notice of the fair
But matters ev'ry day inspect,	But daily those affairs inspect
That naught be wasted by neglect.	That nought be wasted thro' neglect.
Be frugal plenty round you seen,	Be frugal — plenty round you seen
And always keep the golden mean.	And always keep the Golden mien
Be always clean, but seldom fine,	Be always Clean, but seldom fine
Let decent neatness round you shine;	Let decent neatness round you shine
If once fair decency be fled.	If once fair Decency be fled
Love soon deserts the genial bed.	Love soon deserts the Genial Bed,
Not nice your house, tho' neat and clean;	
In all things there's a proper mean:	
Some of our sex mistake in this,	
Too anxious some, some too remiss.	
The early days of wedded life	The Early days of wedded Life
Are oft o'ercast by childish strife;	Are oft o'ercast with Childish strife
Then be it your peculiar care	But be it your peculiar Care
To keep that season bright and fair;	To keep that season bright and fair,

For then's the time by gentle art To fix your empire in his heart. With kind, obliging carriage strive To keep the lamp of love alive; For should it thro' neglect expire, No art again can light the fire.	For then's the time by Gentle art, To fix your Empire in his heart, With kind obliging Carriage strive To keep the Lamp of Love alive. For should it through neglect Expire No art again can light the fire
To charm his reason dress your mind, "Till love shall be with friendship join'd, Rais'd on that basis, 'twill endure, From time, and death itself secure.	To Charm his reason dress your mind Till Love shall be with Friendship Joined, Raised on that Basis t'will Endure From time, and Death Itself, secure,
Be sure you ne'er for power contend, Nor try by tears to gain your end; Sometimes the tears which cloud your eyes From pride and obstinacy rise. Heav'n gave to man superior sway, Then heav'n and him at once obey. Let sullen frowns your brow ne'er cloud; Be always cheerful, never loud; Let trifles never discompose Your features, temper, or repose.	Besure you ne'er for power contend Nor seek by tears to gain your End Most times those tears which Cloud our Eyes From pride and obstinacy rise Heaven give to man superior sway Then Heaven, and him, at once obey, Let sullen frowns your brows ne'er Cloud Be always Chearfull, never loud ~ Let Triffels never discompose Your temper, features or repose
Abroad for happiness ne'er roam; True happiness resides at home; Still make your partner easy there, (Man finds abroad sufficient care). If everything at home be right, He'll always enter with delight; Your converse he'll prefer to all Those cheats the world does pleasure call; With cheerful chat his cares beguile, And always meet him with a smile.	Abroad for happiness ne'er rome True happiness Consists at home. Still make your partner Easy there Man finds abroad sufficient Care If every thing at home be right He'll always meet you with delight Your Converse he'll prefer to all Those Cheats the world do pleasure Call, With Chearfull Chat his Cares beguile, And always meet him with a smile
Should passion e'er his soul deform, Serenely meet the bursting storm; Never in wordy war engage, Nor ever meet his rage with rage. With all our sex's softning art Recall lost reason to his heart; Thus calm the tempest in his breast, And sweetly soothe his soul to rest.	Should Passion E'er his soul deform, Serenely meet the bursting storm Never in wordy war Engage Nor even meet his rage, with rage With all our sexes softning art Recall lost reason to his heart Thus Calm the tempest in his brest And sweetly sooth his soul to rest —
Be sure you ne'er arraign his sense; Few husbands pardon that offence; 'Twill discord raise, disgust it breeds, And hatred certainly succeeds. Then shun, O shun that fatal shelf, Still think him wiser than yourself;	Besure you ne'er arraign his sense Few Husbands pardon that offence 'Twill discord raise disgust it breeds And hatred certainly succeeds Then shun, O! shun, the fatal shelf Still think him wiser than yourself

And if you otherwise believe,	Or if you otherwise belive,
Ne'er let him such a thought perceive.	Ne'er let him such a thought perceive.
When cares invade your partner's heart,	When Care Invades your partner's heart
Bear you a sympathising part,	Bear you a sympathizing part,
And kindly claim your share of pain,	And kindly Claim your share of pain
And half his troubles still sustain;	And half his troubles still sustain,
From morn to noon, from noon to night,	From rising Morn till setting Night
To see him pleas'd your chief delight.	To see him pleased, your sole delight
But now, methinks, I hear you cry,	But now, methinks I hear you Cry
Shall she pretend, O vanity!	Shall she, pretend O! Vanity
To lay down rules for wedded life,	To lay down rules for wedded Life
Who never was herself a wife?	Who never was herself a Wife —
I own you've ample cause to chide,	I own you've ample Cause to Chide
And blushing throw the pen aside.	And Blushing throw my pen Aside
Holt, Wiltshire, May 15, 1752	Dec. ye 8th 1768

Notes

1. "Advice to a Young Lady Lately Married," *Bath Journal*, No. 442, 25 May 1752, 33.
2. Grace Helen Mowat, MS 2/1.
3. See also *Saint John Gazette*, Feb. 6, 1804.
4. Caleff's personal copies of the *Critica Sacra* by Puritan linguist and theologian Edward Leigh (1602–71) and a Latin text on happiness by Puritan divine William Ames both survived into the twentieth century (Jack 1893: 1).
5. "tallboy, caleff." Province of New Brunswick, Heritage Branch, "Image Gallery," Artefacts Canada, Search: "Chests of Drawers," item 5 <www.virtualmuseum.ca/PM.cgi?>.
6. Ibid.
7. "Est. Capt. David Mowat, St. Andrews," *New Brunswick Royal Gazette*, October 29, 1810, and "Est. John Caleff, Surgeon, St. Andrews," *New Brunswick Royal Gazette*, March 22, 1813.
8. "Mehetable Mowat," *St. Andrew's Standard*, January 2, 1861. See also Rees and Rees 2009: 18.
9. Ms. Eng. Poet.e.47.
10. "A young Lady's Advice to one lately married," *Gentleman's Magazine* 22 (May 1752), 234. The same version appeared in the June 1852 issue of the *London Magazine, or Gentleman's Intelligencer*, introduced by the note: "Tho' we had not Room for the following in our last, we doubt not but it will now be acceptable to our Readers," 282.
11. "Advice to a young Lady lately Married," *Pennsylvania Gazette*, 26 Oct. 1752: 1.
12. "Advice to New Married Lady, by her Schoolfellow," *London Magazine*, Oct. 1756: 502–03.
13. "To a Lady, who lately adopted a stolen poem," *London Magazine*, Jan. 1757, 40. In Clark's *Poems Moral and Entertaining* (Bath 1789), this poem follows "Advice to a young Lady lately married," under the title "To a Lady who adopted the foregoing Poem for her own." The authors thank Lonsdale for alerting them to the *London Magazine* exchange.
14. "Advice to a Young Lady lately Married. [By an Unmarried Lady]" *Boston Magazine*, 1783: 529–30.
15. "Advice to a young Lady, lately married," *Gentleman's Magazine* 33 (Dec. 1763).
16. "A young lady's advice to one lately married," *Scots Magazine* 14 (1752), 504-05.
17. "A Young Lady's Advice to one Lately Married," *The Muse in a Moral Humour: Being a Collection of Agreeable and Instructive Tales, Fables, Pastorals, etc., by Several Hands*, vol. 2 (London: Francis Noble and John Noble, 1758), 62–65.
18. "Advice to a young Lady, lately married," Benjamin Martin, *Miscellaneous Correspondence*, vol. 4 (London, 1764): 850–51.
19. "Advice to a new-married Lady," *Gentleman's Magazine* 45 (1775), 595–96.
20. "Advice to a Young Lady, lately married," *New York Weekly Museum*, Oct. 25, 1788: 4.
21. "Proposals, for Printing by subscription two Poems," *Quebec Herald*, April 12, 1790, 164. The poems are "Advice to a New Married Lady" and "Labrador," which was actually written by George Cartwright (see Romkey 1987).

22. This is erroneously described as "For the Philadelphia Minerva," Dec. 10, 1796: 2.
23. Version A appeared as "A Young Lady's Advice to an Acquaintance, lately married" in *The New Lady's Magazine*, Feb. 1786: 44, and as "Advice to a Young Lady, lately married, By A Lady" in *Amatory Pieces. Hammond's Elegies, etc.* [Ludlow 1799]: 51–54. Version A2 appeared as "Advice from a Young Lady to her Female Acquaintance Lately Married" in *A Collection of Interesting Anecdotes, Memoirs, Allegories, Essays, and Poetical Fragments*, ed. Mr. Addison (London, 1793): 238–41, which was reprinted in Sherborne [Dorset] in *The Weekly Entertainer* 11 (1798): 70–72. A large section of version B, titled "Advice to a Young Wife," appeared in the *Philadelphia Album and Ladies' Literary Portfolio*, Dec. 14, 1833: 400. Version C appeared as "To a young lady, lately married" in *The Universalist's Miscellany; or Philanthropist's Museum*, ed. W. Vidler (London, 1797): 469–72.
24. Rather than this final version, Roger Lonsdale chose version B for his *Eighteenth Century Women*.
25. "Verses Addrest to my Niece, Miss S.B. of Chester, Upon Her Marriage," *Poems by Mrs. Pickering* (Birmingham, 1794): 48–51.
26. This gender-reversed version appears after version A2 in *Friendly Hints; which, Being Rightly Observed, May Prove Very Conducive to the Mutual Happiness of both Sexes in the Married State* (Northhampton: T. Dicey, 1787): 4–7.
27. "An Advice to a Young Lady, Lately Married," Patricia Rolland Darling, *Poetical Pieces* (Edinburgh: Oliver and Boyd, 1817): 8–13. See Chantal Lavoie's essay on "Patricia Rolland Darling's *Poetical Pieces*, "Scottish Women Poets of the Romantic Period," on-line.
28. The signature is difficult to decipher but appears to be this name. The word "Bath" is clear.
29. Most recently, access to a new body of digitized periodicals located an example of version A entitled "Duties of a Wife," which appeared in a Liverpool newspaper, the *Kaleidoscope; or, Literary and Scientific Mirror*, April 15, 1823: 332.

References

Bell, D.G. 1983. *Early Loyalist Saint John: The Origin of New Brunswick Politics, 1783–1786*. Fredericton: New Ireland Press.

Branson, Susan. 2001. *Those Fiery Frenchified Dames: Women and Political Culture in Early National Philadelphia*. Philadelphia: University of Pennsylvania Press.

Clark, Esther (Lewis). 1789. *Poems Moral and Entertaining Written Long Since*. Bath: S. Hazard.

Daniell, Jere R. 1981. *Colonial New Hampshire, A History*. Millwood, NY: KTO press.

Drucker, Johanna. 2009. "Blind Spots: Humanists Must Plan Their Digital Future," *The Chronicle Review* B6 (April 3).

Eustace, Nicole. 2008. *Passion is the Gale: Emotion, Power, and the Coming of the American Revolution*. Chapel Hill: University of North Carolina Press.

Gerson, Carole, and Davies, Gwendolyn. 1994 (repr. 2010). *Canadian Poetry: From the Beginnings Through the First World War*. Toronto: McClelland and Stewart.

Jack, David Russell. 1908. "The Mowat Family." *Acadiensis* 8.

Jack, Edward. 1893. "Glimpses of the Past." *Saint Croix Courier*, 17 (January 19).

Kierner, Cynthia A. 1998. *Beyond the Household: Women's Place in the Early South, 1700–1835*. Cornell University Press.

Lonsdale, Roger. 1989. *Eighteenth Century Women Poets: An Oxford Anthology*. Oxford/New York: Oxford University Press.

Matthews, Samantha. 2004. *Poetical Remains: Poets' Graves, Bodies and Books in the Nineteenth Century*. New York: Oxford University Press.

Mowat, Grace Helen. 1976. *The Diverting History of a Loyalist Town*. Fredericton: Brunswick Press.

Punch, Terrence M. 1978. Third printing. *Nova Scotia Vital Statistics From Newspapers: 1813–1822*. Halifax: Genealogical Association of the Royal Nova Scotia Historical Society.

Rees, Diana, and Ronald Rees. 2009. *Grace Helen Mowat and the Making of Cottage Craft*. Fredericton: Goose Lane Editions.

Robinson, Charlotte Gourlay. 1980. *Pioneer Profiles of New Brunswick Settlers*. Belleville, ON: Mika Publishing.

Romkey, Ronald. 1987. "The Canadian Imprint of George Cartwright's 'Labrador' — A Bibliographical Ghost." *Canadian Poetry* 21 (Fall/Winter): 42–51.

Sabine, Lorenzo. *"Sabine's Biographical Sketches of Loyalists of the American Revolution."* Available at < www.archive.org/details/biosketchloyal01sabirich>.

Shields, David S. 2007. *American Poetry: The Seventeenth and Eighteenth Centuries*. New York: Library of America.

Tremaine, Marie. 1952. *A Bibliography of Canadian Imprints*. Toronto: University of Toronto Press.

Woods, Stuart. 2009. "History, Bit by Bit." *Quill & Quire* 25 (May).

Wright, Esther Clark. 1972. *The Loyalists of New Brunswick*. Moncton: Moncton Publishing Company.

_____. 1988. "Cumberland Township: A Focal Point of Early Settlement on the Bay of Fundy." In Margaret Conrad (ed.), *They Planted Well: New England Planters in Maritime Canada*. Fredericton: Acadiensis Press.

Wulf, Karin. 2000. *Not All Wives: Women of Colonial Philadelphia*. Philadelphia: University of Pennsylvania Press.

Yalom, Marilyn. 2001. *A History of the Wife*. New York: Perennial (Harper Collins).

Unearthing an Erased Poet
Gathering up The Fragments of James McCarroll

Michael Peterman

I have a tee-shirt from the Hastings County Historical Society that reads "ARCHIVES ARE FOREVER." I was delighted to receive it several years ago and I wear it often. In so doing I am, in my own mind, honouring projects completed and research still to be undertaken, even as I delight in fielding queries from bemused acquaintances about what the message means. In the case I am about to describe, archives are not only forever and enduring, but they have been essential in my quest to unearth and recreate the narrative of a lost but significant nineteenth-century Canadian writer and artist. It is a story that I have tracked in various archival sites in Canada, the United States, England and Ireland, often to look at specific resources and sometimes to play a calculated hunch. My challenge has been to find as many pieces of the story as possible and to try to make sense of the personal narrative they constitute and the cultural history they inform.

James McCarroll (1814–1892) was a journalist, poet, humourist, story-writer, musician, theatre critic and entertainer in Canada West from the late 1830s until early in 1866. His rise to literary and cultural prominence in the colony was slow, marked by his struggle to earn a living, several professional relocations and a near bankruptcy in 1846. Nevertheless, by 1861, his fame in the province was considerable. While his working life as a Customs officer (he was first appointed in 1849) took him from Peterborough to Cobourg, then to Niagara Falls (Port Stanford) and Port Credit, and finally Toronto (1856), his reputation as a multitalented, amusing and provocative Irish-Canadian literary figure grew apace. Indeed, by 1864, he had established himself as one of the best known cultural figures at work in the city. He excelled as a poet and humourist, but he was also an accomplished flautist and singer who appeared in numerous concerts and benefit performances in Toronto and environs.[1]

However, in February 1866, he disappeared from the pages of the very newspapers and magazines in which he had attained his prominence. Wooed by Fenian friends in Buffalo, he decamped for that city, where he would work for about five years before heading for New York City and an editorial job with the Frank Leslie Publishing Company. Seen by many as a traitor to British interests, he was not long in fading from the attention and even the memory of most Canadian observers. In fact, he would live his final twenty-five years in the United States, working in various capacities as a journalist, poet, editor, songwriter and inventor.

Retrospectively, I see him as a pre-Confederation Humpty Dumpty of sorts, a skilled and sometimes flamboyant writer who suddenly fell from a position of literary eminence atop the colonial wall. In falling from view he lost the very audience he had nurtured and amused in Canada West. In the wake of the excitement of Confederation, as Canada began its slow transformation from colony to Dominion, all that remained of the once prominent McCarroll were archival fragments — sometimes gaudy fabrics, sometimes drab rags — pieces of the literary apparel he once wore for Canadian readers. James McCarroll's story is more than a case of personal overreaching and bad judgement, of failing to protect the literary reputation he had carefully developed. It is a cautionary tale highly indicative of the turbulent times in which he rose to public prominence; as well, it charts the politicized response to some of the more outspoken ways in which, at the peak of his powers, he chose to express his talents. In his narrative the political trumps the literary. For a writer it was, after all, a challenge to try to build, let alone maintain, a literary reputation during an era in which politics, racial identity and issues of national identity were such powerful determining forces. It mattered tremendously who you were and how well you were able to play the political game — particularly the game of loyalty, connections, patronage and verbal give and take — and it mattered whether you were English, Scottish or self-consciously Irish. It also mattered how well you were protected financially from untoward events.

For most Canadians in the pre-Confederation years, the notion of a literary life was a romantic and inherently risky idea; it had little place in the daily scheme of things. Literature was valued, to be sure, but it was regarded as something that was accomplished elsewhere, a special kind of achievement produced by more sophisticated societies where leisure time and education were inherent in the social fabric. Colonial life was all about raw survival and, when possible, personal advancement; cultural achievement was worth supporting in principle but it was of very minor concern in day-to-day realities.

To attempt to become an imaginative writer in Canada in the pre-Confederation years was tacitly deemed a flighty and impractical objective. By contrast, a career in journalism, with its firm commitment to political and economic realities, was worthwhile and substantial. McCarroll understood this and, having had a good training in the polemical journalism of Canada West in his twenties, he consciously developed his growing number of journalistic connections as a means of placing examples of his literary work and promoting his creative undertakings.

These connections were largely Irish and they were many. In 1861 Toronto was a city in which the Irish — Protestant and Catholic together — made up the largest sector among its British citizenry. McCarroll was an Irishman to the core; his Connaught accent was as pronounced in the 1860s as it was when he immigrated in 1831, and over the years in Canada he grew increasingly passionate about Irish history. As well, he had the knack of fellowship, whether his friends were Irish or Scottish, or even English. Nevertheless, in the eyes of most English and Scottish observers, to be flamboyantly Irish and proudly Celtic carried a dangerous whiff of excess, a suggestion of uncertainty and instability; it spoke to a legacy of inherited old-world problems that showed few signs of going away in Canada. In that sense, and with the ease of hindsight, one might conjecture that James McCarroll was on shaky ground as he sought to carve out his personal prominence in Toronto during the decade preceding Confederation. He knew how to waken and sustain attention, but he ran significant risks in the process, especially for a working man without capital to support himself in a pinch.

It is necessary to begin this accounting of archival resources and research challenges with a more detailed description of James McCarroll's lost literary career. Being "lost" to us as contemporary observers, it follows that he needs to be rediscovered. That has been a part of my work for some twenty years. But without a detailed reconstruction of the salient events of his life in Canada — both personal and literary — and thus some sense of his historical place and the kinds of cultural expression that he represented, a reader would lack the context to appreciate the barriers a researcher must face. In such sleuthing there are many disappointing dead-ends, especially the absence of personal letters and the fact of lost (or missing) runs of relevant newspapers and magazines.

At the same time the very extent of extant archival records is daunting, even though those records contain plenty of material — what I shall call fragments — that make the work of archival research very rewarding at times. My focus has been to gather up and make sense of the fragments of James McCarroll that remain to be found. Indeed, this biographical sketch is composed of many such fragments pulled together from a wide range of archival and historical sources.

Born in County Longford, Ireland, and raised in nearby County Leitrim, James McCarroll came to Canada with his parents in 1831. He was seventeen at the time and had already developed an interest in music and literature during his Irish schooling. Neither he nor his father Robert was inclined to farm the land grant near Peterborough, in Upper Canada, that Robert had received as a retired British soldier. He had been the bandmaster of the

Leitrim militia for twenty years. As an alternative, father and son set up a music school in the Peterborough-Cobourg area, which they advertised in the Cobourg *Star* in February 1832, offering training in the music of Carolan,[2] Mozart and Haydn. Likely, they found only a handful of students — certainly not enough clientele in those early days of pioneering and hard travel to provide them with a living.

When Robert McCarroll decided to relocate his family to York (Toronto), young James took up other plans. He liked Peterborough and stayed on, marrying a young woman named Anne Davis. They began a family; to make ends meet financially, he found work first as a shoemaker (his father's military trade) and later as an assistant school master, choir leader and fledgling journalist.

McCarroll may have worked for John Darcus on Peterborough's first newspaper, the *Backwoodsman* (c. 1839–43) — only a few issues survive and all articles are unsigned — but the first identifiable record of his own writing (and writerly aspirations) was his emergence as owner and editor of the *Backwoodsman's* successor, the *Peterboro Chronicle*, a venture in which he was likely backed by local Irish friends. Its first issue appeared in December 1843, and it ran as a weekly newspaper until the summer of 1846, when a fire destroyed his print shop and effectively bankrupted him. During its two-year run, however, he made a provincial reputation for himself as a hard-hitting journalist who supported the cause of responsible government and the Reform party leaders while attacking their Tory opponents with fiery panache and often withering *ad hominum* rhetoric. However, as only two issues of the *Chronicle* have survived (probably as a result of the fire), there is very limited access to his early writing, journalistic style and opinions. Nor can one determine how much of his poetry and fiction he inserted in its pages. He did however place a few poems in newspapers like the *Christian Guardian*.

For three years after his devastating losses in the fire, McCarroll scrambled to make ends meet, both in Peterborough (where his wife and two daughters continued to live) and in Cobourg (where he stayed at the Globe Hotel and taught music). Patronage, he knew, could provide the answer to his long-term needs. His patience was rewarded late in 1849, when he received a coveted government position. In announcing James McCarroll's appointment as a "Landing Waiter" at the Port of Cobourg, Attorney-General Francis Hincks rewarded McCarroll for his loyal journalistic support of the Reform agenda. Hincks himself had edited the *Toronto Examiner* in the 1840s and had emerged as a prominent member of the Baldwin-LaFontaine government. In fact, he would continue to take a friendly interest in McCarroll's career during the next decade.

From 1849 until 1864 McCarroll served as a salaried employee of the Customs Department. His career followed an upward arc — he was promoted to the position of collector in 1851 and was posted to several ports in Canada West; then, in 1856, he was appointed to the more prestigious and higher-paying position of assistant surveyor at the Port of Toronto. His salary rose to 250 pounds a year. Along the way he developed numerous journalistic connections and actively sought to place his poems and short stories with magazines and provincial newspapers, especially those of a Reform stripe. Once he came to reside in Toronto, however, he began to hit his stride as a poet, reviewer and humourist. Certainly his literary reputation blossomed there.

Archival evidence gathered from extant provincial newspapers and magazines suggests that James McCarroll became one of the leading creative writers and musicians in Toronto during the decade leading up to Confederation. This is no small claim. Canada was still a colony, but many cultural activities were astir in the city in those years, and James McCarroll was near the centre of much of that energy and activity. Certainly, he enjoyed his prominence, especially among the Irish readers he sought to please and the Irish editors with whom he liked to fraternize. But his range of admirers was wider still. Henry Morgan saw him as a gifted, many-sided talent, adding that "there has scarcely been… a periodical or newspaper of any note published in U[pper] C[anada] with which he has not had something to do" (1867: 254). The Rev. Edward H. Dewart praised him in 1864 as a poet "long and favourably known to the Canadian public" (237). In Dewart's anthology of Canadian poetry (the first in the colony, published in Montreal that year), McCarroll vied with Charles Sangster, Susanna Moodie and Alexander McLachlan in terms of the number of poems (six in his case) chosen for inclusion. But McCarroll was different from the others. At heart, he was an excitable, passionate and tactile poet, fun-loving and high-spirited, despite his occasional dark moods. He was much more interested in earthly pleasures and in cheeky humour than his contemporaries. In fact, he was inherently anti-Victorian and increasingly anti-English in his outlook. By the mid-1850s he had become more passionate in his commitment to his native — and much beleaguered — Ireland. The famine years of the late 1840s had galvanized his attention even as he began to deepen his knowledge of the long legacy of cultural achievement in Ireland and the damage done to his homeland in the wake of the English conquest.

By the 1850s the Irish comprised the largest single sector of the Canadian population; however, for many non-Irish, Ireland and the Irish in general remained a problematic entity. Plagued by famine, poverty, in-fighting, violence and unrest, Ireland was viewed by many as an ungovernable country; it was deeply split along religious lines, while many of its people, particularly the poor (mainly the Catholic poor), were seen as errant, slovenly, feckless and prone to drunkenness.

For his part McCarroll took a supportive and integrative view of Irish culture. He saw himself as a writer who specialized in the humorous, hearty and occasionally bawdy expressions of the Irish "voice" — he drew here for distinctiveness on the established tradition of the vernacular "stage-Irish voice" — even as he offered his readers a sometimes satiric, sometimes affectionate, view of Canadian life in the present as seen through his Irish lens. He liked to think (and this may qualify as both a noble aspiration and a case of personal hubris) that he could speak for both the Protestants (he was raised in the Church of Ireland) and the Catholics, with whom he sought to be empathetic. For nearly a decade he flourished in his particularized literary niche, publishing touching, often comic poems from his "Irish Anthology," stories with an Irish locale or flavour ("The New Gauger; or Jack Trainer's Story" — serialized in *The Anglo-American Magazine* (1856), was set in County Leitrim) — and comic letters from a Toronto barkeeper, the ebullient Terry Finnegan, to Thomas D'Arcy McGee, the leading Irish politician of the day. Terry, who called himself McGee's "lovin cousin," became a favourite for many Toronto readers beginning in the winter of 1861. In all some fifty of Finnegan's weekly letters have survived, though I know that many more were published.

However, in 1864 things changed suddenly for McCarroll, and that change was very much for the worse. The government of John Sandfield Macdonald, which McCarroll had boldly mocked and criticized in print, suddenly removed him from his Customs position in early September 1864, terminating his comfortable annual salary. Not surprisingly, he was angry and bereft; he began to fester in his hostility and to write, wherever he could find a helpful editorial friend, about the unfairness and injustice that had been done to him. It was an injustice that he saw as mean-spirited and anti-Irish; the maxim, "No Irish Need Apply," took on a highly personalized meaning for him. Feeling betrayed by government and by the Customs officials who criticized his work, and seeing himself at least temporarily neglected by his friends in power (notably, his occasional drinking friend, John A. Macdonald), he bided his time in Toronto for two and a half increasingly difficult years, making what money he could by piecemeal newspaper work and by travelling across the province to perform his one-man show of music and Irish humour. Then in February 1866, when he took his show to Buffalo, New York, he opted to stay there, aligning himself with men of Fenian interests like Patrick O'Dea. For O'Dea, he would edit two short-lived Fenian newspapers (the *Buffalo Globe* [1866] and the *Fenian Volunteer* [1867]) during his first two years in Buffalo.[3]

This was a seismic shift for McCarroll. It led to his being denounced by many in Canada as a traitor.[4] Government border detectives watched his movements closely, fearing that his detailed knowledge of Canadian ports and their respective vulnerabilities might be used in the planning of invasions of the colony. Several Canadian journalists were quick to criticize his decampment while others took a cautious view. A decade later, another Irish emigrant of notable literary ambition, Nicholas Flood Davin, offered a definitive cultural judgement on the Fenian McCarroll. "Terry Finnegan" had chosen to forsake Canada in favour of the Fenian promise that was then flourishing in numerous American border cities. Davin chose to omit him from his comprehensive vanity book, *The Irishman in Canada* (1878), even though, at the very time of its composition, McCarroll was working as a journalist, musician, playwright and editor in New York City, apparently having long since left Fenianism and Buffalo behind. His penalty, as Davin's book implies, was to be dropped from the record of cultural achievement by the country in which he had done his best literary work; moreover, it seemed that he had been abandoned by the Irish themselves.[5]

This was a conspicuous act of erasure. By his own actions McCarroll had made himself *persona non grata*, a notorious figure in the minds of many; he had resisted Confederation in his writings and then had aligned himself with the interests of American Fenians. However, by the early 1870s, many, if not most, of the Irish in Canada were actively distancing themselves from the Fenian cause and the coincident, and still ominous, threat of American invasion.

In fact, Fenianism was never a strong force in Toronto despite its large Irish populace. Patrick Boyle's Hibernian newspaper, the *Irish Canadian* (begun in Toronto in 1863), became the centre for the cause of Irish nationalism in the city, but Boyle and his fellow editors were careful to avoid too much overly heated Fenian rhetoric in its pages. Nevertheless, government officials twice closed down his newspaper because of fear of Fenian activities. Certainly, the 1868 assassination of Thomas Darcy McGee in Ottawa, allegedly by Fenian conspirators, horrified many Canadians. Patrick Whalen was charged with the murder and executed within a few months. For his part, McCarroll, who had been associated editorially with the *Irish Canadian* from its earliest days and had been blamed by his former friend Patrick Moylan, the Irish-born editor of the *Canadian Freeman*, for inciting those who murdered McGee, continued his Fenian literary efforts in Buffalo. In 1868 he self-published *Ridgeway: An Historical Romance of the Fenian Invasion of Canada*. The novel's nominal author was "Scian Dubh," a Gaelic term meaning "Black Knife." Beyond its narrative focus on the progress of Irish nationalism in North America, McCarroll used the "Introduction" to launch a heavy-handed attack upon his old friend, John A. Macdonald. He was, however, careful to avoid mention of the fallen McGee.

It may not sound, from what I have written, that there is very much of a challenge involved in searching for the literary fragments of James McCarroll. Certainly, there is a good deal of archival material that had to be located and then checked, often more than once, with close attention. He published four books during his lifetime even as he contributed to many newspapers and magazines.[6] The problem begins with a lack of accurate and detailed information about the man himself. His Fenian enthusiasm and the residual effects of Davin's act of erasure have left large gaps in subsequent accounts; one finds only a few trustworthy references to him in Canadian biographical sources since his death in New York City in 1892. There are scarcely any scholarly articles about him; indeed, he is seldom noticed in studies of nineteenth-century Canadian writing.

Such was the case when I first tried to find information in order to compose a footnote about him for a book of Susanna Moodie letters (*Letters of a Lifetime*, 1985). I was met, in the few Canadian sources available, by what turned out to be several factual errors and an absence of pertinent detail. For instance, I did not realize at the time that several of the facts cited in the *Macmillan Dictionary of Canadian Biography* were not to be trusted. Still, as he had been a respected literary friend of the Moodies and Catharine Parr Traill, I was curious to learn more about him. I recall suggesting to Frances Halpenny that she might consider him as an entry in Volume 12 of the *Dictionary of Canadian Biography*; however, as that volume's deadline was looming and my quest for reliable facts about him was still in its early stages, we agreed that there was too little time to develop the entry. Only in Norah Story's *Oxford Companion to Canadian History and Literature* (1967) did one find an informed entry on McCarroll; sadly however, it was eliminated when William Toye and Eugene Benson co-edited a new edition of the *Companion*.

Thereafter, as I sought out more information about McCarroll's cultural and political life, I came to realize that he had been a more substantial Canadian writer and public figure than the Canadian record allowed. In terms of the era, his was a fascinating and sometimes sensational story. As a complex, sometimes brilliant, sometimes contradictory writer, he called out for a much larger effort of recovery and restitution. In fact, because his life supplied so much drama and so many historical glimpses, I had to resist the temptation to fictionalize him in a story of my own making.

I soon found that American biographical dictionaries were more helpful than the Canadian ones in tracing his literary life. This is not surprising because he lived his final twenty-five years in New York State and during that time wrote for a variety of American periodicals. Such accounts made me aware that there was a great deal of data to track down both in Canada and the United States and that, once gathered, there would be much to do by way of filling in the gaps and providing a coherent contextual interpretation. Archival resources were clearly the key to my recovery of various aspects of his literary and musical life; I needed those findings to give shape and texture to his lost story.

Archival work is never simple and involves many roadblocks. Those who research nineteenth-century documents will recognize many of the challenges that I have faced in this work. First and foremost is the absence of any McCarroll family papers. I don't know why this is so, though I can speculate, even as I realize that guessing is a dangerous game when one is pursuing factual accuracy.[7] Thus, surviving McCarroll letters are rare (though he appears to have been a keen and able correspondent), and there exists no familial attempt to gather material together and to shape his story for public consumption.

Insofar as McCarroll lives on, he endures largely in the record of what he wrote for publication or, more precisely, what he wrote that has survived in various archives. I should add that he also exists through accounts of his life that he passed on to writer friends like Henry Morgan. I have come to realize that, however much he craved book publication, the essence of his writing life lies less in his books than in the newspapers and magazines to which he contributed, especially those he edited or those edited by friends and colleagues. As Charles Lotin Hildreth noted in his "Introduction" to McCarroll's final book, *Madeline and Other Poems* (1889: v), he "probably has the honorable distinction of having edited or been connected with more newspapers, journals, and magazines than any other man in America." This is no small commendation.

He would have loved to locate publishers and backers for his other book projects, but he lacked the necessary connections and the personal financial resources to bring such plans to fruition.[8] Unlike books, newspapers provided quick publication, immediate authorial gratification and occasionally a (small) fee for providing a poem, a story or a comic letter. McCarroll knew the business well, and he knew the limitations of book publishing in pre-Confederation Canada. He advanced his own literary life by haunting the offices of prominent Toronto newspapers and developing friendships with influential editors like James Moylan, Charles Lindsey, Ogle Gowan and Patrick Boyle.

Second, my sleuthing has been undercut by incomplete runs of newspapers and magazines; in some instances not a single copy of a particular paper or periodical is extant. Such absences are frustrating and can be devastating in terms of the gathering of necessary data. There are only two surviving issues of McCarroll's first newspaper, the *Peterboro Chronicle*; there is a broken run of its successor, the *Peterborough Despatch*, to which he often contributed in the late 1840s; and there are no copies of the *Newcastle Courier* (Cobourg), which he edited for several months in 1847–48. There are no extant copies of certain Toronto satiric magazines, like *Momus* (1861) and *Pick* (1865), to which he contributed; indeed, he may even have owned and edited them. So too only one issue of the two Fenian papers (the Buffalo *Globe* and the

Fenian Volunteer) that he edited in Buffalo has survived, and it dates from a time after he left the employ of the *Fenian Volunteer*.

In many of these instances the brevity of the run likely meant that no yearly cumulative record was kept. It also suggests that McCarroll could be a difficult man in his editorial positions, decamping when he was unhappy with conditions or more simply abandoning the work when monetary support proved inadequate. With regard to the Peterborough-Cobourg region's most important conservative newspaper, the Cobourg *Star*, one finds in its pages during the late 1840s numerous McCarroll poems along with occasional prose contributions and the first of his comic Irish letters. Despite his reputation as a Reformer, he was friendly with the *Star's* editor, who welcomed his creative submissions. Yet even the volumes of the Cobourg *Star* are incomplete. For instance, volumes for 1852 and 1853 are missing and with them any evidence of McCarroll's continuing contributions; he was by then posted to Port Stanford, but he sent back poems and news items as the *Star's* Niagara Falls correspondent.

Tracking his writing as a music and theatre reviewer in Toronto has proved very difficult. In various biographical entries he is described as writing reviews for city newspapers like the *Colonist* and the *Leader*. However, lacking exact dates for such assignments and, in the case of the *Colonist* faced with an incomplete run, it is virtually impossible to track his personal contributions. The problem, in part, is that it was regular practice in those days to leave reviews unsigned. Some can be identified as likely by McCarroll, given the subject matter and emphasis, but there are few that can be deemed so with certainty. Still, enough evidence remains to identify him as a writer who was very keen on both the theatre and musical performances; he would have made it his business to be in the audience for many of the shows that played Toronto theatres in the pre-Confederation decade. As a man about town and cultural figure, there were few performances that he would have wanted to miss.

Third, he is mostly absent from the personal papers and letters of important contemporary figures whom he knew well and with whom he occasionally hobnobbed or corresponded. Only by patient trolling in various archival collections have I found mention of him or a letter or two from his pen. Happily, his numerous letters to John A. Macdonald (1864–67) have been preserved, but I have been frustrated in examining the papers of politicians like Thomas D'Arcy McGee and Francis Hincks, as well as those of early Canadian editors and newspaper owners. His many letters written to headquarters in his capacity as a Customs officer are also revealing, both in terms of work issues and evidence of his personal tastes. As well — and this is disappointing — I have not been able to locate specific references to him in the papers of the many internationally famous, nineteenth-century musicians whom he claimed to know. I include among those acquaintances, in Toronto and New York, such prominent stars as Sir Jules Benedict, Catherine Hayes, Anna Bishop, Lucca, Frederick Griebel, Henri Vieuxtemps, Ole Bull, Maurice Strakosch, Henri Wieniawski and the phenomenally famous Jenny Lind.

A fourth and still more challenging problem is McCarroll's aforementioned delight in using pseudonyms. Early in his career he often wrote acerbic letters using catchy pseudonyms. For the Peterborough *Despatch* in the late 1840s he used the penname Crux to put down and denounce the pretensions of the young editor of the rival (Tory) paper, the *Peterborough Gazette*. His most famous is Terry Finnegan, the name he gave to Thomas D'Arcy McGee's fictional "cousin," who, writing from "Stanly Street" (now Lombard Street) in Toronto, composed delightfully provocative and advisory letters to Canada's leading Irish politician. McCarroll excelled in the composition of comic vernacular letters, redolent with humorous phrasing, comic illiteracy, sharp political observation and edgy cultural commentary. The Terry Finnegan letters appeared weekly (but not consistently) between 1861 and 1865 in a number of Toronto satiric magazines, notably the *Grumbler*. Not only did they help to make McCarroll's name as a literary man in the 1860s, but also, when seen in historical terms, they serve to place him — once his contributions are better recognized by literary historians — in the tradition of humorous Canadian letters, from Thomas Haliburton through Susanna Moodie to Stephen Leacock. Indeed, because students of Canadian literature have overlooked him for so long, he remains a missing link in that tradition.

But Terry Finnegan was only the most prominent of McCarroll's pseudonymic voices. I have already mentioned Scian Dubh (*Ridgeway*) and Crux (the *Despatch*), but there are many more. With help from able research assistants like Janet Friskney and through painstaking re-readings of newspapers like the Toronto *Leader* (later the *Daily Leader* (1854–65) and other newspapers, I have been able to identify several other pseudonyms he applied.

These further gambits — among them Lanty Mullins, Soprano, Yod, Terry Fenian and Professor Pike, UCD — help to expand and define McCarroll's literary range, his playfulness and the complexity of his purposes. With such information in hand (and there may well be more pseudonyms to unearth), I am now able to identify close to a hundred McCarroll poems — up from about eighty without the pseudonyms — that appeared in the Toronto *Leader* between 1854 and 1865. This is a remarkable total in itself and, overall, a testimony to the high regard in which he was held by the paper's founding editor, Charles Lindsey, and his successors, along with the paper's owner, Irish-born James Beaty. It was through the *Leader* as well that McCarroll met the Belford brothers and in particular Robert, the youngest; nephews of James Beaty, the Belford boys would each make his mark in North American publishing.

My inventory of major archival repositories of McCarroll material includes, as indicated above, the papers of John A. Macdonald at Library and Archives Canada. This "collection" is a mother-lode of sorts; it contains fourteen personal letters (1864–66) written by McCarroll to the then-attorney general of Canada West. In them he decries his personal situation, directs blame at his enemies in the Customs Department (Thomas Worthington and Alfred Brunel) and urges Macdonald to provide him with some relief in his increasing distress. The letters become more desperate as his situation worsened, but they also reveal many important aspects of his literary interests and his struggles to get by after he lost his coveted government position.

Increasingly, he had to borrow money from friends even as he sought to implement various projects that might provide modest monetary support for his family as well as a continuing journalistic voice for himself. He reported on his hope of finding an American publisher for his various manuscripts, he continued to write for newspapers and magazines in Canada West (though the pay was at best modest) and filled in as an editor when an opportunity occurred.

On a more demanding scale he described to Macdonald the intensive work he had to undertake in setting up, promoting and performing his one-man evening of entertainment. He took the show across the province to places as various as Ottawa, Hamilton, Lindsay, Peterborough, Yorkville and Dunnville where he had an invitation from the local Mechanics Institute or the support of a well-placed Irish friend.[9] His performances drew local acclaim, but the demands of the work were exhausting. He would open his shows with a comic lecture called "The House That Jack Built," read a letter or two in the Irish brogue from the renowned Terry Finnegan and perform flute solos and duets with his daughter Mary, who accompanied him on piano. But as a last resort he continued to pin his hopes on John A.'s promised support, believing that he should, and would, eventually receive some financial help or restitution through government. Having been lifted out of poverty once before when he received his initial Customs appointment from Francis Hincks, he believed that once Macdonald had the "right" opportunity available to him he would see to his needs as he had promised.

McCarroll also reported to Macdonald that he continued to operate "a small, neat printing office in Toronto which is some service to me now in printing matter connected with my lectures."[10] Doubtless, that office was also useful in his attempts to set up and print the issues of several of ambitious satiric papers (the *Growler*, the *Latch Key* [in its two incarnations] and possibly *Momus* and *Pick*) that he placed before the reading public. Overall, however, these several efforts proved exhausting and did nothing to alleviate his increasing anxiety. In the same letter he wrote to Macdonald, "If I am as poor as a church mouse and as reckless as a highway man, I am as proud as Lucifer and as consistent a friend or enemy as ever breathed." That recklessness, that strong vein of volatile Irish spirit, would soon lead him to leave Canada in anger and despair.

The papers of the Customs Department (Library and Archives Canada) are also a major resource. They include McCarroll's correspondence from his various postings with his superiors, including Francis Hincks and R.S.M. Bouchette; they detail his negotiations with them and a number of the local challenges and controversies that he encountered in pursuing his customs duties. In fact, he was seldom far from troubling local situations as a Customs collector (often because he was an obvious outsider in the region), though in general he was seen by his superiors as a gentleman and a reliable, diligent public servant. While Customs business is always the central issue in these letters, they occasionally provide glimpses of his personal interests and the situation of his family that add colour and texture to what I know of his working life, even as they offer insights into business operations and political factors in pre-Confederation Toronto.

In this same vein of tracking elusive correspondence, I would like to highlight three particular letters to or from McCarroll that I have found in the papers of some of his literary and journalistic contemporaries. How often I dream of finding more such documents! They have helped me greatly in identifying him as an ambitious and multifaceted literary man (in both Toronto and New York City), and they offer suggestive glimpses into his intriguing personality; indeed, they open up new territory and identify important connections that might otherwise be overlooked. Like most writers McCarroll remained hopeful of making a big splash in the larger literary world. He did not lack in self-regard and chudspah even when he found himself in a constraining situation or a depressed state of mind.

The first is a letter that he wrote to the aforementioned Charles Lindsey from New York. Lindsey was William Lyon Mackenzie's son-in-law and had been an influential Reform journalist in Toronto before he became the editor of the Toronto *Leader* in 1853. The Mackenzie fonds at the Ontario Archives include two boxes of Charles Lindsey's papers. In them I found two McCarroll letters, one of which provided a goldmine of information about his post-Canadian literary life and served to open up a whole new area of research for me.[11]

Writing on the stationery of the Frank Leslie Company in the spring of 1873, McCarroll reported that he was currently employed in an editorial capacity by that firm. He described his position as one of "no small influence." Internal evidence in Leslie's major publications suggests that he was involved in the editing of both *Frank Leslie's Illustrated Newspaper* and *Frank Leslie's Chimney Corner*; the former was an illustrated weekly that often sold between 150,000 and 300,000 copies a week and the latter a weekly story magazine aimed at the American middle-class family. He added that for the *Chimney Corner* he was organizing and writing several Canadian portraits to be included in its ongoing series, "Self-Made Men of Our Times." McCarroll wanted his old friend and colleague to know that his profile (both portrait and text) was to appear in the current issue.

This letter led me not only to the identification of many of McCarroll's contributions (signed and, in some cases, unsigned) to Leslie's many periodicals[12] but also, by implication, to his pivotal role in helping young Isabella Valancy Crawford of Peterborough, Ontario, to establish a reliable outlet for her serialized novels and stories. Two of Crawford's serialized novels along with more than twenty-five of her short stories appeared in Leslie's publications while McCarroll worked there in an editorial capacity.

A second document was published a few years ago in *The Collected Letters of Charles Dickens*. McCarroll had written to Dickens in 1861, just as he had written to Thomas Moore in Ireland a decade earlier (and as he would write to leading American writers like Oliver Wendell Holmes and Henry Wadsworth Longfellow in the 1860s) seeking advice and help in finding a publisher.

Dickens's reply, dated 28 February 1862, provided no encouragement regarding specific publishing opportunities in the London marketplace.[13] Dickens answered that he himself had never succeeded in trying to "induc[e] any publisher to accept a book on my recommendation"; he mentioned as an example his failure to get Edgar Allen Poe's work published in England. In response to the writing samples sent by McCarroll, he was also less than optimistic about their appeal to an English audience, though he identified "merit" and originality in them, especially in the poetry. In his reply he mentions "a poem of two thousand lines" and an Indian tale, noting discouragingly of the latter that "on this side of the Atlantic the Indian would scarcely interest any more, though he were in the hands of Scott himself."[14] Nevertheless, his closing words were encouraging: "But I can honestly add that your cultivation of literature evinces an earnestness of spirit, and a love and knowledge of nature, and a purity of taste, all very interesting and suggestive of advance."

In fact, McCarroll's collected poems, which he had hoped to see in print in the 1860s, were not published until 1889 in New York and then by means of special support from Robert Belford, a young Irish friend from his Toronto days. One of the three Belford brothers who became involved in journalism and publishing in Toronto, Robert later became the publisher of *Belford's Magazine* in New York and co-owner of the publishing firm of Clarke, Belford and Company. McCarroll worked at *Belford's* in an editorial capacity for the last five years of his life, writing reviews and occasional essays.

The final letter, which I discovered in the summer of 2008, proved another windfall. I found it through a name-search of the Ontario Archives website. I punched in the *Latch-Key* as a magazine title and was directed to the fonds of a Toronto lawyer and writer, William A. Foster (1840–1888).[15] In Foster's small cache of papers I found two McCarroll letters that had been mis-catalogued in pencil under the name of "Carroll." the *Latch-Key* letter, in McCarroll's fine hand, was dated 5 September [1864] and labelled "Private & Confidential." It invited Foster, a young literary friend, to contribute to "a new series" of McCarroll's current magazine. "Give me some scraps and your name shall be held sacred," he wrote, promising the standard anonymity of the era. The magazine, he added,

> will contain exclusively Terry Finnegan's letters, as well as other articles from the pen of that genius. In addition, the bills [posters] will claim that all the principal writers in *Momus* and the FIRST series of *The Grumbler* will also be contributors.

The smart yet casual tone of the letter took my breath away; so did its allusive content. It assumes and suggests much. Part of my delight lay in the fact that, until then, I had very little documentary evidence about the several satiric magazines that appeared in Toronto during the late 1850s and early 1860s. The letter makes clear that McCarroll was involved in — perhaps even had an editorial hand in — several of these periodicals; it also confirms that he was a major contributor to at least three of them. Terry Finnegan's letters did appear in all three magazines. In addition, the letter implies that there was a small coterie of Toronto writers whose work appeared in both *Momus* and the *Grumbler* (first series).

The *Grumbler* was the most successful of these satiric weeklies; it went through three phases of operation over nearly a decade of publication. Its founders were John Ross Robertson (1841–1918) and Erastus Wiman (1834–1904). Extant issues reveal that it was the second home of Terry Finnegan's weekly letters. The short-lived *Momus* [winter, 1861] was the first, though none of its issues have survived. Likely the versatile McCarroll contributed other satirical and comic pieces to the *Grumbler*, but these would have appeared anonymously.

But there were several other satiric papers in the city during these politically unstable and volatile years. the *Latch-Key*, which appeared in two short-lived series (1863 and, in this instance, in 1864), were McCarroll's own undertakings, providing outlets for his comedic talents and, once he had lost his Customs' position, a forum for his complaints about political machinations and government unfairness. Internal evidence from the few surviving copies of the *Latch-Key* had made it clear that McCarroll was closely involved in the magazine, but this letter provides confirmation of his editorship while implying a good deal more.

McCarroll's reference to the short-lived *Momus* (1861) is intriguing. Published by Warne and Hall and advertised in grandly excessive terms in the Toronto *Leader* for weeks before its initial appearance (the magazine would have 75,000 readers, it announced), it ceased publication within four months of its fanfare.[16] No copies have survived but I did find in the columns of the Toronto *Leader* an excerpt from a Terry Finnegan letter taken from the pages of *Momus*. It is thus evident that *Momus* was the first home of Terry's epistles to Thomas D'Arcy McGee and that the letters found a home in the *Grumbler* only after *Momus* ceased operations.

Still other questions arise. What organizational and editorial roles did McCarroll play in *Momus*? He cites it to Foster as a venture in which they were both involved, hoping to attract Foster's interest in contributing to and supporting the *Latch-Key*. Is it too much to surmise that *Momus*, like the *Latch-Key*, was edited by McCarroll himself? After all, he had his own printing press and was not hesitant to use it. Certainly, in connecting William Foster with both literary undertakings, he offers us a peek into how things were done among writers and editors in pre-Confederation Toronto. One drew on the satiric talents of a few like-minded friends, promised anonymity and tried by means of a small-scale media blitz to make the magazine attractive to hesitant purchasers. There was, however, no hesitation on McCarroll's part to try to be competitive, in this case with the already-established *Grumbler*. But the economics of production and marketing were daunting. Both schemes — *Momus* and the *Latch-Key* — though entrepreneurial in spirit were grossly undercapitalized in fact; no promoter in Toronto, then a city of about 55,000, could be sure that a sufficient market would willingly embrace such ventures. As it turned out, neither magazine lasted for more than a few months, despite the solid production values that McCarroll offered and his ability to draw together a range of amusing material.

McCarroll's editorial hand is also clearly evident in the four issues of the *Growler*, a Toronto magazine that appeared in the summer of 1864, lasting four issues. It appeared before the reincarnation of the *Latch-Key* but included no Terry Finnegan letters, likely because those letters were appearing regularly in the *Grumbler* at the time.

If one casts back to 1859 and examines the eleven surviving issues of the (nearly) year-long run of an early satiric paper, the *Poker* (Toronto), there is reason to speculate that McCarroll, who was by then well-established in the city, may also have been active there. Perhaps he wrote the broadly comic vernacular letters to and by Darcy McGee that appeared in those pages or, as an attentive reader, found himself gauging how he might bring Terry Finnegan to life as the engaging Irish voice deftly tied to the low-life setting of Toronto's "Stanly Street." Whatever the case, such letters make it clear that he was a major player, both creative and managerial, in the flood of satiric writing that appeared in Toronto during these unsettled pre-Confederation years.

A final entry among the satiric magazines of the era is the *Pick*, a lively weekly which ran for about six months in 1865. Like *Momus*, no single copy survives, but it is evident from numerous notices in the Toronto *Leader* that Terry Finnegan's letters (components of the unpublished "Second Series") appeared weekly in its pages — indeed, these would have been the last of Terry's epistles. One such notice of the *Pick* in the *Leader* (March 29, 1865) reads as follows:

> Genial humor and sarcasm are the very condiments of human life — the very salt and pepper of society, when rightly applied. We take shame to ourselves that we have so long suffered to pass unnoticed "The Pick," a humorous weekly, which has for some months made its regular appearance in Toronto. In raciness of touch, true wit, and, above all, the careful abstinence from any expressions which may wound or shock the most critical and fastidious reader, we are bound to say "The Pick" is most excellently conducted. The celebrated letters of the renowned "Terry Finnegan" regularly grace its columns.

Reviews and notices can be very valuable in filling the gap caused by missing material.

Was the *Pick* another abortive and undercapitalized McCarroll literary venture? Was it his final stab — still earnest, plucky and even hopeful — at having his say about his personal situation and at trying to come up with another way of making some money from his writing and his printing press? It would not be long before his patience deserted him, before, in frustration and deeper than ever in debt, he found it necessary to seek refuge among the Fenian brethren in Buffalo.

In living out his final three years in Toronto, McCarroll became more engaged and identified with Fenian politics. He assured Macdonald that this was not so, but those who were watching him closely saw something quite different. 1865 was his year of desperation and living dangerously. He was on the road a great deal with his one-man show; the result, however, was exhaustion and disillusion rather than a monetary success. As well, he was likely producing weekly issues of the *Pick* and struggling to keep Terry Finnegan fresh in people's minds even as he continued to lobby for restitution from government officials like John A. Macdonald. McCarroll's debts abounded, and his wife Anne, who had been seriously ill for some time, was failing.

Not surprisingly, the Finnegan letters he wrote during 1865 became more polemical. (The *Leader* complained on occasion about this in its notices of the *Pick*.) On at least two occasions in 1865 he conspicuously changed the "inimitable Terry Finnegan" into Terry Fenian, a pro-Irish and anti-English polemical poetic voice. Predictably, the *Irish Canadian* provided a home for his Fenian enthusiasm. "A New Song" appeared in the issue of 15 March 1865 and "The Fenian's Vow" in September, 1865. More of the same may well have made the pages of the *Pick* before it ceased publication.

Such then is the record of my major archival successes in tracking down details and finding traces of the literary and cultural life of Canada's lost writer, James McCarroll. In New York, he resurfaced in various old and new capacities — as an editor and reviewer (for Frank Leslie and for *Belford's Monthly* and *Humanity and Health*), a playwright, a popular songwriter (three of his songs, including "Don't, Nellie Dear!," were published as sheet music in the early 1880s) and an inventor who registered several patents. Indeed, until his death he remained a buoyant creative force who continued to write, compose and edit, even as he took on many other projects.

The truth is, he is only partially lost. He may have fallen from grace in Canada West and he was certainly the victim of erasure by another Irishman, Nicholas Flood Davin, but he lives on in many archival collections in North America. Humpty Dumpty did fall and he did break into a thousand fragments. However, by tracking archival records and probing various holdings, I have been able to gather up a considerable number of those fragments, perhaps as much as 60–70 percent of them. I have of course met my share of dead-ends and frustrations, but I remain amazed at and delighted by how much is there to discover. Since McCarroll had so many journalistic connections in North America during his lifetime, there are likely still more archival fragments to unearth. Hence, with optimism I continue my searching; fresh clues still occasionally appear even as I undertake to write his biography and to put together a selected collection of his prose and poetry, the better to connect Canadian readers with his once-lost narrative and his writing.

Notes

1. David John Sale (1968) identifies over twenty Toronto concerts in which McCarroll participated as a flautist and singer.
2. Turlough Carolan (1670–1738) was a famous blind Irish piper and composer whose music is still revered in Ireland and elsewhere.
3. Occasional pieces from these papers were reprinted in Canadian newspapers ("National Music" from the *Buffalo Globe* was reprinted in the *Irish Canadian* [October 19, 1866]), but no issues of either paper have survived, at least from McCarroll's time as editor.
4. James Moylan, the editor of the *Canadian Freeman* (Toronto), who had been a good friend to McCarroll, led the attack on him after his defection to Buffalo. See the *Canadian Freeman* (November 15, 1866; February 14, 1867).
5. Davin included a biographical description of William Cluxton (1819–1901), a successful Peterborough businessman and politician; likely he was well aware that Cluxton had been one of McCarroll's closest friends and his music student during their early days in Peterborough. Cluxton likely helped McCarroll to finance his first newspaper, the *Peterboro Chronicle,* and provided support for him

in the wake of his bankruptcy.
6. His first book was *The Letters of Terry Finnegan, First Series* (Toronto, 1864). *Ridgeway* appeared in 1868. A play, *Nearly a Tragedy: A Comedy*, was published in New York in 1874, and *Madeline and Other Poems* was published by Belford, Clarke & Company in New York (1889).
7. When McCarroll left for Buffalo in 1866 he seems to have abandoned his dying wife and their daughters. Ann McCarroll died that summer in Toronto. Three of their daughters, including Mary, who travelled with her father as his piano accompanist in 1865, later made their living as music teachers. The fourth daughter was the only one to marry. It would appear that none of the daughters made an effort to keep a record of their father's literary pursuits; neither is there evidence of any such effort in New York even though several newspapers and magazines wrote glowing obituaries after his death.
8. For example, McCarroll wrote letters to Thomas Moore, Charles Dickens, Oliver Wendell Holmes and Henry Wadsworth Longfellow asking them to help him find a publisher for such volumes as his "Irish Anthology" and his collected stories. He included replies that he received from Holmes and Longfellow in a postscript to *Madeline and Other Poems*.
9. McCarroll to John A. Macdonald, January 19, 1866.
10. McCarroll to John A. Macdonald, February 16, 1865.
11. Chris Raible, a Mackenzie scholar, brought these Lindsey letters to my attention several years ago.
12. In most American biographical sketches of McCarroll, there is no mention of his work for Frank Leslie and Company (1872–73 into the early 1880s). This is a curious omission for which at present I have no explanation other than that McCarroll himself opted to downplay that part of his career. Numerous McCarroll poems and prose pieces also appeared in *Frank Leslie's Sunday Magazine* in the early 1880s.
13. The letter is held by the Huntington Library.
14. I know of no poem of 2000 lines written by McCarroll. This is a gap in his oeuvre. The Indian tale is likely "Black Hawk, A Tale of the Plains" which McCarroll published in two separate locales, one a magazine that was discontinued and the other a Cobourg newspaper. Neither serial was completed beyond the tenth chapter. One wonders if the full text died in Dickens's hands or if his discouragement about Indian tales had a negative effect on McCarroll's efforts.
15. A lawyer by training, William Foster would become a member of the Canada First group that met in Ottawa. He often wrote on Canada's potential as a nation and was a good friend of Henry Morgan, who also knew McCarroll, judging from the personal details that he was able to include in the sketch of McCarroll he wrote for *Sketches of Celebrated Canadians*.
16. *Momus* set out to sell 75,000 copies at 4 cents per issue, though the proprietors admitted that it was "impossible to divine to how great a circulation *Momus* will ultimately attain." It promised "SPARKLING WIT, PUNGENT HUMOR, and SALIENT HITS, At the Whims and Follies, Political, Theatrical, Fashionable, Musical and Literary" (see the *Leader*, January 31, 1861).

References

Primary Sources

The Papers of Sir John A. Macdonald, Library and Archives Canada, MG26A (Vol. 298).

Records of the Department of National Revenue (Customs), Library and Archives Canada, RG 16 (1849–66).

The Papers of William A. Foster, Archives of Ontario, F70.

The William Lyon Mackenzie Papers, Archives of Ontario.

Microfilm runs of newspapers: The Peterborough *Backwoodsman*. (c1839-43), The *Christian Guardian* (c1840s), The *Peterboro Chronicle* (1843–46), The Peterborough *Despatch* (1846–1850), The Peterborough *Gazette* (1845–49), The Peterborough *Examiner* (1860–66) , The Cobourg *Star* (1832–1860), The Cobourg *Sentinel* (1860–63), The St. Catharines *Journal* (1851–53), The Toronto *Leader* (later the *Daily Leader*) (1854–65), The *Canadian Freeman* (Toronto), The *Irish Canadian* (Toronto).

Magazines: The *Latch-Key* (Toronto), The *Grumbler* (Toronto), The *Growler* (Toronto), *Graham's Magazine*, The *Canadian Gem and Family Visitor* (Cobourg,Toronto), The *Home Journal* (Toronto), The *Anglo-American Magazine* (Toronto), The *Victoria Magazine* (Belleville), The *Literary Garland* (Montreal), The *British North American Magazine* (Toronto, 1863), *Frank Leslie's Illustrated Newspaper* (New York, 1870-80), *Frank Leslie's Chimney Corner* (New York, 1872–1880), *Frank Leslie's Sunday Magazine* (New York, 1875–82), *Appleton's* (New York), *Belford's Magazine* (New York, 1887-92), *Humanity and Health* (New York, 1892).

Secondary Sources

Brown, Joshua. 2002. *Beyond the Lines: Pictorial Reporting, Everyday Life, and the Crisis of Gilded Age America.* Berkeley and Los Angeles: University of California Press.

Dewart, Edward Hartley. 1864. *Selections from Canadian Poets*. Montreal: Lovell.

Dickens, Charles. 1998. *The Letters of Charles Dickens*. Vol. 10 (1862–64). (Gen. ed.) Madeline House, Graham Story, and Kathleen Tillotson. Oxford: Clarendon Press.

McCarroll, James. 1864. *The Letters of Terry Finnegan*. Toronto: Toronto News Co.

_____. 1856. "The New Gauger; or, Jack Trainor's Story." (Serialized in *The Anglo-American Magazine*). Toronto.

_____. 1868. *Ridgeway: An Historical Romance of the Fenian Invasion*. Buffalo: McCarroll Publishing Co.

_____. 1874. *Nearly a Tragedy: A Comedy*. New York: J.F. Trow.

_____. 1889. *Madeline and Other Poems*. New York: Clarke, Belford, Clarke & Co.

_____. 1981. "Some Social and Other Characteristics of the late John A. Macdonald." *Belford's Magazine* (August).

Morgan, Henry J. 1865. *Sketches of Celebrated Canadians*. Montreal: R. Worthington.

_____. 1867. *Bibliotheca Canadiensis*. Ottawa: G.E. Desbarats.

Peterman, Michael. 1996. "James McCarroll, Alias Terry Finnegan: Newspapers, Controversy and Literature in Victorian Canada." Occasional Paper #17. Peterborough: Ontario: Peterborough Historical Society.

———. 2005. "Case Study: Lost From View: James McCarroll, Journalist, Poet, Satirist." *History of the Book in Canada.* Vol. 2, 1840–1918. Toronto: University of Toronto Press.

———. 2009. "From Terry Finnegan to Terry Fenian: The Truncated Literary Career of James McCarroll." In David A. Wilson (ed.), *Irish Nationalism in Canada.* Montreal: McGill-Queen's University Press.

The (Macmillan) Dictionary of Canadian Biography. 1926. Comp. by W. Stewart Wallace. Toronto: Macmillan of Canada.

Sale, David John. 1968. "Toronto's Pre-Confederation Music Societies, 1845–67." Toronto: University of Toronto Press.

Story, Norah. 1967. *The Oxford Companion to Canadian History and Literature.* Toronto: Oxford University Press.

Waters, Maureen. 1984. *The Comic Irishman.* Albany: State University of New York.

The Many Deaths of Tom Thomson

Gregory Klages

Tom Thomson is one of Canada's most well-known and best-loved painters. Even those who do not recognize Thomson's name are likely familiar with his iconic paintings of wind-swept pine trees, choppy lakes and rocky crags. Thomson's rise to fame was a gradual process that rested in large part on characterizations of the artist as an untrained woodsman of singular talent and sensitivity, whose untimely death in the summer of 1917 cut short what promised to be a brilliant career. Misunderstandings or misrepresentations about his death, however, have played a critical role in the building of Thomson's reputation.

Tom Thomson was only becoming recognized as a landscape painter during the last five years of his life, after training and working as a designer and illustrator in Ontario and Seattle. After his death, several of his close friends went on to form the Group of Seven, the informal cluster of painters whose representation of Canadian landscapes during the 1920s revolutionized Canadian painting. Thomson's reputation rose with that of the Group, aided in part by the romance lent to his work by his tragic death in the "Canadian north." During the 1920s, Thomson's works were given privileged position in European exhibitions of Group members' paintings and recognized by critics as some of the strongest contributions to these shows. In 1930, thirteen years after Tom Thomson's death, the first book-length biography of the artist was published (Davies 1930). By the 1940s, a prominent commentator listed Thomson as one of Canada's top ten historical figures (MacLennan 1949). Despite their relative scarcity, Thomson's paintings are now held by all major Canadian collections. His work is the subject of regular academic and public discussion. In 2002, *Tom Thomson*, the first catalogue *raisonné* of his works was published (in tandem with a nationally travelling exhibition), and recently his works have sold for over one million dollars at auction. By almost any measure, Tom Thomson has become, as one biographer recently offered, "a Canadian hero" (Murray 1998).

As is often the case with historical heroes, "myth-making" and "obsessive rescripting" mark writing about Thomson's life (Grace 2004: 3, 8; Silcox and Town 1997: 194–97; Murray 1986, 1, 1994: 79). By 1920, Thomson's friends and supporters were promulgating an understanding of the man as a near-mythological "heroic reincarnation of Canada's pioneering figures, the voyageur and the backwoodsman, a 'man alone' in nature" (MacHardy 1999: 781). Misunderstanding, however, is not the same as hero-worship or willful ignorance. In the mid-1970s, Harold Town, a renowned Canadian painter in his own right, suggested that sloppy research and ill-informed speculation about Thomson's death served to significantly cloud understanding of the importance of Thomson's life and, more importantly, his painting (Silcox and Town 1997: 19).

Despite clear interest in the artist's life (and death) and undisputed national respect for the artist's work, no trained historian has published an assessment of how Thomson died, leaving the issue to be dealt with primarily by amateur historians and journalists. Works produced by these authors have often offered elaborate speculation involving the cause of Thomson's demise. Over time, such theories have gradually spiralled further and further away from what is reflected in the primary, documentary evidence. To clarify what can reasonably be proposed about Thomson's death, we must test the speculation against the available historical records, something that has so far been done in an inconsistent and selective fashion at best. Such a corrective enterprise has been made easier within the last twenty years, as a significant supply of documents has been deposited with archival collections available to the public, many of which were digitized and made available on the Internet in 2008, making for particularly easy access.[1]

The speculation regarding Thomson's death is somewhat surprising, given the availability of a wide selection of relevant primary documents. Blodwen Davies based much of her two 1930s biographies of Thomson on testimony gathered in correspondence with his friends and family members; letters which she later deposited with the National Archives (quite likely during the late 1930s or early 1940s).[2] Correspondence sent by Thomson and some of his friends to their patron, Dr. James MacCallum, was deposited in the archives of the National Gallery of Canada in 1944.[3] Some important documents, however, have not been publicly available until recently. Thomson family members contributed a significant collection of documents to Library and Archives Canada between 1981 and 2001, although researchers were granted access to at least some of these materials during the 1970s (Addison 1969: 88–95; Silcox and Town 1997: 13; Murray 1971: 46–47).[4] These three collections, along with deposits in other publicly-accessible archives (such as the diary of the Park Ranger who led the search for Thomson, held in the archives of Trent University, Peterborough, Ontario), allow reasonably clear sense to be made regarding what was happening at Canoe Lake in the spring of 1917.[5]

Probably a view of the mill-yard of the abandoned Gilmour Lumber Company at Canoe Lake. The man seated on the stump is thought to be Tom Wattie, an Algonquin Park ranger.
Credit: Tom Thomson/Library and Archives Canada/PA-193569.

The mystery surrounding Thomson's death has been fed by testimony offered by those close to the case long after the events in question. For instance, Mark Robinson, the Algonquin park ranger responsible for the Canoe Lake area in 1917, wrote two letters to Blodwen Davies in 1930 and was interviewed by Park historians twice during the 1950s.[6] In 1955, R.P. Little, who lived at Canoe Lake from June 1916 to October 1917, offered an account of the events surrounding Thomson's death that Little claimed he had been told by Annie Fraser, operator of the lodge where Thomson was living at the time of this death (Little 1955: 219). In 1956, two undertakers involved in the case offered their recollections in newspaper accounts (Dixon 1956; *Leader-Post* Oct. 12, 1956). Recollections of Thomson's funeral by friends of the Thomson family were published in a newspaper in 1969 (*Sun-Times*). Charles Plewman, who arrived at Canoe Lake between Thomson's disappearance and discovery of his corpse, also offered his recollections in a magazine article in 1972 (Plewman). All of these persons contributed new information to the case. Of course, the memories of these witnesses may have faded with time, and their testimony often does not entirely fit with the historical record. In Robinson's case, for instance, his stories about Thomson's last hours, as offered in various letters and interviews over the course of thirty years, are not consistent.

Aside from contemporary newspaper accounts of Thomson's death

Tom Thomson.
Credit: Blair Laing / Library and Archives Canada / PA-125406.

and several newspaper articles stemming from the 1956 discovery of an unidentified corpse in what may have been Thomson's original grave in Mowat Cemetery, descriptions of Thomson's death did not become a topic of popular public discussion until the late 1960s. Although Davies wrote two biographies of Thomson, the first, published in 1930, made no mention of suspicions about his death, and the other, published in 1935, received little attention, largely because it was self published in a small edition of 450. Ottelyn Addison, Mark Robinson's daughter, published a biography of Thomson in 1969, in which she included copies or transcripts of key documents: her father's diary entries regarding the events surrounding Thomson's death and excerpts from a 1956 account written by Rose Thomas, who was living at Canoe Lake at the time of Thomson's death (Addison). The same year, the Canadian Broadcasting Corporation produced a program investigating Thomson's death, with the assistance of William Little, who was one of the men who in 1956 dug up what was, he argued, Thomson's original burial site (Canadian Broadcasting Corporation 1969). The next year, Little, now an Ontario judge, published an account of Thomson's death (Little 1970). In response, one of the forensic scientists who assessed the remains found by Little published his perceptions of the case soon thereafter (Sharpe

1970). Roy MacGregor, a journalist whose great-uncle married the sister of Winnifred Trainor, the woman many identify as Thomson's girlfriend, wrote two magazine articles about the case, as well as a novel based on Thomson's death (1973, 1977, 1980, reissued 2002). None of these accounts give any indication of being built upon a comprehensive survey of the relevant primary documents in the Davies or MacCallum collections, or held by the Thomson family.

Several publications by art experts dealing with Thomson's death have made it difficult to know how closely they have consulted primary materials because the authors have chosen to rarely or inconsistently cite their sources (Hubbard 1962; Silcox and Town 1997; Murray 1986, 1994, 1998).

A number of recent texts have tended to draw significantly (and less than critically) upon research and interpretations included in earlier works, rather than consultation with the original documents (Clemson 2002; Poling 2003; MacGregor 2010), or seem to be based on very selective use of available archival material (Silcox 2002). Like MacGregor's 1980 novel, a recent treatment of Thomson's death, *Algonquin Elegy* (2005), is a historical fiction with Thomson's death at its centre, self-published by a Michigan lawyer, Neil Lehto. While Lehto notes many faults in the work of previous researchers not previously addressed in publications dealing with Thomson's death (he goes so far as to accuse William Little of fabricating evidence [96]), he makes no citations of documents in the Davies, MacCallum or Thomson collections.

All of the authors listed above have contributed to discussion of Thomson's death, either introducing new evidence to support (or discount) existing theories or advancing new theories of what occurred. Clearly, however, most of them overlooked the most significant, publicly available collections of primary documents central to the events they were attempting to explain or made use of them in a way that does not easily facilitate critical analysis.

This present study is largely based on comparing key elements in the accounts discussed above against the information that can be found in publicly accessible archival collections, as well as other relevant records, such as Blodwen Davies' 1931 request to the Ontario Attorney General to have Thomson's original Algonquin Park burial site opened, which have recently been made available through formal requests by this author for access to information collected by the Ontario Attorney General's office and the provincial Centre for Forensic Sciences.[7]

To begin to understand how researchers might be presenting inaccurate narratives concerning Tom Thomson's death, let us begin by considering what most accounts agree on with regard to his last days. In the spring of 1917, Tom Thomson travelled several hours north of Toronto by train to spend the summer in Ontario's Algonquin Park, as he had done several times in the past. On the edge of the Canadian Shield, the rough park was home to logging operations, tourists and rangers entrusted with ensuring the safety of residents and visitors, as well as ensuring observance of the park's rules and regulations. Thomson had spent several summers in the park, working as a fire ranger, as a guide for fishing parties and, of course, painting the local landscape. Settling in at Canoe Lake in late March or early April 1917, Thomson had a productive season making small, rough paintings.[8] In late April, he applied for a licence to help fishing parties find their way around the park.[9] He guided a few parties during the spring, and by early July knew more were scheduled during the next two months.[10] He told his brother-in-law that he was debating heading west, however, to paint the Rocky Mountains.[11]

About midday on July 8, Thomson, intending to take a short fishing trip, pushed his canoe away from a dock in the small village of Mowat, on Canoe Lake. His empty canoe was spotted within a few hours, and when this information was brought to the attention of the local park ranger, a search ensued. On July 16, Thomson's body came to the lake's surface, within a kilometre of where his journey began. A doctor holidaying in the area examined the corpse, concluding the cause of death was "accidental drowning."[12] Thomson's body was buried in the village cemetery the day after its discovery. That night, after Thomson's burial, the North Bay coroner spent an evening investigating the death, and without seeing the body, agreed with the examining doctor's conclusion.[13] On July 18, Thomson's body was exhumed and moved to a family plot in the village of Leith, near Owen Sound, Ontario.[14]

Despite its brevity, even the preceding account of events does not contain universally accepted assertions regarding the death and burial of Tom Thomson. There is no shortage of writing on Thomson's death. Such treatments vary widely in tone and quality, often being written by untrained historians intent on advancing arguments regarding a particular cause of death. Theories regarding Thomson's final activities and fate can be grouped into three categories: accident, suicide and murder.

While the official finding was accidental drowning, documents produced at the time indicate other theories were circulating. Five months after Tom Thomson's death, his brother George found it necessary to write an excoriating letter to Shannon Fraser, operator of Mowat Lodge, where Tom had been living at Canoe Lake. George claimed an unnamed source had told him that Fraser had reported to the coroner that Tom committed suicide. Reflecting on what evidence he had heard was considered at the inquest, George concluded Tom's death was "caused either by accident or foul play, and not by suicide."[15] Perhaps out of respect for the sensitivities of the Thomson family, little was written about the suicide theory until the 1970s, when a number of authors proposed that Thomson took his life to avoid marrying a love interest who may have become pregnant (Plewman 1972; MacGregor 1973, 1977). More recently, several commentators have proposed that Thomson may have suffered from manic depression or a similar malady that might have prompted him to commit suicide (Grace 2004; Lehto 2005).

Another theory regarding Thomson's demise that has become very popular is that the artist was murdered. This theory does not appear in the documentary record for more than a decade after Thomson's death, other than in the George Thomson letter referred to above. In 1931, a Toronto-based Thomson biographer intimated foul play might be the most plausible explanation for his death (*Evening Telegram* 1934; Davies 1935). New "evidence" and proposals in support of this theory and variations on the theory have appeared almost every decade since the 1930s (Guillet 1944; Delaplante 1956; Little 1970; Poling 2003; Shaw 1966).

Speculation regarding Thomson's cause of death was given surprising new impetus in the fall of 1956. At that time, four Canoe Lake visitors who had heard stories regarding Thomson's death, burial, and exhumation took it upon themselves to find and excavate the artist's original burial site. After several hours digging at Mowat cemetery (without legal permission), the men discovered skeletal remains in an unmarked grave. The provincial police were called and the remains excavated. Forensic experts consulted by the police concluded the remains were likely those of an Aboriginal, younger than Thomson, buried much more recently than 1917, who showed signs of an operation on his skull.[16]

The discovery of the remains at Mowat Cemetery did nothing to resolve the mystery of Tom Thomson's death, but instead fed speculation that *something* about Thomson's death had been covered up, calling into question almost everything that was believed about the case. Since the late 1960s, a number of researchers have attempted to rewrite the story of Thomson's death. An itemized account of disagreements between these accounts could easily fill an entire book. The following analysis concentrates on how descriptions of events surrounding Thomson's death differ in their descriptions of four critical aspects of the narrative. These moments have been identified as significant based on the degree of variation identified between the secondary accounts and the primary evidence, between the secondary accounts themselves, and the degree to which narrative elements introduced in secondary accounts have been repeated in later narratives.

An examination of the accounts identified above suggests mythologizing of Tom Thomson's death revolves around the following four particular aspects of the story:

1. the events immediately preceding Thomson's decision to go fishing on July 8;
2. the sighting of Thomson's empty canoe on Canoe Lake, and what was done in response to this sighting;

3. the discovery of Thomson's corpse, particularly what condition it was in; and
4. the inquest into Thomson's death, and (possible) later exhumation of his body from its original, Canoe Lake burial site.

It is when considering these four aspects that the secondary accounts most significantly diverge from the primary evidence available and where genuine progress can be made in clarifying what can be reasonably claimed about Thomson's death.

First, let us consider the events preceding Thomson's death. Thomson arrived at Canoe Lake in late March or early April 1917, and took up residence at Mowat Lodge, where he intended to rent a room until the ice came off the lake and he could camp in the park.[17] By his own account, he was having a successful spring of painting, noting to his patron, Dr. James MacCallum, that he had "made quite a few sketches," and although he regarded many as substandard, "I keep on making them."[18] On Saturday, July 7, the day before he died, Thomson wrote MacCallum, who had visited Canoe Lake in late May, that he had had to stop painting until the blackfly season passed but that he intended to send the sketches he had produced to Toronto in a day or two.[19] He also noted his intention to make some more sketches but explained that had been busy guiding parties in the park. He added that he had some more guiding jobs lined up during the next two months. After Thomson's death, Winnifred Trainor, whose family frequently spent time at Canoe Lake, told George, Thomson's brother, Tom had also written her on July 7, but she did not reveal the contents of the letter.[20]

According to Shannon Fraser, who wrote to MacCallum on July 24, Thomson had helped him lift a boat over a nearby dam on the morning of the eighth.[21] Trainor referred to a similar event, suggesting in a September 1917 letter to Tom's brother-in-law that Tom had helped Fraser "cadge a boat" the morning he died.[22] Later accounts of what Thomson was thinking and doing in advance of his death claimed far more was transpiring than correspondence written at the time communicated. Most of these accounts, however, are likely based on hearsay or poor memory.

In 1930, Mark Robinson, the Algonquin park ranger responsible for the Canoe Lake region, responded to a query from Blodwen Davies, who was in the process of writing a book regarding Thomson.[23] Robinson wrote that some of the locals had been trying to catch a particularly large, elusive trout and that on the morning Thomson died he had decided to try and catch a similar fish. Thomson's plan was to offer up the similar fish in order to deceive Robinson that he had caught the elusive trout. However, Robinson's letter does not make clear whether his account is based on personal observation of the events or whether he was relating a story someone else had told him. While Davies did not include Robinson's story in her 1930 biography of Thomson, she did include it in a book published five years later. Almost every biography written since has repeated this story, which first appeared almost fifteen years after Thomson's death.

Along with the "trout story," Davies offered additional information regarding Thomson's final activities in her 1931 letter to the Ontario attorney general.[24] In this account, Thomson rose late in the morning on 8 July and ate breakfast with Annie Fraser. He was in good spirits, Davies claimed, "freshly shaved, hair brushed and shining" (1–2), and about noon went with Shannon Fraser, Annie's husband, to catch the trout intended to fool Robinson. Davies does not supply any information regarding the source of this version of events.

Over twenty years later, Mark Robinson offered an expanded version of his story when interviewed by a Canoe Lake camp operator, Taylor Statten.[25] The morning of Thomson's death, Robinson reported, he had noticed Thomson walking with a couple who operated a lodge on nearby Joe Lake. Some time later, Robinson noticed Shannon Fraser walking towards Canoe Lake, followed soon after by Thomson. The two of them stopped at the dam separating Joe and Canoe Lakes and attempted to catch the elusive trout. Robinson watched the two, eavesdropping on Thomson's plan to trick him. As the plan was hatched, however, Thomson noticed Robinson, responding by waving and saying, "Howdy" (200–201).

In 1956, Rose Thomas supplied another unique account in a personal letter to Ottelyn Addison, Robinson's daughter. Thomas reported that she had seen Thomson and Fraser walk together to Joe Lake, where they left a canoe. Addison did not make this account public, however, until she included an excerpt from it in her 1969 book, *Tom Thomson: The Algonquin Years* (95).

Secondary literature regarding Thomson's death has tried to identify what transpired *before* the day of Thomson's death that could have contributed to the tragedy. In her 1931 letter to the Attorney General, Blodwen Davies refers to "the quarrels between Martin Blecher… and Thomson."[26] The quarrels, she reports, "are said to have been violent" and might have been related to the war in Europe (Blecher was an American of German heritage whose family holidayed at Canoe Lake). She claims Thomson wrote his friend, Arthur Lismer, about the fights, but that the letters had not been preserved (6). Though she makes no accusations, her intent certainly seems to be to suggest that Martin Blecher might have been involved in Thomson's death.

Martin Blecher does not make a prominent appearance again in writing about Thomson's death until 1970, when William Little, in the first published book devoted exclusively to Thomson's death, proposed an additional reason for conflict between Thomson and Blecher. Little stated that at least two persons had told him that Thomson had been engaged to marry

Winnifred Trainor, daughter of a local lumber camp foreman who lived in nearby Huntsville and who holidayed at Canoe Lake. One of these persons assured Little that a honeymoon cabin had already been arranged (66–67). Little intimates that Thomson and Blecher may have come to fatal blows over the woman (38–42). In March 1930, Mark Robinson mentioned to Blodwen Davies that rumours were circulating about Thomson and Trainor being engaged (5).[27] In 1972, Charles Plewman, who claimed to have been one of Thomson's pallbearers at Canoe Lake, picked up on the topic of Thomson and Trainor's relationship, claiming that Winnie had been pressuring Thomson to get married and that a reluctant Thomson was considering suicide as an escape from the problem (8). Several years later, an Algonquin Park researcher interviewed Daphne Crombie, who sixty years before had been at Canoe Lake with her husband (Pittaway 1977). When prompted to tell what she knew about Thomson and Trainor, she related a story she had been told by Annie Fraser regarding how Annie had discovered a letter from Trainor to Thomson that pleaded "we'll have to be married." In response to the letter, Crombie suggested, Tom had approached Shannon Fraser during a drunken party on the night of July 7, asking Fraser to repay a loan Thomson had made him. Fraser punched Thomson, Crombie claimed, and Thomson had fallen, hit his head and passed out. Fraser and Annie, Crombie believed, had panicked and placed Thomson's body in his canoe, then dumped the body in the lake. Roy MacGregor reported this version of the story in a nationally distributed magazine soon thereafter (1977).

In a 1977 book regarding Thomson's life and art, art historian David Silcox proposed an entirely new reason for Thomson's death. Silcox claimed that Thomson had sprained his ankle in the days leading up to July 8, and likely stood up in his canoe — perhaps to urinate — and slipped, hitting his head and drowning (Silcox and Town 1977: 59). As a sprained ankle does not appear in any primary or secondary accounts before this date, this claim is very likely based on testimony provided to Silcox (or another researcher working on his book) by one of Thomson's nephews. In a 1973 interview, the nephew and his wife related how George Thomson's son told them that Tom had sprained his ankle, and that George Thomson felt that his brother had wrapped his ankle with fishing line to give it support and had likely fallen and hit his head while getting out of his canoe.[28]

Throughout the spring, and even the day before he died, Thomson was giving friends and family the impression that he was making plans and promises about the future. A number of people claim to have seen Thomson the morning he disappeared and at the time did not observe anything that seemed outside the ordinary. Many elements of accounts of the events surrounding Thomson's death, such as the idea of a drunken fight on the night before Thomson's death, plans for a wedding to Winnie Trainor and a sprained ankle, were introduced decades after the events being discussed and have a tenuous relationship (if any) to evidence produced during the period of Thomson's death.

A second key narrative interest is when Tom Thomson's empty canoe might have been discovered floating in Canoe Lake, who discovered it, when the discovery was reported and what was discovered in the canoe.

Primary accounts of these events are few. The only reports we have from the time are Mark Robinson's diary entries and telegrams and letters Shannon Fraser wrote to Thomson's family and friends. These reports formed the basis for newspaper coverage of the events in Canoe Lake that were written before Thomson's corpse was discovered. On 10 July, Fraser reported to MacCallum that Tom's canoe had been found upside down.[29] Robinson's diary entry for the day notes that Fraser came to him that morning to report that Martin Blecher had spotted Thomson's canoe floating upside down in the lake.[30] Robinson notes that someone wanted the lake dragged to locate Thomson's body but is unclear as to whether it was Fraser or Blecher making the request. In a letter to MacCallum, sent on July 12, Fraser explained that Thomson's canoe was sighted about 3 p.m. on Sunday, a few hours after Thomson had departed, and when investigated the provisions and both paddles were found tied up in the overturned canoe.[31] The *Owen Sound Sun* and Toronto *Globe* reported that both paddles were strapped into Tom's canoe when it was found.[32] Fraser repeated this claim in a letter to MacCallum on July 24.[33]

While these elements of the Thomson death story seem straightforward in the primary documents, later accounts would vary considerably from these reports. When Blodwen Davies inquired with Mark Robinson in September 1930 regarding the fate of Thomson's canoe paddles, he responded, "One was found tied in his canoe for portaging." She did not mention this claim in her 1935 book, and in a 1955 magazine article, R.P. Little stated that both paddles had been found inside Thomson's canoe (220).[34] When Robinson was interviewed in 1956, though, he made an odd claim.[35] He stated two paddles were found tied up inside Thomson's canoe but that the "paddling paddle" was missing (202). William Little repeated this claim in 1970 (46). In articles written during the 1970s, Roy MacGregor suggested that only one, "sloppily" tied-in paddle was found and that Thomson's favourite paddle was not (1973: 47; 1977: 7). In 2010, MacGregor embroidered his account further, suggesting that Thomson's "preferred" paddle was missing, while two others were "tethered to the seats and thwart [of his canoe] to form a shoulder support for portaging" (100).

Similar variations from the primary accounts can be noted in narratives addressing when Thomson's canoe was found and what was done with it. In March 1930, Robinson told Blodwen Davies that the discovery of Thomson's canoe had been reported on the morning of Monday, July 9, when the canoe was retrieved, but that he was not aware until the inquest on the evening of the seventeenth that Martin Blecher and his sister had first spotted it (3).[36] In 1955, R.P. Little introduced an entirely new version of the story, reporting that after Martin Blecher and his sister spotted the canoe, they had retrieved it and brought it back to their boathouse, where it was noticed on Tuesday morning, July 10, by another Canoe Lake resident, Charlie Scrim (219–20). In the account Mrs. Thomas offered to Ottelyn Addison in 1956, unique elements were introduced as well (Addison 1969: 95). Thomas claimed that Martin Blecher had towed Thomson's overturned canoe to Shannon Fraser's and that Fraser came to the train station on Monday morning hoping to send a telegram to Owen Sound (where Thomson's parents lived) as he feared Tom had drowned. In 1970, William Little introduced yet another variation on the story, reporting that Charlie Scrim actually found Thomson's canoe, after Shannon Fraser related that the Blechers had reported their sighting to him on the Monday. It was Scrim, Little asserts, who reported the find to Robinson (48).

Clearly, secondary accounts regarding how Tom Thomson's overturned canoe was discovered and how many paddles were found in the canoe vary widely. Some of the later versions of these important elements in the narrative of events surrounding Thomson's death may have been the product of poor recollection on the part of those involved. It should be noted, however, how some later writers clearly overlooked primary documentation that was readily available to them and that directly contradicted the version of events they advanced. Like the discussion of events preceding Thomson's death, many of the secondary accounts have a limited relationship to the primary evidence available. As discussed above, evidence from the time indicates that other than its missing passenger, little was regarded as amiss when Thomson's canoe was discovered.

A third component of narratives addressing the events surrounding Thomson's death concerns the condition of Thomson's corpse when it was discovered. Records of observations made at the time are very few. Mark Robinson included some notes in his diary the evening after the body was examined, and Shannon Fraser made some brief comments in a letter to Thomson's father.[37] In 1931, the Crown Attorney's office supplied Blodwen Davies with a copy of the examining doctor's affidavit regarding the condition of Thomson's corpse.[38] The same year, George Thomson wrote Davies, including a transcript of what he claimed was the doctor's handwritten affidavit. These latter two accounts differ in two important ways.[39]

All four of these documents agree that Tom Thomson's body was discovered floating in Canoe Lake on the morning of Monday, July 16, eight days after he had gone missing. On Tuesday, July 17, either Robinson or G.W. Bartlett, the Algonquin Park Superintendent, requested that Dr. G.

Howland, who was holidaying at Canoe Lake, examine the corpse. The coroner had been expected to arrive on the train the day before but had not. An undertaker and his assistant had arrived, however, and were waiting to do their work on the clearly decomposing corpse.

We have several accounts of the condition of the remains. Mark Robinson noted that Thomson's body had a bruise on the left temple about four inches long, "Evidently caused by falling on a Rock," but that, "otherwise [there are] no marks of Violence on Body."[40] The next day, Shannon Fraser wrote Thomson's father that the doctor had found a bruise over Tom's eye and "thinks he fell and was hurt."[41] The copy of Dr. Howland's affidavit supplied to Blodwen Davies in 1931 states: "Bruise on right temple 4 inches long. No other external marks. Air issuing from lungs, some bleeding from right ear."[42] This account, however, differs from the version George Thomson claimed to have in several ways. George's version includes notations regarding the clothes Tom's corpse was wearing, as well as additional details regarding the condition of the body.[43] This version states:

> Body clothed in grey lumberman's shirt, khaki trowsers [sic] and canvas shoes. Head shows marked swelling of face, decomposition has set in, air issuing from mouth. Head has a bruise over left temple as if produced by falling on rock. Examination of body shows no bruises, body greatly swollen, blisters on limbs, putrefaction setting in on surface. There are no signs of any external force having caused death, and there is no doubt but that death occurred from drowning.

The most important aspect of this version of Howland's observation is that it repeats Robinson's statement that the bruise on Thomson's temple was on the left side, not the right, as the copy of the Attorney General's affidavit states.

The question of whether the bruise was on the left or right side of Thomson's temple has certainly vexed later commentators. The location of the bruise, though, is not particularly critical to resolving Thomson's cause of death. Much of the speculation regarding Thomson's cause of death revolves around a different narrative element, which does not appear in primary accounts and was not introduced into discussion of the events surrounding Thomson's death until long after the events in question.

In March 1930, Mark Robinson told Blodwen Davies that there were "no marks on the body except a slight bruise over the left eye."[44] He added, in a tone suggesting this claim was widely known, that Thomson's "fishing line was wound several times around his left ankle and broken" (4). Davies mentioned the fishing line in her 1931 request to the Attorney General (8), but did not include this seemingly important detail in her 1935 book.[45] In 1955, R.P. Little would provide a little more detail to Robinson's claim, stating that Thomson's body was discovered with *copper* fishing line around one ankle (207). In 1952, and again in 1956, Robinson was interviewed about his memories of the artist.[46] In the course of these interviews, he added new information, noting that the fishing line was wrapped "carefully" sixteen or seventeen times around Thomson's ankle.[47] Robinson suggested this observation supported his assertion that Thomson had been murdered.[48]

In the fall of 1956, M.R. Dixon, the undertaker who prepared Thomson's corpse for burial, wrote a letter to the editor of the *Toronto Star* addressing the recent discovery of a body in Algonquin Park, which some suspected was Thomson's. Dixon claimed there was no blood or signs of violence on the body, only post-mortem staining. As discussed earlier, in 1977, David Silcox claimed that Thomson had wrapped the fishing line around his ankle intentionally, to splint a sprain (59). He also repeated Blodwen Davies' claim that the bruise was on Thomson's right temple, as have a number of other recent writers (Silcox and Town 1977: 59; Murray 1994: 79; Silcox 2002: 60; Lehto 2005: 28).

Commentators arguing in favour of the theory that Thomson met with foul play have depended on reference to both the bruise on Thomson's temple and the fishing line around his ankle to argue their case. Both references have critical problems of credibility, however. The bruise on Thomson's temple, regardless of its location, does not seem to have given any observers at the time the impression that foul play was the cause of Thomson's death. Neither Howland nor Robinson noted anything that seemed to give them cause for alarm during the examination of Thomson's corpse. The much later testimony of the undertaker also supports the understanding that the body did not exhibit signs of foul play. Lending support to this conclusion, in 2007, after assessing some of the case materials for *Death on a Painted Lake: The Tom Thomson Mystery*, Dr. Michael Pollanen, Chief Forensic Pathologist, Province of Ontario, noted, "The state of decomposition was probably advanced enough that the 'bruise on the right temple' and the 'bleeding from the right ear' may not be injuries at all."

As for the idea that Thomson's corpse was found with fishing line around its ankle, it is very curious that in their contemporary notes about the condition of the corpse neither Howland nor Robinson made mention of this fact. Given the attention they paid to other details, that neither observer would find this fact worth noting at that time is incomprehensible. That this element of the story was first mentioned thirteen years after Thomson's death, and only really took hold in popular discussion after it had been spun into a much darker, exaggerated version during the mid-1950s, significantly undermines arguments that it is important as an explanatory factor in Thomson's death or even a trustworthy observation.

A fourth important component of narratives addressing the events surrounding Thomson's death concerns the exhumation of Tom Thomson's body from its Canoe Lake burial site on the evening of July 18, 1917.

Debate regarding the facts of the exhumation of Tom Thomson's body from Mowat Cemetery became particularly important after 1956, when a corpse was discovered just outside the Mowat Cemetery grounds, in almost exactly the place where it was believed Thomson was originally buried. If these remains were Thomson's and the story of his exhumation thus false, there would be grounds to argue that other elements in the story of his death might also have been falsified. As well, the condition of the remains, some argued, pointed to the newly discovered person having been murdered (Little 1970).

Primary accounts of the exhumation include Robinson's very brief account from his diary, and a few letters of the time refer to what happened. Unfortunately, these accounts are often short and rather ambiguous regarding who did what and when.

We can tentatively reconstruct what occurred using accounts written between July and September 1917 by those involved. Winnifred Trainor headed toward Canoe Lake from her home in Huntsville, Ontario, likely as soon as she learned of Thomson's death. She later told T.J. Harkness, Tom Thomson's brother-in-law and executor of his estate, that before she arrived in Canoe Lake she had tried to get changes made to the arrangements that were being made there.[49] On July 18, she was billed for a call to the Thomson family in Owen Sound and four calls to R.H. Flavelle, an undertaker in Kearney, Ontario.[50] The undertaker's bill, submitted to Harkness, also includes costs for calls to Owen Sound and Canoe Lake.[51] In September 1917, Tom's sister Margaret reported to Dr. MacCallum that George Thomson (Tom and Margaret's brother) had sent a telegram to Canoe Lake with the family's instructions regarding what to do with Tom's remains and that Shannon Fraser had received the telegram but did not show it to anyone else.[52] Trainor claimed that after arriving in Canoe Lake and after some struggle, she was able to see the telegram from the Thomson family.[53] She then made suggestions about what should be done, and her suggestions were rejected. Later correspondence between Flavelle and Harkness suggests Shannon Fraser made the initial burial arrangements. When Harkness indicated to Flavelle his belief that the undertaker's bill was exorbitant, Flavelle responded that he would simply direct the bill to the buyer, and promptly sent it to Fraser.[54] The same day Thomson was buried, Mark Robinson's diary records that Shannon Fraser received a telegram communicating intentions to exhume Tom's body but that Robinson did not know who had ordered this.[55] Robinson's diary entry for the following day states that Tom's body was exhumed "under direction of Mr. Geo. Thomson." A letter from Harkness later asserted that the family had arranged for Tom's remains to be shipped to Owen Sound in a metal casket.[56] The body was shipped out of Canoe Lake to Owen Sound by train. The July 20 *Owen Sound Sun* reported that George Thomson would be accompanying the body when it arrived that day.

The difficulties caused by the limited communications available between Canoe Lake and the "outside world" may have contributed significantly to the confusion regarding what to do about Thomson's remains. Later descriptions of these events, however, often suggest that darker motivations were at play in the awkward progression of events around the two burials of Tom Thomson.

In fall 1956, when suggestions were made that Thomson's body might not have actually been transferred out of Mowat Cemetery, a Canadian Press representative spoke with the undertaker responsible for exhuming Thomson's body and preparing it for shipment out of the park (*Leader-Post* Oct. 12). The undertaker, F.W. Churchill, had never spoken out publicly regarding his work on Thomson's body. While his account is rife with factual errors, it nonetheless offers an intriguing perspective regarding how the confusion surrounding what to do with Thomson's corpse might have played itself out in July 1917. Churchill asserted:

> Mr. Thomson's relatives and friends were not happy with the burial spot, Miss Blodwen Davies, a friend, wanted him buried at Leith. She phoned the undertaker at Kearney, who had been in charge of the funeral near Canoed [*sic*] Lake, but he refused to exhume the body. Then she phoned me in Huntsville.

While Davies was a mere child in 1917 and never met Thomson or his family (*Leader-Post* Oct. 16), if Churchill had confused Winnifred Trainor with Blodwen Davies (keeping in mind that this interview took place almost forty years after the events in question, and that he had likely seen Davies' name associated with Thomson due to her publishing biographies of the man), his testimony fits closely with the account Trainor provided the Thomson family, as well as the phone bill she provided the estate regarding costs related to Thomson's death.

Churchill added that he had transferred Thomson's "badly decomposed but still recognizable" remains into a metal box that he could seal, and returned the empty coffin and its surrounding "rough box" to the grave, which he then refilled. He also notes that one of Thomson's brothers accompanied the coffin on the train to Owen Sound.

In early 1969, a CBC television feature dealing with Thomson's death led to an outburst of discussion similar to that caused by the discovery of the remains in Mowat in 1956. The special, produced with assistance from William Little, who was involved in the 1956 discovery of the remains in the park and whose book regarding Thomson's death was just about to go to print, suggested that Thomson's remains might be those found in the park.

In his book, Little claims that George Thomson and an undertaker received the body in Owen Sound on the early afternoon of July 19, 1917 (88). Ottelyn Addison, whose book about Thomson was published in 1969, claimed that George Thomson had returned to Canoe Lake on July 19 to accompany his brother's coffin to Owen Sound (94). Recently, Neil Lehto has pointed to a George Thomson letter on Mowat Lodge letterhead, dated July 19, 1917, as proof that George accompanied the body from Mowat to Owen Sound (100). Lehto asserts that George may have lied to Little about his presence in Canoe Lake to cover up that he never actually confirmed if Tom was in the coffin (105).

Churchill's testimony does suggest that Thomson's body was in fact removed from the park. This version of events is supported by testimony provided by the niece of two women who were childhood neighbours of the Thomson family in Owen Sound. This woman came forward in 1969 to report that her aunts clearly recalled their cousin visiting the Thomson family home while Tom's body was there (*Sun-Times*). The cousin had told these women that Tom's father insisted on having the coffin opened, although the undertaker was reluctant to comply, and that the elder Thomson and the ladies' cousin observed Tom's body.

Despite suggestions that a number of people viewed Thomson's corpse between 18 and July 20, 1917, on its trip between Mowat and burial in Leith Cemetery, the idea that Thomson's body might remain in the park persists in popular speculation. For instance, in 1973, Roy MacGregor introduced yet another proposal for what happened to Thomson's corpse after its initial burial. MacGregor reported in *Maclean's* that a seventy-three-year old, long-time Canoe Lake resident had told him that when some of Thomson's Canoe Lake friends had heard that the body would be removed from the park, they took matters into their own hands (50). These friends exhumed the body themselves and relocated it within the park before Churchill arrived to take it back to Owen Sound. MacGregor renewed this claim in 2010, arguing that Thomson was buried in Mowat Cemetery, based on a forensic artists' conjecture of what the owner of the skull found in Mowat Cemetery would have looked like.

Without definitive scientific proof regarding the identity of the remains discovered beside Mowat Cemetery in 1956, or alternatively, identification of any remains that might be exhumed from Thomson's grave in the Leith cemetery, it is impossible to definitively prove that Thomson's body was indeed moved from one site to the other, or that it remained buried beside Mowat Cemetery. Accounts written immediately following Thomson's death and the testimony of those who were involved, however, do provide strong reasons to conclude that the body was exhumed and moved from Mowat to Leith. That being said, the mystery in this case may very likely have less to do with where Tom Thomson is buried, than with who might be buried in a site that is close to or the same as where Thomson was originally buried.

What consideration of these four central themes in secondary narratives of Thomson's death indicates is that an alarming amount of writing about Thomson's death bears little resemblance to the primary evidence preserved in publicly accessible archives. Much of the "proof" upon which common theories regarding the cause of Thomson's death rest was introduced between thirteen and fifty-five years after his death, when the memories of those involved in the events would likely have been significantly coloured by having heard and read the accounts of others. In addition, much of the testimony available is based on hearsay passed between three or more people. To be plausible, arguments based on this type evidence should offer significant support.

The primary documentation surrounding Tom Thomson's death, as well as the later testimony from persons who participated in those events, does allow a reasonably clear idea of what happened at Canoe Lake during the tragic days of July 1917. Based on the preceding analysis of the primary documents, two of the three most-frequently offered theories regarding Tom Thomson's cause of death do not hold much credibility.

Considered against the tone and content of Thomson's letters of July 1917, it seems unlikely that he was considering suicide. Thomson had made commitments to guide fishing parties in July and August and to send his patron in Toronto some art works produced during the spring. A central element in consideration of Thomson's suicide — whether he was being compelled by Winnifred Trainor to consider marriage — did not appear until the late 1960s, more than fifty years after Thomson's death. No one had intimated before the 1960s that they were aware of any such situation, and no documentary evidence linking the two romantically has been produced to support the theory.

The murder theory has little evidence to support it. Testimony offered in July 1917 by multiple witnesses at Canoe Lake indicate that both paddles were tied in Thomson's canoe when it was discovered, suggesting Thomson was either portaging when he died, had tied his paddles in while fishing or had not set out onto the lake at all. At the time of his death, no one noted anything out of the ordinary about the way the paddles were tied into his canoe. As for the condition of his body, the bruise identified on Thomson's body was very likely on his left temple, and the most plausible explanation is that it was a result of putrefaction rather than a blow while he was alive. Finally, as has been shown, the story about fishing line being wrapped around Thomson's ankle was not introduced until over a decade after his death, and evolved considerably, particularly in versions told by the witness who introduced it.

Much of the "mystery" surrounding Thomson's death would be fed by the confusion raised by awkward communication about the Thomson family's wishes for treatment of Tom's remains. Evidence from the time indicates his family never wanted to have him buried in Algonquin Park and tried to communicate their wishes to those at Canoe Lake. For some reason, perhaps simply due to the exceptional challenge of having to deal with a tragic death in the small community or perhaps as a petty play for control in a crisis situation, quick burial of Thomson's remains was pursued at Canoe Lake, perhaps in spite of the family's wishes. The conflict over such an emotional issue clearly caused consternation and frustration at the time, and the ensuing exhumation of Thomson's body created fertile ground for hostility and suspicion among almost all involved. However, these difficult circumstances did not produce significant proof that Thomson committed suicide or was murdered.

Thomson has been characterized as a deft outdoorsman with natural skill at painting a unique, distinctively Canadian environment that he knew well. This is an image that Thomson's friends and supporters worked to promulgate after his death and that was integral to the rise of his reputation. If Thomson died as a result of a canoeing accident on a calm lake, in the middle of the day, this image would be significantly destabilized. It is not, however, an image that is necessary to appreciate Thomson's contribution to the development of Canadian painting. As Harold Town observed, decades of speculation regarding how Tom Thomson died have done little but cloud our understanding of Thomson's life and the importance of his art. Acceptance of what the evidence indicates, that Thomson died by accident and not suicide or murder, points to the importance of understanding his painting not through the lens of romantic myth but as what it was, the rather more mundane but nonetheless inspiring work of a skilled and hard-working artist.

The primary documents available from the time of Tom Thomson's death, particularly those in publicly accessible archival collections, many of which have been available for over sixty years, are integral to an accurate understanding of how this leading figure of Canadian art history died. They also offer a significant body of firsthand knowledge against which to test the understandings of Thomson's personality, values and creative interests that have been offered by many writers since his death. That these archival materials have been so often overlooked, or selectively drawn upon, and that the accounts written to date have veered so significantly from the historical records available, speaks to the importance of the work of archival preservation and of the critical use of archival resources in the reconstruction of full and accurate historical narratives.

Notes

1. In 2008, a significant body of archival material was digitized and made available online. See *Death on a Painted Lake: The Tom Thomson Mystery*, a sub-site within Great Unsolved Mysteries in Canadian History, Research Director, Gregory Klages <http://www.canadianmysteries.ca/Thomson/>.
2. Library and Archives Canada (hereafter LAC), MG30 D38, Blodwen Davies fonds, Vol. 11.
3. Library and Archives, National Gallery of Canada (hereafter LANGC), Dr. James M. MacCallum papers.
4. LAC, MG30 D284, Tom Thomson collection.
5. Trent University Archives (hereafter TUA), 97-011, Addison Family fonds.
6. LAC, MG30 D38, Blodwen Davies fonds, Vol. 11, "Mark Robinson to Blodwen Davies, March 23, 1930." LAC, MG30 D38, Blodwen Davies fonds, Vol. 11, "Mark Robinson to Blodwen Davies, Sept. 4, 1930." Library and Archives, National Gallery of Canada, N.T485.E24, Alex Edmison, Q.C. interviews Mark Robinson, 1952. 1956 transcript of tape recording made at Canoe Lake. Taylor Statten, 1956, interview with Mark Robinson. Excerpted in William Little, *The Tom Thomson Mystery*, 183–210. Original interview transcript: Algonquin Park Museum Archives, ON.
7. AO, RG 4-32, Attorney General Central Registry Criminal and Civil Files, File #2225, "Blodwen Davies to Col. Price, Attorney General, July 27, 1931."
8. In an April 16, 1917 letter to his father, Thomson notes that he has been in Canoe Lake for two weeks. LAC, MG30 D284, Tom Thomson collection, "Tom Thomson to John Thomson, April 16, 1917." In an April 21, 1917 letter to his patron, Dr. James MacCallum, Thomson notes that he has been in Canoe Lake for three weeks. "Have made quite a few sketches this spring." LANGC, Dr. James M. MacCallum papers, File 5, "Tom Thomson to Dr. J. MacCallum, Apr. 21, 1917."
9. LAC, MG30 D284, Tom Thomson collection, Vol. 1 File 21, "Algonquin Provincial Park, Tom Thomson's Algonquin Park Guide License, April 28, 1917."
10. LANGC, Dr. James M. MacCallum papers. File 5, "Tom Thomson to Dr. J. MacCallum, July 7, 1917."
11. LAC, MG30 D284, Tom Thomson collection, Vol. 1 File 21. "Tom Thomson, letter to Tom [T. J. Harkness], April 31, 1917."
12. LAC, MG30 D38, Blodwen Davies fonds, Vol. 11, "T.E. McKee (Crown Attorney and Clerk of the Peace, Nipissing District, North Bay, ON), letter to Blodwen Davies, June 5, 1930, with copy of Dr. G. W. Howland's affidavit, July 17, 1917."
13. AO, RG 80-8-0-631, File 022151, "Return of Death by Other Than Physician, for Tom Thomson, July 19, 1917." The coroner listed cause of death as "Drowning." As he did not alert police that foul play might have been involved after conducting his inquiries at Canoe Lake, it is reasonable to surmise that the coroner agreed that Thomson's death was accidental.
14. TUA, 97-011, Addison Family fonds, "Mark Robinson daily journal," July 19, 1917.
15. LANGC, Dr. James M. MacCallum papers, File 6, "George Thomson, Letter to

J. S. Fraser, Dec. 25, 1917."
16. Dr. Noble Sharpe, 1956, Re: Human Bones Received from Unmarked Grave in Algonquin Park, October 30, "Tom Thompson — Circumstances of Death of." Archives of Ontario, Toronto, RG 4-2, File 475.2, Office of the Attorney General correspondence and subject files.
17. LANGC, Dr. James M. MacCallum papers, File 5, "Tom Thomson to Dr. J. MacCallum, July 7, 1917."
18. LANGC, Dr. James M. MacCallum papers, File 5, "Tom Thomson to Dr. James MacCallum, April 21, 1917."
19. "Tom Thomson to Dr. J. MacCallum, July 7, 1917."
20. LAC, MG30 D284, Tom Thomson collection, Vol. 1, Files 3-6, "Winnifred Trainor to T. J. Harkness, August 11, 1917."
21. LAC, MG30 D284, Tom Thomson collection, Vol. 1, File 3, " J.S. Fraser to Dr. J. MacCallum, July 24, 1917."
22. "Winnifred Trainor to T.J. Harkness, August 11, 1917."
23. "Mark Robinson to Blodwen Davies, March 23, 1930."
24. "Blodwen Davies to Col. Price, Attorney General, July 27, 1931."
25. Taylor Statten, 1956, interview with Mark Robinson.
26. "Blodwen Davies to Col. Price, Attorney General, July 27, 1931."
27. "Mark Robinson to Blodwen Davies, March 23, 1930."
28. LAC, MG30 D404, Harold Town fonds, Vol. 30 File 15, "Interview with Elva Henry, Nov. 15, 1973."
29. LANGC, Dr. James M. MacCallum papers, "Shannon Fraser telegram to Dr. James MacCallum, July 10, 1917."
30. "Mark Robinson daily journal," July 10, 1917.
31. LANGC, Dr. James M. MacCallum papers, File 6, "Shannon Fraser telegram to MacCallum, July 12, 1917."
32. *Sun (Owen Sound)*, 1917, "Tom Thomson's Canoe Found On Canoe Lake," July 13. *The Globe (Toronto)*, 1917, "Toronto Artist Missing in North," July 17.
33. "Shannon Fraser to Dr. J. MacCallum, July 24, 1917."
34. "Mark Robinson to Blodwen Davies, September 4, 1930."
35. Taylor Statten, 1956, interview with Mark Robinson.
36. "Mark Robinson to Blodwen Davies, March 23, 1930."
37. "Mark Robinson daily journal," July 17, 1917. LAC, MG30 D284, Tom Thomson collection, Vol. 1, File 3, "Shannon Fraser to John Thomson, July 18, 1917."
38. "T.E. McKee (Crown Attorney and Clerk of the Peace, Nipissing District, North Bay, ON), letter to Blodwen Davies, June 5, 1930, with copy of Dr. G. W. Howland's affidavit, July 17, 1917."
39. LAC, MG30 D38, Blodwen Davies fonds, Vol. 11, "George Thomson to Blodwen Davies, July 8, 1931."
40. "Mark Robinson daily journal," July 17, 1917.
41. "Shannon Fraser to John Thomson, July 18, 1917."
42. "T.E. McKee (Crown Attorney and Clerk of the Peace, Nipissing District, North Bay, ON), letter to Blodwen Davies, June 5, 1930, with copy of Dr. G. W. Howland's affidavit, July 17, 1917."
43. "George Thomson to Blodwen Davies, July 8, 1931."
44. "Mark Robinson to Blodwen Davies, March 23, 1930."

45. "Blodwen Davies to Col. Price, Attorney General, July 27, 1931."
46. Taylor Statten, 1956, interview with Mark Robinson, LANGC, N.T485.E24, "Alex Edmison, Q.C. interviews Mark Robinson, 1952. 1956 transcript of tape recording made at Canoe Lake."
47. Edmison, 18. Statten, 206.
48. Edmison, 21. Statten 209.
49. "Winnifred Trainor to T. J. Harkness, August 11, 1917."
50. LAC, MG30 D284, Tom Thomson collection, Vol. 1, File 23, "Bell Telephone Company of Canada, Huntsville, phone bill of calls by Miss Traynor [sic] on July 18, 1917."
51. LAC, MG30 D284, Tom Thomson collection, Vol. 1, File 3, "R.H. Flavelle to T.J. Harkness, July 25, 1917."
52. LANGC, Dr. James M. MacCallum papers, File 6, "Margaret Thomson to Dr. J. MacCallum, Sept. 9, 1917."
53. "Winnifred Trainor to T. J. Harkness, August 11, 1917."
54. LAC, MG30 D284, Tom Thomson collection, Vol. 1, File 3, "T.J. Harkness to R.H. Flavelle, July 23, 1917." "R.H. Flavelle to T.J. Harkness, July 25, 1917." LAC, MG30 D284, Tom Thomson collection, Vol. 1, File 4, "R.H. Flavelle to J.S. Fraser, Bill for services rendered, August 2, 1917." Included as an attachment to "J.S. Fraser to T.J. Harkness, Aug. 6, 1917."
55. "Mark Robinson daily journal," July 17, 1917.
56. "T.J. Harkness to R.H. Flavelle, July 23, 1917."

References

Primary

Archives of Ontario, RG 4-2 File 475.2, Office of the Attorney General correspondence and subject files, "Tom Thomson — Circumstances of death of."

Archives of Ontario, Toronto, RG 4-2, File 475.2, Office of the Attorney General correspondence and subject files, "Tom Thompson — Circumstances of Death of." Sharpe, Dr. Noble. 1956. Re: Human Bones Received from Unmarked Grave in Algonquin Park. October 30.

Archives of Ontario, RG 4-32 File #2225, Attorney General Central Registry Criminal and Civil Files.

Archives of Ontario, MU583/F1066 File IIA, William Colgate Collection, "Tom Thomson Correspondence, 1915-1943."

Archives of Ontario, RG 80-8-0-631, File 022151, Return of Death by Other Than Physician, for Tom Thomson, 19 July 1917.

Library and Archives Canada, MG30 D38 Vol. 11, Blodwen Davies fonds.

Library and Archives Canada, MG30 D284, Tom Thomson collection.

Library and Archives Canada, MG30 D404 Vol. 30 File 15, Harold Town fonds.

Library and Archives, National Gallery of Canada, Dr. James M. MacCallum papers.

Library and Archives, National Gallery of Canada, N.T485.E24, Alex Edmison, Q.C. 1952. Alex Edmison, Q.C. interviews Mark Robinson. 1956 transcript of tape recording made at Canoe Lake.

Trent University Archives, 97-011, Addison Family fonds.

Secondary

Addison, Ottelyn; in collaboration with Elizabeth Harwood. 1969. *Tom Thomson: The Algonquin Years*. Vancouver: Ryerson Press.

CBC (Canadian Broadcasting Corporation). 1969. "Was Tom Thomson murdered?" Television broadcast, February 6.

Clemson, Gaye I. 2002. *Algonquin Voices: Selected Stories of Canoe Lake Women* Victoria, BC: Trafford.

Davies, Blodwen. 1930. *Paddle and Palette [The Story of Tom Thomson]*. Toronto: Ryerson Press.

_____. 1935. *A Study of Tom Thomson*. Toronto: Discus Press.

Death on a Painted Lake: The Tom Thomson Mystery. 2008. Research Director: Gregory Klages. Available at <http://www.canadianmysteries.ca/Thomson/indexen.html>.

Delaplante, Don. 1956. "Long a Mystery of Art World Body May Answer Riddle of Tom Thomson's Death." *Globe and Mail*, October 10.

Dixon, M.R. 1956. "I Buried Tom Thomson, No Foul Play." *Daily Star (Toronto)*, October 12.

Evening Telegram [Toronto]. 1934. "Arts & Artists." February 3.

[Fairbairn, Margaret], M.L.A.F. 1916. "Some Pictures at the Art Gallery." *Toronto Daily Star*, March 11.

Globe (Toronto). 1917. "Toronto Artist Missing in North." July 17.

Grace, Sherrill. 2004. *Inventing Tom Thomson: From Biographical Fictions to Fictional Autobiographies and Reproductions*. Kingston, ON: McGill-Queen's University Press.

Guillet, Edwin C. 1944. *The Death of Tom Thomson, Canadian Artist: A Study of the Evidence at the Coroner's Inquest, 1917*. Self-published: October 31.

Hubbard, R.H. 1962. *Tom Thomson*. Toronto: McClelland and Stewart.

Leader-Post (Regina). 1956. "Ex-Undertaker Says He Exhumed Tom Thomson's Body." October 12.

_____. 1956. "Author Did Not Know Artist." October 16.

Lee, Rupert. 1924. "Canadian Pictures at Wembley." *Canadian Forum* 14, August 31, 338–9.

Lehto, Neil. 2005. *Algonquin Elegy: Tom Thomson's Last Spring*. Lincoln, NE: iUniverse books.

Little, Dr. R.P. 1955. "Some Recollections of Tom Thomson and Canoe Lake." *Culture* 16: 210–22.

Little, William T. 1970. *The Tom Thomson Mystery*. Toronto: McGraw-Hill Ryerson.

MacGregor, Roy. 1973. "The Great Canoe Lake Mystery." *Maclean's*, September 31: 30, 44, 48–50.

_____. 1977. "The Legend." *The Canadian*, October 15: 2–7.

_____. 1980. *Shorelines*. Toronto: McClelland and Stewart.

_____. 2002. *Canoe Lake*. Toronto: McClelland and Stewart.

_____. 2010. *Northern Light: The Enduring Mystery of Tom Thomson and the Woman Who Loved Him*. Toronto: Random House Canada.

MacHardy, Carolyn. 1999. "An Inquiry into the Success of Tom Thomson's *The West Wind*." *University of Toronto Quarterly* 68/3 (Summer): 768–90.

MacLennan, Hugh. 1949. "The Ten Greatest Canadians" [Tom Thomson]. *New Liberty* 26, 9: 7–13.

Murray, Joan. 1971. *The Art of Tom Thomson*. Toronto: Art Gallery of Ontario.
_____. 1986. *The Best of Tom Thomson*. Edmonton: Hurtig Publishers.
_____. 1994. *Tom Thomson: The Last Spring*. Toronto: Dundurn Press.
_____. 1998. *Tom Thomson: Design for a Canadian Hero*. Toronto: Dundurn Press.
Pittaway, Ronald. 1977. Interview with Daphne Crombie at her home in Toronto, January 14. Excerpted in Joan Murray, *Tom Thomson: The Last Spring* (1994): 94–96. Original interview transcript: Algonquin Park Museum Archives, ON.
Plewman, Charles. 1972. "Reflections on the Passing of Tom Thomson." *Canadian Camping Magazine* Winter: 6–9.
Poling, Jim Sr. 2003. *Tom Thomson: The Life and Mysterious Death of the Famous Canadian Painter*. Canmore, AB: Altitude Publishing.
Pollanen, Dr. Michael (Chief Forensic Pathologist, Province of Ontario). 2007. "Forensic Pathology Report, Nov. 2007." *Death on a Painted Lake: The Tom Thomson Mystery*. Available at <http://www.canadianmysteries.ca/Thomson/interpretations> (password protected).
Reid, Dennis (ed.). 2002. *Tom Thomson*. Toronto: Art Gallery of Ontario.
Sharpe, Dr. Noble. 1970. "The Canoe Lake Mystery." *Canadian Society of Forensic Science Journal* 3 (June 31): 34–40.
Shaw, S. Bernard. 1996. *Canoe Lake Algonquin Park: Tom Thompson and Other Mysteries*. Burnstown, ON: General Store Publishing.
Silcox, David. 2002. *Tom Thomson: An Introduction to His Life and Art*. Toronto: Firefly Books.
Silcox, David, and Harold Town. 1977. *Tom Thomson: The Silence and the Storm*. Toronto: McClelland and Stewart.
Statten, Taylor. 1956. Interview with Mark Robinson. Excerpted in William Little, *The Tom Thomson Mystery*: 183–210. Original interview transcript: Algonquin Park Museum Archives, ON.
Sun (Owen Sound). 1917. "Tom Thomson's Canoe Found On Canoe Lake." July 13.
Sun-Times (Owen Sound). 1969. "Recall Identifying of Tom Thomson Body Prior to Burial Here." February 10.

Contributors

Kathleen Garay and **Christl Verduyn** established the Archives in Canada Conference Series. They collaborated on editing the selected papers of the first two conferences in special issues of the *Journal of Canadian Studies* (40: 2: Spring 2006), *Topia* (20: Fall 2008) and *Archivaria* (67: Spring 2009). They are also joint editors of *Marian Engel, Life in Letters* (University of Toronto Press, 2004).

Kathleen Garay, a faculty member and former archivist at McMaster University, currently teaches in the Arts and Science Program there. She is also an adjunct member of the Department of History. A medievalist by training, her previous books include translations of the *Life of Douceline de Digne* (Boydell and Brewer, 2001) and *The Distaff Gospels* (Broadview, 2006) with Madeleine Jeay. She is currently working on a translation of a thirteenth-century Latin text, the miracles of St. Elizabeth of Hungary. Recent digital projects include *Peace and War in the Twentieth Century* <http://pw20c.mcmaster.ca>, based on archival resources at McMaster University. <garay@mcmaster.ca>

Christl Verduyn is a member of the Department of English and the Canadian Studies Program at Mount Allison University, where she is the Davidson Chair in Canadian Studies and director of the Centre for Canadian Studies. Her research interests in Canadian women's writing led her to the archives, in particular the Marian Engel Archive at McMaster University, and has resulted in several volumes, including *Lifelines: Marian Engel's Writings* (MQUP, 1995), winner of the Gabrielle Roy Book Prize, and most recently, *Marian and the Major* (MQUP, 2010). She has also published extensively in other areas of Canadian literature and Canadian studies. Recent titles include *Asian Canadian Writing Beyond Autoethnography* (WLUP, 2008) with E. Ty and *Perspectives on Dutch-Canadian Relations* (Barkhuis, 2010) with C. Steenman Marcusse. <cverduyn@mta.ca>

Jodi Aoki works at Trent University Archives and is a student in the Trent/Carleton Canadian Studies Ph.D. program. Interested in letters and diaries of nineteenth-century Upper Canadian women immigrants, Jodi's research is focused on the interconnectedness between gender, memory, landscape and literary representation. Her forthcoming book, *Revisiting "Our Forest Home":*

The Immigrant Letters of Frances Stewart, will be released by Dundurn Press in Summer 2011. <jaoki@trentu.ca>

Emily Ballantyne is working on a PhD in English at Dalhousie University in Halifax, NS, where she holds a SSHRC Canada Graduate Scholarship. She completed her MA in Public Texts at Trent University. Her MA thesis "Exile and Inhabitant: P.K. Page's Brazil" socializes Page's Brazilian poetry with her travel writing in Brazil, her early paintings, the retrospective autobiographical essays and the Brazilian Journal. She received an Editing Modernism in Canada graduate stipend to complete a genetic, parallel-text edition of the Brazilian poetry (1957–1959). As a research assistant for Zailig Pollock she has conducted archival research and transcribed manuscript poetry for *Kaleidoscope* and the Digital Page project. <emily.ballantyne@dal.ca>

Manon Brunet is a professor in the Department of Letters and Social Communication at the Université du Québec à Trois-Rivières. As specialist in the nineteenth century and sociologist of literature, her studies focus on the literary networks arising from correspondence (including manuscripts). Historiographical analysis and an epistemological approach characterize her numerous works for which she received in 2002 the Prize of the Commission de la Capitale nationale du Québec and the Association internationale des études québécoises. Her most widely known publications are *Henri Casgrain épistolier: réseau et littérature au 19ᵉ siècle* (1995), *Discours et pratiques de l'intime* (1993), *Érudition et passion dans les écritures intimes* (1999), *L'inscription sociale de l'intellectuel* (2000). She has also published articles in journals and book chapters in Quebec and abroad. <Manon.Brunet@UQTR.CA>

Kristan Cook works in records and information management for the Department of Education, Nova Scotia Government. She has a master of archival studies from the University of British Columbia and a master of arts from the University of Victoria. <cookkr@gov.ns.ca>

Gwendolyn Davies, FRSC, is professor and dean emerita in English and graduate studies at the University of New Brunswick. The author, editor or co-editor of five books, she has published numerous articles on pre-WW1 Atlantic Provinces literature. She is currently researching a book on Loyalist women in Maritime Canada at the end of the eighteenth century. <daviesg@unb.ca>

Heather Dean is an archivist at the Beinecke Rare Book and Manuscript Library. She has a master of archival studies and a master of library and information studies from the University of British Columbia, and a master of arts from the University of Victoria. <heather.dean@yale.edu>

Carole Gerson is a professor in the English Department at Simon Fraser

University and was an editor of the *History of the Book in Canada*. She has published extensively on Canadian literary history, early Canadian women writers and print culture in Canada, topics that coalesce in her recent book, *Canadian Women in Print, 1750–1918* (2010). <gerson@sfu.ca>

Jocelyn Hallman holds an MA in English from Simon Fraser University and an MLIS degree from the School of Library, Archival and Information Studies at the University of British Columbia. Her research explores the connections between cultural artifacts and networked spaces, particularly in the contexts of the web, information ecologies, and information architectures. <jdr1@sfu.ca>

Grant Hurley is an MA student in the Department of English at the University of British Columbia. He is a graduate of Mount Allison University, where he completed a bachelor of arts in English with an honours thesis titled "Coming of Age: Canadian Children's Literature and National Identities, 1900–1945." A recipient of a 2010 SSHRC Canada Graduate Scholarship, he continues to work in small archives and is presently occupied with research on the Clarke family of St. Andrews, New Brunswick. <gehurley@mta.ca>

Dean Irvine is an associate professor in the Department of English at Dalhousie University. He is the editor of *Archive for Our Times: Previously Uncollected and Unpublished Poems of Dorothy Livesay* (1998), *Heresies: The Complete Poems of Anne Wilkinson, 1924–1961* (2003) and *The Canadian Modernists Meet* (2005), and author of *Editing Modernity: Women and Little-Magazine Cultures in Canada* (2008). As general editor of the Canadian Literature Collection/Collection de littérature canadienne (University of Ottawa Press) and director of the Editing Modernism in Canada project, he is engaged in a wide range of collaborative editorial projects in print and digital media. <dean.irvine@dal.ca>

Gregory Klages teaches Canadian studies at the University of Guelph-Humber and York University in Toronto. Recent publications include *Death on a Painted Lake: The Tom Thomson Tragedy*, one of twelve international award-winning, book-length, bilingual websites produced as part of the *Great Unsolved Mysteries in Canadian History* project <http://www.canadianmysteries.ca>. Other publications include a comparative analysis of the creation of the Saskatchewan Arts Board and the Canada Council of the Arts, as well as a microstudy of late-nineteenth-century fraternal organization membership in a rural Ontario settlement. <gklages@alumni.yorku.ca>

Ronald Labelle completed his doctoral studies in ethnology at Université Laval. He was folklore archivist at the Université de Moncton's Centre d'études acadiennes from 1979 until 2005, and served as director of the Centre from 1988 to 1992. He presently holds the McCain Research Chair in Acadian Ethnology and Folklore in Moncton. His publications include *The Acadians of Chezzetcook* (1995) and *Au Village-du-Bois — Mémoires d'une communauté acadienne* (1985). He has been editor of the journal *Oral History Forum*, has held several posts on the executive of the Folklore Studies Association of Canada and is a member of the editorial boards of *Musicultures*, the journal of the Canadian Society for Musical Traditions, and *Rabaska*, the journal of the Société québécoise d'ethnologie. <ronald.labelle@umoncton.ca>

Melissa McCarthy is the archives advisor with the Council of Archives New Brunswick. She has also worked at the Halifax Regional Municipality Archives and interned at Pier 21, Canada's Immigration Museum. She became interested in archival theory and practice and in the history of the book while studying for her master of library and information studies degree at Dalhousie University. Her professional interests include access and privacy, digitization, archival outreach and the ways in which the technology used by archivists shapes — and is shaped by — these concerns. <melissa.d.mccarthy@gmail.com>

Andrew Nurse is coordinator of Canadian studies at Mount Allison University. His previous work includes the edited collections (with Raymond Blake) *Trajectories of Rural Life* (2003) and *Beyond National Dreams: Essays on Canadian Nationalism, Citizenship, and Identity* (2002). <anurse@mta.ca>

Michael Peterman is professor emeritus at Trent University and spends his time between Peterborough, Ontario, and Lunenburg, Nova Scotia. For nearly two decades he has been working on a biography of James McCarroll and a volume of his collected writings. Other current projects include an edition of Susanna Moodie's "Flora Lyndsay" (1854) and an edition of Moodie's two anti-slavery pamphlets ("Mary Prince" and "Ashton Warner," 1830–31), co-edited with Molly Blyth. An interest in maritime writing in Canada has led to work on an edition of James DeMille's "The Lily and the Cross." <mpeterman@trentu.ca>

Zailig Pollock received his BA at the University of Manitoba and his PhD from the University of London. He teaches at Trent University, where he is director of the English graduate program. He has served as chair of the A.M. Klein Research and Publication Committee, which oversaw the publication of *The Collected Works of A.M. Klein*, for which he edited Klein's poetry and co-edited his notebooks, *The Second Scroll* (2000). He has also served as a general editor of the Collected Works of E.J. Pratt and has co-edited the *Selected Poems of E.J. Pratt* (1998). He is currently a general editor of the *Collected Works of P.K. Page*, for which he is editing Page's poems. <zpollock@trentu.ca>

Ala Rekrut is manager of preservation services at the Archives of Manitoba. She has a master's degree from the Archival Studies Program at the University of Manitoba and a master of art conservation from Queen's University. Her research interests are materiality and the preservation of archival value. She has given workshops, seminars and presentations on a variety of preservation-related topics for organizations ranging from small heritage institutions to the International Conference on the History of Records and Archives, the Society of American Archivists, the Association of Canadian Archivists and the Canadian Association for Conservation of Cultural Property. <Ala.Rekrut@gov.mb.ca>

Noah Richler, an author and essayist, is also a producer and host of documentaries and features. Raised in Montreal, he worked for BBC Radio in London, England, for fourteen years before returning to Canada in1998. His 2006 book, *This Is My Country, What's Yours? A Literary Atlas of Canada*, a compelling travelogue and portrait of Canadian society and Canadian writers, won the British Columbia Award for Canadian Non-Fiction.

Doug Rimmer is an assistant deputy minister in the Acquisitions Sector at Library and Archives Canada. He was previously with the Documentary Heritage Collection Sector and, before that, with Programmes & Services. He has degrees from the University of British Columbia and the University of Toronto. <doug.rimmer@lac-bac.gc.ca>

Robert Summerby-Murray is a cultural-historical geographer with interests in urban and industrial heritage, environmental histories, narrative and place. His research focuses on historical geographies of settlement in the Bay of Fundy, industrial heritage in maritime Canada and environmental histories of Atlantic Canada. His recent publications have appeared in the *Canadian Geographer, Urban History Review* and the *Journal of Geography in Higher Education*. While the research for the chapter in this book was completed while he was a member of the Department of Geography and Environment at Mount Allison University, he is currently dean of the Faculty of Arts and Social Sciences and a professor in the Department of History at Dalhousie University. <rsummerb@dal.ca>

Meagan Timney is a postdoctoral fellow for the Editing Modernism in Canada Project at the Electronic Textual Cultures Laboratory (University of Victoria). Her research interests include the theory and practice of digital scholarly editing, interface design, human-computer interaction, knowledge mobilization and collaborative digital environments, Victorian literature and industrial culture, and working-class women's poetry. Her most recent article is "Mary Hutton and the Development of a Working-Class Women's Political Poetics." <mbtimney.etcl@gmail.com>